Fichte and the Phenomenological Tradition

# Fichte and the Phenomenological Tradition

Edited by
Violetta L. Waibel,
Daniel Breazeale and
Tom Rockmore

De Gruyter

Gedruckt mit Förderung der Universität Wien,
Fakultät für Philosophie und Bildungswissenschaft

ISBN 978-3-11-048170-9
e-ISBN 978-3-11-024528-8

*Library of Congress Cataloging-in-Publication Data*

Fichte and the phenomenological tradition / edited by Violetta L. Waibel, Daniel Breazeale, Tom Rockmore.
 p. cm. – Proceedings of a meeting held Mar. 15–18, 2006 at the University of Vienna.
 Includes bibliographical references and index.
 ISBN 978-3-11-024529-5 (hardcover : alk. paper)
 1. Fichte, Johann Gottlieb, 1762–1814 – Congresses.  2. Phenomenology – Congresses.  I. Waibel, Violetta L.  II. Breazeale, Daniel.  III. Rockmore, Tom, 1942–
 B2848.F515  2010
 193–dc22
                                                                    2010023397

*Bibliographic information published by the Deutsche Nationalbibliothek*

The Deutsche Nationalbibliothek lists this publication in the Deutsche Nationalbibliografie; detailed bibliographic data are available in the Internet at http://dnb.d-nb.de.

© 2010 Walter de Gruyter GmbH & Co. KG, Berlin/New York

Printing and binding: Hubert & Co. GmbH & Co. KG, Göttingen
∞ Printed on acid-free paper
Printed in Germany
www.degruyter.com

# Preface

This volume contains papers from a meeting of the North American Fichte Society entitled "Fichte and the Phenomenological Tradition" at the University of Vienna March 15–18 2006. In addition to Fichte, attention was devoted to the work of thinkers such as Husserl, Heidegger, Merleau-Ponty, Levinas.

The meeting, which included participants from the USA, Canada and several European countries, was organized by Violetta L. Waibel (Universität Wien), Daniel Breazeale (University of Kentucky), and Tom Rockmore (Duquesne University). The meeting was financially supported by Dean Univ.Prof. Dr. Peter Kampits. The publication is financially supported by Deans of the Faculty of Philosophy and Science of Pedagogy Univ.Prof. Dr. Peter Kampits and Univ.Prof. Dr. Ines Breinbauer.

We wish to express thanks to Diana Rosdolsky (Vienna), who revised the English-language papers, and to Max Brinnich (Vienna) who reformatted the papers. We are grateful to Walter de Gruyter Verlag for publishing this volume and especially to Dr. Gertrud Grünkorn in her role as "Lektor".
    Violetta L. Waibel, Daniel Breazeale, Tom Rockmore, March 2010

# Contents

TOM ROCKMORE
Introduction .................................................. 1

## I. Fichte's Wissenschaftslehre as a Phenomenology

TOM ROCKMORE
On Fichte and Phenomenology ........................ 11

CLAUDE PICHÉ
The Concept of Phenomenology in Fichte's *Wissenschaftslehre* of 1804/II .................................................. 25

F. SCOTT SCRIBNER
Reduction or Revelation? Fichte and the Question of Phenomenology. .................................................. 41

ANTHONY N. PEROVICH
Fichte's Phenomenology of Religious Consciousness ......... 57

ELIZABETH MILLÁN
Fichte and Brentano: Idealism from an Empirical Standpoint and Phenomenology from an Idealist Standpoint ............... 71

## II. Fichte and Husserl

ANGELICA NUZZO
Phenomenologies of Intersubjectivity: Fichte between Hegel and Husserl .................................................. 97

FEDERICO FERRAGUTO
Tendency, Drive, Objectiveness. The Fichtean Doctrine and the Husserlian Perspective .................................... 119

ROBERT R. WILLIAMS
Life-World, Philosophy and the Other: Husserl and Fichte .... 141

GARTH W. GREEN
Self-Consciousness and Temporality: Fichte and Husserl ...... 167

VIRGINIA LÓPEZ-DOMÍNGUEZ
Body and Intersubjectivity: The Doctrine of Science
and Husserl's *Cartesian Meditations* ........................ 191

## III. Fichte and Heidegger

JÜRGEN STOLZENBERG
Martin Heidegger Reads Fichte ........................ 207

M. JORGE DE CARVALHO
Fichte, Heidegger and the Concept of Facticity ............. 223

SHARIN N. ELKHOLY
Overcoming the Priority of the Subject: Fichte and Heidegger on
Indeterminate Feeling and the Horizon of World and
Self-Knowledge ..................................... 261

## IV. Fichte, Sartre and Others

DANIEL BREAZEALE
How to Make an Existentialist?
In Search of a Shortcut from Fichte to Sartre ............... 277

GAETANO RAMETTA
Consciousness. A Comparison between Fichte and
the Young Sartre in a Bio-Political Perspective ............. 313

ISABELLE THOMAS-FOGIEL
Fichte and Levinas. The Theory of Meaning and
the Advent of the Infinite ............................. 327

ARNOLD L. FARR
The Other and the Necessary Conditions of the Self in Fichte's
*Wissenschaftslehre* and Paul Ricoeur's Phenomenology of the Will  341

Violetta L. Waibel
Does the Methodology of Phenomenology Involve Dual
Intentionality? Some Remarks on Conceptions of
Phenomenology in Husserl, Fichte, Hegel, Sartre and Freud ...   357

Wayne M. Martin
Fichte's Logical Legacy: Thetic Judgment from the
*Wissenschaftslehre* to Brentano ..........................   379

Notes on Contributors ................................   407

# List of Abbreviations

## JOHANN GOTTLIEB FICHTE: EDITIONS

| | |
|---|---|
| GA | J.G. Fichte-Gesamtausgabe der Bayerischen Akademie der Wissenschaften, ed. Reinhard Lauth and Erich Fuchs, Stuttgart-Bad Cannstatt 1964 ff. |
| SW | Johann Gottlieb Fichtes sämtliche Werke, ed. I.H. Fichte, eight vols. (Berlin: Viet & Co., 1845-1846); Reprinted, along with three vols. of Johann Gottlieb Fichtes nachgelassene Werke, Bonn 1834-1835, Berlin 1971 |

## JOHANN GOTTLIEB FICHTE: INDIVIDUAL WORKS

| | |
|---|---|
| APR | Antwortschreiben an Herrn Prof. Reinhold |
| APT | Annalen des philosophischen Tons (1797) |
| AzsL | Anweisungen zum seeligen Leben (1806) |
| BWL | Über den Begriff der Wissenschaftslehre (1794) |
| DdWL | Darstellung der Wissenschaftslehre |
| EiP | Einleitung WS 1810/11 Nachschrift Twesten |
| EPW | Fichte: Early Philosophical Writings (ed. and trans. Daniel Breazeale, Ithaca, NY 1988) |
| ErE | Erste Einleitung in die Wissenschaftslehre |
| EVWL | Einleitungsvorlesungen in die Wissenschaftslehre |
| FNR | Foundations of Natural Right (ed. Frederick Neuhouser, trans. Michael Baur, Cambridge 2000) |
| FTP | Fichte: Foundations of Transcendental Philosophy (Wissenschaftslehre nova method, ed. and trans. Daniel Breazeale, Ithaca, NY 1992) |
| GdgZ | Die Grundzüge des gegenwärtigen Zeitalters (1806) |
| GNR | Grundlage des Naturrechts (1796/1797) |
| GWL | Grundlage der gesamten Wissenschaftslehre (1794/1795) |
| IWL | Introductions to the Wissenschaftslehre and Other Writings (ed. and trans. Daniel Breazeale, Indianapolis 1994) |
| LEr | Logik Erlangen |
| LWL-1804 | Lectures on the Wissenschaftslehre (trans. Walter Wright, Albany 2005) |
| MEr | Metaphysik Erlangen |

| | |
|---|---|
| NaR | Nachschrift an Reinhold |
| NdSdV | Nach dem Schluße der Vorlesungen |
| Nz1 | Nebenbemerkungen zu 1 |
| PEr | Propädeutik Erlangen |
| PfGD | Privatissimum für G. D. |
| PW | The Popular Works of Johann Gottlieb Fichte (trans. William Smith, ed. by Daniel Breazeale, London 1889, Bristol 1999) |
| SB | Sonnenklarer Bericht |
| Sd1A1808 | Seit d. 1. April. 1808 |
| SE | Systems of Ethics (trans. and ed. Daniel Breazeale and Günter Zöller, Cambridge 2005) |
| SS | Das System der Sittenlehre (1798) |
| StL | Die Staatslehre, oder über das Verhältnis des Urstaates zum Vernunftreiche (1813) |
| TdB | Thatsachen des Bewusstseyns |
| TdB-1811 | Thatsachen des Bewusstseyns 1811 |
| TdB-1811/12 | Thatsachen des Bewusstseyns 1811/1812 |
| ÜVLP | Über das Verhältniß der Logik zur Philosophie |
| UI | Ultima Inquirenda |
| VLM | Vorlesung über Logik und Metaphysik |
| WL | Wissenschaftslehre |
| WL-1804-I/II/III | Wissenschaftslehre von 1804, Erste, Zweite, Dritte Vorlesungsreihe |
| WL-1805 | Wissenschaftslehre 1805 |
| WL-1810 | Wissenschaftslehre 1810 |
| WL-1811 | Wissenschaftslehre 1811 |
| WL-1812 | Wissenschaftslehre 1812 |
| WLaU | Die Wissenschaftslehre in ihrem allgemeinen Umrisse |
| WL-Kö | Wissenschaftslehre Königsberg |
| WLnm | Wissenschaftslehre nova methodo (1796–1799) |
| WLnm-H | Wissenschaftslehre nova methodo („Halle Nachschrift," 1796/97) |
| WLnm-K | Wissenschaftslehre nova methodo (Nachschrift K. Chr. Fr. Krause 1798/1799) |
| ZAdWL | Zur Ausarbeitung der Wissenschaftslehre |
| ZwE | Zweite Einleitung in die Wissenschaftslehre (1797) |

## WORKS BY OTHER AUTHORS

| | |
|---|---|
| Ak | Immanuel Kant's gesammelte Schriften, ed. by the „Koeniglich Preussische Akademie der Wissenschaften" and its successors, Berlin: de Gruyter 1900 ff. |
| AKJ | Heidegger: Anmerkungen zu Karl Jaspers „Psychologie der Weltanschauungen" |
| BN | Sartre: Being and Nothingness |
| BwJ | Heidegger: Martin Heidegger/Karl Jaspers, Briefwechsel 1920-1963 (ed. Walter Biemel and Hans Sanep, Frankfurt a. M./München: Klostermann/ Piper 1990) |
| BwL | Heidegger: „Drei Briefe Martin Heideggers an Karl Löwith," in: Dieter Papenfuss/Otto Pöggeler (ed.), Zur philosophischen Aktualität Heideggers. Symposium der Alexander von Humboldt Stiftung vom 24.-28. April 1989 in Bonn- Bad Godesberg, vol. II, Im Gespräch der Zeit. Frankfurt a. M., Klostermann 1990, pp. 27-39 |
| GAH | Heidegger: Gesamtausgabe (ed. Friedrich Wilhelm von Hermann. Frankfurt a. M.: Klostermann 1975 ff.) |
| HUA | Husserliana, Gesammelte Werke, Den Haag 1950 ff.) |
| KPM | Heidegger: Kant und das Problem der Metaphysik |
| KrV | Kant: Kritik der reinen Vernunft |
| PIA | Heidegger: Phänomenologische Interpretationen zu Aristoteles |
| SuZ | Heidegger: Sein und Zeit |
| VWG | Heidegger: Vom Wesen des Grundes |
| WiM? | Heidegger: Was ist Metaphysik? |

# Introduction

TOM ROCKMORE

Duquesne University – Pittsburgh, PA

If Husserl invented phenomenology,[1] it has nothing obviously to do with Fichte, whom observers understand as the first great post-Kantian idealist, and as widely influential in a variety of ways: as a reader of Kant, with respect to the views of Schelling and Hegel, and as concerns the later debate. According to this claim, which is widely and uncritically accepted, even by leading historians of phenomenology, phenomenology begins in Husserl, whose influence is reflected in the later views of Heidegger, Sartre, Merleau-Ponty and others. These and other figures make up what Spiegelberg, following Husserl, calls *The Phenomenological Movement*.[2] On this "official" version of the history of phenomenology, there is only one such movement, which begins in Husserl, not earlier than Husserl, from whom it dates.[3]

This "official" view is highly questionable, questionable even to those who supposedly accept it. Heidegger, who publicly clearly endorses this view, equally clearly rejects it in private. He seems to have been skeptical, even contemptuous of Husserl's claim to invent phenomenology.[4] In

---

1 He says of this science that "die ich de facto in die Geschichte eingeführt habe". Edmund Husserl, *Die Krisis der europäischen Wissenschaften und die transzendentale Phänomenologie. Eine Einleitung in die die phänomenologische Philosophie*, edited by Walter Biemel, The Hague: Martinus Nijhoff, 1954, Husserliana VI, p. 440.
2 See Herbert Spiegelberg, *The Phenomenological Movement: A Historical Introduction*, The Hague: Nijhoff, 1962.
3 See, e.g., Dermot Moran, *Edmund Husserl: Founder of Phenomenology*, London: Polity Press, 2005.
4 In a letter to Jaspers, he sarcastically remarks that Husserl is wholly taken up with his mission as the inventor of phenomenology, though no one can say what that is. See his letter of 14 January 1923 to Jaspers, in Martin Heidegger/Karl Jaspers *Briefwechsel 1920–1963*, edited by Walter Biemel and Hans Saner, Frankfurt a. M.: Vittorio Klostermann, 1990, p. 42: "Husserl ist gänzlich aus dem Leim gegangen – wenn er überhaupt je "drin" war – was mir in der letzten Zeit immer fraglicher gewordern ist – er pendelt hin und her und sagt Trivialitäten, der er

*Being and Time*, where he states that his own studies are only possible on the ground prepared by Husserl, he at the same time indicates that as concerns this philosophical movement possibility stands higher than actuality.⁵ In short, from Heidegger's perspective Husserl has not yet really begun phenomenology.

If "phenomenology" does not begin in Husserl, then we need to reassess our understanding of it. What if phenomenology began earlier than Husserl? What if the story were more complex and phenomenology and German idealism interacted? What if Fichte were in some sense a phenomenologist? These and related questions are raised by the present volume. The papers collected here concern different aspects of the relation between Fichte and phenomenology. Together they suggest the need to modify received views of the relation between Fichte and German idealism on the one hand and German idealism, Fichte and phenomenology on the other.

As soon as we began to scratch the surface, doubts begin to emerge and questions arise. Certainly the meaning of "phenomenology" has never been clear. Husserl, who uses the term in different ways in his writings as his view continues to evolve, never arrives at a univocal understanding of the term. It is significant that his last unfinished work is still intended as an introduction to phenomenology.⁶ His early descriptive form of phenomenology, expounded in *Logical Investigations* (1900–1901),⁷ later gives way in *Ideas* 1 (1913) to what he calls transcendental idealist phenomenology centering on the phenomenological reduction,

---

einen erbarmen möchte. Er lebt von der Mission des "Begründers der Phänomenologie", kein Mensch weiss, was das ist."

5 "Die folgenden Untersuchungen sind nur möglich geworden auf dem Boden, den E. Husserl gelegt, mit dessen "Logischen Untersuchungen" die Phänomenologie zum Durchbruch kam. Die Erläuterungen des Vorbegriffes der Phänomenologie zeigen an, daß ihr Wesentliches nicht darin liegt, als philosophische "Richtung " *wirklich* zu sein. Höher als die Wirklichkeit steht die *Möglichkeit*. Das Verständnis der Phänomenologie liegt einzig im Ergreifen ihrer als Möglichkeit." Martin Heidegger, *Sein und Zeit*, Tübingen: Max Niemeyer Verlag, 1967, S. 38.

6 See Edmund Husserl, *Die Krisis der europäischen Wissenshaften und die transzendentale Phänomenologie. Eine Einleitung in die phänomenologische Philosophie*, edited by Walter Biemel, Den Haag: Martinus Nijhoff, 1962.

7 See Edmund Husserl, *Logische Untersuchungen*, Tübingen: Max Niemeyer Verlag, 1980.

which he regarded as the cornerstone of his position.⁸ This suggests a link between phenomenology and idealism, which was never clarified and remains unclear in his position. Observers are divided in their reactions to his earlier and later forms of phenomenology. Merleau-Ponty, who was influenced by both Husserl and Heidegger, famously rejects the reduction as an infinite task, hence as regulative but not constitutive. Husserl firmly links his conception of phenomenology to epistemology, which Heidegger rejects in favor of phenomenological ontology. Husserl and Heidegger cannot both be correct about which form of phenomenology is preferable; and they cannot both be correct about the meaning of "phenomenology," which they grasp in obviously incompatible ways.

The relation of phenomenology to German idealism further remains unclear. There are many examples. There is, for instance, no agreement and little discussion about what is phenomenological about Hegel's *Phenomenology*. What does "phenomenology" mean in this context and how does that relate to views formulated beginning with Husserl? What does "German idealism" mean? Is there a single German idealist movement, and if so who are its members? Do they include only Fichte, Schelling and Hegel, but also Kant? What about Hölderlin? Marx? What do the German idealists share in common beyond the fact that they were all German, wrote in German, and were Protestant? Is there an overlapping doctrinal commitment? What does "idealism" mean for these thinkers and is it significant? Ever since G. E. Moore's canonical attack on idealism,⁹ analytic thinkers have been opposed to it. It is at least interesting to note that, since Strawson's important study of Kant,¹⁰ influential analytic observers prefer to discuss Kant without idealism as if it were somehow detachable from the critical philosophy.

The study of the relation of Fichte and phenomenology raises numerous interesting questions, which require discussion, and whose answers are not clear. What is Fichte's view of "phenomenology" and how does it relate to his overall position? Is this interest momentary or more abiding? Is his position in some significant sense phenomenological or even a form of phenomenology? Fichte claims to be a Kantian. How does his

---

8   See Edmund Husserl, *Ideen zu einer reinen Phänomenologie und phänomenologischen Philosophie*, Tübingen: Max Niemeyer Verlag, 1980.
9   See G. E. Moore, "The Refutation of Idealism," in G. E. Moore, *Philosophical Studies*, London: Routledge and Kegan Paul, 1922, 1958.
10  See Peter Strawson, *The Bounds of Sense: An Essay on Kant's Critique of Pure Reason*, London: Methuen, 1966.

interest in phenomenology relate to his self-proclaimed Kantianism? How does it relate to his reading of Kant? It is further well known that Fichte, who is the first really strong post-Kantian idealist, greatly influenced Schelling and Hegel. Is his influence on his idealist colleagues phenomenological, and if so, in what sense? This is particularly important for Hegel's relation to Fichte. Could it be that there is a Fichtean component to Hegel's conception of phenomenology in the *Phenomenology of Spirit*?

Fichte is an idealist and Husserl, for many the prototypical phenomenologist, later claims to be an idealist. What is the relation between Fichtean idealism and Husserlian phenomenology? Is Husserl in some sense a Fichtean? More generally: what is the relation between idealism and phenomenology? Is idealism, or a form of idealism, phenomenological or even phenomenology?

I have formulated a long series of questions since it seems to me that the present volume on Fichte and phenomenology points toward largely unexplored philosophical terrain, which requires exploration. The authors of these studies do so in different ways and from different angles of vision.

This volume is divided into four parts and an appendix grouped, with the exception of the latter, around different approaches to the general theme of Fichte and phenomenology. The first part contains five papers on Fichte's *Wissenschaftslehre* as a Phenomenology. In a study "On Fichte and Phenomenology," Tom Rockmore asks a general question: what, if anything, is phenomenological about Fichte's position? He argues Fichte contributes to the post-Kantian idealist development that should be understood as the development of a phenomenological form of idealism. Claude Piché examines "The Concept of Phenomenology in Fichte's *Wissenschaftslehre* of 1804/II," in sketching a historical survey of Fichte's forerunners in the philosophical use of the term phenomenology, with special attention to Lambert, Kant and Reinhold, whose theories he distinguishes. In "Reduction or Revelation? Fichte and the Question of Phenomenology," Scott Scribner contends Fichte's entire project can be understood to reiterate – or even better, anticipate – the impasse between phenomenology's methodological aspirations for objectivity and its more revelatory accounts. Anthony N. Perovich analyzes "Fichte's Phenomenology of Religious Consciousness" in suggesting that Fichtean religious consciousness exhibits so-called mystical union. In her investigation of "Fichte and Brentano: Idealism from an Empirical Standpoint and Phenomenology from an Idealist Standpoint," Elizabeth Millán contends that interpreting Fichte's idealism as a subject-centered view of reality with nothing much to tell us about the external world is seriously mistaken. She highlights realist strands of his thought through his influence on the development of phenomenology.

The second part contains five papers about Fichte and Husserl. Angelica Nuzzo's topic is "Phenomenologies of Intersubjectivity: Fichte between Hegel and Husserl." She argues that the response to the problem of intersubjectivity raised by Fichte is perhaps best answered in Husserl's late notion of *Lebenswelt*, where a convergence between their views can be indicated. Federico Ferraguto's theme is "Tendency, Drive, Objectiveness. The Fichtean Doctrine and the Husserlian Perspective." He suggests that from a methodological point of view there is a radical difference of intent: the unitary systematization of knowledge beginning with a principle in Fichte and the formulation of an absolute science capable of realizing in an apodictic manner the relationship between knowing and known in their infinitely multiple concrete forms in Husserl. In "Life-World, Philosophy and the Other: Husserl and Fichte," Robert R. Williams insists that Husserl's paradox of the life-world frames a similar issue and problem in Fichte since there is a phenomenological aspect or dimension in the transcendental systematic program of German idealism. He contends that because unity of the Fichtean *Ichheit* trumps synthesis, the I does not become a we, and the unity of the I remains subjective. In his account of "Self-Consciousness and Temporality: Fichte and Husserl," Garth Green shows ways in which Fichte's reception of Kant's conception of time helps to grasp Husserl's phenomenological view of inner time consciousness. He suggests that phenomenology would do well to return to both Fichte and Husserl as a guide to further research. In "Body and Intersubjectivity: The Doctrine of Science and Husserl's *Cartesian Meditations*," Virginia López-Domínguez points out that fifth *Cartesian Meditation* probably constitutes the best proof of the tremendous impact of Fichtean anthropology on Husserl. She contends Husserl's development of this theme is very similar to that laid out by Fichte in Paragraphs V and VI of his *Foundations of Natural Right*.

The short Part 3 offers three papers on the theme of Fichte and Heidegger. In "Martin Heidegger Reads Fichte," Jürgen Stolzenberg analyzes Heidegger's recently published 1929 lecture course: "Der deutsche Idealismus (Fichte, Hegel, Schelling) und die philosophische Problemlage der Gegenwart." Stolzenberg finds this course interesting as the first systematic study of Fichte's early writings since Hegel, and for the light it throws on Fichte's influence, through the concept of freedom, on Heidegger's conception of authenticity. In "Fichte, Heidegger and the Concept of Facticity," Mário Jorge de Almeida Carvalho argues that the concept of "Facticity" plays a key role both in Fichte's *Wissenschaftslehre* and in Heidegger's phenomenological hermeneutics. He thinks that both philosophical undertakings regard themselves as radical attempts to face the problem of facticity. Sharin Elkholy studies the theme of "Overcoming the Priority of the Subject: Fichte and Heidegger on Indeterminate Feeling and the Horizon of World and Self-Knowledge." She aims to free both Fichte and Heidegger, whom she thinks are misunderstood, from the charge of egoism and subjectivism directed primarily toward their earlier work by highlighting the irreducibility of the ground of knowledge to the knowing subject in each thinker's thought.

The fourth part of the volume considers Fichte, Sartre and Others. Daniel Breazeale's "How to Make an Existentialist? In Search of a Shortcut from Fichte to Sartre" addresses some of the more striking similarities between the "systems of freedom" of the early Fichte and of the early Sartre, including the related questions: does Fichte deserve to be called in some sense a "proto-existentialist"? And if not, what might it take to transform him into one? With Foucault in mind, Gaetano Rametta focuses on "Consciousness: A Comparison between Fichte and the Young Sartre under a Bio-Political Perspective". He suggests that Fichte and Sartre give us the possibility of conceiving a *transcendental* concept of life from a *philosophical* point of view, which the transcendental and phenomenological traditions combine with the simply biological dimension of life. In "Fichte and Levinas. The Theory of Meaning and the Advent of the Infinite," Isabelle Thomas-Fogiel compares Fichte and Levinas through the question of the meaning and status of the transcendental in phenomenology. She argues Fichte is closer to Husserl than Levinas because he is a transcendental philosopher. In "The Other and the Necessary Conditions of the Self in Fichte's *Wissenschaftslehre* and Paul Ricoeur's Phenomenology of the Will," Arnold Farr examines Ricoeur's references to Fichte in the context of the attempt to develop a phenomenology of the will. These references shed light on Ricoeur's cryptic references to Fichte in laying the foundation for further work on the Fichte/Ricoeur relationship. Violetta L. Waibel addresses a complex theme: "Does the Methodology of Phenomenology Involve Dual Intentionality? Some Remarks on Conceptions of Phenomenology in Husserl, Fichte, Hegel, Sartre and Freud." She identifies a common phenomenological thread on two levels: a first level is intentionality directed toward objects of research followed on the second intentional level through the uncovering of hidden implications.

The book closes with a paper by Wayne Martin on the theme of "Fichte's Logical Legacy: Thetic Judgment from the *Wissenschaftslehre* to Brentano." According to Martin, it is not usual to think of Fichte as a logician, nor indeed to think of him as leaving a legacy that shaped the subsequent history of symbolic logic. Yet Fichte formulated an agenda in formal logic that his students (and their students in turn) used to spark a logical revolution.

# I. Fichte's Wissenschaftslehre as a Phenomenology

# On Fichte and Phenomenology

Tom Rockmore

Duquesne University – Pittsburgh, PA

The central question that needs to be answered in any discussion of Fichte and phenomenology is: what, if anything, is phenomenological about Fichte's position? This paper will try to answer that question and, in the process, show the importance of Fichte from a phenomenological perspective. I will argue that he contributes to the post-Kantian idealist development that should be understood as the development of a phenomenological form of idealism. The work of the paper will consist in understanding "idealism," and "phenomenology," and in situating Fichte's idealism with respect to the latter.

## I. On "idealism"

To begin to answer this question, and before turning to Fichte, we need to define the terms "idealism" and "phenomenology." Both of these terms are used in different, often incompatible ways. The term "idealism" is apparently first used by Leibniz to refer to Plato. In responding to Bayle, he objects to "those who, like Epicurus and Hobbes, believe that the soul is "material" and adds that in his own position "whatever of good there is in the hypotheses of Epicurus and Plato, of the great materialists and the great idealists, is combined here."[1]

"Idealism" was a badge of honor at the turn of the nineteenth century, which became a mark of incompetence at the beginning of the twentieth century. Though there are idealists, there is no idealism, which is not a natural kind, but rather a normative term employed to designate a number of theories, in practice often those one desires to refute. Marxism, as distinguished from Marx, and Anglo-American analytic philosophy each emerged as a distinctive philosophical tendency through refuting "ideal-

---

[1] Leibniz, Gottfried Wilhelm, *Philosophische Schriften*, edited by C.J. Gerhardt, Berlin: Weidmann 1875–1890, IV, pp. 559–560.

ism," which they understand in different ways. Marxism since Engels understands idealism as the opposite of materialism.[2] The latter term refers to a scientific grasp of the empirical world based on experience. In analytic circles, at least since Moore's pioneer discussion of "idealism," this term refers to a theory, or type of theory, which allegedly denies the existence of the mind-independent external world.[3]

It will be sufficient here to identify detect four main forms of philosophical idealism, which, except for British idealism, concern distinctive, but different epistemological approaches. British idealism is a tendency, which was mainly created by early analytic philosophy, which refuted it. I will have nothing further to say about British idealism, not because I think it is uninteresting, but rather because its main members (Green, Bradley, Bosanquet, McTaggart and others) apparently do not share any single distinctive epistemological thesis.

We do not know and cannot now determine Plato's position. Platonic idealism includes the notorious theory of ideas, which is often attributed to Plato, and which combines ontological and epistemological elements, as well as a distinction between appearance and reality, what Kant later called things in themselves or noumena. In his attack on the cognitive function of art and aesthetic objects, Plato refutes any form of what later came to be known as representational approach to knowledge. He can be read as suggesting that, under the proper conditions, on grounds of nature and nurture some selected individuals can directly intuit the real. Idealism is, from this perspective, a representational approach to reality.

The term "the new way of ideas" was applied to Locke at the end of the 17$^{th}$ century to differentiate his position from Platonism, or the so-called old way of ideas.[4] I will be using this term in an extended sense to refer both to British empiricism and continental rationalism. By the "new way of ideas" I will have in mind a relation between ideas and reality according to which, under appropriate conditions, ideas in the mind "match up" one to one so to speak with the mind-independent world as it

---

2   See Engels, Friedrich: *Ludwig Feuerbach and the Outcome of Classical German Philosophy*, ed. Dutt, C. P., New York 1941.
3   See Moore, George Edward: "The Refutation of Idealism", in: *Philosophical Studies*, London: 1922, 1958.
4   The term was applied to Locke by Bishop Stillingfleet. For an account of the controversy between Locke and Stillingfleet, see "Prolegomena: Biographical, Critical, and Historical," in: *John Locke, An Essay Concerning Human Understanding*, collated and annotated by A.C. Fraser, New York 1959, I, pp. xli-xlii.

is in itself. In all its variants, the proponents of the new way of ideas, the main modern approach to knowledge prior to Kant, are committed to reviving an anti-Platonic, representational approach to knowledge. There is a way the world is and, under the right conditions, we can reliably claim to know it, not directly, say through intuition, but indirectly through ideas, which under the proper conditions correctly represent it. My reason for calling this a form of idealism is that, as we shall shortly see, Kant, who is an idealist, is in part committed to representationalism.

By "German idealism" I will have in mind the philosophical movement that begins with Kant. My view of Kant is frankly "revisionary," that is intended to call attention to a different way of reading Kant. It is often suggested that Kant's position forms a single unitary whole.[5] I contend, on the contrary, that Kant's critical philosophy, the mature position he worked out during the so-called critical period, exemplifies two different approaches to knowledge I will be respectively calling representationalism and constructivism. Though Kant proudly calls attention to his relation to Plato, Kantian representationalism is, as the name suggests, an anti-Platonic representational approach to knowledge, which extends and perfects the new way of ideas. Kant, who already has a role in his theory for the term "idea," uses "representation" (*Vorstellung*) for the role played in the new way of ideas by the former term. In the famous letter to Herz (21 February 1772), Kant formulates the problem of knowledge as analyzing the relation of representations (*Vorstellungen*) to objects (*Gegenstände*). He later develops this approach in the *Critique of Pure Reason*. Yet Kant, who is inconsistent, also has another, different, incompatible approach to knowledge. This second approach is sometimes suggested under the heading of a Copernican Revolution, a term Kant never uses to designate his own position, but that was nearly immediately used by such contemporaries as Reinhold and Schelling to refer to Kant's critical philosophy.

---

5   See Hanna, Robert: *Kant and the Foundations of Analytic Philosophy*, Oxford: 2001, p. 22. "Kant's Copernican Revolution of 1781–7 is in this way an all-things considered answer to the fundamental semantic question he raised in 1772: how can mental representations—and more specifically necessary a priori mental representations—refer to their objects. And the answer is that mental representations refer to their objects because 'objects must conform to our cognitions'; hence our true a priori judgments are necessarily true independently of all sense experience because they express just those cognitive forms or structures to which all the proper objects of human cognition automatically conform."

The interpretation of this concept is difficult. One way to describe it is to notice the difference in the respective approaches to knowledge between representationalism and constructivism. A representational approach presupposes that, on the basis of a distinction between a mind-independent external object, and a representation of it, we can reliably claim to know the object through its representation. This approach makes two presuppositions. First, it distinguishes between phenomena and appearances (*Erscheinungen*), also called representations. Second, it presupposes that representations in fact represent. Yet, as Kant later realized, this cannot in fact ever be shown. The alternative, which Kant later adopted, is to deny the distinction between appearances and phenomena in working out a theory of knowledge based merely on phenomena. From this angle of vision, the problem is not to know something else through a phenomenon that is also an appearance, but merely to know a phenomenon. Kant's famous suggestion, which is the basis of his Copernican revolution, and which has still not received the attention it deserves, can be paraphrased as the claim that a minimal condition of knowledge is that the subject "construct" its cognitive object, in this case the phenomenon.[6] In other words, Kant's theory of knowledge is an effort to explain how, if the cognitive object is a phenomenon, knowledge in general is possible. In that sense, it is and should be understood as a form of phenomenology.

## II. On "Phenomenology"

My rapid remarks on "idealism" culminate in what I am calling the constructivist approach to knowledge based on the construction of phenomena. The term "phenomenology" is used in many different ways. Thus Heidegger's ontological form of phenomenology is inconsistent with Husserl's epistemological emphasis. Husserl understands his position as incompatible with Hegelian phenomenology, which he sharply but incorrectly criticizes as lacking a critique of reason.[7]

In the final chapter of the *Metaphysical Foundations of Science*, Kant discusses a modal approach to matter under heading of phenomenology.

---

[6] For an interpretation of Kant based on the distinction between representationalism and constructivism, see Rockmore, Tom: *Kant and Idealism*, New Haven 2007.

[7] For Husserl's critique of Hegel, see Husserl, Edmund: *Philosophie als strenge Wissenschaft*, ed. by Wilhelm Szilasi, Frankfurt a. M. 1965, p. 11.

If "phenomenology" is taken as referring to description rather than explanation, then it identifies descriptive practices in a wide variety of cognitive and non-cognitive disciplines, including certain kinds of poetry, painting, and even natural science. Analytic philosophy of science, which favors forms of causal explanation, lays particular weight on prediction. Yet this criterion seems overly narrow. Many types of science, including paleontology and archeology, are retrospective and descriptive, not predictive, and, in that specific sense, close to certain views of phenomenology. If phenomenological description means something like pre-predicative or pre-theoretical redescription, then Descartes' famous wax example might be an illustration. A further non-standard philosophical instance might be Wittgenstein, who, in the *Philosophical Investigations*, insists on the importance of description rather than explanation.[8]

If there were more space, it would be interesting to trace the evolution of the understanding of "phenomenology" from Lambert, where the term apparently first emerges in a philosophical sense, to the present day. It will be sufficient here to focus on two very different forms of phenomenology linked to the names of Hegel and Husserl. Though very different, both theories can be understood as interpretations of "idealism."

Kant explicitly suggests that philosophy worthy of the name begins and ends in the critical philosophy. By analogy, it is sometimes, but erroneously, believed that theory of knowledge worthy of the name ends in Kant. Post-Kantian German idealism can be understood as an effort to continue and perfect the critical philosophy, and, if its central insight is the Copernican revolution, to carry it further than Kant in completing his position according to its letter while, if necessary, neglecting its spirit.

Hegelian phenomenology can be described as an outgrowth of the effort to improve on Kant by such important successors as Fichte, Schelling and finally Hegel, leading, in the latter, to a theory of knowledge based solely on phenomena in eliminating appearances in the Kantian sense, more precisely any relation between phenomena and things in themselves. Hegelian phenomenology is explicitly constructivist. The key insight, which is clearly a version of Kant's Copernican revolution, is that when we know we know no more than phenomena that we in

---

8 "We must do away with all *explanation*, and description alone must take its place. And this description gets its light, that is to say its purpose, from the philosophical problems." Wittgenstein, Ludwig: *Philosophical Investigations*, transl. Anscombe, Gertrude Elizabeth Margaret, New York 1966, § 109, p. 47.

some sense construct, not a priori, but from a point situated within the social and historical world.

In Kant's Copernican revolution, in language he does not use, this insight takes the form of a claim for the identity in difference of subject and object, knower and known. Hegel offers an interpretation of this basic insight in what is often referred to as the philosophy of identity (*Identitätsphilosophie*), according to which at the limit subject and object, knower and known coincide. Yet different thinkers understand this claim in diverse ways. Unlike Kant, who takes an apodictic, a-historical approach to knowledge, Hegel takes an experimental, almost pragmatic, deeply historical view of knowledge, very different from its Husserlian counterpart.

Husserl is sometimes mistakenly said to have invented phenomenology or at least to be its first significant representative. Phenomenology is often understood mainly in terms of Husserl's position and the reactions to it.[9] The Husserlian phenomenological tradition includes a series of disparate figures, who, other than their appeal to the common term "phenomenology," arguably do not share any unambiguous doctrinal commitment. Heidegger, who initially characterized his position as phenomenological ontology, is often described as a phenomenologist. Yet he holds a view that is clearly incompatible with Husserl's. If Heidegger's position is correct, then Husserl's is incorrect, and conversely. Husserl's core position changed greatly over time, beginning in an initial emphasis on pure description that later turns into transcendental idealism intended to realize the idea of philosophy as a so-called rigorous science. Typical features in Husserlian phenomenology include stress on apodicticity, anti-psychologism, anti-naturalism, and anti-relativism.

The relations between Hegelian and Husserlian phenomenology have often been misunderstood. The French view (e.g. Kojève, Hyppolite, Derrida) that they share a single phenomenological method is demonstrably false. Hegel's critique of Kant's effort to isolate an identifiable method from the process of knowledge counts against any reading of his position as based on a discernable phenomenological method.[10] What they do share is a generally constructivist approach growing out of Kant, hence a relation to Kantian idealism. Yet the differences here are far more important. Above I attributed to Kant a simultaneous allegiance to represen-

---

9  See, e.g., Sokolowski, Robert: *Introduction to Phenomenology*, New York 2000.
10 See *Enzyklopädie der philosophischen Wissenschaften*, in: *G. W. F. Hegel-Werke*, ed. Moldenhauer, Eva and Michel, Karl Rinus, Frankfurt a. M. 1971, Bd. 8, I, § 10, Bemerkung, pp. 53–54.

tational and constructivist approaches to knowledge. Like other forms of post-Kantian idealism, Hegelian phenomenology, which gives up any vestige of the thing in itself, is concerned solely and wholly with phenomena, not with appearances. Husserl is difficult to interpret since he changes his terminology and often his position from text to text. But broadly speaking, and despite a constructivist dimension, his main emphasis lies on the relation between the intention and the intended, the noesis and the noema, transcendental psychology and empirical psychology, in a distant version of Kantian representationalism. Though there are constructivist aspects of Husserl's position, unlike Hegel and the post-Kantian German idealists, through his understanding of intentionality Husserl remains committed to some form of representationalism, hence to a form of the thing in itself, unlike post-Kantian idealism in which this concept disappears.

### III. Fichtean Phenomenology and the Concept of the Thing in Itself

I believe that, in post-Kantian idealism, Fichte precedes Hegel down the post-Kantian phenomenological road. The key insight is the Copernican idea running throughout the entire German idealist tradition, including Marx, and independently in such thinkers as Hobbes and Vico, that we know only what we in some sense construct, produce or make, as distinguished from uncovering, discovering or finding the cognitive object.

I see Fichte as making at least three important contributions to phenomenology as it arises within German idealism: in the decisive elimination of the thing in itself, leading, despite his claims of faithfulness to Kant, to a theory of knowledge based on phenomena rather than appearances; through a deeply revised view of the subject, pointing toward philosophical anthropology inconsistent with Kant"s antipsychologism; and through an incipient turn to history.

Kant arguably introduces the concept of things in themselves, or nouemena, to solve problems arising in his position. These include the source of the contents of sensory intuition, but above all the ability to make objective cognitive claims. Fichte is the first of the great German idealists to reject the concept of the thing in itself, hence the first centrally important figure after Kant to point to the need to reconstruct the critical philosophy by simply dropping this concept in the critical philosophy, where it is a key theme. It is only if there is in fact a way the mind-uninterpreted external world is, and if further under a selected set of circumstances we can reliably claim to know it as it is, that representations can be said to represent.

Fichte's view of the thing in itself turns on two central insights. First, following contemporaries opposed to Kant's concept, he argues that, on the grounds of the critical philosophy itself, the idea of a mind-independent external world understood as the cause of sensations is indefensible. Second, in both *Introductions* (1797) he suggests there are only two ways of doing philosophy: from the perspective of the subject, which is idealism, or from the perspective of the object, or thing in itself, which is dogmatism. This line of argument leads to the inference that Kant is himself unable to overcome dogmatism in defending a concept of the thing in itself. A striking instance where Kant falls into dogmatism is in the famous Herz letter, mentioned above, where he provides the initial description of the problem of knowledge. This description calls for a solution of the epistemological problem along representational lines, hence for an analysis of the relation of a representation to the mind-independent external world that is not given in experience. It follows that, on the basis of Kant's theory, metaphysical reality cannot be known. It further follows that a claim for objective cognition cannot lie in the relation of a representation to an object understood as lying outside of experience. Any claim for objectivity must occur within the confines of experience, precisely what Fichte takes as the only legitimate sphere of philosophy. Fichte does not pursue this theme further. Yet he offers the essential insight, which will later be worked out by such post-Kantian German idealists as Hegel and such American pragmatists as Peirce and Dewey.

## IV. Fichtean Phenomenology and the Concept of the Subject

Fichte's most important contribution to German idealism, hence, by inference to phenomenology, is arguably his concept of the subject. It is not too much to say that in revising the Kantian view of subjectivity Fichte decisively transforms the problem of knowledge. The debate on knowledge prior to Fichte culminates in an analysis of knowledge in general, which, in Kant, leads to a concept of the subject as a mere epistemological function, or better fiction. After Fichte, the main question concerns grasping the nature and limits of human knowledge on the basis of finite human being.

Fichte's contribution in this respect has not been well understood, in part because of a widespread, but misleading belief that he holds that the subject simply "generates," produces or creates the world out of its own mind. In a letter to Goethe, Schiller writes: "According to Fichte's verbal statements, the self creates through its representations; and all reality is only in the self. The world is to the self like a ball, which the self has thrown out and then caught again through reflection."[11] A more sophisticated, similar interpretation is stated by Josiah Royce: "That this self of philosophy is not the individual man of ordinary life appears from the very outset of Fichte's discussion. The individual man of ordinary life is one of the beings to be defined by philosophy, and is certainly not the principle of philosophy."[12]

If Fichte in fact believed that the subject were in any obvious sense the "source" of the world, then it could not be understood as a finite human being. The point at issue between Fichte and Kant can be briefly described as follows. For Kant, the subject, or transcendental unity of apperception, is the highest point of the critical philosophy. For Kant, who emphasizes an anti-psychological approach to knowledge, the epistemological subject is an epistemological posit, which functions to provide knowledge meeting Kant's normative criteria. Only a fictitious philosophical subject can be wholly free, entirely rational, and beyond time and place, hence a source of perfect knowledge.

In reaction to Kant, Fichte inaugurates a post-Kantian philosophical anthropology that arguably agrees with the spirit if not with the letter of the critical philosophy. Instead of "deducing" the nature of the subject from a normative concept of knowledge, Fichte reverses the procedure in describing a theory of knowledge on the basis of the subject. In beginning from what he understands as human experience, or the contents of consciousness accompanied by a feeling of necessity, Fichte depicts the subject as caught up in the social context as a finite human being. The object is understood in terms of the subject, or what the subject is not. The absolute subject is what the finite subject would be if, at the limit, it were wholly freed from the limitations of its surroundings, against which it strives. The Fichtean subject is depicted from two perspectives, as theoretically limited and as practically unlimited in striving to expand the limits of its activity in order to conform to what should be the case.

---

11 Letter from Schiller to Goethe dates 28 October 1794, in: Johann Christoph Friedrich Schiller: *Briefwechsel zwischen Schiller und Goethe*, ed. Hauff, Hermann, Stuttgart 1856, Vol. I, p. 26 (translation by the author).
12 Royce, Josiah: *Lectures on Modern Idealism*, 1919, reprint ed., New Haven 1964, p. 97.

In turning away from a description of the subject in terms of the requirements of knowledge, Fichte describes finite human beings, who find themselves in a social setting, and desire, as Fichte says, to work out a theory to explain experience. In related ways, all the British empiricists offer theories of human knowledge. This element is quickly lost in Kant's concern to analyze the conditions of knowledge in general in abandoning the limits of the finite subject. From this perspective, one of Fichte's most important contributions lies, in Kant's wake, in redirecting attention to the finite, human subject as the basis of a revised constructivist approach to knowledge.

## V. Fichte and the Historical Turn

Kant is a basically an a-historical thinker. Though he is interested in history, he considers knowledge worthy of the name to be a priori, hence independent of the historical context. Unlike the critical philosophy, post-Kantian German idealism is increasingly historical. The historical turn, which is implicit in Kant's Copernican revolution, and which implied that knowledge relies on the activity of the knowing subject, is clearly not taken by him. In different ways in Kant's wake a historical turn, which is absent in Kant, is undertaken by all the major post-Kantian idealists, including Fichte, Schelling, Hegel, and Marx. Fichte's own "historical" turn is arguably less successful than other aspects of his position since, unlike later post-Kantian idealist figures like Hegel and Marx, he is never able to bring his interest in history and his interest in knowledge together in a historical conception of knowledge.

Kant, who systematically maintains a wholly a-historical approach to knowledge, reacts to his former student, Herder, in creating the bases of an a-priori analysis of the very possibility of history. His a-historical approach further extends to the history of philosophy. Though he is clearly influenced by a number of earlier thinkers (e.g. Hume, Wolff, Leibniz, Plato, Aristotle and others), at least in an "official" sense he treats all prior philosophy as dogmatic, hence unworthy of the name. According to Kant, though there is historical knowledge, knowledge, including philosophical knowledge, is not itself historical.

Fichte does not himself undertake a historical turning. Yet he provides an important stimulus to the historical turning which is everywhere in post-Kantian philosophy, especially in Herder, but also in F. Schlegel, Schelling and Hegel. History depends on practice, but practice is not yet history. Practice is a stage situated between theory and history. Kant, who fails to subordinate theory to practice, absorbs practice into theory. Fichte, on the contrary, understands theory as arising out of practice.

Part of the difficulty of ascertaining Fichte's view of history is that he provides no more than a semi-popular presentation of it. The two main sources are the *Discourse on the German Nation* and *The Character of the Present Epoch*. In the "First Introduction," he says that the chemist and the ordinary person see the same thing from different perspectives, the former a priori and the latter a posteriori.[13] This suggests the possibility of identifying the main lines of history in independence of experience. In his "Conference on the destiny of the savant (1805)," he suggests the possibility of applying this approach to history.[14]

We can distinguish between Fichte's theories of history and knowledge of history. He summarizes his division of history into five different epochs in writing:

> In the preceding presentations, we have interpreted the present moment as an integral part of the overall plan concerning the terrestrial life of our species in revealing its hidden meaning. We have striven to understand the signs of the present moment on the basis of this concept, to deduce them as the necessary results of the part and to foresee their immediate consequences for the future.[15]

This claim reminds us of both Kant and Hegel. With respect to Kant, Fichte appears to differ in providing, in Kantian terms, not a regulative but a constitutive view of the nature of human history. Like Hegel, Fichte describes the present epoch as the historical moment in which freedom and necessity overlap.[16] We see here how Fichte, in the space between Kant and Hegel, restates the Kantian antinomy between freedom and causal necessity, in this case individual freedom and logical determinism, in anticipating Hegel's solution, based on Spinoza, of freedom as the manifestation of reason.

There are numerous parallels on this point between Fichte and Hegel. As Hegel will shortly do, Fichte stresses reason, freedom, development as a conceptual and historical process, more precisely the way in which different nations momentarily incarnate the spirit of an epoch before giving way to other nations. He further insists on the importance of the present

---

13  See IWL, p. 34; "Erste Einleitung in die Wissenschaftslehre," in: SW I, p. 449.
14  GA I/2, p. 53.
15  GdgZ, p. 248.
16  See GdgZ, p. 56.

epoch, what Hegel, in the *Phenomenology of Spirit*, later calls, in the wake of the French Revolution, "eine Zeit der Geburt und des Übergangs".[17]

The difference between the two perspectives, which is perhaps even more important than the similarity, concerns the distinction between reason and freedom. Fichte, who is close to Kant, hence to the Enlightenment view, arguably underestimates the difficulty of realizing reason in a social context, which he describes as "the plan" consisting in "educating the human species through reason to freedom."[18] Hegel, who differs on this point, holds that reason is always rational, but never in a final sense. Unlike Kant and Fichte, for Hegel freedom is not merely a "given," not, like Descartes, something that is always already there, but rather the aim to be realized in history.[19]

## VI. Fichte, Representationalism and Phenomenology

It might be objected that I am misdescribing Fichte's position as related to Kantian constructivism and not to Kantian representationalism. For Fichte's analysis of theoretical knowledge in the initial and most influential version of the *Wissenschaftslehre* (1794) culminates in a "Deduction of Presentation" (*Deduktion der Vorstellung*).

Here as in his other writings, it is important to notice that Fichte knowingly or unknowingly simply overestimates the extent to which he is faithful to Kant. We can detect this exaggeration of his fidelity to the author of the critical philosophy as early as the well known review of Aenesidemus. The upshot of his complex discussion of Aenesidemus' critique of Reinhold lies in refuting a causal theory of representation on both Kantian and general grounds. Fichte's reason is obvious. A representational theory of knowledge depends on causality, also called the principle of sufficient reason, to suggest that the object causes its representation in the subject. This is a linear analysis of knowledge running from object to subject and back again. Yet since he understands the object as ultimately dependent on the subject, Fichte introduces a circular model of knowledge he perhaps abusively attributes to Kant in claiming that the thing or object affecting the subject is constituted or constructed by it.

---

17  G. W. F. *Hegel-Werke*, III, p. 18.
18  GdgZ, p. 20.
19  See *Vorlesungen über die Philosophie der Geschichte*, in: G. W. F. *Hegel*-Werke, XII, p. 32.

This line of analysis has two consequences. First, Fichte attributes to Kant the denial of a representational theory of knowledge in favor of a constructivist approach. This attribution is problematic in two ways. First, it overlooks the representationalist dimension of the critical philosophy that Kant maintains even after he introduces the constructivist strategy for knowledge in the Copernican turn. Second, in removing the obvious tension, or the contradiction between representationalism and constructivism in the critical philosophy, Fichte's reading of Kant makes the critical philosophy better than it is. There are many passages where Kant straightforwardly appears to expound a representational, but not a constructivist view of knowledge. Yet Fichte's interpretation of Kant suggests that, if Fichte is a Kantian, then Kant, like Fichte, also holds a constructivist, but non-representationalist approach to knowledge.

We see this clearly in Fichte's "Deduction of Representation" in the *Grundlage*, where he understands the crucial term "representation" ("*Vorstellung*") in a non-Kantian sense. From the point of view of philosophy, we are in fact wholly self-determining; but from the perspective of life we are determined by our surroundings. In explaining the determination through its own nature, the subject accounts for the fact of being determined only by itself. To put the same point differently, Fichte is dealing with, to use his term, two opposing trains of reflection: the subject which is determined and the subject which is self-determining, The second series is merely the reverse of the first. The union, or unity of these two utterly opposed trains of reflection, viz. the objective and the subjective, the real and the ideal, or again the fact of consciousness and its philosophical explanation, can only be brought about through the productive imagination. At the close of this difficult line of argument, Fichte concludes" dass alle Realität—es versteht sich *für uns*, wie es denn in einem System der Transzendentalphilosophie nicht anders verstanden werden soll—bloss durch die Einbildungskraft hervorgebracht werde."[20]

In this respect, Fichte's view is both Kantian and non-Kantian. Kant holds that what is real for the subject, is, hence, intuitable by it, precisely for the reason that we bring it forth as a condition of experience and knowledge of objects. Yet unlike, say, the partisans of the new way of ideas, and unlike Kant in his representationalist mode, Fichte does not link representation to the hopeless task of correctly representing things in themselves, or the way the mind-independent world is. In fact, he clearly breaks on this point with Kant who, in the famous Herz letter,

---

20 SW I, p. 227.

seems to formulate the problem of knowledge as precisely requiring an analysis of how representations relate to metaphysical reality. On the contrary, Fichte says that we represent no more than what we ourselves construct through the productive imagination.

## VII. Conclusion: Fichte and Phenomenology

As a post-Kantian German idealist, Fichte belongs to a transformation by many hands of Kant's critical philosophy in an increasingly phenomenological direction. Kant hesitates between two versions of the theory of knowledge. These include a theory based on the distinction between appearance and phenomenon, or representationalism; and another, incompatible theory based solely on phenomena, or constructivism, which is a form of phenomenology. The difference lies in the difference between phenomena and appearances. All appearances are phenomena but only some phenomena are appearances. In cutting the link between phenomena and mind-independent reality, Fichte opens the way for phenomenology understood as a science of phenomena that are not appearances since they give up any claim to represent things in themselves or again the mind-independent reality.

Post-Kantian idealism is phenomenology, to which Fichte makes a three-fold contribution: he decisively rejects the concept of the thing-in-itself, leading to a very different kind of idealism that, as phenomenological, no longer relies on a mind-independent, but unknowable real; he completely rethinks the concept of the subject as finite human being, hence overcoming the Kantian division between the conditions of knowledge and human mental activity; and, like others in Kant's wake, he begins a historical turn leading away from an apodictic concept of knowledge toward a conception of human beings, hence human knowledge, as situated within, hence limited by, history. From this perspective, the limit of Fichte's phenomenological approach lies less in the turn to history than in his inability to integrate knowledge and history in a fully historical conception of human knowledge.

# The Concept of Phenomenology in Fichte's *Wissenschaftslehre* of 1804/II

CLAUDE PICHÉ

Université de Montréal

The topic of this presentation is the concept of phenomenology as we find it in Fichte's *Doctrine of Science* of 1804. I refer here to the second series of lectures given during that year, between April 16 and June 8.[1] I do not want to go into the concrete details of this phenomenology, since it represents the second part of an undertaking that is extraordinarily dense and speculative. As we know, the 1804 *Wissenschaftslehre* is composed of two main parts, the first being a theory of truth, or what we could now call an "alethology,"[2] as the counterpart of phenomenology. It consists of an ascending movement, whereby the pure "insight" (*Einsicht*) gives access to the absolute, and of a descending movement, from the absolute back to the phenomena. Taken together, these two movements make up a complete exposition of Fichte's *philosophia prima*. In fact, this version of the *Wissenschaftslehre* has a special status within the Fichtean corpus since it is "one of the most accomplished texts"[3] that he has left us, and because it announces the further developments of the doctrine of science.

The reason why it might be helpful here to concentrate primarily on the concept of phenomenology is that it deserves particular attention due to a certain ambiguity in the formulation of its definition. Therefore, understanding the correct articulation of the two elements included in this concept may be rewarding. In lecture 13, Fichte defines phenomenology as a "theory of phenomenon and of appearance".[4] The question is then:

---

1  For an account of the circumstances under which these lectures were held, see Lauth, Reinhard: "Über Fichtes Lehrtätigkeit in Berlin von Mitte 1799 bis Anfang 1805 und seine Zuhörerschaft", in: *Vernünftige Durchdringung der Wirklichkeit. Fichte und sein Umkreis*, Neuried 1994, pp. 191–232.
2  Goddard, Jean-Christophe: *Fichte (1801–1813). L'émancipation philosophique*, Paris 2003, p. 39.
3  Vetö, Miklos: *Fichte. De l'Action à l'Image*, Paris 2001, p. 102.
4  WL-1804-II, p. 138. (all translations are my own)

how is the word "and" to be read here? Does it mean "or in other words" or does it link two different things, namely phenomenon and appearance? One might be tempted to opt for the first reading of the definition of phenomenology if we compare it with the twofold definition given by Fichte in the first part of his lectures: the *Seynslehre* is a "theory of reason *and* of truth".[5] Here, in contrast with the definition of phenomenology, we suspect no opposition between reason and truth, whereas phenomenon (*Erscheinung*) and appearance (*Schein*) have very different meanings. A phenomenon can be considered as something that is neutral with respect to its propensity to lead to truth or falsehood. On the other hand, the German word *Schein* (translated henceforth by the word "appearance") bears the sense of an illusion and the possibility of deception. Thus, I think that we might be well advised to maintain a clear distinction between the two elements of Fichte's idea of phenomenology and to opt for the second reading. His concept is a complex one and, as we will see, there are good reasons for this.

In what follows, I would like to proceed to a historical survey of Fichte's forerunners in the philosophical use of the term phenomenology. The fact is that Fichte does not quote his sources in this matter and it is not altogether clear from whom he has borrowed his concept of phenomenology. One thing is certain, however. The history of the term phenomenology as used to designate a philosophical discipline goes back 40 years. Johann Heinrich Lambert employs it for the first time in his *Neues Organon* in 1764. We later find it in Kant's *Metaphysische Anfangsgründe der Naturwissenschaft* (1786) and then in Reinhold's *Beyträge zur leichtern Uebersicht des Zustandes der Philosophie am Anfang des 19. Jahrhunderts*, more precisely in the fourth issue (1802) of this series of contributions. To be sure, the meaning of the term "phenomenology" varies considerably according to the philosophical context in which it is used. Therefore, the perspective I shall adopt here will be a more or less formal one. We will study the semantic content of this concept through its short history solely in order to draw structural analogies; otherwise we would lose sight of the uniqueness of Fichte's project in the *Wissenschaftslehre* of 1804. In fact, phenomenology is associated here with the externalisation of absolute being: In the second part of his lecture course, Fichte aims at tracing the genesis of phenomena as part of the manifestation of the absolute in order to prevent their being mistaken for ontologically independent objects and becoming, therefore, false appearance.

---

5  WL-1804-II, pp. 150–151.

Fichte's definition of phenomenology is composite insofar as it unites two elements that can be treated independently from one another. And this is precisely the case if we consider the use of this concept found in Lambert and the one found in Kant. For the former, phenomenology deals exclusively with appearance, while for the latter it deals with phenomena.

In Lambert's *Neues Organon*, the word 'phenomenology' is used to designate the fourth and last part of the book. Lambert is considered to be the inventor of phenomenology as a philosophical discipline, and we must take notice of the fact that at first this discipline was designed to deal with illusion and delusion. The subtitle of the fourth part of his book corresponds to one of the two components of Fichte's definition: "*Lehre von dem Schein*" – Fichte writes *Scheinlehre* – and there is no doubt, according to the definition found in the foreword to Lambert's whole work, that it is a theory elaborated in order to prevent appearance from leading the knowing subject into error: "Finally Phenomenology, or the theory of appearance, is the fourth [science] and has to single out appearance and provide the means to avoid it and to create our way [durchdringen] to truth".[6] The word *Schein*, which is at the center of this definition, clearly has a negative accent, as opposed to the more neutral term *Erscheinung* (phenomenon), which Lambert does not use in his phenomenology as a technical term. Appearance is conceived as a serious obstacle in the search for truth. Its role is stated in the following passage, taken from §1 of the Phenomenology: "[Appearance] very often leads [us] to represent to ourselves the things in another form, and to easily take what they appear to be for what they really are, or to confuse [reality] with [appearance]."[7] According to Lambert, it is "always a mistake"[8] to take the appearance for the thing itself, for the thing as it is in reality. Nevertheless, the mere appearance of things, when it is unmasked and recognized as such, may become an incentive to the search for truth and lead to the discovery of the real nature of things. As a model for the phenomenological project, Lambert refers to the way an astronomer proceeds. For example, if an astronomer observes a certain movement of the stars, he might suspect this movement to be a mere appearance, and can take it as a starting point in order to search for the hidden laws of this

---

6 Lambert, Johann Heinrich: "Vorrede", in: *Neues Organon, Philosophische Schriften* I, ed. Arndt, H.-W., (Hildesheim : Olms, 1965), not paginated.
7 Lambert, Johann H.: *Neues Organon, Philosophische Schriften* II, pp. 217–218.
8 Lambert, Johann H.: "Vorrede", in: *Neues Organon, Philosophische Schriften* I, not paginated.

movement. In the end, he might even come to the conclusion that it is the spectator and the earth under his feet that are moving, and not the stars.

Let us now turn to Kant. We know that he was familiar with the *Neues Organon*, to which he occasionally refers, especially in his lectures on logic.[9] In view of this fact, it is all the more interesting to note that in his *Metaphysical Foundations of Natural Science* from 1786 he presents a definition of phenomenology that is not only different from the Lambertian conception, but that moreover seems to be stated in direct opposition to Lambert. Kant conceives phenomenology as a theory of phenomena (*Erscheinungen*), or more precisely as a theory that explains how phenomena become experience. I do not intend to go into the details of the specific form of phenomenology developed in the fourth part of Kant's book. It might suffice to point out that it deals with the movement of bodies from the standpoint of the categories of modality. This means that the phenomena in this case are material ones and that the concept of experience is considered not in the context of transcendental philosophy, but rather of the metaphysics of nature. But this specific use of the term here does not matter too much, since what Kant has to say about the difference between *Erscheinung* and *Schein* holds for the "whole" of philosophy.

Kant argues that it is of the utmost importance to distinguish *Erscheinung* from *Schein*, because *Schein* as opposed to *Erscheinung* already implies a judgment. And in this case the judgment might very well lie on subjective grounds instead of objective ones. Involving as such no judgment, the *Erscheinung* is not exposed to such a "danger". It is still neutral, so to speak, with regard to truth or falsehood.

> What is in question here is not the transformation of appearance [*Schein*] into truth, but rather of phenomenon [*Erscheinung*] into experience; because in appearance the understanding with its judgment determining the object is always involved, even though it runs the risk of taking the subjective for the objective; in the phenomenon no judgment at all from the understanding is involved. This remark is useful not only here but for philosophy as a whole, since otherwise, when dealing with phenomena we take this expression as having the same meaning as appearance, we always expose ourselves to misunderstanding.[10]

---

9   Kant, Immanuel: *Logik* (Jäsche), Ak IX, p. 21.
10  Kant, Immanuel: *Metaphysische Anfangsgründe der Naturwissenschaft*, Ak. IV, p. 555.

This explicit warning seems to be directed at those, like Lambert, who would be tempted to confuse Kant's conception of the phenomena with mere appearances. For the reader of the first edition of the *Critique of Pure Reason*, this warning sounds familiar. For instance, at the beginning of the Transcendental Dialectic, Kant makes this point in similar terms: appearance involves a certain claim to truth, whereas the phenomenon, critically understood, does not involve any such claim.[11] *Erscheinung* in fact is a term that is introduced in the Transcendental Aesthetic, that is, prior to dealing with the role of concepts and judgments in knowledge. But even at this early stage, the reader might be tempted, with regard to the distinction between phenomenon and thing in itself, to declare the phenomenon to be mere illusion deprived of any reality; which is another case of the confusion between *Erscheinung* and *Schein*, as Kant indicates.[12] Kant's other remark, made this time in the Aesthetic, was provoked by the objection brought up by "men of intelligence" such as Mendelssohn and Sulzer. But it might be relevant to note that Lambert (who died in 1777) was also among those who had voiced this objection, because he could not help but interpret Kant's *Erscheinung* in terms of his own concept of *Schein*. The fact that, in Kant, time is considered as a mere *Erscheinung* means for Lambert that the whole of experience and the changes taking place in it are nothing more than pure illusion.[13]

With Lambert and Kant, we are facing two very different conceptions of phenomenology and, at first glance, it is not clear how these conceptions could be reconciled or, moreover, combined into a coherent one, as will be the case in Fichte's *Wissenschaftslehre* of 1804/II. For instance, Kant does not even think of using the word phenomenology in his *Critique of Pure Reason* to designate his theory of phenomenon in the Transcendental Aesthetic, in all likelihood because he feared spreading confusion in the minds of readers acquainted with Lambert's definition. On the other hand, and for the same reason, it is out of the question for him to use this expression to characterize his own "logic of appearance" because of the confusion caused by the etymology of the word '*phenomeno*-logy'

---

11  KrV A293/B349–350.
12  KrV A36/B53.
13  See Lambert's letter to Kant of October 13, 1770, Ak. X, pp. 103–111. In the immediate aftermath of his *Dissertation* of 1770, Kant defined the positive part of this work as a *phaenomenologia genaralis*. See his letter to Lambert of September 2, 1770, Ak. X, p. 98. I have treated this question in my article "Kant, heredero del metodo fenomenológico de Lambert", trans. J. Rivera de Rosales, Madrid 2004, No. 18, pp. 45–68.

itself. This is precisely the ambiguity he wants to prevent, so he chose for his theory of transcendental illusion in the first *Critique* the classical term "dialectic".

But before Fichte, it is Reinhold, in his phenomenology of 1802, who undertakes to combine both meanings. In fact, he is the first to use the term "phenomenology" in the title of a philosophical work: *Elemente der Phänomenologie oder Erläuterung des rationalen Realismus durch seine Anwendung auf die Erscheinungen*.[14] In the *Vorbericht* to this work he gives a precise definition of the new understanding of the term: "[Phenomenology] completes the exposition of rational realism through the application of its principles to the phenomena, which it teaches us, with the help of these principles, to distinguish and separate from mere appearance."[15] Firstly, we find in this definition a move that reminds us of Lambert: in our knowledge, appearance must be identified as such and we must find the means to get rid of its spurious aspects. But there is, secondly, a Kantian element in this conception, in that the phenomenon serves as the basis of every appearance. We understand now the need felt by Kant to distinguish carefully between *Erscheinung* and *Schein*. The confusion is easily arrived at. But it is nevertheless the case that the theory of appearance presupposes, at least here according to Reinhold, a well-founded theory of phenomena, because appearance is nothing other than a misinterpreted phenomenon. The illusion occurs when the phenomenon is taken for more than what it is in reality, i.e., when the *Erscheinung* is mixed up "with the essential being, with the archetype" of all things.[16] If, on the other hand, we consider the matter closely, we realize that Fichte's conception of the problem of false appearance is in full agreement with that of Reinhold. It is also the case for Fichte that appearance occurs when the phenomenon is "taken for the essence itself."[17] This common conception of the articulation of *Erscheinung* and *Schein* at the basis of their respective phenomenologies, however, is not the only thing over which they agree. There are also striking similarities

---

14 Reinhold, Karl Leonhard: *Beyträge zur leichtern Uebersicht des Zustandes der Philosophie beym Anfang des 19. Jahrhunderts*, Heft IV, Hamburg 1802, p. 104.
15 Reinhold, Karl L.: *Beyträge*, Heft IV, p. IV.
16 Reinhold, Karl L.: *Beyträge*, Heft IV, pp. 108, 155. See also *Beyträge*, Heft VI (1803), pp. 69–70. I have tried to show what Reinhold's concept of phenomenology owes to Kant, and in particular to the Transcendental Dialectic, in: "Der Phänomenologiebegriff bei Kant und Reinhold" in: *K. L. Reinhold. Am Vorhof des Idealismus*, ed. P. Valenza, Pisa and Rome 2006, pp. 59–72.
17 WL-1804-II, p. 115.

between both philosophical projects and they are significant enough to be taken into consideration. It might suffice here to mention three of them, leaving aside momentarily the question of the possible influence of Reinhold's phenomenology of 1802 on Fichte's *Wissenschaftslehre* of 1804.

The first point worthy of mention concerns their views of the philosophical system. In both cases we find a twofold structure of the system. In Reinhold, rational realism consists of an ontology and of a phenomenology. The former deals with the essence of things as such, and it is made possible through the new approach set forward by Bardili: "thinking as thinking" (*Denken als Denken*), which is the only appropriate theoretical channel to gain access to the essence of things. The latter, phenomenology, elaborates, as we have read in the extensive title of this part of the system, an "application" of the results of the ontology to the phenomena. These phenomena are the elements of the sensible world, so that Reinhold's phenomenology has to be understood as a philosophical discourse on nature, as a "pure philosophy of nature".[18] Because the phenomena are thematized according to the ontological principles arrived at in the first part of the system, they do not run the risk of being taken for the "objects themselves" (*Objekte selbst*), but grasped strictly as what they are: phenomena. Taken together, these phenomena are involved in the "manifestation of the originary being [*Urwesen*] in the essence of things,"[19] or, put more simply, they contribute, as a mere "condition,"[20] to the "manifestation of God in nature".[21] From here, it is quite easy to draw a parallel with Fichte's *Wissenschaftslehre*, since we already know that the lectures of 1804 to which we are referring contain an ascending and a descending movement. In the first part, we are led from the multiplicity of things in the world to an insight into the one absolute being as such, while the second part exposes the manifestation of pure being through a multiplicity that is composed of what now has to be considered as mere phenomena. This is to say that the phenomenology developed in the second part has to produce the "deduction (of the diversity of phenomenal reality)"[22] which means that the world as we know it now has to be envisaged as the "phenomenon of the one true existent".[23]

---

18 Reinhold, Karl L.: *Beyträge*, Heft IV, p. 110.
19 Reinhold, Karl L.: *Beyträge*, Heft IV, pp. 104, 132.
20 Reinhold, Karl L.: *Beyträge*, Heft IV, p. 108.
21 Reinhold, Karl L.: *Beyträge*, Heft IV, p. 106.
22 WL-1804-II, p. 89.
23 WL-1804-II, p. 90.

The second similarity to which I would like to draw attention concerns the status of appearance. It is clear that Reinhold in his *Beyträge* as well as Fichte in his 1804 lectures deal extensively with the different philosophical systems in their historical forms. Specifically, they both take a very strong stand toward the systems of their contemporaries. But in this they have one point in common: they do not limit themselves to denouncing the false appearances present in the philosophical discourse of their opponents, for the simple reason that the problem of truth or falsehood is not just a matter of philosophical science, but also a problem for mankind in general. If their respective phenomenologies are to have universal reach, they have to show to what extent illusion and deception are facts that are not confined to classical systems. This is the reason why they both try to show how the mistakes found in highly technical metaphysical theories have their origins in everyday knowledge. The philosophical mistakes are just the consequences of a *Schein* already at work in ordinary knowledge.

For example, Fichte criticizes realism and idealism as two unilateral philosophical positions, which share the same prejudice in that they each in their own way claim to have access to the truth of things. As two diametrically opposed philosophical systems, both of them are refuted in the *Wissenschaftslehre*. But in order to refute them, the doctrine of science has to trace their origins – and the force of the illusion that they carry – in everyday knowledge. Therefore, the *Wissenschaftslehre* has to deal with

> the natural idealism and realism that stem, without our conscious intervention, from ordinary knowledge, at least in its derived occurrences and phenomena [...] It is also the goal of the Doctrine of Science to deduce [idealism and realism] as entirely natural and spontaneous disjunctions and unilateralities of ordinary knowledge.[24]

If we now turn to Reinhold, we can notice a similar attitude toward the origin of falsehood in philosophy. For Reinhold, the ultimate appearance in philosophy lies in the duality between subjectivity and objectivity and in the fact that they have come to be considered identical. It goes without saying that, in his eyes, Schelling's system of identity is the most perfect expression of this fatal mistake, which is nevertheless already at work in ordinary knowledge. Let us read the very first words of Reinhold's text on phenomenology:

---

24 WL-1804-II, p. 118.

The error which is contained in every other error and under which every other error is contained, lays [...] precisely in the appearance of the objectivity of the subjective, and of the subjectivity of the objective, which is held for the truth itself. This appearance, which according to its essence is one and the same in the common and in the speculative error, takes moreover in the latter case the appearance of an elevation above itself.[25]

To be sure, we also find a criticism of the dual structure of subjectivity/objectivity[26] in the *Wissenschaftslehre* of 1804, a criticism that Fichte pursues in his own terms. But more interesting here is their common concern to show that, beyond philosophical speculation, there is a certain kind of diffuse dogmatism that makes the ordinary person think that he or she is in presence of the things themselves. No wonder then that Fichte claims that almost all of mankind lives in the "world of error".[27] It is precisely the role of phenomenology to remind us that this world consists of mere phenomena and that they must be regarded as such.

The third point these authors have in common concerns what has come to be characterised as the philosophy of subjectivity. It is clear that Reinhold in his *Beyträge* stigmatizes Fichte's *Wissenschaftslehre* for being the quintessence of a philosophy based on the subject. And Fichte for his part is certainly authorized to claim that this accusation does not bear upon the Doctrine of Science, even at the time of its first inception in Jena. But be it as it may, the fact is that Reinhold, from 1800 on, not only turns his back on his *Elementarphilosophie*, among other things, but he further criticizes this earlier position systematically. We know that the *Elementarphilosophie* was based on a first principle that Reinhold designated as the "principle of representation" or as the "principle of consciousness". Both terms, representation and consciousness, refer to modern philosophy insofar as it is considered to be a philosophy of subjectivity. But now in his phenomenology, Reinhold, while not dismissing representation outright, does place it in the proper perspective in view of his new allegiance to rational realism. And the same goes for Fichte, who stigmatizes consciousness, envisaged as the ultimate ground of truth.

In his *Beyträge*, Reinhold relativizes the status of representation in that it is, from then on in his work, limited to the field of phenomenology as opposed to ontology. Ontology has access to the object "in itself"

---

25 Reinhold, Karl L.: *Beyträge,* Heft IV, p. III.
26 See WL-1804-II, pp. 24–25, p. 45.
27 WL-1804-II, p. 75.

while phenomenology can only disclose it as representation. In other words, representation is henceforth restricted to the realm of phenomena.

> The object of representation [...] as such, the represented, or the object as represented, is the phenomenon, and as the phenomenon, which is not a contradiction, which is therefore no mere appearance, it is as such in reality [Wirklichkeit][28]

As long as representation is restricted in its scope and limited to the correctly interpreted phenomena, there are no risks of delusion. In comparison, Fichte's position toward consciousness is quite similar. Consciousness certainly continues to play an all-important role in knowledge and the *Wissenschaftslehre* no doubt intends to describe it. The problem is, though, that one might be tempted to confer upon immediate consciousness the function of a foundation of knowledge, in which case it becomes nothing more than "vain appearance and error":

> the ground of truth as truth certainly does not lay in consciousness, but rather directly in truth itself [...] [consciousness] remains only the outer phenomenon of truth [...] whose ground still has to be given to you. But if you think that in this consciousness lays the ground for truth to be truth, then you fall under the spell of appearance.[29]

As we can see, consciousness itself is, in light of the absolute, a mere phenomenon, and it is consequently evident that it cannot serve as the ground for the truth of being.

The three points that I have just stressed are intended to show analogies between the Reinholdian and the Fichtean conceptions of phenomenology: (1) the phenomenal world as a manifestation of the absolute, (2) the natural illusion present in ordinary knowledge as the condition of philosophical appearance and (3) the critique of the philosophy of subjectivity. It goes without saying that both phenomenologies belong to philosophical systems that are appreciably different, and that we can not speak with certainty of an influence on Fichte of Reinhold's texts published in the *Beyträge* between 1801 and 1803. In fact, Fichte does not acknowledge any debt toward Reinhold in his *Wissenschaftslehre* of 1804. When mentioned, the name of Reinhold is an object of criticism. Jean-François Goubet, who has studied this problem in detail in an interesting article entitled "Fichte's Phenomenology in the WL-1804/II: a Historical Approach," admits that he could not arrive at anything conclu-

---

28   Reinhold, Karl L.: *Beyträge*, Heft VI, p. 69.
29   WL-1804-II, p. 137.

sive.³⁰ The only thing we know is that Fichte had read the first issues of the *Beyträge*, but we do not know exactly whether he studied the fourth issue, which contains the remarks on phenomenology. In a letter to Bardili from November 21, 1803, Reinhold writes that he has sent Fichte the sixth issue of his *Beyträge*, and in a letter dating from the same period to Friedrich Christian Perthes, Fichte acknowledges the reception of Reinhold's "writings" – in plural, – which leads the editors of the *GA* to conjecture that he received the fifth together with the sixth issue.³¹ But no conclusion can be drawn from the simple fact that he was in possession of these issues dealing abundantly with *Erscheinung* and *Schein*.

Before coming to my conclusion, it might be useful to focus on Fichte's phenomenology for its own sake and to briefly sketch its status within the economy of the 1804 *Wissenschaftslehre*. If the first part of the lectures is a long ascending path toward truth, it does not mean that the second, descending part brings us back to the realm of illusion. In other words, the fact that the "theory of truth" of the first part is followed in the second by a "theory of appearance [*Schein*]" does not mean that the latter contains only a theory of deception. We have come to realize that the *Erscheinungslehre* – also constitutive of the second part – does not mean the same as *Scheinlehre*, so that the phenomenology laid out in the second part is intended to provide a positive appraisal of the phenomenal world.

The first part can be called a 'theory of being' insofar as it aims at reaching being as such, as pure life, in its total autarchy. Being remains therefore within (*in*) itself, it exists from (*von*) itself and through (*durch*) itself.³² In the first part of the *Wissenschaftslehre* we therefore witness the "self-construction of being,"³³ which brings us to an absolute knowledge of being. Now, this knowledge of being is not separated from being as such; rather, it takes part in it. This is why Fichte in his Berlin lectures tries to guide his audience to what he calls pure *Einsicht*, the insight through which a person rises to the level of this knowledge, a knowledge from within, momentarily leaving aside any external point of view. Such an external standpoint is represented by consciousness. Un-

---

30 Goubet, Jean-François: "La phénoménologie de Fichte dans la WL-1804/II: une approche historique", in: *Fichte. La doctrine de la science de 1804*, ed. J.-C. Goddard and A. Schnell, Paris, forthcoming.
31 For the two letters and the note of the editors, see GA III/5, p. 5.
32 WL-1804-II, p. 151.
33 WL-1804-II, pp. 161–162.

doubtedly, consciousness is always present in knowledge and is in a certain way inescapable, but nevertheless the audience is asked to "abstract" from it,[34] because, as we already know, immediate consciousness has a tendency to "objectivize" everything, to put it at distance, before itself, in a way that blurs the true origin of the object, its genesis. In other words, the object of consciousness is the result of a projection, of a "proiectio per hiatum irrationalem"[35] as Fichte puts it. Consciousness is always content with mere *Fakta*, while the aim of the *Wissenschaftslehre* has always been to trace the genesis of these *Fakta*.

In view of this, the task of phenomenology, as the descending movement of the *Wissenschaftslehre*, is to reintroduce consciousness in the limited scope of its legitimate functions. Reintroducing consciousness means at the same time reintegrating all the elements that had been left aside in the first part in order to gain access to the truth of pure being. In this manner, the phenomena, as objects of consciousness, are taken into account, but only for what they are in truth, i.e., mere phenomena of the absolute and not some kind of independent reality endowed with an autonomous existence. Phenomenology is therefore a theory of the "true [*wahrhafte*] phenomenon"[36] in contradistinction with the misinterpretation that makes of it a mere appearance, *Schein*. And it is the task of phenomenology to "present", in their true light, the phenomena and to "deduce"[37] them correctly; that is, in consideration of the results of the first part: reached through the insight into the absolute. In this regard, Jean-Christophe Goddard is certainly right when he argues that this *Wissenschaftslehre* gives back to the phenomenal world its legitimate claim to truth.[38] At the end of his lectures, Fichte enumerates the different strata of this phenomenal world. He mentions themes that are so many domains for the concrete elaboration of his *Wissenschaftslehre*, namely (1) the principle of sensibility (our belief in nature), (2) the principle of legality, (3) the standpoint of morality and (4) the standpoint of religion.

When we endeavour to search for the sources of Fichte's concept of phenomenology in 1804, we are facing a problem similar to the one Hegel's

---

34  WL-1804-II, pp. 142–143.
35  WL-1804-II, p. 157, see also p. 147.
36  WL-1804-II, p. 160.
37  WL-1804-II, pp. 89–90, p. 200.
38  Goddard, Jean-Christophe: *Fichte (1801–1813) l'émancipation philosophique*, Paris 2003, p. 47.

commentators are confronted with when they investigate the sources of the title of the *Phenomenology of Spirit*. Since they find no clear indication on Hegel's part, they are obliged to draw parallels with Lambert, Kant, Reinhold and Fichte, although, here again, they do not know if Hegel had read more than the first of Reinhold's *Beyträge*, which was one of the main targets of the *Differenzschrift*, and although there is very little chance, on the other hand, that Hegel could have had access to the detailed content of Fichte's Berlin lectures of 1804[39]. Therefore, since in Fichte's case the evidence concerning possible influences has also been absent, we might ask ourselves what Fichte could have retained from authors that we have taken into consideration. Aside from the various semantic elements on which I have focused until now, together with certain formal analogies, what in these authors can be regarded as relevant from the point of view of Fichte's philosophy?

Apart from the fact that they place appearance at the center of phenomenology, it is not clear at first glance in what way Fichte could have profited from of the concrete developments of the fourth part of the *Neues Organon*. Effectively, Lambert deals mainly with a *Schein* that is empirical, namely the "sensible", the "psychological" and the "moral" appearance,[40] in which case the attention is primarily focused on the interference of sensations and passions in moral life. If there is, however, one thesis of Lambert that remains valid for Fichte, it is likely to be found in what Lambert calls the "method of the astronomers". For example, in a letter dated from October 13, 1770, Lambert urges Kant to adopt in metaphysics the same attitude as the astronomers; that is, to make the assumption from the start that "everything" is mere appearance (*Schein*), and then try to distinguish what is illusion and what is reality. This means that the reality behind appearances must be sought out and exposed with the help of laws. This could be brought together with Fichte's conclusion in the phenomenology, according to which every phenomenon, having no separate existence of its own, as long as it has not been interpreted as part of the manifestation of the absolute, is nothing more than a mere *Schein*.

In the case of Kant, as we have seen, the strict distinction established in the *Critique of Pure Reason* between *Erscheinung* and *Schein* is only a

---

[39] See the introduction of W. Bonsiepen to his edition of Hegel's *Phänomenologie des Geistes*, Hamburg 1988, p. XVI.
[40] Lambert, Johann H.: *Neues Organon, Philosophische Schriften* II, pp. 237, 276, p. 300.

methodological clarification. As soon as we consider the content of the *Critique* and in particular the goal of the Transcendental Dialectic, we recognize the usefulness of this distinction. In fact, it is in the *Prolegomena* (1783) that Kant is most explicit about the need to distinguish, but also, in a second step, to bring together phenomenon and appearance, in order to refute the claims of dogmatic metaphysics. In a remark following §13, he argues that the world of phenomena has to be clearly established – as the realm of truth – if one is to be in a position to identify metaphysical appearance[41]: *Erscheinung* and *Schein* are here presented in their complementary functions. But already in 1781 in the first *Critique* Kant had no doubt made use of this distinction, for example when he claimed that the source of the transcendental Antinomy lies in the fact that phenomena are taken for things in themselves, thereby giving rise to dialectical appearance. And the same can be said of the two other ideas of reason: the origin of the illusions of the *omnitudo realitatis* (God) and of the immortal soul are also anchored in the phenomenal world. So this means that Fichte could already have learnt from Kant that metaphysical *Schein* necessarily presupposes a world of *Erscheinungen*.

But the distance between the two thinkers is still enormous, and this is true even though Fichte claimed in 1804 that Kant's transcendental philosophy is the only philosophical discourse with which he is ready to associate his own enterprise. The gap between them, however, comes to the fore in the central line of criticism that Fichte develops against Kant in the 1804 *Wissenschaftslehre*. The criticism amounts to saying that Kant as a philosopher cannot surmount mere factuality. This term must be understood, as we know, as the opposite of genesis. For instance, Kant's goal in the third *Critique* is to find the "root" common to nature and freedom, to "empirical experience" and the "moral world", each of them considered as an absolute.[42] But in the end, Kant is unable to attain this common ground. The unity of the system is for him something certain, but it remains mere "factual" evidence, whereas it should have been "genetic". This means that Fichte has doubts as to Kant's capacities as a genetic philosopher. And this failure has consequences for Kant's ability to deal with *Schein* in general.

This argument is developed at the beginning of the 1804 *Wissenschaftslehre*, and since it is part of Fichte's methodological remarks con-

---

41 Kant, Immanuel: *Prolegomena*, Ak. IV, p. 292.
42 WL-1804-II, p. 28; see also p. 20, p. 38, p. 88.

cerning the problem of "attention", Kant is not mentioned by name. But the same criticism had already been explicitly directed at him in the *Second Introduction to the Doctrine of Science* (1797). The argument in Section 10 takes the form of the following question: How can Kant still claim to be in danger of a relapse into transcendental appearance after having philosophically explained its origin? This led Fichte to think that Kant, when writing the *Critique of Pure Reason*, could not be entirely "convinced" by his own philosophy, since it is utterly absurd to constantly fear a reversion into the delusion of metaphysics, when one has deciphered all of its workings[43]. This only confirms Fichte's view according to which Kant remains at the surface of things: that he remains a philosopher of factuality, and this precisely because he is not enough of a genetic thinker. As such Kant does not provide us with an extensive theory of the relation between *Erscheinung* and *Schein*, with an authentic phenomenology.

Concerning Reinhold, finally, we have come to the conclusion that it is impossible to know exactly what Fichte could have taken from him for his own philosophy. The three parallels already pointed out between the two thinkers are only analogies and they do not allow us to conclude anything with certainty. As I have said, the references to Reinhold in the *Wissenschaftslehre* of 1804 are all critical. One of these critical remarks has to do with the fact that Reinhold in his exposition of the first part of rational realism "does not refer" to consciousness. He develops the doctrine of pure thought, the doctrine of thinking as thinking, without being able to assign the proper place to consciousness. It is as though Reinhold had experienced difficulties in articulating his conception of the absolute, of the thinking of the originary essence (*Urwesen*) with consciousness. But the fact of the matter is that this is a very difficult question indeed, a question that Fichte is also confronted with, and that he himself is led to solve through recourse to pure factuality. As Miklos Vetö aptly remarks, Fichte's *Wissenschaftslehre* succeeds at disclosing the genesis of every phenomena, but in the end it fails to articulate the genesis of consciousness itself[44]. For Fichte, consciousness must be accepted as a fact, attributed to a *proiectio per hiatum* stemming from being itself. And until the end Fichte asks himself how he should conceive of the "hiatus" in question, so that it might not be considered a hiatus *irrationalis*.[45] Facing such a

---

43 Fichte, Johann G.: *Zweite Einleitung in die Wissenschaftslehre*, GA I/4, p. 264.
44 Vetö, Miklos: *Fichte. De l'Action à l'Image*, Paris 2001, p. 107.
45 WL-1804-II, p. 217.

difficult problem for himself, Fichte could have adopted a more conciliatory attitude toward Reinhold, or he could at least have entered into a more extensive discussion with the developments of the *Beyträge*.

# Reduction or Revelation?
# Fichte and the Question of Phenomenology.

F. SCOTT SCRIBNER

University of Hartford

The task and scope of what counts as phenomenological method is indelibly shaped by the impasse between Husserl and Heidegger. If, for Husserl, the call for a return to the 'things themselves' looked toward a transcendental reduction to eidetic essences as a means for achieving objectivity, Heidegger would argue, in effect, that a true relation to things cannot be sought within the epistemological framework of adequation and objectivity, but rather only in the manifestation of Being itself. Such an overview is a necessary prelude to any account of Fichte's own transformation of transcendental philosophy in terms of phenomenological method insofar as, I will argue, his entire project can be understood to reiterate – or even better, anticipate – the impasse between phenomenology's methodological aspirations for objectivity and its more revelatory accounts.

While certainly the Fichte of the first period could be understood to undertake something like a transcendental phenomenology in which concepts or essences are not pre-given, but rather arise out of his own unique conception of transcendental philosophy as an experimental practice undertaken in the first person, in the last period of his work the transcendental subject is clearly displaced by the discourse of Being. In more Twentieth Century language, transcendental phenomenology is transformed into a phenomenological ontology.

The suggestion that Fichte enacts within his own work the central tension within the phenomenological method is itself a significant claim. What is further unique, however, is the way this tension is ultimately articulated within his own project. In the *Wissenschaftslehre of 1804*, he will speak of the intimate relation between immanence and emanation (*der Emanenz und der Immanenz*).[1] Here, I will argue, he uses this language

---

1   WL-1804-p. 45. I generally follow the English translation with only minor alterations. Fichte, Johann G.: *The Science of Knowing. J.G. Fichte's 1804 Lectures on*

as part of his continued effort to bring coherence to his early and later projects by attempting to align the aspirations for transcendental phenomenology and phenomenological ontology. The core project of this paper then is a critical analysis and assessment of Fichte's own unique appropriation and approach to the paradoxical demand at the heart of phenomenology's methodology. The call to 'the things themselves' situates itself at the cross-roads of the seemingly impossible demand for *both* epistemological objectivity and the immediacy of Being. The question then is whether Fichte ultimately escapes this methodological paradox, and is thus able to offer insight to more contemporary approaches to phenomenology, or whether he too will be forced to choose between reduction and revelation.

## I. Fichte and Phenomenological Methodology

The interrogative in the title of this paper underscores that what one calls phenomenology is not singular; it is not a rigid method, or a parcel of philosophical territory that stands as absolute measure, determining the rightness or wrongness of all who take up the spirit of its experimental practice. In some ways, Husserl himself was slow to come around to such a view. Husserl's disappointment in the direction of Heidegger's work is in some way reiterated with Kant's reception of Fichte's experimental approach to transcendental philosophy. And, in the same way it makes sense to articulate the Fichtean transcendental project by beginning with Kant, so too does it make sense to begin with Husserl.

It's worth noting that for all Husserl may have learned from Fichte and the idealist tradition, he does work hard to distance himself from it. He remains suspect that in Kantian and Post-kantian transcendental idealism, the empirical and transcendental are inexorably bound. In section 57 of the *Crisis* he writes,

> I myself, as transcendental ego, "constitute" the world, and at the same time, as soul, I am a human ego in the world. [...] Can the ego which posits itself, of which Fichte speaks, be anything other than Fichte's own? If this is supposed to be not an actual absurdity but a paradox that can be resolved, what

---

the *Wissenschaftslehre*, trans. Walter Wright, Albany 2005. [Henceforth abbreviated as LWL-1804]

other method could help us achieve clarity than the interrogation of our inner experience and an analysis carried out within its framework?²

Husserl's approach to transcendental phenomenology, and his solution to the above paradox of the transcendental and empirical, ironically, relegates Fichte and all of idealism to a form of unscientific introspection, or in his words an "obscure metaphysics and mythology," – as if denying the very source of his own revelation that "consciousness of intersubjectivity, then, must become a transcendental problem."³ This of course, is a gross misunderstanding of Fichte. After all, the method of introspection would approach the I directly as complete self-awareness. Phenomenology is the inverse of introspection: the I also arrives late, or at least indirectly by means of reflexivity.⁴ In this respect, Husserl is mistaken: Fichte is far more phenomenological than introspective.

As a way to articulate phenomenological aspects within Fichte's work, despite Husserl's own "distancing," I would like to offer a few basic aspects or principles that guide Fichte's project. First, like a return to Aristotle's characterization of philosophy in terms of an originary wonder about the world, phenomenology begins in observation. Observation precedes any categorization. It works to avoid axiomatic-constructive ideas, theories, and formal systems in order to return, in the well worn phrase, to the things themselves. Its method then is by nature highly experimental; it is always beginning, revising, and correcting; its conclusion and definitions are always practical constructs open to revision that, if they arrive at all, come quite late in the game.

Fichte's project of the *Wissenschaftslehre* is also a study in beginnings. With at least sixteen versions of the *Wissenschaftslehre*, none more definitive than the next, the question is always, which Fichte, which *Wissenschaftslehre*? In the *Second Introduction to the Wissenschaftslehre* Fichte differentiates his work from other philosophical systems by pointing out that such projects begin with constructs and "dead concepts". The *Wissenschaftslehre* alone is "vital, active," it "generates cognitions out of itself by means of itself"⁵. Further, he says of the philosopher,

> his task is to engage in this living subject in a purposeful activity, to observe this activity. [...] He conducts an experiment. [...] It is up to him to attend

---

2   Husserl, Edmund: *The Crisis of European Sciences and Transcendental Phenomenology*, trans. David Carr, Evanston, Ill. 1970, sec. 57.
3   Ibid.
4   Ihde, Don: *Experimental Phenomenology*, New York 1977, p. 50.
5   IWL, pp. 36–37.

to these appearances, to survey them accurately and to connect them with one another. But *it is not for him to decide how the object should manifest itself. This is something that should be decided by the object itself.* Other philosophies engage in the manufacture of an 'artificial product'.[6]

Here Fichte embraces a foundational phenomenological rule: attend to phenomena as they appear.

Now despite our early reference to Husserl's somewhat over-zealous discrediting of idealism, in the *Cartesian Meditations* we see him affirming the fraternity between the transcendental projects of both idealism and phenomenology. In suprisingly strong language Husserl affirms,

> The proof of this idealism is therefore phenomenology itself. Only someone who misunderstands either the deepest sense of intentional method, or that of transcendental reduction, or perhaps both, can attempt to separate phenomenology from transcendental idealism.[7]

The near identity between these methods lies in the genetic-descriptive account whereby one is led back to the apriori conditions of possibility. For Husserl there are two moments that are crucial. He explains, "we attain the methodological insight that, along with phenomenological reduction, eidetic intuition is the fundamental form of all particular transcendental methods".[8] The phenomenological reduction, as a method, clears the field and determines how the world is to be approached. These basic hermeneutic rules, however, are raised to the level of a transcendental shaping of experience through the directionality of intentionality. Intentionality dictates the conditions of possibility of how things show themselves. And what Husserl refers to as eidetic phenomenology refers to a free variation of imagining that explores the horizon of possibility as a possible ideal perception apart from any factualness. Husserl explains, "Eidetic phenomenology, accordingly explores the universal apriori without which neither I nor any transcendental Ego whatever is 'imaginable' [...]".[9]

As a transcendental idealism, Fichte adopts the Kantian-like view that this world of empirical appearances arises with law-like necessity from non-empirical, apriori cognitions. His widened conception of transcendental philosophy as an experimental practice, and as a practical activity

---

6 IWL, p. 37, emphasis added.
7 Husserl, Edmund: *Cartesian Meditations: An Introduction to Phenomenology*, trans. Dorian Cairns (The Hague: Martinus Nijhoff, 1960), p. 86.
8 Husserl, Edmund: *Catersian Meditations*, p. 72.
9 Ibid.

that allows apriori cognitions to be interpreted on the order of act and activity readily transforms the rigid, ideal aspects of idealism into an expansive phenomenological-like practice. While Fichte still seeks a priori grounds, the method of genetic deduction gives way more and more to observation and experiment.

Fichte's account of intellectual intuition is established as a fact-act, as a fact of consciousness. Intellectual intuition defines the transcendental I as activity. The *Tathandlung* is a fact-fact, a fact of consciousness in which the I is intuited in doing. In Fichte's own words it is the "act of intuiting himself while simultaneously performing the act by which it originates for him".[10] For Fichte it is the ultimate reduction because its form of consciousness is not "derived from anything else," but is instead a form of "immediate consciousness".[11] Yet its account of Being, as an activity, is nevertheless a practical choice that sides with freedom. I would suggest that the realization of intellectual intuition is achieved by means of a phenomenological reduction, by bracketing more substantial reifications of the ego and simply observing without judging, and remaining open to how the ego is given originally.[12]

For Fichte, it is the guiding touchstone of his philosophy to the degree that he can assert of it that "it contains within itself the source of life, and apart from it there is nothing but death".[13] As we will soon see, the question arises whether this is the ultimate act of transcendental reduction or a springboard to a phenomenology that exceeds the transcendental framework in revelation. Fichte's own talk of intellectual intuition in terms of life is quite suggestive of this. He writes: "it must be an intuition of sheer activity . . . not a being, but something living".[14] With the notion of intellectual intuition, Fichte, of course, was offering a phenomenological account of the very ground of the transcendental ego. It would seem that as a "fact of consciousness," the *Tathandlung* and its claim of intellectual intuition would stand as a transcendental ground, an *epoche* or reduction beyond which nothing more can be said. Fichte is clear that intellectual intuition is the intuition of life. His reformulated conception of transcendental philosophy as a process begins in the bedrock of intellec-

---

10 IWL, p. 46.
11 IWL, p. 49.
12 See Husserl, Edmund: *Ideas Pertaining to a Pure Phenomenology and to a Phenomenological Philosophy*, trans. Kersten, Fred, Dordreckt 1982, p. 4.
13 IWL, p. 47.
14 IWL, pp. 46–47.

tual intuition which, in his words, stands at once as a practical necessity and as "a product of iron necessity".[15]

Now while this fact of consciousness would seem to be the reduction to an ultimate ground, upon further investigation it reveals itself to be a mere conduit to the absolute. The Twentieth Century French phenomenologist Michel Henry offers a phenomenological account of transcendental consciousness, as the pure appearance of appearance, and as the immanence of life itself. His interpretative tact, I have found quite insightful in helping articulate the phenomenological aspects of Fichte's own project, and in particular, the transition of Fichte's project from a transcendental to an ontological concern with life (*Leben*). Thought phenomenologically, Fichte's notion of intellectual intuition does indeed seem to be an instance of sheer phenomenality. Henry writes, "a thinking thing means what shows itself in self-showing since what shows itself is not a thing but self-showing itself. The something of substance [...] is nothing but appearance's apparition and luminescence".[16] Henry's language sounds much like Fichte's account of intellectual intuition in terms of the *Tathandlung*. The idea of there being no substantive I, just 'doing,' as translated into the register of life, does indeed result in the appearing of appearance, a self-showing without a self. Or again, as Henry affirms, "A thing that thinks is nothing but lightning's flash, a self-illuminating light. It's substantiality is phenomenological actuality, the materiality of phenomenality as such."[17] What Henry is suggesting is that the kind of auto-affective self-generative capacities, like that of Fichtean activity presents us with the very givenness of life, the self-presentative, emergent force of life he sees in terms of the materiality of phenomenality.

Fichte's embrace of intellectual intuition as a *Tathandlung* is a recognition that one cannot embrace Being abstractly. He is all too aware that the "ground always lies outside what it grounds" and as such, abstraction, as "impossible,"[18] will require him to proceed phenomenologically from the self-feeling of life to the generative source of the essence of the absolute. As Fichte himself rapidly realizes in the coming years, this bedrock of intellectual intuition, as life itself, goes far deeper than he initially imagined. The reduction that revealed the transcendental ego in in-

---

15　Ibid..
16　Michel, Henry: *Genealogy of Psychoanalysis*, trans. Douglas Brick, Stanford 1993, p. 14.
17　Ibid.
18　IWL, S. 49.

tellectual intuition as the ultimate ground in self-activity finds itself losing traction as Fichte's quest for the source of life takes him to sources far deeper than the transcendental subject. Intellectual intuition is indeed life. It is the intuition of life itself. In positing oneself, he notes, "I am given to myself, by myself [...] I possess life within myself and draw it from myself".[19] Fichte's remark that intellectual intuition "contains within it the source of life, and apart from it is nothing but death," is a first indication of the true depth of this notion as a research into the source of life itself.[20]

## II. Phenomenology in the *Wissenschaftslehre 1804*

The highly experimental character of Fichte's transcendental idealism proceeded through regressive, genetic arguments, phenomenological observation and a phenomenological reduction that would delineate the transcendental as a process, and point to apriori *modes* of consciousness as apriori facts of consciousness. Yet despite this apriori fact, in the preceding sections I have argued that intellectual intuition provided only a very tentative ground for transcendental consciousness. The problem for Fichte, as for Husserl, was that while the mode of givenness stood as a transcendental apriori, from another perspective such givenness signaled existential concerns. The transcendental ground of the ego in activity was not merely an epistemological concern, but readily led one to wonder about the ontological status of the very Being of the ego. In the words of Jean-Luc Marion, "Does the return to the things in question lead back to their objectivity or to their Being? Does that which effects the re(con)duction act in the capacity of the transcendental I or in that of *Dasein?*".[21] I will suggest that, after 1800, the deepening notion of intellectual intuition forces Fichte to confront precisely this same question. As a consequence, the reduction to a priori facts of consciousness, at least ones that are grounded in transcendental subjectivity, seem to be superceded by a discourse of Being, in which the event of the appearance of Being eclipses any possible recourse to the transcendental ground of reduction.

---

19 Ibid..
20 IWL, S. 47.
21 Jean-Luc, Marion: *Reduction and Givenness*, trans. Carlson, Thomas A., Evanston, Ill. 1998, p. 2.

I will argue that Fichte's notion of life, and in particular his emphasis on inner life (*inwendiges Leben*), is an extension and deepening of intellectual intuition and the existential aspects of the *Tathandlung* of the first period. In the second period we see Fichte working with both hands. He suggests repeatedly that the intuition of life is the highest ground, suggesting the profoundly phenomenological character of his new work. On the other hand, he still sees his own method in the transcendental vocabulary of a largely genetic account. Fichte's genetic account of the origin of self-conscious subjectivity leads him to seek the Being of the absolute through phenomenological analysis of the immediacy of appearance of life itself.

What Fichte is forced to confront, I believe, is what Heidegger encountered in Husserl. At the utmost reduction of consciousness, one encounters Being itself. For Fichte, as for Heidegger, Being itself is inaccessible. While many, like Max Wundt, have suggested a neo-Platonic influence that reads Fichte's later work from the perspective of an emanationist account of Being, Fichte's emphasis on the appearing of appearance (*Schein der Erscheinung*) and in particular, a unity with the absolute in radical immanence, constantly leads itself to phenomenological concerns – concerns, I will suggest, that are quite close to the phenomenology of Michel Henry.[22]

While Fichte's analysis of the absolute in the later periods of the *Wissenschaftslehre* are largely genetic in structure (that is, it argues from transcendental conditions of possibility), it is in the *Wissenschaftslehre* of 1804 that he makes explicit the way in which the shift in the I from a transcendental subject to a mere medium for the imaging of the absolute is developed precisely as a problem of existence (*Existenz*). And to the extent such a transformation arises from a crisis of transcendental subjectivity, in which the transcendental I cannot ground all meaning, but requires a turn to an absolute beyond it, all the *Wissenschaftslehren* after 1800 are motivated principally by existential concerns.

Now apart from these more general characterizations of Fichte's method as phenomenological, it's worth looking at a specific instance of the role he accords phenomenology within his own idealism as he outlines it in the *Wissenschaftslehre of 1804*. Here, once again, Fichte continues to differentiate his form of transcendental idealism from others by emphasizing that the "I" is not a product but a process. And his account

---

22 Henry's conception of radical immanence was inspired by Meister Eckhart. It is less clear whether Fichte read Eckhart.

of the *Tathandlung* and intellectual intuition is further explored and deepened through his account of "life". The centrality of "life" for this project becomes clear with his assertion that "life is the true absolute".[23] Thus, if in the Jena period Fichte understood intellectual intuition as activity, as the ground of the transcendental I, his shift away from a subject-centered transcendental knowing toward Being would result in a correlative reformulation of intellectual intuition in terms of the activity of life itself as the new ground of his transcendental project. He writes, "Being – understood by language as a noun – cannot literally be active except as immediately living".[24] As he explains, and as we will develop further, the former transcendental I in its activity exhibits life; but this inner life stands as a mere medium, or in his words "a through" (*Durch*) to the life in itself of the absolute. This explanatory prolegomena is the key to understanding aspects of his project as phenomenological to the extent that this "through" or medium is an image, a structure of appearance for the manifestation of the absolute. Fichte explains his new understanding of intellectual intuition as life as follows:

> If there really is to be a 'through,' then – as a condition of its possibility – we must presuppose an inner life, independent in itself from the 'through,' and resting on itself. [...] since everything depends on this [...] that the *inward life* of this concept was the principle of the energetic insight into a life *beyond*, which grasped us, and which was *intuited* in this insight as self-sufficient. Thus it was the principle of intuition and of life in the intuition.[25]

The investigation into life is a genetic or transcendental project that uses the *concept* of life to seek a life that perhaps stands beyond any conceptual understanding.

The real difficulty, of course, is how, or by what method, one approaches the absolute. One point of entry for an understanding of the role he accords phenomenology is his distinction between reason and appearance. He explains, "on a particular occasion I divided the science of knowledge into two main parts; one part that it is a doctrine of reason and truth, and second, that it is a doctrine of appearance and illusion, but one that is indeed true and grounded in truth".[26] The last part here is the key. Thus, when Fichte defines phenomenology as "a doctrine of appearance and illusion," it is not a doctrine of deception, but a meth-

---

23 LWL-1804, p. 90.
24 LWL-1804, p. 116.
25 LWL-1804, p. 94.
26 LWL-1804, p. 115.

od of approaching appearance and as a way of access to truth, the truth of the absolute.[27] While earlier versions of the *Wissenschaftslehre* aligned truth with the transcendental subject, in the 1804 version the key role of phenomenology is to help sort appearance from the absolute, consciousness from truth. As he explains, "consciousness remains only an outer appearance of truth. [...] But if you believe that the grounds why truth is truth are found in consciousness, you lapse into illusion".[28] It is for this reason then, the fact that "the primordial fact and source of everything factical is consciousness", that "the science of knowing keeps its promise and, as a doctrine of truth and reason, expunges all facticity from itself".[29] Fichte is explaining that the truth of idealism no longer resides with the I of subjective consciousness. Indeed, it is only by the eradication of consciousness that truth might be possible at all. While not altogether clear in his exposition, Fichte seems to be suggesting that phenomenology operates as a method that ultimately helps move individual factical consciouness beyond itself to the absolute. Thus while "life is the true absolute",[30] "we stand [...] between life itself and the image of life".[31] Fichte explicitly uses the word "phenomenology" to describe his 1804 project because it is by means of this method that we must read the appearance of "the image of life" as a conduit to life itself. Fichte seems to inscribe something like a two worlds theory, not unlike Kant's distinction between the thing-in-itself and the realm of appearance. The notion of life, or "living" is the inaccessible holy grail he continually hopes to access by means of the roughly correlative terms of concept, image, or Being.[32] He envisions life a near inaccessible in-itself. He explains,

> The presupposed life in itself therefore should be unconditionally in-itself; and it is intuited as such. Therefore all Being and life originates with it, and apart from it there can be nothing. The reported subjective condition of this perspective and insight was this: that one not stubbornly hold onto the principle of idealism, the energy of reflection, but rather yield patiently to its opposite insight. The realistic perspective.[33]

---

27 LWL-1804, p. 107. Fichte writes, "To the extent that this science in its second part is a phenomenology, a science of appearance and illusion."
28 LWL-1804, p. 107.
29 Ibid.
30 LWL-1804, p. 90.
31 LWL-1804, p. 91.
32 Ibid.
33 LWL-1804, p. 95.

Fichte plays out the central tension or dualism between realism and idealism through the respective terms of "life" and "concept". As he notes "realism (=genesis of life) and idealism (=genesis of the concept)".[34] Fichte struggles with the capacity of the concept to express the absolute. He repeatedly, at one moment sides with the realism of the immediacy of life, then with his true idealist aspiration to grasp it intellectually, and then waffles again. Admittedly, Fichte sees such movement as a dialectical ascension in which he posits a new realism, only to in turn be countered by a new idealism.[35]

Fichte's view of the relation of the real and the ideal can be illuminated by looking further at his approach to the problem of the "in-itself" of life. Fichte vigorously reflects on the process of reflection itself to recognize that the in-itself, the notion of oneness, is itself a conceptual figment, a projection no more real than its conceptual opposite, the not-in-itself. He refers to this empty conceptual projecting as "an irrational gap," a *projection per hiatum*. He explains this irrational gap as "the absolute projection of an object whose origin is inexplicable, so that between the projected act and the projected object everything is dark and bare".[36] This irrational gap that defines the reciprocal negation of conceptual opposites might also be said to apply to the very categories of realism and idealism.

The problem of access to the absolute, however, remains bound up with the continuing impasse between realism and idealism. At times, then, Fichte asserts that life stands as an immediacy. Fichte, explains, "we live immediately in the act of living itself, therefore we are the one undivided Being itself, in itself, of itself, through itself, which can never go outside of itself to duality".[37] Yet still, he recognizes without "knowing" we have no chance of grasping "Being": his project remains transcendental. He writes,

> (h)ence we in no way depend here on an empirical perception of our life. [...]; rather we are depending on the genetic insight into life and the I, which emerges from the construction of the one Being and vice versa. We already know, and abstract completely from, the fact, that this very insight as such [...] is irrelevant and vanishes; we will need to look back at it again in deducing phenomena.[38]

---

34 LWL-1804, p. 101.
35 For Fichte's reference to his achievements of a "new realism" and then a "new idealism", see the LWL-1804, pp. 98, 108.
36 LWL-1804, p. 119.
37 Ibid., 116..
38 LWL-1804, pp. 116–117.

Fichte seems to renounce any possible empirical access to the immediacy of life. Life for him is transcendentally deduced. Yet since life is aligned with activity, and his transcendental approach itself remains a vital process that – by his own attestation – can only be undertaken in the first person, it might be best to understand this changing dual series relation on the order of what Husserl identified in terms of founding and founded acts. In other words there is no pure thing-in-itself. The object of transcendental phenomenology influences the method as much as the method in turn shapes the object.

Now Fichte seems to recognize the tentative nature of any of his conclusions. Indeed, Fichte himself seems to confess the extreme difficulty and ultimate ambiguity of the situation. He explains, "Thus it remains completely ambiguous whether thinking originates from this intuition, the intuition comes from thinking, or whether both might only be appearances of a deeper hidden oneness which grounds them".[39] His acknowledgment of this ambiguity is sharpened as a distinct 'impasse' with his recourse to the language of 'disjunction'. For instance, he will further acknowledge that the work of phenomenology, as a transcendental phenomenology, reveals the appearances of individual consciousness as merely inadequate moments of the concept of life on its way towards an articulation of the life of the absolute. And he explains this inadequacy explicitly in the language of disjunction. He affirms that the "first remaining disjunction – between Being and the we (absolute I) – is completely annulled," and he sees the repetition of this impasse or doubling as the work of transcendental phenomenology's method "undoing" of consciousness. Thus he can query, "[b]ut, as the first stage of our descent into phenomenology, we will have to explore whence this empty repetition and doubling may arise".[40] Here we see something like the Husserlian phenomenological reduction at work. Fichte uses the term "phenomenology" with much restraint, but he clearly invokes the use of its method as a way to clear away inadequate moments of consciousness on its way to the absolute.

Fichte seems to distinguish between two forms of reason. On the one hand, there is the inadequate rationality of a discriminating consciousness that simply generates appearances in its attempt to grasp the world. On the other hand, beyond the subjectively grounded transcendental consciousness, there is a reason he associates with Being itself. It is a ration-

---

39  LWL-1804, p. 103.
40  LWL-1804, p. 118.

ality beyond any transcendental I. Yet to the extent he explicitly associates this reason with light (*das Licht*) and the power of manifestation, his exploration of it continues as a transcendental phenomenology beyond the transcendental subject. Without the transcendental subject, the *Wissenschaftslehre* becomes a transcendental phenomenology of pure appearance. Thus Fichte can suggest that a dualist consciousness is the "familiar death of reason"[41] and that *the real "question about the possibility of philosophy depends on whether the I can perish and reason can come purely to manifestation"*.[42] If, as Fichte calls it, "the first stage" of phenomenology is to read the images of life in the appearance of consciousness as a *Durch*, the "second part" or stage of phenomenology pursues the "unconscious law of reason working in us,"[43] with the explicit recognition that "Being and light are one".[44] Reason is equated with pure appearance and light. It is a phenomenology where the I perishes along with all phenomena: it is a phenomenology of *phainomenon*, one of pure light.

The first stage of this phenomenology might be said to be a phenomenology of reduction; a phenomenology whereby one aspires to arrive at some absolute fact of consciousness by bracketing, – in more Husserlian language – the everyday illusions of the natural attitude. Of course, Fichte's recognition that the reduction to activity as a *Tathandlung* was but a temporary moment, a foundation without bottom, that revealed itself as "life," as a revelatory manifestation, that led him to that phenomenology beyond phenomena. The second stage of phenomenology Fichte outlines seems more like a phenomenological ontology, a phenomenology of revelation that arises in the face of the inadequacy of the transcendental subject and the ultimate failure of self-conscious cognition. This second moment of phenomenology is less about phenomena than the appearing of appearance itself. Here "Being and light are one".[45] Yet still, "the principle of appearance is a principle of disjunction"[46]. As a consequence of our finite consciousness, many aspects of the absolute are conveyed by Fichte as a necessary disjunction or contradiction. The principle of appearance is a disjunction because light is the manifestation of Being; yet Being, as wholly immanent, needs no exteriorization. There is a dis-

---

41 LWL-1804, p. 144.
42 LWL-1804, p. 139, emphasis added.
43 LWL-1804, p. 118.
44 LWL-1804, p. 147.
45 Ibid.
46 LWL-1804, p. 160.

junction between absolute life in itself and its mode(s) of appearance. Appearance, or what appears, is the realm of phenomena and phenomenology proper. Light, by contrast, is the condition of any possible appearing. To paraphrase Fichte from an earlier version of the *Wissenschaftslehre*, the ground always stands outside of what it grounds. Fichte's pursuit of the appearance of appearance or pure phenomenality (in the words of Henry), takes him beyond phenomena and to the very limit of what one might call phenomenology.

For us, another significant and allied disjunction stands between these two forms of phenomenology we have just outlined: reduction and revelation. Fichte explains,

> The two highest disjunctive terms stand here absolutely opposed to one another, life's inner and outer life, the form of immanent and eminent existence as well, separated by an impassable gulf. [...] If one wishes to think them as united, then they are united exactly by this gulf and by this contradiction.[47]

I take Fichte to mean that the grounded and the ground, phenomena and its conditions of possibility, represent radically different frameworks that cannot readily be understood except by finding the hinge upon which this paradox swings.

Both elements of representation and life are necessary. In the same way that a genetic account of the source of self-consciousness in life is only possible by means of the achievement of the representational capacities of representational self-consciousness, so too does thought (*Denken*) require Being (*Sein*). Fichte, however, more and more, affirms the interchangeability of this terminology. He explains, "In the insight of insight of the foundational division, in Being (*Sein*) and thought (*Denken*) as one, and sensible and super-sensible as one, rests the key to the form of knowing (*ruht der Schlußpunkt dieser wissenschaftlichen Form*).[48] Fichte worked relentlessly to establish the interpenetration and reciprocity between sensible and super-sensible worlds. His language may take on a transparency that yields the greater force of its epistemological meaning to a phenomenology of pure appearance, but to the degree those terms retain an epistemological residue, and his phenomenology still seeks the source of Being as a transcendental ground, Fichte intends to articulate life through Being and representation, *Sein* und *Denken*.

---

47 LWL-1804, p. 91.
48 SW X, p. 136–137.

This notion of 'between two worlds' is most powerfully articulated with Fichte's description of the role of the now former transcendental subject in terms of the preposition *Durch*. The I is no longer the self-generating self of the world. Rather it stands between worlds as a transparent medium of the absolute, that is nevertheless the refractory lens by which the world comes to be. Even reason itself capitulates to Being in its operation between two worlds as a *Durch*. For instance, reason is aligned not only with making, but with pure appearance. In fact, Fichte explains, the "inner life of reason as a living *Durch*".[49] This sense of inter-worldly transparency is also clear in Fichte's repeated references to light (*das Licht*). He writes, "the insight of insight of light stands here between both the immanent and emanation (*der Emanenz und der Immanenz*)".[50] The unifying principle of light and love culminates in the unifying force of life itself.

While Michel Henry sees the burgeoning and bustle of all emerging life as instances of life itself, and thus Being, Fichte sees life not as the ground of Being, but as its principle.[51] Life is not Being itself, but the principle that unites Being's self-enclosed immanence with a self-productive emanation: it unifies sensible and super-sensible worlds. The idea of life as a unifying principle is emblematic of the difficult task Fichte is attempting. Faced with the choice of reduction or revelation, Fichte seems to want both. His phenomenology, as the appearing of appearance, seems to affirm a phenomenological ontology that nevertheless remains strongly committed to a transcendental project. In the *Thatsachen des Bewusstsein*, he continues to make reference to his genetic method, and explains that the *wissenschaftliche* use of reason requires that "phenomena (given purely in factical consciousness) come to be grasped from their ground or law (*Gesetz*)".[52] Still more explicitly he explains that "The I intuits itself as substance to accident as an absolute law of imaging (*absoluten Gesetz des Bilden*)".[53] Here Fichte affirms the revelatory capacity of Being, but

---

49 LWL-1804, p. 109.
50 SW XIX, pp. 130–131. LWL-1804, p. 75.
51 Drechsler, Julius: *Fichtes Lehre vom Bild*, Stuttgart 1955, p. 190.
52 SW X, p. 403. This paper offers a close textual reading of Fichte's reference and application of phenomenology as a method within limited sections of the *Wissenschaftslehre* of 1804. Nevertheless, I have made mention to some of his later work to shed light on some of the issues present in the 1804 version. I do not pretend to present a thorough account of Fichte's later theory of imagining. This remains well beyond the scope of this paper.
53 Ibid..

this self-enclosed Being, as radical immanence, generates reality (*Wirklichkeit*) in which emanation, as thought, arises as a *reines Denken*. Thought is one with imagination, or the productive power of imaging, that is both revelatory in its pure giveness, yet one whose generative power, Fichte believes, nevertheless is determinable according to transcendental laws of imaging (*das Gesetz des Bildens*). And this law of imaging, which delineates the former transcendental subject, as a *Durch*, is indeed the hinge which gives unity to this paradox. And it is perhaps also the key to embracing and retaining the best aspects of the phenomenological method and its disjunctive terminology of reduction and revelation. If, as Fichte suggests, there is an interpenetration and transparency of Being (*Sein*) and thought (*Denken*), then we can be sure that the gulf between phenomenology's epistemological and ontological concerns is much smaller than we imagine. It is a disjunction, at least, that Fichte would encourage us to move beyond.

# Fichte's Phenomenology of Religious Consciousness

ANTHONY N. PEROVICH

Hope College, Holland, Michigan

Fichte's account of religious consciousness may be discussed in terms of two old-fashioned senses of "phenomenology". From the perspective of each of these forms of phenomenology puzzles arise about Fichte's account of religion and the religious life, puzzles that I will try to solve below. One puzzle concerns the relation of Higher Morality to Religion, the other concerns the mystical character of Fichte's outlook, and the solutions for both involve distinguishing different senses of the key terms. First, in his *Way towards the Blessed Life* Fichte presents us with a graded series comprised of different ways of viewing the world and maps out the progression from the least to the most adequate, "the various possible stages and grades of development of the inward Spiritual Life"[1] as he puts it. This of course recalls a notion of phenomenology familiar from Hegel's famous "voyage of discovery". In treating of the actual number of stages and the proper interpretation of Fichte's own divisions I shall suggest that in one sense Higher Morality is, but in another it is not, to be included in the Religious Life (*Religiosität*) as Fichte understands it. Second, in attempting to untangle the relations between Higher Morality, the Religious Standpoint, and the Religious Life and in giving what I take to be their proper interconnection, I will perhaps be offering a version of that sort of phenomenology of religion that attempts to identify the essential features of religious consciousness, in this particular case the essential features of Fichtean religious consciousness. In any case, the characterization that emerges provides a basis for addressing the mystical character of that state: once a distinction is drawn between two sorts of mystical union, Fichtean religious consciousness is seen to yield an experience of mystical union in one, but not in both, of these senses.

---

1 SW V, p. 464; PW II, London 1889, p. 368.

## I. The Stages of Phenomenological Development and Their Relations

Fichte had a fondness for fivefold divisions, and the phenomenology of the spiritual life that he presents in *The Way towards the Blessed Life* is no exception, at least formally. Thirty years ago C. K. Hunter presented a discussion of what he called Fichte's fivefold "Phenomenology of Love", based on the popular writings; however, as he noted, it was in fact drawn primarily from *The Characteristics of the Present Age* and *The Addresses to the German Nation*.[2] Here I intend to focus on the phenomenology of the *Way*, where Fichte presents five different modes of viewing, apprehending, and understanding the world, modes that he considers "reciprocally exclusive".[3] His terminology is flexible, but, as most typically described, these stages are Sensuousness, Stoicism, Higher Morality, Religion, and Science. Yet it is not entirely clear that the development of our spiritual life differentiates itself into precisely five stages: there are reasons to consider the number of stages both greater and fewer than five. The number is greater, because Skepticism seems to form an additional moment in Fichte's schema. It is not a part of his five-fold division, because it does not represent a point of view on the world but rather an unwillingness to adopt a point of view. Thus Fichte sometimes refers to this state of mind as a "Nullity", perhaps giving rise to the thought that he might accept a six-fold division, but only if he could begin the numbering with zero. Fewer than five, because there are reasons to question whether some of these latter stages are really distinct worldviews. This is certainly the view of some recent commentators.

Verweyen observes that, for Fichte, the blessed life

> unfolds itself in the three standpoints of "Higher Morality," "Religion," and "(Doctrine of) Science" ["*Wissenschaft(slehre)*"]. They do not actually represent different worldviews of the one life that conceives the world, not as the dispersion of things existing in themselves [i.e., as Sensuousness] or as freedoms subsisting for themselves [i.e., as Stoicism], but rather as the still hidden image of God that discloses itself only in the devotion of human freedom to the call for actual being.[4]

---

2  Hunter, Charles K.: "The Problem of Fichte's Phenomenology of Love", in: *Idealistic Studies* 6 (1976), p. 183.
3  SW V, p. 511/PW II, p. 430.
4  Verweyen, Hansjürgen: "Fichtes Religionsphilosophie. Versuch eines Gesamtüberblicks", in: *Fichte-Studien* 8 (1995), pp. 217–18.

Ceming maintains that "insight about the cause of action differentiates points three, four, and five [i.e., Higher Morality, Religion, and Science]. Otherwise, these can hardly be distinguished from one another".[5] The person of Higher Morality acts as the Divine instrument but not necessarily with any knowledge of God or of His relation to us and to the world; the Religious individual has such knowledge but only as a bare fact, whereas the person of Science through a genetic principle is able to deduce what, as just noted, is merely a fact to Religion.[6]

It is certainly true that the Religious Standpoint possesses an awareness, namely, the awareness that the energy working through the individual is God's will, that is not shared by the Higher Morality. But this is not the only distinction between these two states. It is characteristic of each standpoint that it "should place the real and independent being and root of the World in one definite and unchangeable principle", and as we move from one worldview up to another, we observe that "each higher step abolishes the lower as an absolute and highest standpoint, and subordinates it to itself".[7] Fichte explicitly carries out this replacement in the transition from the Higher Morality to Religion, so it is misleading to say that they are distinguished only epistemically. Moreover, Fichte notes that persons of Higher Morality are invested in the success of their projects and are thereby distinguished from those engaged in the Religious Life, who are indifferent to whether their aims are realized: the former strive after a certain result, whereas the latter strive after the development of the Divine life within themselves—for them the actualization of their goal is a side issue.

---

5   Ceming, Katharina: *Mystik und Ethik bei Meister Eckhart und Johann Gottlieb Fichte*, Frankfurt a. M. 1999, p. 180.
6   SW V, p.472/PW II, p. 377. This is not exactly how Ceming presents the different relations to God but seems to me more accurate; in any case her general claim that the three standpoints are largely indistinguishable is what is of most concern here. (Edith Düsing is properly more circumspect. She notes that Higher Morality already exhibits essential characteristics of the standpoint of Religion and observes that, while on the one hand, the independence of the ethical over against the religious sphere is not fully preserved, for its part the genuinely religious life rests on morality for Fichte and is unthinkable without it. Precisely how these two are interrelated is explored below. See Düsing, Edith: "Sittliches Streben und religiöse Vereinigung. Untersuchungen zu Fichtes später Religionsphilosophie", in: *Religionsphilosophie und spekulative Theologie. Der Streit um die göttlichen Dinge (1799–1812)*, Jaeschke, Walter (ed.) Hamburg 1994, p. 114.
7   SW V, p. 468/PW II, p. 373.

Of course, one may object that, for Fichte, when it comes to the final two stages both the Religious and Scientific viewpoints are, as he insists, merely "percipient and contemplative", not "active and practical".[8] Now, the Religious standpoint divorced from living activity is just the "mysticism" in the pejorative sense that he has contemptuously rejected earlier in *The Way towards the Blessed Life*.[9] Therefore, Religion cannot represent by itself a higher stage on the road toward the blessed life but must be combined with Higher Morality in order to attain a further level of development. In a way this is correct, but it is not a simple additive process: "unpurified" Higher Morality does represent a separate stage, a separate worldview, from Religion, but Religion does need to be integrated with a refined Higher Morality—a Higher Morality whose purification integrates it into the worldview of religion so that it no longer represents a distinct stage even though it remains distinct from the purely contemplative aspect of Religion—in order for a more comprehensive blessed state to be attained. We can see this most clearly by juxtaposing comments Fichte makes only a few lines apart: First, as already noted, he says that the Religious and the Scientific points of view "are only percipient and contemplative, not in themselves active and practical". Only a few sentences later he insists, "The true and real Religious Life is not alone percipient and contemplative, does not merely brood over devout thoughts, but is essentially active. It consists, as we have seen, in the intimate consciousness that God actually lives, moves, and perfects his work in us".[10] We may take it, then, that Fichte distinguishes between the Religious point of view and the Religious Life. The Religious Life, however, does not simply turn out to be the combination of the Religious standpoint with Higher Morality, first, because Fichte has claimed that different stages are mutually exclusive, second (and the basis for the first claim), because these acknowledge different absolutes, and third (and the basis in this particular case for the second claim), because one only arrives at the Religious standpoint by overcoming Higher Morality (in its unpurified state). We shall find that the Religious Life consists of the Religious viewpoint along with a version of the Higher Morality that has been transformed by the knowledge represented by the higher point of view.

---

8  SW V, p. 473/PW II, p. 378.
9  See SW V, p. 474/PW II, p. 379.
10  SW V, p. 473/PW II, p. 378.

To see this more clearly, let us briefly recount the stages of Fichte's phenomenology of "the inward Spiritual Life" and focus on what distinguishes each stage from its prior. If we begin, as Fichte does not, with the stage of Skepticism or Nullity, we note that it has no absolute: for this view there is no "unchangeable principle", nothing toward which it makes good sense to strive and in whose attainment we might seek to find our blessedness. For this standpoint, if, for the sake of courtesy, we call it that, the "despair of all salvation" is "the only true salvation".[11] When we move to the first standpoint, properly speaking, we find that its unchangeable principle consists in the objects of our outward sense. Because this mode of consciousness acknowledges nothing but the world disclosed to the senses, it hopes to find satisfaction there. But because, as Augustine famously remarked, our souls are restless until they rest in God, no sensible object turns out to be satisfactory. At first, this consciousness explains the failure by holding out the hope that the problem is with this particular object, that some other may do the trick. After repeated failings, consciousness either degenerates toward Skepticism or advances toward Stoicism, or what Fichte sometimes calls Legalism. The unchangeable principle for this view is the Law, a moral law of order, of equal rights in a system of reasonable beings. The sensible world of the previous viewpoint now occupies a subordinate position: it exists only "because free action necessarily assumes the existence of objects of such action".[12] Kant is the most striking instance of this position, although Fichte notes that he himself, in his *Rechtslehre* and his *Sittenlehre*, has also investigated this view of the world; in his case, however, he assures us that he was never so naïve as to regard it as the highest.[13] The third level, that of Higher Morality, also locates its unchangeable principle in a law, but now in a creative law rather than a law of order.[14] It is a law of the production of "the Holy, the Good, [and] the Beautiful";[15] both the law of morality as well as the world of sense are here demoted to mere means for the realization of this aim. The fourth level, however, no longer regards a law for the production of the Holy, the Good, and the Beautiful as the ultimate and the absolute; indeed, it no longer sees the realization of these as essential. What is essential is God's acting through

---

11 SW V, p. 409/PW II, p. 305.
12 SW V, p. 467/PW II, p. 371.
13 See SW V, p. 467/PW II, p. 372.
14 See SW V, p. 469/PW II, p. 373.
15 SW V, p. 469/PW II, p. 374.

the individual in the pursuit of these goals. The outward result—the Holy, the Good, the Beautiful—is no longer willed absolutely and unconditionally: "it therefore would not, even for a single moment, disturb his Peace and Blessedness should it nevertheless remain unaccomplished;— his Love and his Blessedness return into his own proper Life, where they always, and without exception, find their true satisfaction".[16] Only when we reach the fifth stage, that of Science, do we plausibly encounter a new position in which the unchangeable principle remains the same as in the preceding stage: Science goes beyond Religion's mere identification of that principle with Being or God to a comprehension of how being serves as a foundation for the manifold. That is to say, the relation between the fourth and fifth stages of Fichte's spiritual phenomenology is made in terms of his familiar distinction, already alluded to, between what is taken as a mere fact and what is understood in terms of a genetic development.[17]

The key point on which I wish to focus is the transition from Higher Morality to Religion: even though Fichte at one point says that the latter is conjoined with the former,[18] it is only a purified version of the former of which this is true, for in fact the stage of Higher Morality prior to its purification by Religion is incompatible with the latter. The Higher Morality arises with the renunciation of self and self-will, which permits God to will and to act through us so as to produce the Holy, the Good, and the Beautiful[19] but without realizing, at this stage, *that* it is God who is willing and acting through us. For the person of Higher Morality, then, what is important is the holy, good, or beautiful result. And when efforts to produce such a result fail, "then his Love, which has still an uncertain object, is dissatisfied with this failure, and thereby his Blessedness is disturbed and destroyed".[20] This failure generates introspection: in reflecting on what it is that we really aim at, this individual discovers that it is not the result but the "development of the Divine Being and Life in him"[21] that is his goal, and that this development is not dependent on

---

16 SW V, p. 535/PW II, p. 458.
17 See SW V, p. 472/PW II, p. 377.
18 See SW V, p. 470/PW II, p. 375.
19 Thus, this is the point at which Düsing locates the transition from "autonomous" to "theonomous" morality. See Düsing, Edith: "Sittliches Streben und religiöse Vereinigung", in: *Religionsphilosophie und spekulative Theologie. Der Streit um die göttlichen Dinge (1799–1812)*, Jaeschke, Walter (ed.) Hamburg 1994, p. 111.
20 SW V, p. 534/PW II, p. 457.
21 Ibid.

the realization of any result. "So long as joy in the deed is mixed up with desires regarding the outward result of the deed, even the possessor of the Higher Morality is not yet perfect in purity and clearness".[22] The Religious standpoint may be purely contemplative, but the Religious Life is not: it essentially involves activity, but unlike (unpurified) Higher Morality, it does not essentially involve the achievement of what this activity aims at. As Fichte puts it, "the Blessedness of such an individual will not be disturbed by the failure of this result, provided only that he raise himself to a true comprehension of that which he strives after *unconditionally*, as distinguished from that which he seeks only *conditionally*".[23] What the Religious Life strives after unconditionally is that God acts through us; what it strives after conditionally is the Holy, the Good, or the Beautiful, because these have value not in themselves but only insofar as they are produced by God through us. Thus, the place of the Higher Morality in Fichte's religious phenomenology is ambiguous: in its unpurified state, in which the production of the Holy, the Good, and the Beautiful functions as its basic principle, it merits a separate stage; in its purified state, in which we aim for a condition in which God works through us in such a way that, if unobstructed by the activity of others, the Holy, the Good, and the Beautiful will result, the Higher Morality is the active component of the Religious Life that has the Religious standpoint as its cognitive component.

## II. Religious Consciousness and the Question of Mystical Union

In describing the essential traits of that consciousness represented by Religious Life the features of infusion, vocation, and love are certainly central. The precondition for their emergence is the denial or renunciation of self: "as soon as man, by an act of the Highest Freedom, surrenders and lays aside his personal, individual freedom and independence, he becomes a partaker of the Only True Being, the Divine, and of all the Blessedness that is contained therein".[24] Or as the *Theologia Germanica* put it four and a half centuries earlier: "the more the Self, the I, the Me, the Mine, that is, self-seeking and selfishness, abate in a man, the more

---

22 SW V, p. 529/PW II, p. 452.
23 SW V, p. 538/PW II, p. 464.
24 SW V, p. 524/PW II, pp. 445–446.

doth God's I, that is, God Himself, increase in him".[25] Roman Catholic writers have sometimes identified a state of prayer as infused when the prayer is no longer produced through our own efforts but rather through God working in us; hence the prayer is sometimes described as passive and supernatural as well. A situation comparable to this is described by Fichte: once the self is denied, nothing prevents God's flowing forth through us into the world: "So long as man cherishes the desire of being himself something, God comes not to him, for no man can become God. But so soon as he renounces himself sincerely, wholly, and radically, then God alone remains, and is all in all".[26] In the Religious Life, one's will "forever flows forth from the Divinity, immediately and unmistakeably,"[27] and is thus experienced as infused. Not only does the Divine will flow forth from us, but it also does so in a particularized way. It is telling that Fichte uses artistic genius so extensively in his depiction of Higher Morality, for the notion of the genius traditionally brings with it not only the idea of a divine infusion but also the idea of a unique form of expression. This unique expression is our vocation, and Fichte makes it clear that for the consciousness of the Religious Life vocation is not inferred but revealed. This vocation completely takes over the individual raised to the level of the Higher Morality: it "penetrates him wholly, and takes possession of all his Life".[28] The individuals who are thus infused by the Divine, who are so permeated with their vocation, express themselves in Love, or rather Love expresses itself through them. The Quaker Thomas Kelly once spoke of the need to live life in the passive voice, and something of this comes through in Fichte's description of the blessed life: "Love necessarily enters into Reflexion, and manifests itself there immediately, as a life which employs as its instrument a personal, sensuous Ex-istence [*Dasein*],—and thus as Individual Action".[29] The Religious Life thus experiences itself as infused by God with its own vocation, and in the carrying out of that vocation it experiences itself as the conduit whereby love enters into the world. Only a part of this Religious Life is what Fichte calls the Religious stage, and this stage is marked not by the experiences we have just described but by knowledge of the fact

---

25 *The Theologia Germanica of Martin Luther*, trans. Susanna Winkworth, Mineola, NY 2004, pp. 59–60.
26 SW V, p. 518/PW II, p. 438.
27 SW V, p. 549/PW II, p. 476.
28 SW V, p. 543/PW II, p. 455.
29 SW V, p. 544/PW II, p. 470.

that God and the human being are at bottom one, a knowledge grasped by thought and by no other means. This knowledge, however, transforms the Higher Morality, enabling it to understand the life being lived through it as God's own.

This detailed description of the consciousness represented by the Religious Life helps us to resolve one controversial question, namely, whether it is a mystical consciousness, and if so, of what sort. This general attribution has been challenged, particularly by some more recent commentators. Christoph Asmuth, for example, writes, "So far as by 'mysticism' something is understood like *mystical experience, unio mystica, irrational union with the Divine essence*, etc., the concept of mysticism is hardly in keeping with Fichte's texts, especially *The Way towards the Blessed Life*".[30] Regarding the more general issue of whether Fichte's thought deserves to be described as mystical, everything depends on how we understand the term, but if, following what I take to be the best contemporary scholarship, we understand mysticism in terms of an immediate awareness of the Divine presence, then, as I have suggested elsewhere, there is little question that Fichte's religious thought deserves this characterization.[31] In the Religious Life we live out of a Divine center as God loves through us. Fichte leaves no doubt that this manifestation is immediately experienced. Understanding mysticism as the awareness of the Divine presence, there can be little question but that Fichte's standpoint qualifies as mystical. But Asmuth also raises the further issue as to whether such more specific terms as "*unio mystica*" can be appropriately attributed to Fichte's position. The account we have just given helps us to understand in what sense Fichte acknowledges a mystical union, and in what sense this is to be denied.

Fichte recognizes two divisions in *The Way towards the Blessed Life*. One, which has already been described, is Fichte's phenomenology of the different modes of apprehending the world. The second is that whereby Being is transformed in consciousness into a world, and indeed into a world of infinite variety. The divisions are quite different from one another. Obviously the latter division produces an infinite variety of

---

30 Asmuth, Christoph: "Wissenschaft und Religion. Perspektivität und Absolutes in der Philosophie Johann Gottlieb Fichtes", in: *Fichte-Studien* 8 (1995), p. 17, n. 70.
31 See my "On the Mysticism of Fichte's *The Way towards the Blessed Life*", in: *Idealistic Studies* 36 (2006), pp. 1–11. In referring to "the best contemporary scholarship, I have in mind McGinn, Bernard: *The Presence of God: A History of Western Christian Mysticism*, vol. 1, *The Foundations of Mysticism*, New York 1991, p. xvii.

forms and shapes, while the former is finite. More importantly, the latter "separates and divides the World itself", whereas the former "does not immediately separate and divide the object itself, but only separates and divides reflexion on the object".[32] Most significant for our purposes, however, is the fact that the latter division, the division whereby Being is changed by the nature of knowing into a determinate, infinitely varied world, "is absolutely original, and in actual Consciousness can never be abolished nor superseded by anything else".[33] Thus, although Fichte often insists on the identity of the individual with God, these statements must always be understood philosophically and not experientially: the manifold is inescapable, preventing us from ever immediately experiencing the One behind it. The former division, on the other hand, is one in which our separation from God can be overcome: while in the earlier stages our personal will prevents us from becoming the instrument of the Divine will, this is exactly what we do become at the level of the Higher Morality: "modified only by the form of Infinitude, [the Divine Life] reappears in the life and action of the God-inspired man. In his actions it is not man who acts,—but God himself, in his primitive and inward Being and Nature, acts in man and fulfils his work through man".[34]

Thus there are two ways in which our relation to God can be "veiled" from us. First, consciousness changes true Being into a variegated world and our inexpungible consciousness of the manifold obscures any perception of our identity with the one Being. As Fichte puts it, in Smith's charming rendering and in what looks like a variation on a famous Hindu text, "What thou seest, that thou art: but thou art it not as thou seest it, nor dost thou see it as thou art it. [...] Only reflexion—which likewise thou thyself art, and which therefore thou canst never put away from thee—only this causes it to separate before thee into innumerable rays and shapes".[35] Second, our personal will and pursuit of our personal aims prevent true Being from acting through us. But, and unlike the first, the second veil can be pulled aside: by the renunciation of self, Higher Morality is able to open the portals whereby the Divine flows through us and into the world. Thus, while the first relation to God is obscured by the manifold and known only to thought, the second relation to God is known in the immediate experience of Higher Morali-

---

32  SW V, p. 463/PW II, p. 367.
33  SW V, p. 459/ PW II, p. 362.
34  SW V, pp. 475–476/PW II, p. 381.
35  SW V, p. 458/PW II, p. 361–362.

ty by which vocation is revealed: "it is clear that we cannot by any means comprehend *mediately*, through any other conception, and thus *a priori*, how this Being will disclose itself; but that it can only be *immediately* perceived and experienced, and only apprehended in the act of its living forth-flowing from Being into Ex-istence [*Dasein*]".[36] Fichte himself draws attention to this asymmetry when he remarks how the sensible world becomes a sphere for Divine activity, ultimately a means for

> the inward Essential Being of God himself, as it is absolutely, in itself and through itself, immediately, purely, and without intervening medium, *without being modified, veiled, or obscured by any Form contained in the personality of the Ego*, which is on that account obstructive and limiting;—but *broken only by the indestructible Form of Infinity*.[37]

The veil of the manifold remains, but the veil whereby the personal will had hitherto blocked the activity of the Divine will in us has now parted.

This has all been a prelude to asking whether Fichtean teaching offers a mysticism of union or whether the idea of the *unio mystica* is, as Asmuth suggests, "hardly in keeping with Fichte's texts, especially *The Way towards the Blessed Life*". At this point it is useful to introduce a distinction made by Bernard McGinn between two sorts of mystical union. Only in the twelfth century does union become the basic category in the West for the experience of the divine presence, and from the high to the late Middle Ages, according to McGinn, two different conceptions of mystical union are prominent, what he calls the *unitas indistinctionis* and the *unitas spiritus*. The *unitas indistinctionis* is found most prominently in Meister Eckhart and resembles the idea of union found in later antiquity in the writings of Plotinus and Proclus. This union emphasizes an essential or ontological union between God and the soul.[38] Eckhart, for example, gave expression to this idea of union when he stated, "But between man and God there is not only no difference, there is no multiplicity, only one"[39] and "I am converted into Him in such a way that He makes me *one* with His being, not *similar*. By the living God it is

---

36 SW V, p. 525/PW II, p. 447.
37 SW V, p. 525/PW II, p. 447, emphasis added.
38 McGinn, Bernard: "Love, Knowledge, and *Unio Mystica* in the Western Christian Tradition", in: *Mystical Union and Monotheistic Faith: An Ecumenical Dialogue*, ed. Moshe Idel and Bernard McGinn, NewYork/London 1989, p. 70.
39 Meister Eckhart: *Sermons and Treatises*, trans. Maurice O'C. Walshe, vol. 2, Longmead, Shaftesbury, Dorset 1979, p. 118. (This passage comes from Sermon 40 [as numbered in the edition of Eckhart's *Deutsche Werke* edited by Quint] and is quoted by McGinn in "Love, Knowledge, and *Unio Mystica*", p. 76.)

true that there is no distinction".[40] McGinn contrasts this union with a *unitas spiritus*, an idea that finds prominent adherents in St. Bernard, St. Bonaventure, and the Victorines. This notion of union with God is a union of willing and loving, not a union of essence or substance.[41] For example, in speaking of Thomas Gallus McGinn notes that a "study of his use of the word [for union] in the *Song of Songs* commentaries indicates that he takes it, not in terms of ontological unity with the divine being, but rather to indicate transcendent union of wills, as the constant imagery of love suggests".[42] These can, of course, be seen as alternatives, but they need not. In the case of Fichte, I want to suggest that they map directly onto the two ways we have seen him discuss the relation of the individual to God.

While an "insight into the absolute unity of the human existence with the Divine is certainly the profoundest knowledge that man can attain"[43], Fichte nevertheless also maintains that "only in pure Thought can our union with God be recognized".[44] Although there thus may be textual support for attributing the *unitas indistinctionis* to Fichte as a philosophical thesis, there is not support for attributing to him the experience of such a union. To the extent that experience is regarded as an essential component of mysticism,[45] it is difficult to put Fichte forward as providing an instance of the *unio mystica* in his religious philosophy, provided, that is, that we interpret mystical union in terms of the *unitas indistinctionis*, the union of essence or substance. The case is quite otherwise, however, when we view Fichte's thought from the perspective of the *unitas spiritus*, the union of will. Consider, for instance, the individual's entrance into the Higher Morality: with the renunciation of self and self-love "the previously existing Ego" disappears "in the pure Divine Ex-istence [*Dasein*]; and we can no longer say, strictly speaking, that the Affection, the Love, and the Will of this Divine Ex-istence is *ours*, since

---

40  Meister Eckhart: *Sermons and Treatises*, vol. 2, pp. 135–6 (Sermon 6).
41  McGinn, Bernard: "Love, Knowledge, and *Unio Mystica*", p. 63.
42  McGinn, Bernard: "Love, Knowledge, and *Unio Mystica*", p. 69.
43  SW V, p. 483/PWII, p.390.
44  SW V, p. 445/PWII, p.345.
45  For a scholar who thinks that "experientialism" in mysticism stems from a modern, psychologizing misreading of the medieval tradition, see Denys Turner: *The Darkness of God*, Cambridge 1995: "whereas our employment of the metaphors of 'inwardness' and 'ascent' appears to be tied in with the achievement and the cultivation of a certain kind of experience […] the mediaeval employment of them was tied in with a 'critique' of such religious experiences and practices" (4).

there are no longer two Ex-istences and two Wills; but now one Ex-istence, and one and the same Will, is all in all".[46] As noted above, this infusion is not known merely by Thought, but is, in Fichte's words, "*immediately* perceived and experienced". And in the purified Higher Morality that forms a part of the Religious Life, the will of the individual is God's will: "the innermost root of his Life—his Will—for ever flows forth from the Divinity, immediately and unmistakeably".[47] Thus it seems appropriate to speak of the Religious Life in terms of a union of wills or of an *unitas spiritus*, and, unlike the case of *unitas indistinctionis*, it seems appropriate to claim that this union is a matter of immediate experience and is not merely a philosophical thesis. With the crucial element of experience now in place, we can say that Fichte's religious philosophy truly does make a place for mystical union, but not in those passages where he affirms an ontological union after the fashion of Meister Eckhart—for the identity of essences affirmed there is accessible only to thought—but rather in the union of wills, in "the fountain of Divine Love which has burst forth" and is immediately experienced in the Religious Life. Or to state the position more compactly if more cryptically, Fichte is indeed a teacher of the *unio mystica*, but only when that is understood as the *unitas spiritus*, not as the *unitas indistinctionis*. Parenthetically, what this means is that the many comparative studies between Eckhart and Fichte, for all their merits, are not helpful for resolving the question as to whether Fichtean religious consciousness instantiates mystical union; for if we answer this question in the affirmative, we shall also, I think, discover that the type of union it represents is to be distinguished from that found in Eckhart.

The Religious Life, then, includes for Fichte both Higher Morality and Religion, but these two can be integrated into a single Religious Life only when we understand that Higher Morality exists in two forms, as unpurified and as purified. Unpurified Higher Morality represents a separate stage of its own, while purified Higher Morality represents the active facet of the Religious Life, just as Religion represents its contemplative and more cognitive aspect. In Religion we find knowledge of our substantial union with God, whereas in purified Higher Morality we experience union with the Divine will. In consequence, we may accurately conclude that Fichtean religious consciousness exhibits mysti-

---

46 SW V, p. 518/PW II, p. 438.
47 SW V, p. 549/PW II, p. 476.

cal union, but only provided we are careful to qualify this by noting that it is an experienced union of wills, not of essences.

# Fichte and Brentano: Idealism from an Empirical Standpoint and Phenomenology from an Idealist Standpoint

Elizabeth Millán

DePaul University, Chicago

All too often idealism is indiscriminately associated with an anti-realist position, according to which the "ideal" of idealism refers to that which is "not real." This sort of "not real" idealism, however, does not hold for all of those thinkers who can be classified as idealists. It was Berkeley, whose famous *esse est percipi* view of reality essentially promulgated a view of idealism as world-eclipsing, a view vehemently attacked by G. E. Moore in his famous "refutation" of idealism. Yet critics of idealism continue to believe that Moore effectively refuted idealism *tout court*, including, of course, Fichte's idealism. In what follows, I argue that interpreting Fichte's idealism as a subject-centered view of reality with nothing much to tell us about the external world is seriously mistaken. Indeed, I shall highlight the realist strands of Fichte's thought by revisiting his influence on the development of phenomenology.

Consider the promising connection between Fichte's thought and Brentano's work on intentionality made by Julian Marías:

> Beginning with Brentano, philosophers have once again defined human actions as intentional actions; that is, an action is always directed toward an object, the object of that action. An action presupposes the following: a subject to execute it, the action itself and the object towards which the action is directed. This idea of the fundamental *intentionality* of man has shaped all of present-day philosophy. And it is not strange that this philosophy has looked back to Fichte as a classic forerunner of its position.[1]

Following Marías' lead, yet slightly amending it, I shall present a reading of Fichte as a classic (albeit too often overlooked) supporter of the idea of the fundamental intentionality of human mental activity and argue that this idea helped pave the way for Brentano, whose work was pivotal in the

---

1 Marías, Julián: *History of Philosophy*, trans. Appelbaum, Stanley and Strowbridge, Clarence C., New York 1967, p. 310.

development of the protean movement of what is known today as phenomenology.

The fact that Marías, in one quick stroke, puts Fichte and Brentano into such a close historical relation will certainly bother some contemporary Brentano scholars. Amongst Brentano scholars, it is commonplace to complain that he does not receive the attention he deserves – this is the so-called "Brentano puzzle." As Dallas Willard, in discussing Brentano's work, has emphasized:

> Brentano's visibility or invisibility depends upon how we understand what 'real' philosophical work is. For if what he was doing is not regarded as *real* philosophical work—if some view of *what philosophy is* other than his own is dominant—then no one is going to worry about his relevance to their own work. And that 'not worrying' is really the heart of the 'invisibility' in question. And let us face it and say once and for all, that if 'real' philosophical work can be done just as well, or even significantly as well, with Brentano in oblivion as not, then no one needs him. Any interest in him will be essentially antiquarian. And that is exactly what Analyticus now thinks.[2]

Brentano scholars strive to make the philosophical community aware of Brentano's relevance, yet those scholars are quite narrow in sketching out *which* Brentano we need. Strangely, at least to my ears, those Brentano scholars who are puzzled by the lack of interest paid to Brentano, not only have absolutely no interest in looking carefully at Brentano's German roots: they dismiss all of post-Kantian German idealism as anti-scientific and situate Brentano's historical relations in the more philosophically respectable company of figures such as Aristotle, Aquinas, Augustine, and more modern thinkers such as Mill. Certainly, there can be no doubt that Aristotle and the Scholastics were a strong influence on the development of Brentano's thought, he was after all a Catholic priest, and Aristotle and the Scholastics were required reading for such a vocation. Moreover, Brentano himself, with his emphasis on "empirical standpoints" wished to distance himself from idealism (although, like the term 'idealism', 'empiricism' is a term that has many shades of meaning, so there is work to be done in unpacking what Brentano's 'empirical standpoint' really amounts to). Finally, Brentano himself has few kind words

---

2  Willard, Dallas: "Who Needs Brentano? The Wasteland of Philosophy without its Past", in: Poli, Roberto (Ed.): *The Brentano Puzzle*, Aldershot 1998, pp. 15–44, at p. 19.

for the German post-Kantian tradition.[3] Good reasons for looking away from idealism when coming to terms with Brentano's contributions to philosophy notwithstanding, I think that looking carefully at Brentano's relation to Fichte may shed much needed light on the precise meaning of German idealism in the post-Kantian period, and, at the same time, uncover important strands of that philosophical tradition to which Brentano belonged. Thus, we bring more visibility to both Brentano's insights and to the contemporary relevance of Fichte's thought.

## I. Brentano's Idealist Standpoint

Franz Brentano (1838–1917), the nephew of Clemens Brentano and Bettine von Arnim, was related to key figures of the German intellectual tradition, and not just biologically. In his *Psychology from an Empirical Standpoint* (1874), Brentano develops his view that every mental phenomenon contains its object within itself and that intentional inexistence is the mark of the mental. If this thesis sounds like a decidedly idealist angle of an empirical standpoint, consider further what Brentano says in the foreword to the book:

> My psychological standpoint is empirical; experience alone is my teacher. Yet I share with other thinkers the conviction that this is entirely compatible with a certain ideal point of view.[4]

---

3   The following claim puts Brentano's own view of post-Kantian philosophy into sharp relief: "Kant was followed in Germany by Fichte with his method of thesis, antithesis and synthesis. Fichte, in turn, was followed by Schelling with his 'intellectual insight' that is supposed to be a type of absolute knowledge in and of itself: it cannot be taught, nor is it clear why philosophy should be obligated to pay special attention to any such monstrous power. Indeed, one is supposed to infer the mode of access to it from our common knowledge, even though no connection at all exists between them. Schelling was followed by Hegel with his philosophy of the absolute, which asserts of itself that it contains the knowledge of all truth and that it reproduces the totality of the natural and the spiritual world from within itself. Hegel wants to take as his point of departure a thought completely free of content, and then make 'negation' the vehicle of dialectical progress. By means of a series of cavortings of this sort, he hoped to rise up to an eventual lofty end." Brentano, Franz: *The Four Phases of Philosophy and Its Current State*, trans. Smith, Barry and Mezei, Balász, Amsterdam, Atlanta 1998, p. 102.
4   Brentano, Franz: *Psychology from an Empirical Standpoint*, eds. Oskar Kraus and Linda L. McAlister, trans. Rancurello, Antos C., Terrell, Daily B. and McAlister, Linda, London 1995, p. xxvii.

Now, this "ideal point of view" and the obvious idealist implications of "intentional inexistence" vexed some of Brentano's students (especially Meinong, Höfler, and Twardowski), and it creates problems for proponents of the Austrian Brentano, for whom, as I shall discuss below, Brentano is Austrian because of the rigorous methods for philosophy that he endorses and the scientific tradition of which he was a part, a tradition that they read as sharply at odds with any elements of idealism at all. Yet, there is just no getting around the intersection between Brentano's early philosophy (in particular the intentional inexistence thesis) and a connection to idealism. Dale Jaquette writes:

> Hardline empiricism might be said to lead to idealism in Brentano's early philosophy just as it does in Berkeley's. The dilemma of respecting both empiricist methodology and common sense pre-theoretical beliefs about the mind-independence of objects of experience is dramatically, dialectically played out in the transition from Brentano's acceptance to his rejection of the immanent intentionality thesis.[5]

Of course, the proponents of the Austrian Brentano have much riding on his rejection of the immanent intentionality thesis: accepting the immanent intentionality thesis brings with it the problem of duplicating intended objects, violates the sort of theoretical frugality respected since Ockham, yields counterintuitive consequences,[6] and, most importantly, connects Brentano's fundamental insight regarding the intentionality of all mental phenomena to certain idealist strands. And any path connecting Brentano to idealism is one that those in the Austrian camp want to avoid.

The essential intentionality of mental phenomena is categorized by Brentano as follows: 1) One may think of A or "have it before the mind" or "present to consciousness"; this sort of mental act is what Brentano calls *Vorstellungen*, ideas, thoughts, presentations, in short, anything present to consciousness; 2) One may take an intellectual stand with respect to A: either accepting or rejecting A; this is the group of mental acts that Brentano calls judgments; 3) One may take an emotional stance with respect to A, of loving or hating A, Brentano calls this sort of mental act

---

5   Jaquette, Dale: "Brentano's Concept of Intentionality", in: Jaquette, Dale (ed.): *The Cambridge Companion to Brentano*, Cambridge 2004, pp. 98–130, at p. 122.
6   Jaquette, Dale: "Brentano's Concept of Intentionality", p. 110.

emotive phenomena and includes emotions and volitions.[7] The most basic types of mental phenomena are *Vorstellungen* (ideas, thoughts, presentations) and as Brentano's principle makes clear: "Every mental act is either a presentation or is based on a presentation," so that the other two types of mental phenomena presuppose *Vorstellungen*. Furthermore, as Brentano tells us in what has come to be known as the "intentionality passage:"[8]

> Every mental phenomenon is characterized by what the Scholastics of the Middle Ages called the intentional (or mental) inexistence of an object, and what we might call, though not wholly unambiguously, reference to a content, direction toward an object (which is not to be understood here as meaning a thing), or immanent objectivity. Every mental phenomenon includes something as object within itself, although they do not all do so in the same way. In presentation something is presented, in judgment something is affirmed or denied, in love loved, in hate hated, in desire desired and so on.
> This intentional in-existence[9] is characteristic exclusively of mental phenomena. No physical phenomenon exhibits anything like it. We can, therefore, define mental phenomena by saying that they are those phenomena which contain an object intentionally within themselves.[10]

In this passage, Brentano makes a clear announcement that all mental phenomena and only mental phenomena are intentional, thus locating a feature essential to thought in intentionality. Furthermore, we are given a glimpse into Brentano's view of the mind, for our acts of thought are directed to what exists immanently within it.[11] For the early Brentano,

---

7 Roderick Chisholm gives this clear account of Brentano's basic insights in his entry on Franz Brentano for the *Encyclopedia of Philosophy*, Volume 1, New York 1967 pp. 365–368.
8 Brentano, Franz: *Psychology from an Empirical Standpoint*, from Chapter 1, "The Distinction Between Mental and Physical Phenomena," of Book Two of *Psychology from an Empirical Standpoint*, "Mental Phenomena in General," pp. 88–89.
9 As Jaquette reminds us, it is important to keep in mind that "when Brentano speaks of 'intentional in-existence,' he means to say that an intended object, if not 'a reality', exists in or has 'in-existence,' existing not externally but in the psychological state by which it is thought, as the thought's internal content. The sense of 'in' in Brentano's phrase 'intentional in-existence' is thus locative rather than negative. It specifies where the intended object of thought is to be located, rather than qualifies it negatively as nonexistent (Jaquette, Dale: "Brentano's Concept of Intentionality", in: *The Cambridge Companion to Brentano*, pp. 98–130, at pp. 101–102).
10 Brentano, Franz: *Psychology from an Empirical Standpoint*, pp. 88–89.
11 Barry Smith, who really does not want to allow any proximity between Brentano and the German tradition, does admit that the immanentistic views of Brentano

intentionality is understood as a relation between an act and immanent content or 'object of thought.' Now, a Brentano scholar like Barry Smith, that is, a proponent of the Austrian Brentano, even if he cannot deny the immanentist views of Brentano, views which Brentano shares with some idealists (especially if we do not confine idealism to an anti-realist doctrine), can chalk up the early Brentano's immanent intentionality thesis to a flaw in his thought. I want to emphasize what the Austrian Brentano camp would like to keep at a distance: namely, the elements of the early Brentano's intentionality thesis that bring him in the close company of idealism in general, and of Fichte's idealism in particular.

Let us recall that Husserl held that without Brentano's doctrine of intentionality, "phenomenology could not have come into being at all." If it is true that without Brentano's doctrine of intentionality, phenomenology could not have come into being at all, and if Marías is correct in asserting that Fichte is a classic forerunner of that position, then we have an incredibly important historical relation in the story of the connection between Brentano and Fichte. Why, then, would any serious Brentano scholar wish to deny this kinship?

## II. Brentano: Austrian or German Philosopher?

In his article, "Brentano and Hussserl," Robin Rollinger makes some claims that give us important clues regarding Fichte's exclusion from any discussion of Brentano's work. As he tells us:

> Though Brentano's philosophical views certainly went through various phases of development, what is clearly present in all phases is the conviction that philosophy can and must be scientific.[12]

A few pages later, Rollinger continues with this portrait of the "scientific Brentano":

> Brentano's empirical orientation, according to which concepts are to be derived from either inner or outer intuition, naturally makes him a close ally with the empiricist tradition. It also makes him an enemy of the inflationary

---

that come from his intentionality thesis do indeed bring him into some overlaps with Kant, yet that the similarities are "superficial only". (Smith, Barry: *Austrian Philosophy. The Legacy of Franz Brentano*, Chicago 1996, pp. 41–42.)

12 Rollinger, Robert: "Brentano and Husserl", in: *The Cambridge Companion to Brentano*, pp. 255–276, at p. 256.

philosophy that established itself in Germany in the wake of Kant and eventually discredited philosophy itself for many in the second half of the 19th century.[13]

According to Rollinger, Brentano has no connection at all to the German post-Kantian idealist tradition; quite the contrary, he was an *enemy* of any such tradition. Rollinger stresses that Brentano, in developing his empirical psychology, "sets out from what we actually experience [...] and not from mere speculative notions such as "soul" or "spirit"."[14] As we shall see, certain post-Kantian German idealists also set out from "what we actually experience" rather than from empty speculations.

Arguably, the most forceful proponent of the Austrian Brentano is Barry Smith, who defends the claim that there is a distinctively Austrian style and "mode of philosophizing," which gave rise to scientific philosophy, and which is sharply at odds with German philosophy. Here is what Smith has to say about the German tradition in his seminal (and highly provocative) article, "The Neurath-Haller Thesis: Austria and the Rise of Scientific Philosophy":

> Brentano was not only sympathetic to the idea of a rigorously scientific method in philosophy; he also shared with the British empiricists and with the Vienna positivists an anti-metaphysical orientation, manifesting an especially forceful antipathy to the 'mystical paraphilosophy' of the German idealists and stressing in all his work the unity of scientific methods.[15]

Smith leads the chorus of voices speaking in favor of the scientifically-minded, empirically-grounded Austrian Brentano, and against anything smacking of German Idealism, which is demoted from philosophy to "paraphilosophy." Another voice speaking for the Austrian Brentano and with great suspicion towards the almost haunted specter of the post-Kantian German idealism that emerges in these "Austrian sketches," is Peter Simons, who, following Barry Smith's lead, characterizes Brentano as an analytic thinker and the German Idealists as muddle-headed:

> Philosophy in Austria had, as Neurath put it, spared itself the Kantian interlude [...] [Austrian philosophy] was characterized by a rejection of all forms of idealism, an emphasis on psychological and linguistic analysis, respect for empirical science, a general mistrust of philosophical speculation, and stylis-

---

13 Ibid, p. 258.
14 Ibid.
15 Smith, Barry: "The Neurath-Haller Thesis: Austria and the Rise of Scientific Philosophy", in: Lehrer, K. and Marek, J.C. (eds.): *Austrian Philosophy Past and Present*, Dordrecht 1996, pp. 1–20, at p. 7.

tically by an eschewal of profound sounding obscurity in favor of plain clarity of exposition and thought.[16]

For both Simons and Smith, to categorize Brentano as an Austrian philosopher, is not to make a mistake of biography or of physical geography. Their peculiar academic geography requires that Brentano be placed on the Austrian rather than German map. Brentano fits squarely onto Austrian territory because he is an enemy of obscurity, a philosopher who never fell prey to the aimless wanderings of post-Kantian German idealism, a philosopher, in short, who was rigorous, empirical, and sensible: a philosopher who valued logic, argument, and technical competence. So, the question of whether Brentano was a German philosopher or an Austrian philosopher is not a question of philosophical nationality at all, but rather a question of Brentano's relation to post-Kantian German idealism. Brentano *is* an Austrian philosopher, because he is clear and scientific. He is *not* a German philosopher, because he does not lose himself in empty speculations only to mislead the reader with obscure language. Karl Schumann, another prominent Brentano scholar echoes this sentiment:

> [For Brentano] the method of natural science is also the method of philosophy. Philosophy, in other words, is a scientific enterprise. This has been cashed out in terms of the necessity of logical argument, exact language, and the orientation toward narrowly circumscribed, well-defined, and therefore solvable problems. Such virtues were considered to be the hallmark of "Austrian" philosophy, as distinct from its German counterpart, which indulges in the construction of holistic systems, employing profound and therefore obscure language.[17]

All of this inflated talk of the alleged "obscurity" and "speculation" into which post-Kantian German idealism or "paraphilosophy" falls is based, I shall argue, on a superficial reading of the movement. And those scholars who champion an Austrian Brentano, a Brentano liberated from any German idealist roots, claim to do so in the name of a philosophy focused on the search for truth. Smith even emphasizes that,

> it is the proper business of philosophy to search for "truth simpliciter," including truth in the various fields of the history of philosophy. This, surely,

---

16 Simons, Peter: "Bolzano, Brentano and Meinong: Three Austrian Realists", in: O'Hear, Anthony (ed.): *German Philosophy since Kant*, Cambridge 2000, pp. 109–136, at p. 109.
17 Schumann, Karl: "Brentano's Impact on Twentieth-Century Philosophy", in: *The Cambridge Companion to Brentano*, pp. 277–297, at p. 295.

must imply also a search for truth even in relation to those byways of philosophical history and of philosophical concern which do not fit well into the customary and rather narrow picture of philosophical history that has been favoured by analytic philosophers hitherto.[18]

Clearly, although not on the horizon of Smith's map of philosophy, the byway announced in Marías' claim, regarding Fichte's role in the development of Brentano's thought, opens an inquiry, a search for the truth concerning the relation between Brentano's philosophy and a key figure of the post-Kantian German Idealist Movement. Upon my reading of the Fichte-Brentano connection, it becomes clear that Brentano's serious, scientific philosophy is not sullied by an association with a German idealist like Fichte, quite the contrary; an understanding of their relation leads us to new truths regarding both German Idealism and Brentano's pathbreaking work on intentionality.

### III. The True Story of German Idealism and Its Relation to Reality

Those who argue that Brentano is an Austrian rather than a German philosopher use the distinction between German and Austrian philosophy to distance Brentano from any connection to the dreaded influence of German idealism: these thinkers are guilty of associating idealism with an anti-realist position, in this sense, the "ideal" of idealism refers to that which is "not real". As I mentioned at the outset, this sort of idealism is rooted in Berkeley's idealism and his famous *esse est percipi* view of reality: according to this view, idealism is essentially a negative metaphysical doctrine. It was this sort of idealism that formed the basis of G.E. Moore's famous refutation. Yet, as Frederick Beiser has recently argued, the sort of idealism behind the German philosophical movements of the 1700s was rooted not in Berkeley, but in Plato. Indeed, Beiser's book, *German Idealism: the Struggle against Subjectivism, 1781–1801*, tells a story of German Idealism according to which this philosophical position is compelling *not* because it leads us to the subject, trapping us there in some sort of egocentric predicament which makes it impossible to determine whether our ideas of the world actually correspond to

---

18 Smith, Barry: "The Neurath-Haller Thesis: Austrian and the Rise of Scientific Philosophy", in: *Austrian Philosophy Past and Present*, pp. 1–10, at p. 13.

something objective in the external world, but rather because it leads to the development of a robust realism and naturalism.[19]

The dismissive reading of German Idealism would have the post-Kantian period represented as a slow eclipsing of the world by an overgrown subjectivity. Yet, according to Beiser's account, "the story of German Idealism becomes a story about the progressive *de-subjectivization* of the Kantian legacy, the growing recognition that the ideal realm consists not in personality and subjectivity, but in the normative, the archetypical, and the intelligible."[20]

To prevent general misunderstandings of the post-Kantian period, we do well to keep in mind that German Idealism is *not* a threat to a subject independent reality, *not* a breed of anti-realism according to which all of reality depends on the subject, and so it is *not* a position that reduces all of reality to the mental or spiritual realm. Alas, the Brentano scholars who declare Brentano to be an enemy of German Idealism read Fichte and his ilk as a threat to realism, empiricism, and a truly "scientific" philosophy. Yet, Fichte, as even a cursory look at the title of his main work indicates, *was* interested in scientific philosophy. Admittedly, his version of what counts as *Wissenschaft* and of what a *Wissenschaftslehre* would look like, is certainly different than what Brentano had in mind with his development of a *scientific* philosophy, but to abruptly announce that Fichte, because he is part of the German idealist tradition, must, of necessity then be anti-scientific, is to recklessly disregard the detail of Fichte's philosophical contributions.

In order to highlight the idealism of German Idealism in general and of Fichte's idealism in particular, what I am after here is not a definition of idealism in the basic sense of an ontological doctrine according to

---

19 At first blush, it seems counter-intuitive to read German Idealism as leading to a robust realism. Yet, a closer look reveals that the most prototypical absolute idealist of the period, Hegel, did hold that human thought reflects the nature of reality itself, not its own subjectivity, which would seem to be a kind of absolute realism or materialism, rather than any form of idealism at all. Yet, since Hegel holds that the "deepest fact about the nature of reality is that it is a product of God's thought" (Guyer, Paul: "Absolute Idealism and the Rejection of Kantian Dualism", in: Ameriks, Karl (ed.): *The Cambridge Companion to German Idealism*, Cambridge 2000, pp. 37–56, at p. 37.), Hegel's position remains a form of absolute idealism, though not one that takes anything away from the real, but rather an idealism that attempts to make the real accessible to us in a way that Kant's dualism between appearance and reality did not.
20 Beiser, Frederick: *German Idealism: the Struggle against Subjectivism, 1781–1801*, Cambridge, MA 2002, p. 6, emphasis added.

which things in the universe are dependent, in some way or another, on mental structures. Fichte's idealism is much more a response to the problem of knowledge introduced by Kant's critical philosophy and ultimately leads him, in the good company of several other post-Kantian German Idealists, to a careful examination of mental phenomena and a search for what is essential to all thought, objectives that were shared by Brentano. In the space I have here, my sketch of Fichte's idealism shall be limited to a focus on how Fichte dealt with the problem of knowledge introduced by Kant's philosophy, for in looking at how Fichte dealt with Kant's troubling dualisms, we begin to see the meaning and relevance of his idealism for the development of phenomenology.

Kant's transcendental idealism presented his contemporaries with a dualistic conception of human nature that was found to be highly problematic. What Kant sought to explain with his transcendental idealism was how the mental and the physical, so utterly different in nature, were nonetheless related in such a way that it was possible for us to have knowledge of the external world, a world that was at once independent of us and yet accessible to us. In admittedly complicated ways, the term 'transcendental idealism' brings together Kant's epistemological (the transcendental is that which lays out the conditions for the possibility of knowledge) and ontological (idealism is a position about the nature of the things in the world) commitments – commitments that are fully laid out only when we consider his system in its entirety as a combination of transcendental idealism and empirical realism. In working out his system, Kant was led to posit a duality between the *phenomenal* world, the world we can know, and the mind-independent or *noumenal* world, to which we can never have determinate access. To deny any relation at all between this move in Kant and the development of phenomenology, in whichever of its varied forms we choose, is peculiar at best and blind-sighted at worst, but it is one that the adherents of Brentano as an Austrian philosopher seem all too eager to make.

A decidedly idealist focus in the entire immediate post-Kantian period can be found in the view that the role of reason is constitutive in shaping human experience, yet that there must be some ground of reason, some unity underlying thought and reality that would enable us to move beyond Kant's troubling dualisms and so escape the threat of skepticism – a skepticism that leaves us without clear access to the world as it is.[21] Kant sets limits to knowledge in order to avoid the mistakes of unreason (fallacies, amphibolies, antinomies, paralogisms and other "monsters" born of the sleep of reason).[22] Furthermore, Kant saw his "critical method" as a way to provide an account of knowledge that would resist Cartesian and Humean doubts. Kant viewed his transcendental idealism as the only truly critical idealism, that is, the only position that would enable us to avoid the skepticism of whether or not our beliefs actually correspond to something in the world. Quickly, however, Kant's critics found problems with exactly how the sensible and intellectual realms, utterly different in nature, were supposed to interact. And so began a host of well-known attempts to finish Kant's revolution, by tending to its true spirit (Fichte), providing the missing premises for his conclusions (Schelling), or to finding a principle that truly grounded the critical philosophy (Reinhold). To reduce all of these attempts as jargon-filled, obscure exercises in useless speculation is to ignore the important advances in work on the concept that was to be central to Brentano's work, that is, work on intentionality. In fact, if we look carefully back to one key intellectual dispute of the period, we begin to see just how "scientific" post-Kantian philosophy in Germany was, and just how closely related it is to matters very much on the mind of a certain "Austrian philosopher" of the late 19th/ early 20th century.

## IV. The *Aenesidemus* Debate: Reinhold's Move from *Satz* to Fact of Consciousness

The debate upon which I have chosen to focus in order to vindicate post-Kantian German Idealism from its slanderous image as an anti-scientific movement that had no regard for clarity or rigor is the famous *Aenesidemus* Debate. A close look at the philosophical points that took shape as a result of this debate shall enable us to shed light on both Reinhold and

---

21 Much of the work of the post-Kantian idealists was focused on overcoming the dualisms that they found troublesome in Kant's system, most notably, the one between intellect and sense, which is arguably *the* fundamental dualism in Kant (underlying the dualisms between, for example, concept and intuition, reality and appearance). For more on this matter, see Guyer, Paul: "Absolute Idealism and the Rejection of Kantian Dualism", in: *The Cambridge Companion to German Idealism*, pp. 37–56.

22 This is how Beiser refers to Kant's project. See Beiser, Frederick: "The Enlightenment and Idealism", in: *The Cambridge Companion to German Idealism*, p. 22.

Fichte's conceptions of philosophy as a rigorous science, and to see how central the notions of *Vorstellung* and intentionality were to their philosophical contributions.

Reinhold was one of the first popularizers of Kant's critical philosophy and also one of the first to attempt to move beyond the critical philosophy in his search for its foundation. Reinhold was interested in establishing the *logical* relation (as opposed to Kant's goal of establishing the *transcendental* conditions) between actual knowledge and its cause and arrived not at a *principle* of consciousness, but at a *fact* of consciousness. To accomplish this goal, he develops the concept of *Vorstellung* (which is typically translated in the works of the post-Kantians not as 'presentation', but rather as 'representation'), thereby making reference to a thing-in-itself obsolete. On Reinhold's model, the establishment of objective truth no longer requires any object that is not already a representation [*Vorstellung*].

> Every possible demonstration of objective truth would call for a comparison between a representation and an object different from it; but at the same time this comparison could only take place through representations, and indeed it would have to be between the one representation that consists in the impression itself, and the other through which the impression is represented; consequently, the comparison would never be set up between a representation and an object that is not already a representation.[23]

Reinhold believes that he has found the most fundamental concept of knowledge and truth, and so the very concept which must be secured if philosophy is to be a science. According to Reinhold, the first principle of philosophy (and since he follows Kant in identifying philosophy with the problem of knowledge, his first principle has everything to do with the essence of thought) must be one which secures and defines representation and that which can be represented. Is it far-fetched to make a connection with Reinhold's post-Kantian contribution and the insight articulated by Brentano as he posits intentionality as the mark of the mental and insists that philosophy must be scientific?

Beiser, in fact, describes Reinhold's project as guided by the following convictions: 1) philosophy must be systematic; 2) it must begin with one self-evident principle; 3) only phenomenology can fulfill the

---

23 Reinhold, Karl Leonhard: "The Foundation of Philosophical Knowledge", in: Di Giovanni, George and Harris, Henry S. (eds.): *Between Kant and Hegel, Texts in the Development of Post-Kantian Idealism*, Indianapolis 2000, p. 57.

ideal of a "first philosophy."[24] If philosophy is to be systematic, it must be deduced from one principle and this must be a self-evident principle, for if it were in need of a demonstration, it could not be absolute. But if only phenomenology can fulfill the ideal of a "first philosophy", then this principle must be a fact. This fact of consciousness is the first principle of Reinhold's philosophy. It is expressed in his *Satz des Bewußtseins*:

> A representation is what is distinct in consciousness from object and subject and related to both. (*Eine Vorstellung ist was im Bewußtsein vom Objekt und Subjekt unterschieden und auf beide bezogen wird*).[25]

Reinhold's examination of the methods and presuppositions of Kant's critical philosophy led him to a fact of consciousness which he posited as the essence of mental activity. Hence, the structure of Kant's transcendental argument and its transcendental method are undermined and replaced by Reinhold's phenomenology. Thinking is always thinking of something, a representation is always a representation of something; philosophy must by systematic, and this systematic philosophy will be guided by a connection to objects in the world. This does not sound much like the wild, speculative crazy ravings that proponents of the Austrian Brentano impute to the post-Kantian German Idealists: in fact, what Reinhold is developing seems very much in keeping with where Brentano wanted to go with his philosophical system.

But the story of Reinhold's role in the development of phenomenology does not end with these early attempts. The post-Kantians were committed to a search for truth, so the charge of "paraphilosophy" is unwarranted; in fact, a strong critical spirit infused the movement. Post-Kantian German Idealism developed in a series of attempts to establish systems, and critical responses to those systems, which necessitated refinements and corrections to the systems. Consider the ways in which philosophers such as Reinhold and Fichte searched for truth: they distributed their work to colleagues, were open to criticism, making appropriate changes to certain claims or to the development of certain points in light of such criticisms, all in order to come closer to the truth. To depict German Idealism as an unsystematic movement with no serious commitment to the search for truth is to disregard important historical evidence which clearly demonstrates that these philosophers were interested in ver-

---

24  Beiser, Frederick: *The Fate of Reason. German Philosophy from Kant to Fichte*, Cambridge, MA 1987, p. 228.
25  Ibid., p. 72.

ifying their claims and with establishing truth via a clear, shareable method. A frequent hurdle in the way of a claim's acceptance was its explanatory weakness, as we shall see below.

One example of the scientific method of the post-Kantians was the famous attack against Reinhold's *Elementarphilosophie*, which was published anonymously in 1792: this attack quickly dashed any of Reinhold's hopes that he had definitively settled the problem of the first principle of consciousness and so had saved philosophy from skepticism.[26] The author of the attack was soon discovered to be Gottlob Ernst Schulze (1761–1833), a professor of philosophy at the University of Helmstadt.[27] *Aenesidemus* is written as a collection of letters in which Hermias, an enthusiastic admirer of critical philosophy, declares to Aenesidemus his complete conviction (founded especially upon Reinhold's philosophy of the Elements) of the truth and universal validity of this philosophy. Aenesidemus responds to these enthusiastic claims with a skeptical examination of both Reinhold and Kant's philosophy.

Aenesidemus claims that:

> The philosophy of the Elements, by deriving actual representation from a faculty which it takes to be something objectively actual, and by defining it as the cause of the representations, contradicts its own principles as well as the results of the *Critique of Reason*.[28]

---

26 This was Gottlob E. Schulze's *Aenesidemus or Concerning the foundations of the Philosophy of Elements issued by Prof. Reinhold in Jena together with a defense of Skepticism against the Pretensions of the Critique of Reason* (*Aenesidemus, oder Über die Fundamente der von dem Herrn Professor Reinhold in Jena gelieferten Elementarphilosophie*), trans. and edited by George di Giovanni as Aenesidemus in: Between Kant and Hegel, Indianapolis 2000, pp. 104–135.

27 Beiser indicates that Schulze's historical influence went beyond the controversy surrounding Reinhold's philosophy. In 1803, Hegel wrote a review of Schulze's *Kritik der theoretischen Philosophie*, a work that refined and systematized the criticisms of Kant developed in *Aenesidemus*. According to Beiser, Schulze's skepticism caused Hegel to re-think the relation between philosophy and skepticism. Beiser claims that "the conclusion of these reflections – that a true skepticism plays a positive role in every system of philosophy– was an important step toward the development of Hegel's dialectic in the *Phänomenologie*". (Beister, Frederick: *The Fate of Reason: German Philosophy from Kant to Fichte*, Cambridge 1993, p. 268.) Schulze also influenced Arthur Schopenhauer, who was his student at the Unversity of Göttingen in 1810. Beiser notes in particular the influence of Schulze's critique of Kant and Schopenhauer's mention of this in *Die Welt als Wille und Vorstellung* (Ibid.).

28 Schulze, Gottlob E.: *Aenesidemus or Concerning the foundations of the Philosophy of Elements*, in: Between Kant and Hegel, p. 109.

Why does Aenesidemus claim that Reinhold contradicts his own principle? Reinhold claims that the form of representations must be produced, and this presupposes an active subject. Consciousness is presented by Reinhold as an intentional relation to objects. Of course, this leaves us with the problem of self-knowledge. If there is no un-thing-like consciousness, if the very structure of consciousness consists in "something that is conscious and is called the subject, and something of which one is conscious and is called the object and something through which one is conscious of [something else] and is called representing,"[29] then we cannot have any knowledge of the subject as subject but only of the subject as object, thereby making self-consciousness impossible. If the first principle of philosophy is a fact of consciousness which cannot explain self-consciousness, then we are in need of another principle to explain self-consciousness and this is clearly at odds with Reinhold's claim that he has discovered the first principle of philosophy. Moreover, according to Aenesidemus, Reinhold's fact of consciousness cannot explain the most basic act of consciousness we have, intuition.

> The definition of the faculty of representation laid down in the Philosophy of the Elements could only make comprehensible those representations that are referred to an object and subject and are distinguished from both, if indeed it explained anything at all; for it is drawn only from this type of representation. It would not, however, establish the possibility of anything in us which, even without being referred to an object or subject and being distinguished from both, is nonetheless a representation and rightly deserves to be called so.[30]

Again, a first principle which is capable of explaining *some* rather than *all* acts of consciousness is no first principle at all. Ultimately, Schulze, through his mouthpiece Aenesidemus, claims that Hume's skeptical attacks on the possibility of uncovering the origin of representations have left us without any materials with which to build a system of philosophy and therefore without a means of saying anything about the origin of human knowledge.[31]

These were charges to which Reinhold, undoubtedly interested in rigor and clarity, felt compelled to respond. This response is found in the *Beyträge zur Berichtigung der bisherigen Missverständnisse der Philosophie,*

---

29 "etwas das sich bewusst ist, und Subjekt heisst, etwas, dessen man sich bewusst ist und Objekt heisst und etwas wodurch man sich bewusst ist, und *Vorstellen* heißt." (*The Foundation of Philosophical Knowledge*, in: *Between Kant and Hegel*, p. 64).
30 Schulze, Gottlob E.: *Aenesidemus*, p. 111.
31 Ibid., p. 132.

*Vol. II* (1794).³² In the foreword, Reinhold informs his readers that he had completed this part of the work before the appearance of Aenesidemus' review in the *Allgemeine Literatur Zeitung*. Nonetheless, Reinhold claims that Aenesidemus' objections have been answered: "Aenesidemus will find that his desire not to remain within the confines of my previous foundation for the *Elementarphilosophie* is also my desire."³³

If Reinhold does not wish to remain within the confines of the foundation developed in the *Philosophy of Elements*, then where does he want to go? It was futile, Reinhold concluded, to attempt to establish a first *principle*, but his *Satz des Bewusstseins* was not a first *principle* but a fundamental *fact* of human knowledge.

Reinhold continues to hold that representation is the most fundamental concept, the concept which must be explained if we are to establish a first principle for philosophy, yet in light of the criticisms of his work, he does acknowledge that the structure of his argument must be revised. In this restructuring, the relation between common understanding and philosophizing reason takes on a new meaning. In his response to his critics, Reinhold focuses upon the justification of his fact of consciousness and how this differs from a principle of consciousness, and then goes on to develop a new way of viewing the relation between common understanding and philosophizing reason. But another critique of Reinhold's work would show this line of defense to be the wrong one.

---

32 The work is divided into four parts, with Part I dedicated to a defense of the fact of consciousness as the first principle for philosophy, Part II to a discussion of the status of metaphysics, Part III to the type of skepticism which can properly be directed against the *Critique of Pure Reason* and Part IV to the development of the concept of will that Reinhold had begun to develop in Vol.II of his *Letters on Kantian Philosophy* (*Vorrede*, vi-vii). All references to this work are from the edition published in Jena by Johann Michael Mauke, 1794. All translations are my own. In the section entitled, *Über den Unterschied zwischen dem gesunden Verstande und der philosophierenden Vernunft in Rücksicht auf der Fundamente des durch beyde möglichen Wissens*, we find Reinhold's responses to Schulze's criticisms.
33 "Aenesidemus wird finden, dass sein Wunsch, bey meiner bisherigen Begründung der Elementarphilosophie nicht stehen zu bleiben, auch der meinige ist."(Ibid).

## V. Fichte's Review of *Aenesidemus:* the Move from Fact to Act of Consciousness

In a review of Aenesidemus' criticisms (*Allgemeine Literatur Zeitung* 11, 12 February, 1794), Fichte defends Reinhold against all the claims made against him by Aenesidemus, and this defense marked an important turning point in post-Kantian philosophy.[34]

> It appears to emerge from what has been said so far that all the objects of Aenesidemus are groundless in so far as they are to be taken as directed against the truth of the principle of consciousness as such, but that they are relevant to it as first principle of all philosophy as mere fact; thus the objections make a new justification necessary.[35]

According to Fichte, the problem is not the search for a first principle for all philosophy, but with Reinhold's presupposition that the most fundamental concept is that of representation and the ensuing attempt to locate the principle in a *fact* of consciousness. Fichte criticizes Aenesidemus for failing to aim his skepticism against Reinhold's claim that representation is the most fundamental concept of philosophy. For Fichte, the most fundamental concept is not representation.

> It remains dubious in the eyes of this reviewer whether philosophy itself would benefit from their [Reinhold's and Aenesidemus'] unanimity as regards the second point [that the first principle of philosophy must be that principle which defines and secures the concept of representation]; it might turn out, some time in the future, that what can be justifiably said against the principle of consciousness as the *first* principle of philosophy as a whole will lead to the suspicion that there must be for the whole of philosophy (and not just for theoretical philosophy) yet a *higher* concept than that of representation.[36]

---

34 According to Daniel Breazeale, "The Aenesidemus review turned out to be much more than a defense of Kantianism against skepticism. It implies a fundamental reassessment of both Kant's and Reinhold's work and – in tentative but unmistakable terms – announces the discovery of a new standpoint and of a new foundation for transcendental philosophy. Fichte's review of Aenesidemus thus not only signals a revolution in his own philosophical development but marks a genuine watershed in the history of German Idealism" (Breazeale, Daniel: "Fichte's Aenesidemus Review and the Transformation of German Idealism", in: *Review of Metaphysics 34* (1980–1981), p. 546).

35 Fichte, Johann G.: *Review of Aenesidemus*, trans., George di Giovanni, in *Between Kant and Hegel*, (*op. cit.*), pp. 136–157, at p. 142.

36 Ibid., p. 135. This is precisely what Fichte attempts to show in his *Wissenschaftslehre*. On p. 154, note 13 of *Between Kant and Hegel* (op. cit.) Di Giovanni refers us specifically to the *Grundlage der gesamten Wissenschaftslehre* (1794), §§8–10.

Throughout the review, Fichte uses his criticisms of both Aenesidemus and Reinhold to clear openings for his own thought. On the issue of whether Reinhold's *Satz* is analytic (Reinhold, of course, claims it is) or synthetic (as Aenesidemus claims it is), Fichte finds himself in the middle and is led to a question which his philosophy will answer.

> Suppose that no consciousness can be thought without these three parts [subject, object, representation]; then these parts would certainly be contained in the concept of consciousness, and in regard of its logical validity the proposition specifying them would certainly be, as a reflective proposition, analytical. But obviously the performance of representing, the act of consciousness is itself a synthesis all the same, for it differentiates and refers; indeed, it is the highest synthesis, and the ground of all other possible ones. And with this consideration there arises, then, the very real question, how is it ever possible to trace back all the performances of the mind to the one [act of] putting together? How is *synthesis* to be thought without the presupposition of *thesis* and *antithesis*?[37]

This concern with the acts involved in consciousness became the basis of Fichte's conceptual framework. In addressing another point of contention between Aenesidemus and Reinhold, that of whether Reinhold's *Satz* is an abstract proposition expressing what *some* manifestations of consciousness have in common or what *all* of them share, Fichte finds another opportunity to introduce his own solution to the problem of securing a first principle for philosophy. If the principle is abstracted from empirical self-observation, then the principle is based on an abstraction, and this hints that the proposition must be based on something more than a mere actual fact.

> This reviewer at any rate has convinced himself that the proposition is a theorem based upon another principle, but that it can be rigorously demonstrated a priori from that principle, and independently of all experience.[38]

Fichte is in agreement here with Aenesidemus's critique of Reinhold's claim that his proposition of consciousness is based on no abstraction at all, for insofar as Reinhold claims that we come to it from empirical self-observation, it must be based on an abstraction. Nevertheless, Fichte does not accept Aenesidemus's ensuing skepticism regarding the fate of all first principles.[39] For as Fichte suggests above, if the principle can be

---

37 Ibid., p. 140.
38 Ibid., p. 141.
39 Breazeale details the "delicate position" in which Fichte finds himself throughout the review of having to agree with many of the skeptics' objections while at the

demonstrated a priori and independent of all experience, then the problem of its being an abstraction is removed – Fichte does indeed believe that he can remove this problem and establish philosophy as a science. According to Fichte, both Reinhold and Aenesidemus err in believing that philosophy's starting point can be found in a fact of consciousness.

> To be sure, we must have a real principle, and not merely a formal one; but – if I may venture a claim which can be neither explained nor proven here – such a principle does not have to express a fact just as content (*eine Tatsache*, actual fact); it can also express a fact as performance (*eine Tathandlung*, actual deed).[40]

Reinhold's attempt to establish an absolute starting point for philosophy was met with skepticism by both Schulze and Fichte. Yet the skepticism involved was different. For Aenesidemus, the fact that Reinhold had failed in his attempt to secure a first principle for philosophy amounted to evidence of the impossibility of any such attempt. For Fichte, Reinhold's failure meant only that a first principle for philosophy could not be a fact of consciousness (for a first principle would have to be demonstrated a priori and independently of all experience), and furthermore that a concept more fundamental than representation must be found.

## VI. Fichte as Classic Forerunner of the Idea of the Fundamental *Intentionality* of Mental Activity?

With Reinhold, Fichte held that in order to be a science of knowledge, philosophy must be based upon an absolute first principle; with Schulze, he believed that Reinhold had not provided it. But for Fichte, this was not because the search for a first principle was misguided, but rather because Reinhold's approach was wrong. The *Wissenschaftslehre* is Fichte's attempt to solve the problem of philosophy's starting point and thereby to establish the foundation for Fichte's own version of Kant's transcendental idealism. The problem that Reinhold had failed to solve became the task Fichte set forth for himself.

In his review of *Aenesidemus*, Fichte had hinted that there was a real principle for all philosophy, one which did not express only a fact as con-

---

same time defending the fundamental correctness of the search for the "highest principle of philosophy." Breazeale, Daniel: "Fichte's Aenesidemus Review", in: *Review of Metaphysics* 34 (March 1981), pp. 545–568.

40 Fichte, Johann G.: *Review of Aenesidemus*, p. 141.

tent (*eine Tatsache*) but also a fact as action (*eine Tathandlung*). In his review he neither explained nor proved this, yet almost all that he wrote afterwards was an attempt to do just this or to defend this claim from its detractors.

The fundamental principle of the *Wissenschaftslehre* is contained in the sentence, "The I posits itself purely and simply." (*Das Ich setzt sich schlechthin*). For in this formulation we find the primacy of the I not merely as thinking subject, but as active subject. For Fichte, reality consists in pure activity, an activity of the I. Fichte's idealism begins with a self-positing I, hence with an act (*Tathandlung*) of consciousness rather than with a fact (*Tatsache*) of consciousness:

> If philosophy begins with a fact, then it places itself in the midst of a world of being and finitude, and it will be difficult for it to discover any path leading from this world to an infinite and supersensible one. If, however, philosophy begins with an Act, then it finds itself at the precise point where these two worlds are connected with each other and from which they can both be surveyed in a single glance.[41]

Fichte calls this most fundamental self-positing, which is presupposed by all facts of consciousness but is not itself a fact, an act (*Tathandlung*). The I posits itself and upon doing so posits the Non-I as well. This Non-I serves to limit the I and this limitation gives the I its reality. For, according to Fichte, a pure I, one which would exist unconditionally (that is, without limits), would be indefinite and unreal. This concept of *Begrenzung* and the pivotal role that the I plays in limiting the world so that it can be known, is linked to Brentano's key point that all of mental activity is intentional. For though Fichte does not use the term 'intentional,' in his classification of mental phenomena, there is significant overlap between Fichte's portrait of human mental activity and Brentano's talk of 'intentional mental activity.'

It is well known, and not at all controversial, that Fichte saw his contribution as an extension of Kant's philosophy, in particular of Kant's transcendental deduction, for it is there that the establishment of objective validity through the subjective conditions of representability is carried out. Fichte was also addressing the problem of Kant's positing of a thing-in-itself as the necessary source for all experience: Fichte believed that this thing-in-itself was unnecessary. As Roger Scruton observes:

---

41 IWL, p. 51/GA I/4, p. 221.

> For Fichte, Kant's great achievement was to have shown that the mind has knowledge only through its own activity; in an important sense, the objects of knowledge are a *product* of that activity.[42]

What are the products of the activity of the mind? They must be related to an object and a subject, yet distinguished from both. The only way in which the realm of objects and the activity of the I can be "surveyed in a single glance" is through the fundamental self-positing that is presupposed by all facts of consciousness. Brentano, too, wanted to locate the fundamental or essential mark of the mental, that would distinguish mental from physical phenomena, and he, too, found it in a way of distinguishing the subject from the object via the directedness announced in the fundamental intentionality of thought. Given the Austrian reading of Brentano and the demonizing of German Idealism, it is worse than unorthodox, it is heretical, for me to suggest that in his work, Fichte shares many of the concerns that Brentano was later to address. But I think that this is the case, that is, I think that Marías is correct when he places Fichte as a "classic forerunner" of the move to describe human mental activity in terms of its fundamental intentionality.

In an article for the *Philosophisches Journal*, "Comparison of the System Presented by Prof. Schmid with the *Wissenschaftslehre*,"[43] Fichte, while defending himself from a set of charges which he took Schmid to be making against his idealism, goes on to give a new presentation of his *Wissenschaftslehre*, and one which highlights his interest in looking carefully at the fundamental ways in which the subject relates to objects in the world:

> In my opinion, the question which philosophy must answer is the following: how are our representations joined to its objects, to what extent can one say that these objects are independent and correspond to something outside of us?[44]

---

42 Scruton, Roger: *Kant*, Oxford 1982, p. 93.
43 "Vergleichung des vom Herrn Prof. Schmid aufgestellten Systems mit der Wissenschaftslehre," *Philosophisches Journal* III, Nr. 4 (1796): 267–320. The title sounds innocent enough, but it hides what has been described as an act of annihilation (See Frank, Manfred: *The Philosophical Foundations of Early German Romanticism*, trans. Millan-Zaibert, Elizabeth, Albany 2008, p. 3.), a vituperative attack by Fichte against Schmid's very tentative questions regarding the need for first principles in philosophy.
44 "Meines Erachtens ist die Frage, welche die Philosophie zu beantworten hat, folgende: wie hängen unsere Vorstellungen mit ihren Objecten zusammen; in wiefern kann man sagen, dass denselben etwas, unabhängig, und überhaupt von uns,

According to Fichte, the goal of philosophy is to give an account of the status of our representations and hence the objects of philosophy are *Tathandlungen* (acts of the mind) rather than facts. Brentano, too, in stressing the intentional inexistence thesis, first works out the problem of what the fundamental mark of the mental is before he moves on to the problem of the mind-world connection. Fichte, in his response to Schmid, informs us that his principle task in the *Wissenschaftslehre* was certainly not to leave the non-mental world neglected, but rather to address the matter of whether our representations correspond to something outside of us. He writes:

> What are the reasons for our claim that our representations correspond to something external to us? To address this question is the task of all philosophy and the *Wissenschaftslehre* takes this task on and answers this question in the following way: The representation and the object which should correspond to it are one – indeed the same – only looked upon from two different perspectives. That it [the representation] must be looked upon from these two different perspectives lies in the knowing and representing nature of reason, this is necessary and is to be seen as necessary. The *Wissenschaftslehre* provides insight regarding how and why the rational being distinguishes both, even though they are one, and then later must judge that both are completely equal, accounting for the quality of freedom which the representation as such has and necessity which the object as such has.[45]

This identity is uncovered in the self-positing I. Fichte claims that the method of the *Wissenschaftslehre* is simply the method of abstracting from all contingent parts of the I and thereby uncovering it as a pure activity.

---

ausser uns entspreche?" (Fichte, Johann G.: "Vergleichung des vom Herrn Prof. Schmid aufgestellten Systems mit der Wissenschaftslehre," *Philosophisches Journal III*, Nr. 4 (1796): pp. 267–320 at p. 287.

45 "Welches ist der Grund unsrer Behauptung, dass unsern Vorstellungen etwas ausser uns entspreche? Diese Aufgabe, die eigentliche Aufgabe aller Philosophie […] nimmt die Wissenschaftslehre auf, und beantwortet sie folgendermassen: Die Vorstellung und das Objekt das ihr entsprechen soll, sind Eins, und eben dasselbe, nur angesehen aus zwei verschiedenen Gesichtspunkten, dass es aber aus diesen zwei verschiedenen Gesichtspunkten angesehen werden muss, liegt in der erkennbaren und darzustellenden Natur der Vernunft, ist sonach nothwendig, und ist einzusehen, als nothwendig. Die Wissenschaftslehre giebt die Einsicht, wie und warum das vernunftige Wesen beides, das doch nur eins ist, unterscheiden, und hinterher doch urtheilen müsse, dass beide, den Charakter der Freiheit, den die Vorstellung als solche hat, und den der Notwendigkeit, den das Objekt als solches hat, abgerechnet, völlig gleich sind." (Fichte, Johann G.: "Vergleichung", Ibid., pp. 295–296.)

According to Fichte, the task of the *Wissenschaftslehre* is to place together what has been separated through abstraction.[46] This is because if we proceed via abstraction, we may miss certain links in the chain; this cannot happen when we bring different elements together.[47] He characterizes Reinhold's philosophy as one which begins with facts and then looks for underlying principles and describes his own philosophy as the inverse of this. He also emphasizes his commitment to empiricism and a dedication to scientific method in his search for truth:

> The *Wissenschaftslehre* ends with the set up [*Aufstellung*] of pure empiricism; it brings to light what we can really experience, what we must necessarily experience, and so establishes truly the possibility of all experience. We may reason about this pure experience, it can be combined and become systematic; and that is for me *Wissenschaft*, that which continues where philosophy ends and which is infinitely rich in new developments. So, *Wissenschaft* and philosophy are not for me the same.[48]

So, at the end of a story which is just part of a longer tale, we come to what perhaps can be called Fichte's "Idealism from an Empirical Standpoint" and perhaps some way to think about phenomenology from an idealist standpoint. I end with the humble, albeit provocative, claim that, on both counts, is sure to sound off all sorts of alarms from the Austrian Brentano camp, namely, that there is a bit of an Austrian empiricist in Fichte and some traces of a German Idealist in Brentano.

---

46 "setzt unter ihren Augen zusammen, was durch die Abstraction getrennt war" (Ibid., p. 310.)

47 "Auf dem Wege der Abstraction können Glieder übersprungen werden, auf dem Wege der Zusammensetzung nie." (Ibid.)

48 "Die Wissenschaftslehre endet mit der Aufstellung (set up, organization) der reinen Empirie; sie bringt ans Licht, was wir wirklich erfahren können, nothwendig erfahren müssen, begründet sonach wahrhaft die Möglichkeit aller Erfahrung. Über diese reine Erfahrung nun kann weiterhin rasonniert, dieselbe combiniert und systematisch werden; und dies heisst mir Wissenschaft, welch da angeht, wo die Philosophie sich endet und von unendlichen Umfange ist. Wissenschaft und Philosophie sind mir sonach nicht einerlei." (Ibid., p. 317).

# II. Fichte and Husserl

# Phenomenologies of Intersubjectivity: Fichte between Hegel and Husserl

ANGELICA NUZZO

City University of New York

## I. Transcendental I: Solipsism and Intersubjectivity

As early as 1795, Goethe reacts to the *Grundlage der gesamten Wissenschaftslehre* of 1794 by ironically referring to Fichte himself as the 'absolute I' and to the stones that the Jena students threw to his window as impolite 'not-I s.' In an array of more serious variations, Goethe's remark will be repeated time and again in the history of Fichte readings and interpretations. To this choir of voices Husserl will add an important dimension. His remarks are relevant to the assessment of Fichte's contribution to the development of transcendental philosophy toward transcendental phenomenology. Generally, what all these accounts have in common, despite their different motivations, is to view Fichte as positing the I as absolute (even as identifying it with god)[1] thereby sanctioning a deeply problematic, unbridgeable separation between absolute I and empirical I. In addition, the philosopher is seen as immodestly placing himself in the position of the absolute I, whereby the *Grundlage* receives an almost biographical interpretation. In the personal immodesty voiced in this way lies also a crucial difference between Kant's and Fichte's transcendental philosophy. For Kant's transcendental subject is not yet declared absolute and Kant does not dare place himself in its position. Significantly, a quasi-phenomenological stance is implied in the alleged identification between Fichte the philosopher and the absolute I. In it, however, can be detected the root of another long-standing charge against

---

1 * All translation from German texts are my own (A.N.).
  See Lauth, Reinhard: "Das Problem der Interpersonalität bei J.G. Fichte", in: *Transzendentale Entwicklungslinien von Descartes bis zu Marx und Dostojewski*, Hamburg 1989, pp. 180–196, p. 182 (originally appeared as "Le problème de l'interpersonnalité chez J.G. Fichte," in: *Archives de Philosophie*, 25, 1962, pp. 325–344). Lauth refers to this position as an interpretive "Grundirrtum."

Fichte's *Wissenschaftslehre* – in fact, already against Kant's transcendental philosophy – namely, the charge of solipsism or egoism.

In a letter to Reinhold of 1795, Baggesen qualifies Fichte's philosophy as "philosophical egoism."[2] The position of the I *qua* absolute is the position of a solipsistic subject unable to break the circle of its subjective isolation and reach out to a world of real objects and other subjects – the not-I is always already product or "position" of the I. In a similar way, the specter of idealism haunted Kant in the first *Critique*, while practical egoism emerged as an important target in the second *Critique*. In Kant's view, the "logical egoist" is the person who refuses to test his own judgment in a confrontation with others "as if he did not need this external criterion of truth (*criterium veritatis externum*)." To the position of the logical egoist Kant opposes the mental habit of the person who considers himself not as "someone who embraces in his own singularity the entire world but rather as a citizen of the world"[3] – a *Weltbürger* as it were. Fichte fundamentally agrees with Kant on this point. He himself fights practical "egoism" throughout his career, seeing in it the worse disease of his age. Yet the theoretical problem does not cease to present itself to his philosophy. As Baggesen observes, a philosophy that starts with a unique I – be it *Ichheit* or *Ich* – unavoidably faces the problem of justifying a *plurality* of subjects.

The discussion on egoism and solipsism goes back to the end of the seventeenth century. A century later, it crystallizes around Kant's transcendental philosophy and its contemporary variations and corrections. At this point, "egoism" is yet another way to express the charge of Spinozism (and accordingly of atheism). In its Spinozistic variation, solipsism is egoism (and this in turn is atheism) to the extent that the world (of objects and other subjects) is ultimately reduced to the monistic absolute I now replacing Spinoza's substance.[4] Thus, from the outset the version of transcendental philosophy that Fichte expounds in the 1794 *Wissenschaftslehre* has to meet the charge that denies to its foundational transcendental

---

2   Baggesen to Reinhold, September, 5, 1795, in: Fuchs, Erich (Hg.) in Zusammenarbeit mit Lauth, Reinhard und Schieche, Walter: *Fichte im Gespräch: Berichte der Zeitgenossen*, Stuttgart 1978–1991, vol. 1, p. 46.
3   Kant, Immanuel: *Anthropologie*, Ak VII, pp. 128–129. For a discussion of Kant's position see De Ligiorgi, Katerina: *Kant and the Culture of Enlightenment*, Albany, NY 2005, p. 82.
4   See George Di Giovanni's reconstruction of this discussion in: *Freedom and Religion in Kant and His Immediate Successors. The Vocation of Humankind, 1774–1800*, Cambridge 2005.

subject the capacity to reach the individuality of the empirical subject, the reality of a world of objects, and a plurality of other subjects. This is precisely the point where the discussion around the nature of the 'not-I' – i.e. its more or less authentic or positive otherness in relation to the I – enters the picture.

The solipsistic or egoistic interpretation of Fichte's philosophy dominated Fichte's scholarship until Lauth's 1962 influential essay on the notion of "Interpersonalität" in Fichte. Lauth concludes his essay contending that while Fichte was the first to provide a thought-out "Theorie der Interpersonalität" (Fichte was its "Schöpfer"), which was then further developed by Hegel, Husserl, Heidegger, and Sartre, he has also been unsurpassed in such theory up to the present day.[5] To be sure, the theme – and the very term – of intersubjectivity or interpersonality – emerged in the philosophical discussion only after Feuerbach; while its interest grew significantly only after the crisis of political totalitarianism in the twentieth century.[6] By contrast, Fichte's contemporaries not only did not see in Fichte a philosopher of intersubjectivity – as he is now increasingly regarded; as mentioned above, they labeled him as an outright "egoist." The problem, for them, was not so much the philosophical justification of another human being but rather the foundation of an empirical plurality out of a unique absolute I. To this extent, a discussion of the problem of interpersonality within Fichte's philosophy necessarily leads to the broader issue of the ways in which philosophy after Fichte has 'created' and developed the topic of intersubjectivity as an independent category between subject and object. What do the concept – and the problem – of intersubjectivity indicate? And what are the alternative philosophical perspectives or methodologies that allow one to approach or solve the problem of intersubjectivity? These are the general background questions that I pursue in this paper.

In §57 of the *Krisis der europäischen Wissenschaften,* Husserl presents his own variation of Goethe's remark on Fichte mentioned above. At stake herein is the problem of the development of transcendental philosophy in the trajectory that goes from Locke's psychologically oriented empirical theory of knowledge through Kant's own transcendental philosophy to the metaphysical and indeed "mythical conceptual constructs" of his followers (Fichte and Hegel). More specifically, at stake is the crisis

---

5  Lauth, Reinhard: "Das Problem der Interpersonalität", p. 195.
6  See Cesa, Claudio: "In tema di intersoggettività", in: *J.G. Fichte e l'idealismo trascendentale,* Bologna 1992, pp. 189–233, p. 210.

that the transcendental tradition encounters after Kant and that prompts the need for a phenomenological development or correction of transcendental philosophy. The last station of this itinerary is represented by Husserl's own phenomenology that, as transcendental phenomenology, is introduced as the true heir of the transcendental turn. The "crux" of transcendental philosophy is indicated by Husserl in the "difference between transcendental and empirical subjectivity" – a difference that incomprehensibly as well as unavoidably turns into their "identity." Fichte provides Husserl with the clearest case in point. Laying out the problem and bringing in the concept of "constitution," Husserl does not hesitate to engage in a first-person narrative. "As transcendental I, I 'constitute' the world." Two issues are connected at this point. Transcendentally, the understanding plays a "legislative" role toward the world. Phenomenologically, the understanding is *my* understanding, that is, the understanding of the philosopher who inhabits the world: "the transcendental understanding forms me according to its laws." Hence Husserl's remark: "The self-positing I of which Fichte speaks: can it be something else than Fichte's own I?" Husserl realizes that one can indeed take this claim as a "real absurdity" – very much in the sense given to it by Goethe. But one can also take it as the challenge of a "solvable paradox," in which case the task is to find the "method" that can lead us out of it.[7] Significantly, for Husserl, to solve the paradox does not mean to abandon the first-person perspective (according to which the transcendental I is Fichte's own I) but to abandon the perspective of solipsism to which the philosopher is otherwise condemned. While Fichte was unable to solve the paradox, consequently remaining trapped in the position of solipsism, Husserl's phenomenology is meant to provide the right method out of it. On Husserl's view, the problem of the not-I is explicitly the problem of intersubjectivity. Its question is now more precisely the following: "how can I have a universal, transcendental-intersubjective consciousness beyond my individual self-consciousness?"[8] With this question, Husserl does not abandon Fichte's seemingly paradoxical position. He rather pushes its phenomenological potentiality farther. This marks an important difference between the issue of solipsism raised respectively by Husserl and by Fichte's contemporaries. On Husserl's account, the question of the extension of subjectivity to intersubjectivity cannot be answered in a purely transcendental

---

7  Husserl, Edmund: *Die Krisis der europäischen Wissenschaften und die transzendentale Phänomenologie*, Husserliana, vol. 6, The Hague 1962, p. 205.
8  HUA VI, p. 206.

way; nor can it be handed over to psychology, which still appeared as the only way out of solipsism to both Kant and Fichte. The answer can only be given by a transcendental phenomenology.

It is clear from this discussion that for Husserl, as for the entire post-Kantian and post-Hegelian tradition of the late nineteenth and early twentieth century, in Fichte's philosophy we find more the issue of solipsism than the idea of intersubjectivity. And yet, intersubjectivity is considered by Husserl to be the positive conquest of transcendental phenomenology, and the latter, in turn, is seen as the corrective of the mythical and metaphysical shortcomings of transcendental philosophy. Hence, with Husserl we gain a common methodological framework within which to articulate the connection between solipsism or egoism and intersubjectivity.

In what follows, I will address the issue of intersubjectivity by raising the general problem of the *philosophical method* or perspective that allows one to disclose the meaning and the specific reality of intersubjectivity. Or alternatively, I will ask the question of the different aspects of the concept and reality of intersubjectivity that different philosophical methods allow one to bring to light. In so doing, I repeat the question raised by Husserl in the *Krisis* (but already discussed in *Cartesianische Meditationen* V): what is the *method* that takes us out of Fichte's alleged solipsism and places us in an intersubjectively shared world? I will discuss three different possible approaches to the problem of intersubjectivity: respectively, the one provided by Fichte's transcendental philosophy, then by Hegel's dialectic (and dialectic phenomenology), and finally by Husserl's transcendental phenomenology. Accordingly, I will not attempt to trace the development of the problem or give a comprehensive account of it in the work of these three philosophers individually.[9] Instead I will limit my discussion to the systematic and methodological plane assuming as its leading thread the following general question: What do we indicate with the philosophical problem of intersubjectivity? On this basis I concentrate on a few relevant moments in these philosophers' respective itineraries. Hence, I will address three issues: What does it mean to raise the question of intersubjectivity within a *transcendental* perspective? What does *dialectic* contribute to the thought of interpersonality? And finally, what are the intersubjective structures that a *transcendental phenomenology* brings to light?

---

9  This work has been done exemplarily by Lauth and Cesa, among others.

## II. Fichte: Philosophical Egoist or Philosopher of Intersubjectivity?

Let me start again with my general question. What is meant, exactly, by the problem of intersubjectivity or interpersonality, i.e., what is problematic about intersubjectivity? The question should be raised in particular when at issue is either (with Baggesen and his contemporaries) the charge of Fichte's philosophical egoism or (with Lauth and many of our contemporaries) the view that Fichte is the "creator" and champion of a philosophy of intersubjectivity.

First, let us consider the problem of intersubjectivity as expressing the need for a theoretical justification or foundation of (the existence or representation of) other human beings as such.[10] Within an empiricist perspective intersubjectivity hardly needs justification; the problem simply does not arise. On Locke's account, for example, we recognize another human being by discerning an analogy with ourselves – an analogy that plays itself out first and foremost at the physical level (a point that in the *Grundlage des Naturrechts* becomes important for Fichte as well).

> I think I may be confident, that whoever should see a creature of his own shape or make, though it had no more reason all its life than a cat or a parrot, would call him still a man; or whoever should hear a cat or a parrot discourse, reason, and philosophize, would call or think it nothing but a cat or a parrot; and say, the one was a dull irrational man, and the other a very intelligent rational parrot.[11]

On a merely factual plane, in the 1794 *Bestimmung des Gelehrten*, Fichte ascertains that experience teaches us "that the representation of rational beings outside of ourselves is contained in our empirical consciousness"[12] as a fact. The problem of the theoretical justification of the assumption of other rational human beings outside us is not an empirical problem. It is a specifically *transcendental* problem. In a transcendental perspective it is not enough to factually ascertain the existence of others. Such existence must be justified (or deduced) in relation to the I and its activity. To this specifically transcendental problem Fichte offers a first – and purely formal – answer in the *Grundlage* of 1794. The issue that divides the

---

10  As discussed below, at stake is alternatively the foundation of the *existence* of other human beings or the justification of *our representation* of other human beings.
11  Locke, John: *An Essay Concerning Human Understanding*, II, XXVII, p. 8.
12  SW VI, p. 303.

transcendental philosopher and the theoretical egoist is precisely "whether this representation [of another rational being] corresponds to something outside of it;"[13] which in turns leads to the further question of how we distinguish between objects and other subjects.[14]

In the *Bestimmung des Gelehrten* as later in the *Grundlage des Naturrechts*, Fichte attempts to solve this *transcendental* problem *practically*. In investigating the relation between the *Grundlage*, in which intersubjectivity seems absent, and the contemporary *Bestimmung des Gelehrten*, Lauth projects the material conclusions of the latter on the formal principles established by the former. His claim is that already in the *Grundlage* Fichte's aim is to posit the not-I as an I, that is, as a second I in communication and (moral) community with the positing I. The not-I stands here already for interpersonality.[15] We may or may not follow Lauth in this conclusion. It remains true, however, that for Fichte the problem of interpersonality is a *material* problem (or a problem for the material part of the *Wissenschaftslehre*) that first arises out of the specific formal questioning of *transcendental* philosophy. This point will become relevant in assessing Husserl's attempt to overcome the alleged difficulties of Fichte's theory.

In bringing to the fore one of the meanings he attributes to 'transcendental', Fichte argues that "the transcendental philosopher must assume that all there is, is only *for* an I; and that what ought to be for an I can be only *through* an I."[16] In Fichte's transcendental philosophy, the I as starting point requires the "deduction of our conviction that there exists a world outside of ourselves."[17] Relevant in this claim is that the deduction required by the transcendental standpoint does not concern the existence of a world or the existence of other subjects. At stake is rather the justification or deduction *of our conviction or representation* of the existence of a world and other rational subjects. This point is important in assessing the extent of Fichte's commitment to intersubjectivity and his overcoming of egoism. We can push the transcendental thesis further and argue, with Cesa, that Fichte's central interest is not a deduction of intersubjectivity as such. His aim is rather to use the intersubjective world in order to determine the cognitive as well as practical subject as I. Since at stake is still primarily the transcendental foundation of the

---

13  GA I/3, p. 35.
14  See for example *Zweite Einleitung in die Wissenschaftslehre*, SW I, pp. 501–502.
15  Lauth, Reinhard: "Das Problem der Interpersonalität", p. 187.
16  GA I/3, p. 335/SW III, p. 24.
17  GA I/3, p. 335/SW III, p. 24.

I, not the foundation of the other, Fichte's perspective remains subjective. It is not intersubjective in the sense later attributed to this term by Husserl or Sartre. The relationship to the other established by the central concepts of *Aufforderung, Anmutung, Anerkennung,* and *Anstoss* in the 1796/97 *Grundlage des Naturrechts* can indeed be read in this (still subjective) sense. Ultimately, Fichte's chief question is: "How can the subject find itself?"[18] On this view, intersubjectivity is indeed a transcendental function of subjectivity; yet, precisely in its transcendental function, intersubjectivity is also immediately absorbed into subjectivity. Transcendentally, the other makes the I possible; that is, intersubjectivity is transcendentally constitutive of the I to the extent that the I can posit itself only as interpersonal I. The I, however, remains the starting point and the limit that cannot be transcended. The foundation of an interpersonal I is not exactly identical with the foundation of interpersonality as such. This fundamental ambiguity, I suggest, is proper of the transcendental standpoint. It will still be met in Husserl's transcendental phenomenology.

The way out of philosophical egoism may be searched by underscoring an additional meaning of the concept of intersubjectivity. Intersubjectivity is not only a specifically transcendental issue, it is an *ethical* issue as well. And this is clear to Fichte from the very outset. In this perspective, intersubjectivity refers to a set of reciprocal relations that are constitutive of the I as such. The I is interpersonal or constitutively intersubjective because of the fundamental relations and activities indicated by Fichte as *Anerkennung, Anmutung, Aufforderung* in which and by which the I is first constituted as subject. It is *transcendentally* necessary for the I to attribute reality to other rational beings – otherwise the I cannot posit itself as an I; but this is also *ethically* necessary, i.e., is a command of the moral law – because otherwise the I cannot realize itself as a *free* being. Intersubjectivity constitutes the very idea of subjective freedom. Does this ethical correction or integration of the transcendental perspective lead us out, this time, of practical egoism? This would indeed be the case if the ethical perspective were the place where the deduction of the other is no longer a function of the I but discloses an independent dimension beyond subjectivity and objectivity. This is the point where Hegel's critique of Fichte's position can be brought to bear on our discussion.

In a letter to Jacobi of 1795 Fichte connects the moral-juridical problem of the *Naturrecht* to the charge of egoism raised against the work of 1794.

---

18  SW III, p. 33.

> My *absolute I* is clearly not the *individual*; this has been explained to me by offended gentlemen and angry philosophers in order to attack me with the shameful doctrine of practical egoism. And yet, *the individual must be deduced from the absolute I*. To this task the *Wissenschaftslehre* will proceed in the *Naturrecht*.[19]

A finite sensible being can be thought of only within a sphere of similar sensible beings with whom it is in a "reciprocal relation (*Wechselwirkung*). To this extent this being is called individual." In this sphere, Fichte argues, "the conditions of individuality are called rights."[20] Herein we meet the complex articulation of the structure of *Aufforderung* developed in the *Grundlage*. This represents the systematic center of Fichte's doctrine of interpersonality. The deduction of the individual places it in an intersubjective context. In the *Grundlage des Naturrechts*, the deduction of the other human subject takes place within a practical framework in which the ethical problem is connected to a juridical one. The sphere of right, however, is the sphere where mutually self-limiting egoisms find their legitimate place. Herein, intersubjectivity coexists with egoism; it is indeed the multiplication of egoisms.

### III. Hegel: *Sittlichkeit* and Intersubjectivity

From this examination of the problem of intersubjectivity in Fichte's works of the years 1794–97 the following conclusion can be drawn. The issue of intersubjectivity is implied by the *transcendental* perspective of Fichte's work and carries within itself a fundamental ambiguity. The suspicion is, with Cesa's interpretation, that intersubjectivity is brought into the picture not for its own sake or as a third category beyond subjectivity and objectivity but as the condition for the foundation and transcendental justification of the individual subject. However, a more advanced result beyond this interpretation may be gained by underscoring the *moral* and *juridical* significance of the notion of intersubjectivity. The *Grundlage des Naturrechts* develops two distinct, yet related questions: on the one hand, the problem of how the subject finds itself as a subject; on the other, the problem of how the subject recognizes other rational beings outside of itself – beings with whom its activity is necessarily connected

---

19 Letter to Jacobi of August, 30, 1795.
20 GA III/2, p. 392.

to constitute the moral world of spirit. Thereby the specific social dimension of intersubjectivity is gained.

At this point, however, an assessment of the type of social context disclosed by Fichte's *Grundlage des Naturrechts* is in order. I attempt such an assessment indirectly, bringing in a second perspective by which intersubjectivity can be philosophically investigated, namely, dialectic. I concentrate on Hegel's 1821 *Philosophy of Right* and examine the relation that dialectic establishes between individuality and ethical life or *Sittlichkeit*. What place does intersubjectivity have in Hegel's *Philosophy of Right*? Indeed, in this work, the tension between individuality (and individualism) and intersubjectivity appears as a crucial interpretive problem. Among the many answers that such a problem has received I want to mention only Ilting's reading of this work as a "phenomenology of the consciousness of freedom" and Theunissen's thesis of Hegel's "repressed intersubjectivity."

Although I will not compare Hegel's phenomenological development of *Anerkennung* to Fichte's, one word on Hegel's 1807 work is unavoidable.[21] In the "Self-consciousness" chapter of the *Phenomenology of Spirit*, Hegel famously shows how self-consciousness implies a necessary "duplication" (*Verdopplung*),[22] whose movement is the process of *Anerkennung*. In this regard I want to make two points. First, the necessity of this movement for the constitution of self-consciousness is due to Hegel's phenomenological and dialectic investigation, which is explicitly mobilized against a transcendental framework such as Kant's or Fichte's.[23] Second, the dialectic of *Anerkennung* leads to the threshold of the higher "concept of *Geist*." Spirit is the overarching unity encompassing the conflict of different, independent self-consciousnesses. In a famous formulation, *Geist* is the reciprocity of "the *I* that is *We*, and the *We* that is *I*."[24] Hegelian *Geist* does not speak in a first-person perspective; and yet at the level of the struggle for recognition it does not voice an intersubjective 'We' either. In the later *Encyclopedia*, the moment of recognition still belongs to subjective spirit, namely, to a level of spirit's development that is still individualistic – i.e., not yet social and not yet active in the objective framework of shared institutions. *Anerkennung* may be the necessary be-

---

21 A comprehensive account of this issue can be found in Williams, Robert R.: *Hegel's Ethics of Recognition*, Berkeley 1997, which is relevant also for a critique of Ilting (see below).
22 Hegel, Georg Wilhelm Friedrich: *Werke in zwanzig Bänden*, ed. Eva Moldenhauer, Karl Markus Michel, Frankfurt a.M. 1986, vol. 3, pp. 146–147.
23 This is clear from the preface and introduction to the work.
24 Hegel, Georg Wilhelm Friedrich: *Werke in zwanzig Bänden*, vol. 3, p. 145.

ginning of intersubjectivity. It is not, however, a sufficient condition to it. Where, then, do we find intersubjectivity in spirit's dialectic development? What is the place of intersubjectivity in Hegel's systematic of spirit?

On Hegel's view, Fichte's account of intersubjectivity – or of the social context arising from the interaction of mutually recognizing subjects – is too subjective, too psychological, and ultimately too individualistic. Fichte's understanding of mutual recognition remains individualistic insofar as the agents are conceived as "compelling" each other only as isolated individuals. For Hegel, Fichte's I "retains [...] the significance of being an individual actual self-consciousness, opposed to the universal, the absolute, or *Geist*, in which it itself is only a moment; for the individual self-consciousness is just this, that it remains fixed on one side against an other."[25] In other words, the subject of action remains for Fichte the isolated individual who never reaches *Geist* as a collective integrated structure. No normative authority, however, can be established on this ground.

In Hegel's system, intersubjectivity emerges as a fundamental concept of dialectic within the objective reality of spirit. The highest manifestation of spirit's objective reality is *Sittlichkeit*. The dialectic *Darstellung* of this realm is the topic of Hegel's 1821 *Grundlinien der Philosophie des Rechts, oder Naturrecht und Staatswissenschaft im Grundrisse*. This work fulfils a fundamentally critical function with regard to the natural right tradition, which is attacked first and foremost for its individualism. The *Grundlinien* is no longer a treatise on natural right; to it Hegel consigns the radical critique that ends that tradition. While there is consensus among the interpreters on this point, it does not cease to be puzzling that Hegel opens his work with the highly individualistic, even atomistic standpoint of "Abstract Right." How can this beginning be reconciled with Hegel's stark critique of natural right individualism? To answer this question, Ilting has proposed to view the *Philosophy of Right* as a "phenomenology" meant to present the experiential process of human consciousness thinking and acting from a progression of different standpoints. The difficulties that this interpretation presents, however, are numerous and cannot be discussed in this essay. I cite Ilting's interpretation,

---

25 Hegel, Georg Wilhelm Friedrich: *Werke in zwanzig Bänden*, vol. 20, p. 408. See Pinkard, Terry: "Subjects, Objects, and Normativity: What Is It Like to *Be* an Agent?", in: *Internationales Jahrbuch des deutschen Idealismus*, 2003, 201–219, p. 204 ff.

however, to show how a phenomenological path is open within the dialectic approach to our problem.[26] The most relevant objection to this view is systematic. Briefly put, Ilting's reading cannot account for the systematic function that Hegel attributes to the sphere of objective spirit in the articulation of the reality of *Geist*.

Hegel's critique of Fichte's subjective individualism is framed by his broader critique of the tradition of *Naturrecht*. Hegel's true alternative to Fichte's all too individualistic, pre-social (inter)subjectivity is to be found at the level of *Sittlichkeit*. My claim is that the *Grundlinien* fulfils its critical function of natural right individualism on the basis of the dialectical method that articulates its different spheres. Hegel's most significant and general critique is expounded in the systematic progression of its three spheres: Abstract Right-*Moralität*-*Sittlichkeit*. How should this progression be read and what is its relation to the issue of intersubjectivity? I can give here only a short answer to this vast problem.[27] Within the systematic structure of the *Philosophy of Right*, the dialectic articulation of Abstract Right and *Moralität* functions as a *reductio ad absurdum* of individualism. Hegel's claim is that precisely because of their inescapable individualistic constitution the spheres of Abstract Right and *Moralität* are unable to ground truly intersubjective, social life. No transition from those to the latter is possible; or, to put it differently, any attempt at a deduction of intersubjectivity from the solipsistic, isolated individual is destined to fail. For Hobbes as for Rousseau as ultimately for Fichte, the limited individual consciousness of the juridical subjects is simply replaced, within the political state, by higher, allegedly rational institutions. To this extent, Fichte's *Naturrecht* can indeed be viewed as the most advanced, yet in principle still fundamentally impossible attempt to integrate an intersubjective dimension into the contractualist foundation of social and political life and institutions.

The dialectical method exposes this shortcoming in two ways. First, dialectic proceeds to an immanent critique of abstract right and morality using their respective intersubjective deficiency as the leading thread. Sec-

---

26 See Ilting, Karl-Heinz: "Rechtsphilosophie als Phänomenologie des Bewußtseins der Freiheit", in: Henrich, Dieter/Horstmann, Rolf-Peter (eds.): *Hegels Philosophie des Rechts*, Stuttgart 1982, pp. 225–254, and in the same volume Siep, Ludwig: "Intersubjektivität, Recht und Staat in Hegels *Gundlinien der Philosophie des Rechts*", pp. 255–276. See the critique of Ilting's position in Williams, Robert R.: *Hegel's Ethics of Recognition*.
27 To this issue I have dedicated my book *Rappresentazione e concetto nella logica della Filosofia del diritto di Hegel*, Napoli 1990.

ond, dialectic resolves the negative *impasse* to which abstract right and morality lead – namely, the blocked figures of *Unrecht* and moral *Böse* – with the *Aufhebung* of those structures into the higher sphere of *Sittlichkeit*.[28] Hegel's point is to show that abstract right and morality being, as it were, nothing but "abstractions," cannot function as the starting point of a *philosophy of right* (they are the starting point of *Naturrecht* but this never reaches true intersubjectivity). The starting point of a philosophy of right can only be the sphere of *Sittlichkeit*, within which right and morality gain their concrete and effectual meaning. Now this sphere alone is the realm of true intersubjectivity.

Hegel's critique of the contract can be offered as example of his strategy of *reductio ad absurdum* of abstract right. The contract implies a 'relation to other', and yet, to the extent in which the individual subject keeps her property and leaves the other its property, the subject is "indifferent" to the other and bound to no relation with her. Moreover, the communality and mutuality ("*Gemeinsamkeit*" and "*Gegenseitigkeit*") of the contract rest on *Willkür* and are utterly accidental.[29] Deception constantly menaces the validity of the contractual relation. In sum, the a-social world of abstract right is a construct based on abstraction from reality. This abstraction is revealed by the ways in which intersubjectivity is systematically erased from the picture. Hence Hegel's deliberate insistence on the solipsistic character of the subject of right.

Hegel's critique of morality proceeds along the same lines. Just as right, morality is possible and real only in the context of civil society. Taken outside of this sphere, by contrast, while morality seems to establish a positive relation to the other will, it ultimately (and hypocritically) revokes all intersubjectivity by closing itself up in the fixed form of a pure self-relation. If my "welfare" (*Wohl*) in order for me to be moral must be "the welfare also of another,"[30] this demand is nothing more than an empty abstraction since this result can be reached only in civil society. At the end of the development of morality, the moral subject is as abstract, empty, unreal, and socially and intersubjectively irrelevant as the

---

28 See Theunissen, Michael: "Die verdrängte Intersubjektivität in Hegels Philosophie des Rechts", in: Henrich, Dieter/ Horstmann, Rolf-Peter (eds.): *Hegels Philosophie des Rechts*, Stuttgart 1982, pp. 317–380, p. 339. For a discussion of this transition (and a critical discussion of the literature) see Nuzzo, Angelica: *Rappresentazione e concetto*, chapter 3.
29 See Hegel, Georg Wilhelm Friedrich: *Grundlinien der Philosophie des Rechts*, §§75, p. 81.
30 Hegel, Georg Wilhelm Friedrich: *Grundlinien der Philosophie des Rechts*, §125.

subject of abstract right.³¹ In the sphere of abstract right as well as in the sphere of morality, Hegel shows that the intersubjective, social deficiency of their initial abstraction cannot be recuperated or corrected within the same standpoint. Such deficiency leads rather to the degeneration of the juridical and moral standpoint as such. Dialectically, the only solution of this *impasse* is their *Aufhebung* within the dimension of *Sittlichkeit*. As Theunissen has observed, there is no *Entwicklung* or progress within these spheres; herein, the double negation does not lead to a positive result *within the same sphere*; we assist rather to a blocked movement that has a dead end as result: *Unrecht* and *Böse*.³² Thus, *Aufhebung* in the dimension of *Sittlichkeit* is the answer of dialectic to the unsolved contradiction of the previous standpoints.³³

Ethical intersubjectivity is the alternative that Hegel's dialectic proposes between the atomic, a-social individuality of natural right and the all-embracing organic totality of the metaphysics of substance.³⁴ Within the structure of *Sittlichkeit*, freedom is from the very beginning and constitutively intersubjective. Herein, the other is no longer a limit (or something *Fremdes*) for the individual. Nor is it that in relation to whom the individual is posited as individual.³⁵ Rather, within the sphere of *Sittlichkeit* both the other and the individual in their relationship are moments of the development of intersubjective freedom. On Hegel's dialectical account, the notion of a pre-social, transcendentally grounded or deduced intersubjectivity as condition for social interaction is a sterile concept that leads only as far as the atomistic individualism of abstract right and morality in which social interaction is but an illusory appearance or a *Schein*. The dialectic structure of freedom, which is the very dialectic structure of objective *Geist*, reverses the transcendental standpoint. Accordingly, since an intersubjectively view of mediated freedom is now the foundation of the process, no need for a "deduction" of intersubjec-

---

31  Hegel, Georg Wilhelm Friedrich: *Grundlinien der Philosophie des Rechts*, §141.
32  See Theunissen, Michael: "Die verdrängte Intersubjektivität in Hegels Philosophie des Rechts", p. 339, p. 342 ff.
33  Hegel, Georg Wilhelm Friedrich: *Grundlinien der Philosophie des Rechts*, §141.
34  See Hegel's claim in R§156 Zusatz. This is the expectation that guides Theunissen in his investigation. His analysis, however, leads to the disappointing conclusion that this alternative is "repressed" or revoked by the development of Hegel's theory, in particular, by his theory of the state. On Theunissen's account, intersubjectivity plays for Hegel a role only in the perspective of the critique. His positive doctrine of intersubjectivity remains "repressed."
35  See for example R§147 and Anm.

tivity is present in this perspective. At the level of *Sittlichkeit*, dialectic shows that the "abstract right" and the "abstract good" of the previous two spheres are developed into and replaced by the figure of the "*lebendiges Gute*."[36] Within *Sittlichkeit* the good is a living reality (is *wirklich* as "wirkliche[r] Geist"[37] instead of merely "abstract good") insofar as it is enacted by the intersubjective universality that constitutes ethical life as "*allgemeines Leben*." Out of this structure, which in its first figure is presented as family, arises the individuality that populates Hegel's civil society.

### IV. Husserl: Intersubjectivity and Transcendental Phenomenology

By placing the problem of intersubjectivity at the center of the constitution of ethical life in its articulation through family, civil society, and state, Hegel's dialectic significantly removes it from the realm of a *prima philosophia* concerned with the task of its own scientific foundation. Such was, instead, the crucial concern of the transcendental investigation of Fichte's *Wissenschaftslehre*. In a similar way, this is also Husserl's concern in his transcendental phenomenology.[38] From a general transcendental perspective, it can be argued that Hegel's dialectic *displaces* the notion of intersubjectivity. Perhaps this is also one of the reasons motivating Theunissen's thesis of Hegel's "repressed intersubjectivity." More than repressed, intersubjectivity for Hegel is restricted; it is confined within the realm of ethical life and hence, ultimately (and here lies Theunissen's chief discontent), within the state.

As I have argued above, §57 of the *Krisis* places on the same plane Fichte's and Hegel's "mythical" and metaphysical attempts to abandon the solipsistic standpoint of the transcendental I. At stake, for Husserl, is the problem of a phenomenological foundation of intersubjectivity. On Husserl's reading of the history of transcendental philosophy, with his strict separation of psychology and transcendental philosophy (a separation that must be maintained and yet also emended)[39] Kant has missed

---

36 Hegel, Georg Wilhelm Friedrich: *Grundlinien der Philosophie des Rechts*, §142.
37 Hegel, Georg Wilhelm Friedrich: *Grundlinien der Philosophie des Rechts*, §156.
38 See the analysis in Siemek, Marek: "Fichtes und Husserls Konzept der Transzendentalphilosophie", in: Hogrebe, Wolfgang (ed.): *Fichtes Wissenschaftslehre 1794. Philosophische Resonanzen*, Frankfurt a.M. 1995, pp. 96–113.
39 See Fisette, Denis: "Husserl et Fichte: Remarques sur l'apport de l'idéalisme dans le développement de la phénoménologie", in: *Symposium* (forthcoming).

the crucial phenomenological aspect of Locke's empiricism. Fichte's merit, instead, is to have distinguished empirical and transcendental I – although this is precisely the point in which the major problem of solipsism is encountered and the transcendental I is reduced to an empty metaphysical postulate. Ultimately, on Husserl's view, the fault of the entire post-Kantian idealistic tradition is to have lost contact with the realm of human experience and to have considered empirical or descriptive psychology the only possible way out of this predicament. The task of phenomenology is precisely to recuperate a non-empirical relation to experience, that is, to find that access to experience which alone makes experience itself possible. To this extent Husserl places his own phenomenology (with its procedure of reduction and its notion of constituting intentionality) squarely within the transcendental project. We should now ask: How does Husserl's transcendental phenomenology lead us out of the impasse of Fichte's position? And what does a phenomenology of this kind contribute to the problem of intersubjectivity?

At the end of the nineteenth and the beginning of the twentieth century the philosophical debate revolves as much around the issue of individuality and subjectivity as around the issue of community and intersubjectivity. Embracing the historicism of the Hegelian tradition, Dilthey offers a different perspective on this issue than Husserl – a non-transcendental, realist-empiricist perspective, which Husserl confronts critically on different occasions. What interests me in this confrontation is precisely the opposition between historicism and transcendentalism. "The secret of the world" argues Dilthey in 1870 "is individuality, indivisible and indissoluble individuality. This extends also to history."[40] While Dilthey rejects the possibility of a dialectic mediation between individuality and community, his aim is to ground the historical sciences in the psychology of the subjective *Erlebnis*. Husserl's critique of Dilthey's psychology betrays his different conception of the nature and foundation of intersubjectivity. His chief motivation is to fight psychologism both in logic and in the theory of consciousness. A non-psychological but rather transcendental investigation of consciousness becomes the *locus* of the foundation of philosophy as "rigorous science." However, while Husserl opposes Dilthey's psychologistic account of the subject, he agrees with him in rejecting an abstract view of the foundational subject. The concept

---

40 Dilthey, Wilhelm: *Gesammelte Schriften. Die Wissenschaften vom Menschen, der Gesellschaft und der Geschichte*, ed. by Johach, Helmut and Rodi, Frithjof, Göttingen 1977, p. 193 ff.

of intersubjectivity is now invested with these different tasks: against the abstraction of idealistic metaphysics, one must regain for subjectivity a meaning close to experience; yet, one must avoid the path of psychologism; and ultimately, against the irrationalism and skepticism of the time, provide the ground for the foundation of philosophy as *strenge Wissenschaft*.

For Dilthey, once *Erlebnis* is situated as the basis of the historical sciences, the problem concerns, once again, the transition from the atomic individuality of *Erlebnis* to the intersubjective, communal context of history. How can the world of historical inter-human relationships display *objective* reality and yet be exclusively obtained from the individual, subjective *Erlebnis* of the experiencing consciousness? It is relevant in the connection that I have pursued throughout this essay that in his late years (in the *Studien zur Grundlegung der Geisteswissenschaften*), taking into account Husserl's critique, Dilthey will look for an answer to this crucial problem in Hegel and, in particular, in Hegel's theory of objective spirit. Objective spirit is meant to counterbalance the subjectivist tendencies of the immediate experience of life disclosed by the *Erlebnis*. On this basis, Dilthey revises his position with regard to the foundation of history in the subjective *Erlebnis*. In Hegel's aftermath, the claim is now that the essence of history is the *Objektivierung* of the spirit of a community. The original unity of *Erlebnis* is seen as *objectified* in the historical reality.

In his 1925 *Phänomenologische Psychologie*, Husserl criticizes Dilthey's concept of historical and social intersubjectivity for not being phenomenological. Ultimately, for Husserl, Dilthey's historicism is unable to account for a "pure spiritual community bound by a purely spiritual communal life."[41] Opposing Dilthey's psychologizing view of history, Husserl's task is to find the permanent, transcendental structures of intersubjectivity, saving their transcendental purity from the empirical contingency of historical relations, and thereby gaining the unshakeable foundations of science. Thus, intersubjectivity on a transcendental basis (or alternatively the extension of the transcendental to intersubjectivity) serves Husserl both to avoid Dilthey's psychologism and to steer clear of the solipsistic abstraction of Fichte's transcendental subject.

However, in Husserl's demand for a "*pure* spiritual community" and in the idealizing, purifying function of phenomenological reduction, we encounter the first specific difficulty of his phenomenological account of intersubjectivity. As Fichte rightly saw, within the transcendental perspec-

---

41 HUA IX, p. 354.

tive the problem of intersubjectivity belongs to the *material* part of transcendental philosophy.[42] How, then, can intersubjectivity be brought within the horizon of a *pure* phenomenology? Does this require a split or at least a differentiation within the very concept of intersubjectivity? How does the purity of the phenomenological account meet the charge of social deficiency raised by Hegel and, in a different perspective, by the realist demand put forth by Dilthey's science of history?

In *Ideen II*, the constitution of the intersubjective world (the correlate of intersubjective experience based on *Einfühlung*), must be subjected to a propedeutic phenomenological reduction whereby it is purified of all transcendence.[43] Moreover, in a manner reminiscent of Fichte's notions of *Wechselwirkung* and *Aufforderung*, Husserl presents the reciprocity of the constitution of the I as fundamentally intersubjective. Significantly, however, for Husserl the experience of intersubjectivity is mediated by the communal world in which the correlative experience of myself as an intersubjective being and of the other in relation to myself takes place. Two are the issues that the phenomenological account of intersubjectivity must address at this point. On a first level, at stake is the comprehension of the other as a person or the one-sided intentionality of the I toward the other. One's personal world, however, is intersubjective in the additional sense of being social. Clearly, these two interconnected issues replicate the two problems previously addressed by Fichte and Hegel.

> The social character is constituted by specifically social and communicative acts. By way of these acts, the I addresses others and is conscious of others as those whom it addresses and who understand its address. Eventually, in their behavior, the others will orient themselves according to that address [...]. These acts constitute a higher unity of consciousness among people who already 'know' each other.[44]

In the *Ideen*, Husserl's theory of intersubjectivity is affected by an unreconciled dichotomy. The original, pre-communicative, and "merely subjective sphere of the individual" remains separated from the "external world of spirit" in which intersubjective communication takes place. The original constitution is based on the distinction between a "pre-social subjectivity" not yet touched by the *Einfühlung* (i.e., the transcendental

---

42 Obviously, to say that intersubjectivity belongs to the "material" part of transcendental philosophy is not to say that it is an empirical problem.
43 Husserl, Edmund: *Ideen zu einer reinen Phänomenologie und phänomenologische Philosophie*, Halle 1928, II, Appendix IV, p. 571.
44 Husserl, Edmund: *Ideen*, II, p. 590.

function of all *Fremderfahrung*), and the "social subjectivity" of the communal world. Intersubjectivity—even the intersubjective form of my own reality—can never be accessed or experienced "directly"[45] as it always needs the mediation of *Einfühlung*. Fichte's separation between the absolute I and the empirical I seems to resurface at this point of Husserl's analysis. Although intersubjectivity is brought back to the intentional horizon of consciousness, it still remains transcendent with regard to the constituting original subjectivity. As Masullo has observed, Husserl does not overcome the position of "subjective idealism since the 'world of spirit', namely, the objectivity characterized by intersubjectivity [...], is paradoxically constituted as transcendence posited by consciousness and related to it in its singularity."[46] Despite all its efforts, phenomenology does not seem to substantially advance beyond Fichte's transcendental position and Hegel's critique thereof. And yet, the separation between the pre-social, monadic and foundational subjectivity and its intended intersubjective objectivation signals Husserl's attempt to escape Fichte's problem of solipsism. According to the original program laid out in *Formale und transzendentale Logik*, intersubjectivity should be entirely absorbed within the horizon of a pure transcendental phenomenology. In this framework, however, the problem of the transition between the I conscious of itself as "logical" I, and the world appears yet again. Such world is not only a world of things but is also the "world of us all"—it is an intersubjective world of persons.[47]

To sum up these developments in a first conclusion, the alternative faced by Husserl's transcendental phenomenology seems to be either to stick to a rigorous phenomenological foundation of intersubjectivity in the constituting subjectivity—in which case Fichte's problem of solipsism and the problems connected to the split between absolute and empirical I present themselves again; or to distinguish between a pre-social subjectivity and the social subjectivity of the communal world—in which case Hegel's critique of the social deficiency of this type of intersubjectivity must be confronted.

In the *Cartesianische Meditationen*, the problem of the constitution of intersubjectivity is solved by way of a radical reduction on the basis of the

---

45 Husserl, Edmund: *Ideen*, II, p. 595.
46 Masullo, Aldo: *Lezioni sull'intersoggetività. Fichte e Husserl*, Napoli, (ms. 1963), p. 113.
47 See Husserl, Edmund: *Formale und transzendentale Logik*, Halle 1929, pp. 209–210 where Husserl mentions the specter of solipsism.

"primordial sphere of my transcendental ego" already thematized in *Formale und transzendentale Logik*. Phenomenological reduction eliminates all that which does not belong to that primordial sphere—the world is reduced to "my" world. A relation is established between a "primordial transcendence" which is "immanent" in the sense of not being due to the others' constitutive activity, and an "objective transcendence,"[48] within which other and different transcendences are recognized. The problem, at this point, is expressed by Husserl in the following crucial question: "How can a real and effectual being that is for me, be not only something intended by me but really something that, taking place in me with its own coherence, is nonetheless other than the intersection of my constitutive syntheses?"[49] Once the other is brought within the horizon of constitutive intentionality, this threshold can no longer be crossed and the problem of the *reality* of this other becomes urgent. The other is not a mere representation in me; s/he is the *"singemäß eben Andere."* Indeed, Husserl recognizes that the "appearance of solipsism" seems to menace yet again the phenomenological investigation.[50] On this point, Husserl's Fichtean phenomenological constitution of the "objective world" is indeed the radical alternative to Dilthey's Hegelian, historicist path of objective spirit.

## V. Conclusion

With his phenomenology, Husserl has driven the transcendental investigation into the notion of intersubjectivity to its extreme consequences. In this perspective, I submit, none of the problems opened for the first time by Fichte reaches a definitive solution. The alternative path followed by Hegel's dialectic investigation of objective spirit, and taken up again in Husserl's time by Dilthey's historicist realism remains the other viable perspective for an understanding of the social and historical reality of intersubjectivity. With regard to this problem, however, Fichte's transcendental philosophy and Husserl's transcendental phenomenology have indeed a much more ambitious aim. In the transcendental framework, intersubjectivity is brought to the very center of the foundation of philosophy as rigorous science. The challenge offered by the concept of inter-

---

48  See Husserl, Edmund: *Cartesianische Meditationen*, V, §§47–48.
49  Husserl, Edmund: *Cartesianische Meditationen*, V, §42.
50  See Husserl, Edmund: *Cartesianische Meditationen*, V, §42.

subjectivity is the following: intersubjectivity claims to go beyond a purely logical and epistemological foundation of philosophy and to recuperate the dimension of the multiform inter-human reality in its growing cultural, social, and historical complexity. Husserl's late notion of *Lebenswelt*, which attests to the final transformation of his concept of intersubjectivity, is perhaps the place where a convergence of the two traditions followed throughout this paper can be indicated.

# Tendency, Drive, Objectiveness. The Fichtean Doctrine and the Husserlian Perspective

FEDERICO FERRAGUTO

Università di Roma

I. The Trieblehre in Fichte and Husserl

The first temptation that presents itself when facing philosophical projects – transcendental phenomenology and *Wissenschaftslehre* – so factually distant from one another and yet, so surprisingly contiguous in certain basic instances, is that of constructing some idea of the history of philosophy or, perhaps even a stronger temptation, is that of transmitting a philosophical idea of the history of philosophy[1]. Thus, the "Husserlian Perspective" would come to be configured as a progressive reprise on Husserl's part of reasons implicit in Fichte's *Trieblehre*, in light of the different demands of transcendental phenomenology or, in the opposite direction, clarifying as much of the "phenomenological" as might already be found in Fichte. Proceeding in this way, however, leads to difficulties which are hard to support, such as those connected to the clarification of issues both general and of principle, regarding Fichte and Husserl, such as the nature of transcendentalism, the I, the notions of experience or concreteness and of history. On the other hand, the relationship between instinctive life and definition of the "object" as the sphere of action of the same I – between *instinct and presence*[2] – is one of the most frequented places in the critical literature on Fichte[3] and has been presented themati-

---

1   See for example Siemek, Marek J.: "Husserl und die Erbe der Transzendentalphilosophie", in: *Fichte Studien Bd 1*, 1990, pp. 145–152.
2   Maldiney, Henri: *Penser l'homme et la folie*, Grenoble 1991, pp. 145 and following.
3   For a lucid clarification of the systematic function of the *Trieb* in Fichte see de Pascale, C.: "Die Trieblehre bei Fichte", in: *Fichte-Studien Bd. 6*, 1994, pp. 229–251.

cally much in depth in its psychological, anthropological[4] and philosophical-natural[5] dimensions, and in respect to the aesthetic[6] or ethichal[7] perspectives implicit in it.

As regards Husserl, the issues tied to the relationship between instinctive life and/or the instinct of the subject and the constituition of the object represent, on the one hand, one of the principal driving reasons of the phenomenological project, while, on the other hand, they constitute one of the most significant achievements of transcendental phenomenology in its more mature and radical forms. Even in this case the critical Husserlian literature has constantly maintained in a more or less explicit way the double faces of Husserl's reflections on *Trieb*, from time to time bringing to light the different implications[8], from Marbach's by now celebrated monograph[9], and the more recent expressions of Bernet[10].

It is possible to view everything that has been thus far exposed from a different angle. I maintain, in fact, that it is possible to effect a phenomenological reading of Fichte's *Trieblehre*, not beginning from theoretical generalizations or from variations on the "transcendental philosophy"

---

4   See on this point, Fabbianelli, Faustino: *Impulsi e Libertà. Psicologia e trascendentale nella filosofia pratica di Fichte*, Genova 1998; or Id., *Antropologia trascendentale e visione morale del mondo. Il primo Fichte e il suo contesto*, Milano 2000.
5   See Moiso, Francesco: *Natura e cultura nel primo Fichte*, Milano 1979; Lauth, Reinhard: *Die transzendentale Naturlehre Fichtes nach den Prinzipien der Wissenschaftslehre*, Hamburg 1984.
6   See Pareyson, Luigi: *L'estetica dell'idealismo tedesco. I. Kant, Schiller, Fichte*, Torino 1950.
7   See for example. Fonnesu, Luca: *Antropologia e idealismo. La destinazione dell'uomo nell'etica di Fichte*, Bari 1993; Ivaldo, Marco: *Libertà e Ragione. L'etica di Fichte*, Milano 1992; Soller, Alois: *Trieb und Reflexion in Fichtes Jenaer Philosophie*, Würzburg 1984.
8   Reference has already in fact been made on the constitutive function of this notion of Husserlian phenomenolgy by, Holenstein, Elmar: *Phänomenologie der Assoziation*, Den Haag 1972; Rang, Bernhard: *Kausalität und Motivation. Untersuchungen zum Verhältnis von Perspektivität und Objektivität in der Phänomenologie Edmund Husserls*, Den Haag 1973; Yamaguchi, Ichiro: *Passive Synthesis und Intersubjektivität bei E. Husserl*, Den Haag-Boston-London 1982; A complex thematical treatment of this issue is offered by Nam-In Lee, *Edmund Husserls Pänomenologie der Instinkte*, Dordecht-Boston-London, 1993.
9   Marbach, Eduard: *Das Problem des Ich in der Phänomenologie E. Husserls*, Den Haag 1974.
10  Bernet, Rudolf: *Conscience et existence*, Paris 2004. Bernet orients himself, rightly so in my opinion, in pointing out Husserl's greater adherence to authors like Leibniz or Aristotle, rather than Fichte, in as much as the thematical setting of the instinctive life of the I is concerned.

theme, but from the affirmations that Husserl himself made directly about Fichte, in one of the most explicit expressions of his understanding of the *Wissenschaftslehre:* the *Fichtes Menschheitsideal.* If one suspends judgment on the "edifying" tenor of these Husserlian lectures and reads the judgments expressed on the merit of the *Wissenschaftslehre* in light of the developments of the phenomenological-transcendental project just before the '20 s[11], it is possible to acquire important reading keys in order to continue thinking of Fichte's *Trieblehre* and, perhaps, repropose on different bases the problem of the research on the relationships that exist between the transcendental point of view of the *Wissenschaftslehre* and that of the transcendental phenomenology. Thus, the Husserlian perspectives do not remain isolated terms *ad hoc* for extrinsic comparisons, but become "points of view", interpretive instruments for studying the *Wissenschaftslehre* in depth as a global idea of philosophy in its outcomes and in its limits.

## II. Husserl and Fichte: Freiburg 1917

The lectures held for the first time in Freiburg between the 8th and the 17th of November 1917, more than being just an isolated historical incursion by Husserl into the classical German philosophical background, represent the beginning of many dates of Fichtean philosophy[12]. In 1917 Husserl returns to Fichte after having already held seminars in 1903 and 1915, with explicitly didactic intentions and presents us with the philosopher of Rammenau as a *Bannenträger* of German idealism and as a symbol of the *Existenzkampf* which Germany conducted at the time of the battle of Jena. Under the profile of his intellectual activity, Fichte is presented to us as a man endowed with an imperious force of will and as an "ethical-religious reformer, prophet, visionary (*Seher*)". And

---

11 A first attempt in this sense was performed by Rocco, Donnici: *Intenzioni d'amore, di scienza e d'anarchia. L'idea husserliana di filosofia e le sue implicazioni etico-politiche*, Napoli 1996.
12 Husserl had already held a seminar on Fichte in 1903 which had as its subject the *Bestimmung des Menschen.* The philosopher also repeated a seminar on the *Bestimmung des Menschen* in 1915 and, in 1918, conducted a seminar on the Fichtean *Bestimmung des Gelehrten.* For a first examination of the other Husserlian lectures on Fichte see Baratta, Giorgio: *L'idealismo fenomenologico di E. Husserl*, Urbino 1974.

so, Husserl continues, "his entire philosophizing is placed at the service of this powerful practical impulse"[13].

The interpretive line these lessons consolidated is that whereby Husserl in the *Fichtes Menscheitsideal* does not make his philosophy the subject, although he employs a terminology congenial to him and speaks *pro domo sua*[14]. The consequence of this interpretive scheme is that of placing the figure of Fichte in the margins as much as concerns research on the genesis of specifically theoretical developments which transcendental phenomenology took on in those years.

Whoever takes the Husserlian text apart in light of the foundations which transcendental phenomenology set about maturing just before the '20 s, from the constitutive problematics to the passive synthesis and the structure of the *Erweckung*, accompanied by a progressive deepening of the reflection as to the possibility of giving life to a phenomenology of the instincts, finds himself in the condition of being able to effect three orders of observation.

The first regards the theoretical basis upon which the edifying aspect of Fichte is described which, Husserl maintains, cannot be rejected for a genuine understanding of his philosophizing[15]. Fichte's philosophy is "philosophizing", a practice which has its support in a theoretical discourse that cannot be disregarded.

The second order of observation is tied to the radicalization of the Kantian philosophy which Husserl sees in Fichte's work. Fichte's theoretical questioning, in fact, places the issue of the "existence or the way of existence of the space-time reality, of the world in the natural sense of the term"[16]. But, differently from Kant, Fichte is largely oriented towards placing this issue in terms of the *constitution*, or in terms of research as to the thinkableness of the matter of the constituting of nature[17]. The passage from Kant to Fichte is, thus, presented in such a manner that "according to Kant, subjectivity produces objectivity, after it has been passively felt beforehand" whereas in Fichte the problem of feeling is placed and remains inside of subjectivity[18]. The passage from Kant to Fichte for Husserl leaves open the issue:

---

13  Husserl, Edmund: *Gesammelte Werke*, hrsg. von Hermann Leo van Breda and Samuel Ijsseling, Den Haag 1950, XXV, p. 269.
14  See the introduction to HUA XXV, p. XXVIII.
15  HUA XXV, p. 270.
16  HUA XXV, p. 271.
17  HUA XXV, p. 274.
18  HUA XXV, p. 274.

Is it possible that in subjectivity there is something that it itself has not produced? No, being a subject means nothing more than being an agent (*Handelnder*). And that which the subject always has before it, as a substratum of the action, as the object of its activity, that must be something immanent, which is obtained through itself [19].

Precisely in developing this interpretation, beginning with an interesting lecture on the Fichtean concept of *Tathandlung*, Husserl found himself making reference to the notion of drive[20], in order to explain the contemporaneously active and passive dimension of the same *Tathandlung*, here understood as *Handeln zu Handeln*. On this basis, the novelty of the Fichtean discourse is inscribed by Husserl on the horizon of the definition of the conditions of possibility for the thinkableness of a conscience unburdened by dogmatic elements like sensations or *sense data*[21]. In the years in which Husserl gave lectures on Fichte, in fact, a significant revision or deeper study of the phenomenological project which Husserl conducted on the genetic phenomenology had to be collocated. In relation to the Fichtean context which we are trying to bring into focus, this passage might be understood as a reconfiguration of the *zu* contained in the *Tathandlung* as *Handeln zu Handeln*[22], and thus as an explanation of the origin of the subjective intentionality starting from the principles immanent to the subject itself [23].

The third observation, finally, the passage from the theoretical clarification of Fichteanism to the practical dimension to which Husserl sees the *Wissenschaftslehre* destined. After having explained the Fichtean I as *Handeln zu Handeln*, Husserl connects it to the issue of the concrete life of the I in the world in terms of a teleology. The action of the I as such can not be irrational:

"The infinite chain of purposes, aims, tasks, can not be heterogenous (*zusammenhangslos*), otherwise the I would not be an I, otherwise an achievement would not be motivated, the fulfilment (*Erfüllung*) of a task". The action of the I must therefore be included in the unity of a *telos*[24].

This interpretation of Fichte, which fully takes in the applicative aspect of the *Wissenschaftslehre*, is important in the Husserlian context for various reasons, it may be synthesized with a passage taken from the

---

19 HUA XXV, p. 275.
20 HUA XXV, p. 277.
21 HUA XXV, p. 274.
22 HUA XXV, p. 275.
23 HUA XXV, p. 276.
24 HUA XXV, p. 274.

manuscripts of the late phase of Husserlian meditation, in which it is maintained that "the phenomenology of the instincts is at the basis of transcendental teleology"[25].

In the first place, in fact, the instinctive action of the I must be included in light of a unity of a task, which have to be practical. This necessity, in the second place, is connected to that of not abandoning instinct to its blindness, but to rationalize it. This rationalization, lastly, must happen inserting the emotional life of the I inside of a history of this latter, or, to put it better, inside of an explicative horizon which permits the fathoming of the motivations for its rational action. Teleology and history therefore represent those theoretical aspects which allow for the connecting of the subtle and abstruse theorist image of Fichte to that of the "prophet-visionary" in a lucid way, unitary and theoretically legitimated.

In this perspective I see very little difference between the speaking *pro domo sua* on the part of Husserl and the reflection, occasioned by the lessons on Fichte, on themes implicit in the developmental phase through which phenomenology is passing.

Immanency of feeling, the making problematic of giving oneself to the world in terms of constitution and relationship between history of the I and practical *telos* represent the perspectives according to which Husserl meditated on Fichte between 1917 and 1918. These themes represent *de facto* problems immanent to the maturation of the *Wissenschaftslehre* and they collocate precisely on the systematic horizon occupied by drives. This last one is set out by Fichte on different levels, distinct yet interconnected, which contribute to a definition of the transcendental

---

25 Husserl's manuscript E III, p. 9, p. 6, cit. by Nam-In-Lee, op. cit., p. 3. It is however underscored that Husserl has the notion of the *Trieb* present in depth enough since 1909, when he concentrated on this issue in the as yet unpublished *Studien zur Struktur des Bewusstseins*. In these writings, Husserl dedicates an analysis of the *Trieb* in its multiple specifications understood as a way of acting or doing of the subject considered as a "psychic phenomena". In the course of this analysis the *Trieb* is presented as a mark of' "passive action" of the subject, it is seen, that is to say, as that unconscious element able to motivate every human and rational action and, finally, it is meticulously differentiated compared to other phenomena of the concrete psychic-appetite life of the I of the *Wünschen* and the *Begehren*. Already in this function, the Husserlian *Trieblehre* – precisely because it characterizes subjectivity in its *psychic* dimension and not *psychologic* – is presented as a uniting band between the *coté* metaphyical-transcendental of phenomenological research and its changing to the life activity of the ego in its multiple varieties and concrete modalities.

*status* of the *Wissenschaftslehre* which I think can comprehend how "the life required of the consciousness is exposed by itself, through itself in its unity"[26].

### III. The Fichtean Transcendentalization of the Drive

The term *Trieb* does not refer to a particular dimension of philosophical comprehension. In Fichte, as a noetic specification of a more general notion of *Streben*, as in Husserl, the *Trieb* touches different levels upon which philosophical discourse is articulated, denoting a vast and difficult to comprehend semantic field.

The semantic hypertrophy of the *Trieb* is that of bringing condensation back to the work, just before the Age of Enlightenment, the German *langue* had functioned in terms of exquisitely anthropological origin, such as *nisus, appetitus, impetus, conatus, instinctus* or, even, with expressions in vogue in the philosophy of nature of the time such as *propulsus* or others. The *Trieb* is then significantly associated with other "dynamic" expressions such as *Bewegung, Neigung, Anstoss, Streben* etc. I do not wish to hazard a *Begriffsgeschichte*[27] in this place. What is, however, important to underline is first and foremost how the concept of *Trieb* sets itself out even historically upon four different levels: psychological, anthropological, ethical-moral and philosophical-natural.

---

26  Fichte, Johann G.: "Die Tatsachen des Bewusstseins", in: von Manz, Hans Georg (Hg.): *Die späten wissenschaftlichen Vorlesungen I*, Stuttgart-Bad Cannstatt 2000, p. 300.

27  On this point see Linden, Mareta: *Untersuchungen zum Antropologiebegriff des 18. Jahrhunderts*, Bern-Frankfurt 1976; Cesa, Claudio: "Der Begriff 'Trieb' in den Frühschriften von J. G. Fichte (1792–1794)", in: Cesa, Claudio/Hinske, Norbert (Hg.): *Kant und sein Jahrhundert. Gedenkschrift für G. Tonelli*, Frankfurt a. M. 1993, pp. 165–186; Fabbri-Bertoletti, Stefano: *Impulso, formazione e organismo. Per una storia del concetto di "Bildungstrieb" nella cultura tedesca*, Firenze 1990; Buchenau, S.: "Trieb, Antrieb, Triebfeder dans la philosophie morale prékantienne", in: *Revue germanique internationale*, 18/2002, pp. 11–24. As regards the lexicons used for my passage see Walch, Johann Georg: *Philosophisches Lexicon*, Lepzig 1733, art. "Naturtriebe" and *Deutsches Wörterbuch von Jacob und Wilhelm Grimm*, Leipzig 1965, Bd. 22, pp. 434–451. For a reconstruction of the historical context in which the Fichtean doctrine is matured see Fabbianelli, Faustino: *Impulsi e Libertà*, cit. and Id., *Antropologia trascendentale e visione morale del mondo. Il primo Fichte e il suo contesto*, Milano 2000; and Fonnesu, Luca: "Entre Aufklärung et idéalisme: L'antropologie de Fichte", in: *Revue germanique internationale* 18/2002, pp. 133–147.

This means that the origin of philosophical comprehension of the *Trieb* must be found not only in the development of the philosophy of nature[28] but in a specifically ethical-anthropological context. "Anthropology" must here signify that aspect of research on the nature of the human being which still had not separated body and soul, as it tends to maintain the realm of psychological research united, concerning the faculty of the human spirit, and the ethical-moral reflection. The introduction of the notion of the *Trieb* in this context renders possible the explanation of the human being understood as a "finite rational being" and thus as a being that acts in the world, in interaction with other rational beings external to it and on a natural horizon.

This is exactly what motivated Fichte to his *Trieblehre*. To the degree in which the object of the WL is the "finite rational being", it becomes necessary to realize in all of its aspects, not investigated in its contingent determination but in its transcendental character. It is here then that the assuming of an expression of the I in front of its own sensitive nature – and in front of the same external nature – acquires an essential value for the test of the conditions of possibility of factual knowledge, the principal reason of the *Wissenschaftslehre*. This process of integrating the sensitive factors on the horizon of a transcendental test of the knowledge of its principles, leads to an understanding of nature which does not present other aspects if not those of the relationship to man. At this level of explanation of the nature, the "constitution" of the "objectuality" comes to invest the possibility of a particular comprehension of the feeling in virtue of which the mechanical relationships that regulate the I-world relationship are reconducted into a dynamic relationship of forces, drives and tendencies without reducing themselves to a simple metaphsics of things[29].

On the basis of these passages it can be observed that the integration of the natural life of the I and transcendental exigence render a philosophy of nature as a particular philosophical discipline superfluous[30]. If an

---

28 On the other hand as Pierre-Philippe Druet seems to intend, "L'Anstoss fichteéen: essai d'elucidation d'une metaphore", in : *Revue philosophique de Louvain* 70, 1972, pp. 384–392.
29 See Moiso, Francesco: *Natura e cultura*, pp. 77–78.
30 Exactly from this problem came the dissension between Fichte and Schelling which was irremediably ended by Fichte's letter to Schelling of 31 May 1801 (GA III/5, pp. 43–53.) in which Fichte explains that: "Eine NaturPhilosophie mag wohl von dem schon fertigen, und stehenden Begriffe einer Natur ausgehen: aber dieser Begriff selbst, und seine Philosophie sind in einem Systeme des ge-

object is not given that is not a known object, then the problem of objectuality must needs place itself on the horizon of a *philosophia prima* and not into a special philosophy. In this every danger of arbitrariness is dispersed in posing to Fichte the question about the relationship between drive and constitution of the object in the area of the maturation of his conception of the *Wissenschaftslehre* as a first philosophy, that is as an investigation of his principles of the knowledge of knowledge, that which will represent our principle textual level of reference.

## IV. Strive, Thetic Conscience, Passive Synthesis

As much in the maturation phase of genetic phenomenology, as in that of the *Wissenschaftslehre*, the theme of the relationship between drive and constitution of the object is tied to a problem of a clarification of the thetic conscience in relation to the diverse modalities of aesthetic syntheses, that is sensitive[31]. In Husserl, this problem is already posed in § 9 of *Ideen 2*. The constitution of the object requires, according to Husserl, the reference to a subjective spontaneity that does not exhaust itself in the predicative performance of the I[32]. The constitution of an object starting from the aesthetic synthesis begins, rather, from a synthesis of elements which in their turn are not products of the synthesis itself[33], they organize themselves according to associative motivations[34] compared to these the I seems to be "passive". To explain this *passivity* of the I, Husserl asks himself if the *Erlebnis* rendered possible by the thetic conscience might be "given" to the thetic conscience itself or whether, and how, it might be its "product"[35].

The problem of the possibility of the thetic conscience receptive a/o productive in the dependency relationship of the I to the object is the characteristic point of Fichte's transcendental philosophy and coincides, already in *Eigene Meditationen über Elementarphilosophie* in 1793, to be

---

sammten Wissens erst aus dem absoluten X. bestimmt durch die Gesetze der endlichen Vft. abzuleiten. Ein Idealismus aber, der noch einen Realismus neben sich duldete, wäre gar nichts: oder wenn er doch etwas seyn wollte, müste er die allgemeine formale Logik seyn." (p. 49)

31  HUA IV, pp. 18–19.
32  HUA IV, p. 18.
33  HUA IV, p. 19.
34  HUA IV, p. 19, pp. 276–277.
35  HUA IV, p. 224.

later studied in more depth in the *Praktische Philosophie* of Zurich in 1794. Fichte's task in these first writings is the deduction of the nexus between the absolute spontaneity of the I as *Tathandlung* and the referring of the I to an external term (not-I), necessary so that the I understands itself as such, that is as an active principle of knowing. Fichte's proceeding does not aim, however, to find in the spontaneity of the I a metaphysical principle that explains the constituting of the not I as its product. Rather, Fichte here poses the question of the comprehension of the *modalities* according to which the relationship between I and object can be understood in terms of intentional activity of the I itself [36]. In other words, Fichte's attempt is that of finding the conditions to attribute the *Ichlichkeit* both to the representative synthesis, as well as to that perceptive through a "practical" foundation of theoretical knowing [37] in terms of *strive* [38].

In order to achieve this aim, Fichte performs two passages. The first regards the distinction of the level upon which the philosophical comprehension of representation moves and the level of the self-development of the *fact* itself of representation. This differentiation, rooted in Fichte's rethinking of the Maimonian distinction between *Darstellung* and *Vorstellung* [39], permitted him to insert the immediate self-awareness that the I has of itself as *Tathandlung* inside of an expositive process, artificially constructed by a philosopher, which hypothetically develops according to a reasoning of the apagogic-reflexive sort. This method renders possible the genetic analysis of the stratifications of the conscience which lead from the *Tathandlung* to the I- not-I relationship – attribuited by Fichte to the "dependent I" or "intelligent activity" – and, thus, to set out the laws which regulate the connections between these stratifications. It is precisely from the developing of this genetic dynamic that the notion of *strive* (*Streben*) emerges. The *Streben*, which is characteristic of the practical activity of the I, has the function of recomposing the apparent contradiction between the absolute activity of the pure I and the depend-

---

36 See. Moiso, Francesco: *Natura e cultura*, p. 129.
37 On the peculiarity of the meaning "pratical" in Fichte see Cesa, Claudio: "Sul concetto die pratico in Fichte", in: Id.: *J. G. Fichte e l'idealismo trascendentale*, Bologna 1992.
38 GA II/3, p. 48.
39 For the role of Maimon in the gestation of the WL see. Breazeale, Daniel: "Fichte's Philosophical Fictions", in: Breazeale, Daniel/Rockmore, Tom (Ed.): *New Essays on Fichte's lather Jena Wissenschaftslehre*, Northwestern University Press 2002.

ency of the intelligent activity of the not I[40]. In this sense, the strive "is an activity that does not relate to its object as a cause in the face of the effect. The aim of the strive is that rapport"[41]. Through the strive, in fact, the contradiction between absolute receptive-dependent activity of the I is not recomposed through the annullment of a term in the other but through the exhibition of the nexus that exists between them. This nexus is a "tending", whose function is exactly that of keeping alive the relationship between the two poles, beyond every simple logical contradiction[42]. The tending is first of all understood as tending of the own receptivity of the dependent I to loose it from its passivity with respect to its sensitive datum, felt subjectively as *drive*. This feeling, through which the *Streben* is specified as treated and self-generating causality[43], is that which moves the dependent I to free itself from the bond represented by not-I, and thus to submit itself to it, through the breaking free of the figurative power of the productive imagination which "elaborates" the bond and makes of it a real and true object of the intelligent activity of the I. The feeling connected to the drive is, in fact, a subjective state that does not however exhaust itself in an arbitrary positioning of the I but is bound by the encounter (*Anstoss*) with an otherness.

The encounter with the otherness is clearly made thematic by Fichte as *Anstoss*, an expression which clarifies not only the irreducibility of the meeting between I and not-I in theoretical knowledge, but also exhibits the *tendency to* as function of the practical activity in the constitution of the object. The development of the notion of *Anstoss* likewise shows how it is possible to conclude from a reciprocal action of the I with itself to the independent and autonomous character of the object itself[44]. If, indeed, at the encounter with the otherness there is always a feeling attached, this latter is understood by Fichte as a feeling of perennial impotence or constriction, as a *state*, a *being* or a *nature* of the I from which the I itself must liberate itself through the work of the productive imagination. This limiting characteristic from the origin connected to the feeling and to the drive, respectively the objective and subjective specifications of the *Streben*, confers the character of *necessity* to the representation and

---

40 GA II/3, p. 187.
41 GA II/3, p. 183.
42 The contradiction bewtween absolute activity and dependent activity is not taken away but rather pushed to the infinite. See Fichte's note in GA II/3, pp. 183–184.
43 GA I/2, p. 418.
44 GA I/2, p. 416.

that of *realty* to the constituted object explaining in immanent terms to the I the dynamic according to which an object is perceived as an external object.

Likewise, also the *Gegenstreben*, from necessarily attributing to the not-I so that the *Streben* may be understood as "tending" and not as directed causality, is not reconducted to an extraneous force to the I but, rather, clarified in its relationship to the I itself, through the laws of reflection. Fichte's aim here is not that of explaining how the absolute I "produces" external objects and which ontological connotations have external objects produced by the I, but that of explaining the renewal of the *fact* of the rapport of the I with an otherness (the irreducible *Anstoss*) with explicative laws that leave no space for dogmatic residuals and that is such as to be deduced in the course of the deduction itself which operates using these same laws. Without this observation one would not be able to understand in his epistemological tenor how much Fichte affirms in the methodological consideration premised in the introduction of the notion of *Gegenstreben*, when he asked himself: "How must the things be constituted in themselves? Well, one could respond: just as we should (*soll*) make them"[45]. The reference to *Soll* is configured here as an heuristic instrument turned to the explanation of the constitutive character of experience for the definition of the intentional activity of the I, configuring as a consequence the possibility of a self-legitimization of knowledge beginning from its principle. A topical study of the nexi upon which the concrete exposition of the *Wissenschaftslehre* is based shows, in fact, how the *Soll* does not specify the ontological character of the object which is produced by the I but, rather, the epistemological level at which it collocates the WL as theory of knowledge[46].

It is thus perhaps obvious to underline that the explanation of the *Anstoss* in relation to the reciprocal action of the I with itself does not represent so much of an annihilation of reality. With his theory, Fichte shows, instead, the transcendental principles for which the I, in order to become conscious of itself, needs a complete opening to the wealth

---

45  GA I/2, p. 416.
46  On this point see Janke, Wolfgang: *Vom Bilde des Absoluten: Grundzüge der Phänomenologie Fichtes*, Berlin-New-York 1993 and Siemek, Marek J.: "Bild und Bildlichkeit als Hauptbegriffe der transzendentalen Epistemologie Fichtes", in: Fuchs, Erich. et al (Ed.): *Der transzendentalphilosophische Zugang zur Wirklichkeit*, Stuttgat-Bad Cannstatt 2001, pp. 41–64.

of experience as irreducible reality and incomprehensible dominion[47]. In this profile, in fact, the object is neither "given" nor "produced" but "required" as objective correlate of the feeling of constriction concomitant with the drive and deduced beginning from the *Streben* as a transcendental structure at the basis of the concrete I[48]. This means that the topical path of the *Wissenschaftslehre* cannot reach, not even methodically, a unitary systematization of the *Streben*'s specification dynamic in a multiplicity of drives and feelings. So, the *Praktische Philosophie* is constrained to proceed in "episodes", that is to say by example[49].

Now, the impossibility of completely developing the analysis of the specific relations between strive and feeling is exactly Fichte's limit, as has already been shown by Lauth. According to Lauth, in fact, the Ficthean *Trieblehre* does not succeed in filling in the disparity which exists between enucleation of the transcendental function of the *Trieb* and "the presentation of everything that is practically intended in the representation and that which is represented"[50]. In other words, according to Lauth, Fichte, stopping himself at the notion of *Gefühl*, as that through which the I receives consciousness of its instinctive nature[51], cannot come to a theming of the sphere of the receptivity in all of its variety and reveal the doxical-pratical dimension. These implications connected to the Fichtean *Trieblehre* generate a sort of theoretical crossroads for transcendental philosophy starting from that which foresees at least two possible directions.

The *first* direction is organic to the work of immanent deepening of the nexi of the *Wissenschaftslehre* as *first philosophy*, which Fichte conducted after the re-elaboration of the *Wissenschaftslehre* in the mid and late Berlin phase of his thought. In the Fichtean *Spätwerk*, the notion of *Trieb* is no longer understood as characteristic of the I but as the capacity

---

47 See Hyppolite, Jean : "L'idée fichteenne de la doctrine de la science et le project husserlien ", in : Breda, Herman Leo/Taminaux, Jacques (Ed.) : *Husserl et la pensée moderne*, Den Haag 1956, pp. 184–196.
48 GA I/2, p. 356.
49 GA II/3, p. 199.
50 See Lauth, Reinhard: "Il Problema della completezza della 'dottrina della scienza' nel periodo 1793–1796", in: Id.: *Il pensiero trascendentale della libertà*, pp. 99–183, in part pp. 146–152.
51 On this point see Kinlaw, J.: "Reflection and feeling and the primacy of the practical reason in the Jena Wissenschaftslehre", in: Breazeale, Daniel/Rockmore, Tom (Ed.): *New Eaasys on Fichte'a lather Jena Wissenschaftslehre*, Northwestern University Press 2002, pp. 140–156.

of the Absolute to come out of itself and place itself as the main generator of the *Erscheinung* in its autonomy[52]. In this sense, the *Trieblehre* becomes functional to the deduction of the dynamic of the "seeing of the seeing" and it belongs in the attempt of transcendental legitimization of the difference between Absolute and *Erscheinung*. This is the basis of a notion of "phenomenology" that Fichte elaborates autonomously in the *Wissenschaftslehre* 1804 and which is strictly functional to the proceeding of the same *Wissenschaftslehre*[53].

The *second* direction leads to the inclusion of the questions inherent to the *Trieb* in the realm of an investigation about the transcendental structures of receptivity and especially a scrutinizing of the intentional constitution of perception and its object.

If the limit present in *Praktische Philosophie* would therefore render it impossible to follow a phenomenological reading of the Fichtean *Trieblehre*, Husserl's recourse to the associative motivations in his investigation on the passive constitution of the object of perception would seem to lead to a genetic analysis of the habitual apperceptive systems[54] in their singularity and, thus, to the phenomenological exhibition of the essential form, and not factual or simply exemplificatory, of the perceptive process. In this context, and that is to say in the area of a rationalization of the various modalities of the "giving" of sensitive material, with which Husserl responds to the question about thetic conscience the Husserlian recap takes place in the notions connected with the terms *Streben, Instinkt, Tendenz, Trieb, Triebintentionalität*[55].

Each perception, according to the husserlian *Analysis of Passive Synthesis*, refers to an implicit perceptive system or empty horizon, which is constituted by an implicit tendency to a full consciouness, and that is to a *plus ultra* of the single perception[56]. The perceptive system in

---

52 Fichte, Johann Gottlieb: *Die Wissenschaftslehre. Zweiter Vortrag im Jahre 1804*, hrsg. von Reinhard Lauth und Joachim Widmann, Hamburg 1986, p. 360.
53 See also GA II/8 p. 206. On the concept of Phenomenology in Fichte see at least the most recent essays of Goubet, Jean-François: *La Phenomenologie d Fichte dans la WL 1804/II. Une approche historique du concept*, text presented at the international convention at Poitiers on Fichtean WL/1804 in November 2004 and Ferrer, Diogo: *La Phénoménologie de Fichte (1804): le savoir entre la vérité et la certitude*, text presented at the Fichtean convention at Poitiers, November 2004.
54 See the unpublished manuscript D 13, 4, 40 cit. in Nam-In Lee, *Edmund Husserls Phänomenologie der Instinkte*, cit. p. 18 and pp. 58–9.
55 HUA XI, p. 178, see. also Nam-In Lee, *Edmund Husserls Phänomenologie der Instinkte*, cit. p. 55.
56 HUA XI, p. 20.

which the single perception is inserted may be comprised on the basis of two fundamental notions. The first is that of *Triebintentionalität*[57], with which Husserl denotes the implicit and preconcious structuring of the perceptive datum according to a particular direction which forms the same perceptive system (which in its turn is structured progressively by the formation of perceptive unity up to the *Ichzuwendung*). The second phenomenon is that of the immanent conscience of time[58], which allows for the unifying of every single feeling, of connecting to the others and to placing itself in a horizon which permits an understanding of the laws[59].

In this manner Husserl acquires a point of view which allows the exhibition of the essential form of every single perceptive act, to bend to the phenomenological demands the dynamic of the be given/be product of the object to the/from the thetic conscience and, thus, to reach a more advanced level even in static anlyses[60]. Furthermore, Husserl's analysis seems to begin exactly at the point in which Fichte's comes to a stop.

Upon close examination, however, these Husserlian problems are not completely foreign to the *Wissenschaftslehre* in its Jenean evolution (1794–1799) even if they are developed in a different direction. If Husserl's reference to the *plus ultra* implicit in every perceptive act must be comprehended in light of a teleological process, the theming of the feeling-impulse-limitation nexus is from Fichte properly with respect to the conditions of possibility for the I to project a "concept of task" (*Zweckbegriff*) which is an essential element for the comprehension of the concrete consciousness. The concept of task, used as a pivot for the articulation of the exposition of the *Wissenschaftslehre nova methodo* (1796–99), configures itself as an actualization on the part of the concrete conscience of specific possibilities, which the subject selects beginning from a horizon, identified by Fichte as "determinable" for the self-determination of the I. The analysis of the perception, as a constitution of the basis upon which the concrete project of the I stands, is at the basis of the introduc-

---

57 This term, although present in Husserl only at the beginning of the '30 s, seems however to appear in his basic structure in the phase chronologically prior to the phenomenological reflection. For a more in depth study of this point see Yamaguchi, Ichiro: *Passive Synthesis und Intersubjektivität bei E. Husserl*, p. 33 and following. See also HUA XI, p. 83 where Husserl speaks of the "tendentiöse Intention".
58 HUA XI, pp. 127–128.
59 For a clear exposition of the studies of passive synthesis see Yamaguchi, Ichiro: *Passive Synthesis und Intersubjektivität.*, p. 37.
60 HUA I, p. 110.

tion, in the *Wissenschaftslehre nova methodo*, of the notion of *sensitivity system* (*System der Sensibilität*)[61]. The introduction of this element has the function of exhibiting the condition of possibility in virtue of what is possible transcending the perceptive act and of constituting the horizon inside of which a multiplicity of perceptions may connect themselves in unity and articulate themselves in a temporal series[62]. The sensitivity system thus represents the "a priori materials" for the concrete conscience, it carries itself in a way analogous to that empty horizon essential to the passive constitution in Husserl[63], and represents a clear systematization of the specificity of that which in *Wissenschaftslehre* was characterized as *Gegenstreben*. This horizon, of which the I can not be conscious being set aside from a single feeling, configures the "limitedness" of the I, which we have seen arise in respect to the notion of *Anstoss*, as a potential field in which the conscience might practice its action, both under the cognitive profile as well as in the conative one. On the other hand, the potentiality of the I can not be understood, in the frame of the *Wissenschaftslehre*, as the progressive diversification of effort in a multiplicity of drives[64]. It is precisely in this role that the notion of *Trieb* liberates itself from its specifically psychological dimension to take on a categorial function[65]. This function does not identify the drive as a simple term which unifies or explains presupposed sensitive datum, but it poses itself as the condition of possibility so that the sensitive datum might be understood in its autonomy and independence from subjective activity.

With a desire to generalize, it can be affirmed that, through the connection of the notions of strive, conflict, feeling, drive and sensitivity system, Fichte enucleates the "transcendental protohistory" of the *Bewusstsein*[66], both in respect to theoretical knowledge, and in relation to each

---

61 GA IV/2 § 5, *passim*.
62 GA IV/2, pp. 63, p. 120.
63 HUA XI, pp. 83–84. In WLnm-H Fichte defines the sensitivity system precisely as an "empty" horizon. On this notion, scarcely analyzed in the realm of critical literature about Fichte, see Ivaldo, Marco: *Libertà e Ragione*, p. 98.
64 GA IV/2, p. 73.
65 On the categorial function of the *Trieb* see Claudio Cesa, "Praktische Philosophie und Trieblehre bei Fichte", in: *Fichtes praktische Philosophie. Eine systematische Einführung*, ed. by Zöller and Von Manz 2006, pp. 21–37; and Id. "Sensibilité et Conscience. Remarques sur la théorie des *Triebe* chez Fichte", in : *Revue Germanique internationale*, 18/2002, pp. 121–132.
66 For this expression see Zöller, Günter : " L'idéal et le réel dans la théorie transcendentale du sujet chez Fichte : une duplicité originaire ", in : *Le bicentenaire de la*

of its practical effectuations. In order to understand the modalities of these forms of subjective action signifies, then, inserting this protohistory in the horizon of a "history" of the I or of self-awareness that must coincide with an enucleation of the elements for which the I understands itself as concrete-reflecting subjectivity.

## V. Drive in the Self-Reflective Understanding of the Wissenschaftslehre

We have seen how at the basis of the Fichtean egology there is a theory of the instinctive character of the I, connected to a study of the dynamic constituting of its experience. This is not, however, the final resting place of the Fichtean *Trieblehre*. The *Wissenschaftslehre* is and remains the attempt of a foundation of knowledge in its practical-theoretical nature led by the accentuation of the practical character of knowledge itself.

Thus, the theme of the instinctive constitution of the objectuality is inserted into the framework of the transcendental investigation as to the occurance of spiritual fact. By this expression is meant the attempt at speakable enucleation of the elements which constitute the concrete consciousness, not understood as empirical determination or as being in the world, but as a functional structure in the making concrete and self-comprehending of reason as reason in act. Each element constituted by the concrete conscience must resolve itself, that is, in the reflective self-transparency of the reason that is principle to it. This concept in Fichte is tied to the formation of a history of self-consciousness, or to the exposition of the laws for which the discursive configuration of reason might actuate itself on the basis of the theoretical-practical performances of the I and that is, first of all, as *Wissenschafts-Lehre*.

The theoretical configuration of the rationality of the action of the concrete I operating in the world takes place specifically in the *Wissenschaftslehre nova methodo*. For our aims it is sufficient to read this text as a metaphilosophical clarification of the systematization of the *Trieblehre*. In this profile, in fact, the *Trieb* is taken on as an unitary systematic figure employed for clarifying the *situation* of the concrete-reflective I in the process that this latter performs a philosophical comprehension. If the primary function of the instinct consists in the focalizing of that limited character of the concrete consciousness in virtue of that which it can

---

*doctrine de la science chez Fichte (1794–1994)*, "Les Cahiers de Philosophie" 1995, pp. 211–225.

self-determine, then it must also be functional in clarifying that particular way of subjective self-determination necessary for giving life to the *Wissenschaftslehre* as that fictionalistic process that renders it possible to place the nexi which individuate the same concrete conscience into discursive terms. This latter is understood to be that which is always realized *in* and *as* actuation of a task, loosed from the idea of reason, specified by the meeting of the I with a variety of resistance, and finally brought about through a doxical-factual position in interpersonal interaction with others.

In the clarification of this plexus, the *Trieb* is understood as "drive to intuition, drive of the intelligence or drive to the representations [...] and therefore a power of intuitions"[67]. In particular, the introduction of the notion of *Trieb* is instrumental to the deduction of the action of the philosophizing I as *Bilden*. The *Bilden* represents, generally, the character of projectiveness which individuates the concrete consciousness as the faculty of "forming" or of "figuring" goals for its action in a direction read from its limited form. In relation to this particular meaning of *Bilden*, the *Trieb* clarifies the power of the philosophizing I to make an object of itself and thus of actuating the particular possibility to act in planning that characterizes philosophical understanding and renders possible the genetic and figurative *Darstellung*. Now, without the drive to intuition the expositive dynamic of the *Wissenschaftslehre* can have no place. On the other hand, however, the drive to representation does not appear to be an irreducible element. It is configured as an element of the phenomenology of the concrete consciousness in the *Wissenschaftslehre* and is therefore deduced in its necessity on the basis of a principle, which in the *Wissenschaftslehre nova methodo* is clarified as "pure will", and thus as the practical-theoretical instance which regulates the sphere of possibility of the action of the consciousness. Pure will, in its turn, is not as a factual element but confirmed by the circular proceeding of the *Wissenschaftslehre* to the conclusion of its concrete *Darstellung*.

Analogous to what occurs for the constitution of the objectuality external to the I, and also for as much as regards the constitution of the "object" of the *Wissenschaftslehre* as theory of knowledge, the *Trieb* is consequently revealed as a fundamental term for the constitution of objectuality. In this case it clarifies itself as an expression of the state of limitedness or fundamental passivity which attests to the passage to the act that ratifies the beginning of philosophical-genetic comprehending. This has

---

[67] GA IV/2, p. 80.

nothing to do with different phenomena or tendencies which alternate in the course of separate phases of the psychic life of the I but of a same fundamental structure seen from different perspectives without losing in that its unitary character, maintained by the recursivity of the *Wissenschaftslehre*.

In phenomenological terms, the issue of the *passage to the act* that connects the instinctive life of the I to its reflective operations, may be read both as the movement of awakening of the intentional conscience in relationship to the concrete materiality of life, and as a reflection of the problem of manifesting itself in the awakened life with a hold on the theoretical-practical position of the I[68]. The arranging of the notion of drive in the self-reflective game of transcendental understanding implies, then, the position of the problem of the relationship between "internal teleology" which regulates the apperceptive fabric of the I, on the basis of its motivational nexi, and an "external teleology" that characterizes that which Husserl calls *universale Selbstregelung*, which we can signify as the universe of a self-regulated rational life[69].

To clarify this issue, the analysis of the awakening, as it is so conceived in the *Analysis of Passive Synthesis*, becomes a key passage. In the *Analysis of Passive Synthesis*, in fact, this level is clarified through the investigation on the problem of gaining consciousness of past and future life, which, without awakening, represent a void and indeterminate horizon[70]. Also in this case we are faced with a circular structure. Intentional activity takes place in a context which, recursively, cannot but be understood as such if not in the light of reflective awakening. The possibility of awakening finds its source in the strengthening of the reflectivity through its emotional encounter with the world, understood as causality of motivation[71]. Conversely, the encounter with the world, and the comprehension of this as a motivational network, are not possible except in light of the reflective glance of the awakened life[72].

---

68  On this point see Dedeurwaerdere, Tom: *Action et contexte. Du tournant cognitiviste à la Phénoménologie transcendentale*, Hildesheim-Zürich-New York 2002.
69  HUA XXVII, pp. 29–30. Very interesting in these pages, and for our context, are the variations with which Husserl employs the semantic field connected to the *Trieb* in relation to a "habituelle Kritik der Ziele".
70  HUA XI, p. 125 and 177.
71  HUA XI, p. 427.
72  For an in depth study on this point, also connected to a clarification of the theme of phenomenological reduction in terms of genetic phenomenology see Keiser, Ulrich: *Das Motiv der Hemmung in Husserls Phänomenologie*, München 1997.

It is important to note in this passage the need to focus upon the connection between the instinctive sphere of the feeling and receptive life of the I and the "tending" character of the predicative life in the strict sense. Even objectifying operations, in fact, are guided by an "active impulse of the will" and are presented as "new types of operations"[73] compared to those characterizing the perceptive process. Nevertheless, it is precisely the phenomenological investigation of the constitution which shows how "the objectivities which are constituted in these logical operations result in such a manner as to always return to their lower foundation but nevertheless can detatch themselves from it and lead their own lives as judgments which in their multiple forms are the theme of formal logic"[74].

Now, this consideration of Husserl is important because it shows how the recursive proceeding that characterizes phenomenology does not exhaust itself, nor diminish, not even from a methodological point of view, with pure self-referencing, but is maintained in its multiplicity and variety of singular forms. Thus, the distinction between the tendencies of the perceptive life and tendencies characterizing the predicative life of the I return, to more than two circumscribed sectors of the same life of the I, with the necessity of investigating the *continuum* which renders possible the passagge from one to the other. From this point of view the *Selbstbesinnung* itself in the reflective life is configured rather as knowledge of "the whole arch of typicalness of singular operations and their intersubjective forms"[75] than as the subjective knowledge of being reset to a project which transcends the singular and sensitive life of the I, as one might think in the case of Fichte.

The Husserlian understanding of life according to reason therefore does not result in an anullment of the subjective motivations in an "external teleology", in a purpose or in an intention exterior to the subject, but is always understood in relation to the internal motivational fabric of the single subject[76].

The observation of the points of contact and the analogies between this Husserlian understanding of the *Trieb* and the Fichtean exposition would necessitate, for its completion, a reference to the relationship be-

---

73 Husserl, Edmund: *Erfahrung und Urteil. Untersuchungen zur Genealogie der Logik*, ed. by L. Landgrebe, Hamburg 1948, p. 180.
74 Husserl, Edmund: *Erfahrung und Urteil*, p. 181.
75 HUA VI, p. 204.
76 See on this point Kühn, Rolf: " Besoin, Nature et animalité ", in: *Annales de Philosophie* 1996, pp. 65–79.

tween impulse, will and God both in the late Berlin phase of the *Wissenschaftslehre* (1809–1814) and in the last phase of Husserlian phenomenological meditation. I will not explore these themes because their explication requires a conceptual framework that is difficult to synthesize in a brief space. It seems enough for me to note here how the reflection upon these themes seems to orient itself in two opposing directions. In the case of Husserl one is faced with a radicalization of the function of instinct as a metaphysical-genetic foundation for the reconstruction of the active life of the world up to the most complex manifestations of reason, clarified in its irreducible factuality. In the case of Fichte we instead witness a withdrawal from the instinctive dimension of the life of the subject with respect to a path that tends to progressively conceive of the emotional side of the real as the reflection of the capacity of the Absolute to give itself in images and of this latter to self-deduce the Absolute as an apparition.

In both cases, nonetheless, we are not dealing with a metaphysical-dogmatic drift. Instead, I think it correct to speak of a thought of the "limit" which implies a progressive in depth look at transcendentalism and tends to conceive of the conscience knowing itself, at all of its levels of explication, as the "sense" of the world.

In this way, the dialogue between these two complex philosopical discourses might provide points of reflection about the possibility to enlarge upon, through the consideration of themes which circumscribe the notion of drive, the recursive model of transcendental self-reflection with the integration of a study of the ontic-existentive constitution of the philosophizing subject, which in Husserl seems to be already at work, while in Fichte, more than being implicit, seems to be laid out on a different level.

From a methodological point of view the unattainable distance between the Fichtean project and that of Husserl, is to go back again, beyond that particular *milieu* in which this latter takes on life, even to a radical difference of intent: the unitary systematization of knowledge beginning with a principle, on the one hand, and the formation of an absolute science capable of realizing in an apodictic manner the relationship between knowing and known in their infinitely multiple concrete forms of the other. Nonetheless a parallel reading of these two philosophical perspectives would seem to be productive, not so much for comparisons, but acquiring linguistic and conceptual instruments to reflect upon the possibility of forming an integrated transcendental perspective. This expression could lead to the construction of knowledge which, without renouncing the genetic theming at the lower stratum of the experiential sphere of the I, does not lose sight of, through a gradual reflection upon single aspects of the transcendental life of the I, the task of a properly self-legitimating concrete and complete transcendental. In consequence of this concrete and gradual work on single notions, and not on the basis of a matter of principle, I believe that the reflection on the scientific nature of philosophy might be reproposed.

# Life-World, Philosophy and the Other: Husserl and Fichte

ROBERT R. WILLIAMS

University of Illinois at Chicago

## I. Husserl: Transcendental Phenomenology and the Life-World

Husserl carried out a life-long struggle against positivism. From his early critique of psychologism (*Logical Investigations*) to his critique of naturalistic misconstructions (*Ideas*) to his late *Crisis of European Science*, Husserl sought to show that positivism decapitates reason and suppresses the fundamental problems of reason. Positivistic science downgrades the life-world as merely subjective. Reality is acknowledged only as a mathematical construct. He sought to expose the displacement and downgrading of the life-world in favor of "pure facts" and "pure theory". This reductive move generates fundamental confusions by truncating philosophy and the sense of reality. This impoverished reality sense is the crisis of European culture.

The way out of the crisis is to correct the scientific inversion and displacement of the life-world. The first phase of Husserl's critique of science is to show that it presupposes and is grounded in the life-world. Science is but a garb of ideas that we construct for the life-world. The life world thus becomes a major topic in Husserl's later phenomenology, a topic not without ambiguity.

As is well known, Husserl's elaboration of his program is marked by tensions between his transcendental method of explication which focuses on subjective meaning-bestowal, and the ontological sense of the primordial life-world to which he calls attention in his critique of science. Phenomenology criticizes the natural sciences by showing that they presuppose and take for granted the life-world. The life-world is presupposed by theoretical science as the subsoil of ordinary meaning and intersubjective communication. Husserl writes: "The life-world is the world that is constantly pre-given, valid constantly and in advance as existing, but not valid because of some purpose of some investigation according to some universal end. Every end presupposes it, *even the universal end of knowing it in scientific truth presupposes it*, and in advance".[1] Husserl maintains that the life-world is a realm of immediate evidences that we neither construct nor constitute. All theoretical inquiry presupposes this original environment and immediate evidence in the sense that, if ordinary life-world interhuman communication were invalid or merely subject-relative, then science itself would be invalidated. If phenomenology were to displace the life-world or declare it invalid, then phenomenology would have nothing to describe except its own machinations, and thus would become formal and empty.

Yet Husserl also insists that phenomenological method is transcendental, and he calls for transcendental phenomenology to be a science of the life-world. It is not to be confused with empirical psychology, for the latter is a mundane natural science. Explication within the phenomenological epoché, is always explication of sense, not metaphysical-causal explanation. This explication of sense consists in a reversal of ordinary life world consciousness – which intends and focuses on objects. Phenomenology examines the subjective acts through which life-world objects and meanings are constituted. As Husserl indicates, "By virtue of our present method of epoché, everything objective is transformed into something subjective."[2] Instead of explaining the world by causal analysis like science, phenomenology inquires into the world as phenomenon, and seeks to uncover its primordial sense by examining the meaning-bestowing acts through which that sense is constituted.

> The point is not to secure objectivity but to understand it. One must finally achieve the insight that no objective science, no matter how exact, explains or ever can explain anything in a serious sense. To deduce is not to explain. To predict, or recognize objective forms [...]– all this explains nothing but is in need of explanation. The only true way to explain is to make transcendentally understandable.[3]

Nevertheless, the status of transcendental phenomenology remains elusive. On the one hand, the life-world is the pre-given, pre-theoretical foundation of all scientific and philosophical praxis. On the other hand, the explication of the life-world is provided by transcendental phenomenology. But is transcendental phenomenology itself a theoretical attitude and discipline, providing a *Wissenschaft* of the *Lebenswelt?* Does it

---

1   Husserl, Edmund: *Crisis of European Science,* trans. D. Carr, Evanston 1970, p. 382.
2   Husserl, Edmund: *Crisis*, p. 178.
3   Husserl, Edmund: *Crisis* , p. 189.

# Life-World, Philosophy and the Other: Husserl and Fichte    143

ground the life-world or presuppose it? If transcendental phenomenology presupposes the life-world, why isn't it dragged into the subjective-relative sphere with everything else? Would not that make "pure theory" an illusion? How can Husserl contend (as he does) that the life-world is transcendentally constituted? In order to deal with this issue, Husserl speaks of a special sort of constutitive activity, namely, *passive genesis*. Like the world of the natural attitude described in *Ideas*, the life-world does not have, nor does it depend on, any particular subjective act which 'bestows' meaning on it. The life-world is not only not constituted, its sense is pregiven. All that transcendental phenomenological reflection can do is recover the pregiven sense the world always already has, including others who are also co-present in the world.[4]

Some critics claim that Husserl's transcendental method, while successful as a critique of natural science, shipwrecks on his equal insistence on the irreducible priority of the life-world. According to transcendental idealism, the transcendental subject takes priority over the sense(s) it constitutes. Its relation to sense is asymmetrical. But according to ordinary consciousness, relations of self and world, self and other are inherently two-sided and reciprocal. Can these be reconciled? Husserl wrestles with the following question: assuming that the transcendental subject is a universal intersubjectivity, i.e., humankind, how can a part of the world, human subjectivity, constitute the world as its intentional formation and correlate? As far as I can tell, Husserl's answer to this difficulty is to affirm both sides of a paradox: human subjectivity is both transcendental, i.e., a subject intending the world, and an object in the world (self-and other-constituted).[5] Husserl refuses to choose finally one side or the other. Both are necessary. The two standpoints cannot be identified or separated. One price of this paradox is that the human ego and transcendental ego are called ego by equivocation.[6]

Husserl runs into difficulties in making good on his affirmation of both sides of the paradox in his Fifth Cartesian Meditation. Affirming the paradox generates two opposing requirements: 1) All sense is constituted by the transcendental ego as part of its self-explication, and 2) the other must be constituted as *other*. In ordinary life-world experience, one

---

4    Husserl, Edmund: *Cartesian Meditations*, trans. D. Cairns, Hague 1960, p. 151.
5    Husserl, Edmund: *Crisis*, §§53–55.
6    Husserl himself does not always observe this distinction. He blurs it in a reference to Fichte: "Can the ego which posits itself, of which Fichte speaks, be anything other than Fichte's own?" (*Crisis*, p. 202.)

person is just as "real" as another; neither takes absolute priority over the other. However the reflective turn of transcendental phenomenology commits Husserl to a first-person account; in phenomenological reflection only one is the 'primordial I,' and all the rest are 'others'. This implies a fundamental asymmetry between the primordial I and the other. The other is not self-presenting or self-manifesting. The excess of sense attaching to the experience of the other must have its roots in 'my' primordial experience.

Husserl seeks to work out his account of intersubjectivity through the concepts of pairing and appresentation, i.e., an analogical transfer of sense. Husserl denies that appresentation is an inference or an argument from analogy. It is something like a mediate intentionality or mediate apprehension, an apprehension of the other mediated by his body. However, Husserl never succeeded in clarifying this mediate apprehension or its status. Interpreters such as Paul Ricoeur tend to interpret the appresentation of the other as kind of analogy, or analogical argument. But this is incorrect, for Husserl denies that appresentation is an argument from analogy.

Consider the following text which shows how the two requirements of Husserl's phenomenology, the descriptive-realistic, and the constitution-idealistic, come together.

> Let us assume that another man enters our perceptual field. Under the primordial reduction this means that in the perceptual field of my primordial nature there appears a body (*Körper*) which, so far as primordial, can only be a determinate modification of myself (an immanent transcendence). Since in this nature and in this world my own body (*Leib*) is the only body (*Körper*) that is or can be constituted originally as an organism (*Leib*) (a functioning organ), that other body (*Körper*) over there – which, however is also given as an organism (*Leib*) – must have derived this meaning through an apperceptive transfer from my body-organism (*Leib*) and in a way that excludes a truly direct and primordial justification (that is, by perception in the strict sense of the term) of the predicates belonging to that organism (*Leiblichkeit*) in its specificity. From this point on, it is clear that only a resemblance established with my primordial sphere that connects the other body (*Körper*) with my body can provide the foundation and the motive for conceiving that body 'by analogy' as another organism (*Leib*).[7]

---

7   Husserl, Edmund: *Cartesianische Meditationen*, Hg. Elisabeth Ströker, Hamburg 1977, p. 113. I have corrected Ricoeur's translation, found in Ricoeur, Paul: *Husserl: An Analysis of His Phenomenology*, trans. Edward G. Ballard and Lester E. Embree, Evanston 1967, p. 126.

In this passage we can see appresentation as a kind of mediate intentionality, or analogy at work in experience. The body of the other is *like* mine, an organism; it is not a mere machine or *Körper*. Note that the passage both sets up an analogy, and that the analogical transfer of sense runs asymmetrically from my own to the alien. On the one hand, the other must already be present prior to the construction of the analogy as the condition of its construction, for if the other were not already given in passive genesis, we could not even construct the analogy. On the other hand, given the analogy as constructed, the other's presence is a contradictory one whose meaning seems exhausted in its exclusion of itself from primordial presence. Hence from this point on constitution always runs from the own to the alien. Ricoeur comments on the above passage

> Right up to the end the descriptive spirit and the requirement of constitution tend to meet but fail to blend into each other, for according to the idealistic requirement of constitution, the other must be a *modification* of my ego, and according to the realistic character of description the other never ceases to *exclude himself from the sphere of 'my monad'*.[8]

We will discover a similar problem of the non-merger of the two requirements in Fichte.

The problem in Husserl's account of intersubjectivity is that only one ego, the primordial ego, is presented. All others are appresented, and this appears to mean a derivative mode of presence. This asymmetry creates difficulties when the other is treated by means of or through analogy. As Ricoeur observes, all other analogies proceed from object to object in the same sphere of experience, but here in the pairing of alter ego with primordial ego, the transfer of sense is asymmetrical, i.e., it is always from the own to the 'alien'.[9] Assuming that this one-way transfer of sense succeeds, is the other still other? On the other hand, if it does not succeed, then doesn't the other amount to a failed cognition?

A full treatment of Husserl's Fifth Cartesian Meditation lies beyond our present task. However we must note a second issue in Husserl's account: to wit, the relation between primordial ego and the appresented ego in Husserl's analysis of constitution is asymmetrical. Upon this asymmetry, all communal reciprocity must be constructed.[10] This is the well-known weakness of Husserl's phenomenological sociology. The primordial asym-

---

8 Ibid. p. 130. Italics mine.
9 Ricoeur, Paul: *Husserl*, p. 126.
10 Ricoeur, Paul: *Husserl*, p. 131.

metry appears to exclude the reciprocity which is insisted on by ordinary consciousness. Ricoeur claims that "one must renounce the asymmetry of the relationship me-other required by [Husserl's] monadic idealism" in order to account for the reciprocity and equalization required by empirical and sociological realism.[11] If that is so, then there are serious problems in Husserl's attempt to work out and demonstrate that the transcendental standpoint and the empirical standpoint are not self-canceling, and that both are necessary. Fortunately the *Cartesian Meditations* is not Husserl's only attempt, and probably his least successful attempt, to present an account of intersubjectivity. In his posthumously published studies on intersubjectivity, Husserl's approach is through an analysis of empathy, *Einfühling, Mitgefühl*.[12] Nevertheless, Husserl's execution of his project of providing an account of the other and life-world through phenomenological idealism in *Cartesian Meditations* may succeed only in demonstrating that the project itself is impossible.

## II. The Standpoints of Life and of Reflection in Fichte's Introductions to Wissenschaftslehre

Husserl's paradox of the life-world frames a similar issue and problem in Fichte. There is a phenomenological aspect or dimension in the transcendental systematic program of German idealism. Implicit in Kant, phenomenology becomes explicit in Fichte, and yet more explicit in the title of Hegel's first book, the *Phenomenology of Spirit*. In his second introduction to the *Wissenschaftslehre* 1797, Fichte distinguishes between the standpoint of life and the standpoint of the philosopher. This distinction corresponds roughly to the Husserlian distinction between Lebenswelt and the standpoint of transcendental philosophical reflection. Fichte articulates the distinction thus:

> In the *Wissenschaftslehre* there are two very distinct series of spiritual action: that of the ego which the philosopher observes, and that of the observations of the philosopher. In opposing philosophies [...] there is only one line of thinking, namely that of the philosopher, and the content of his thought is not itself understood to be thinking and reflective, but rather as mere *Stoff*.[13]

---

11  Ricoeur, Paul: *Husserl*, p. 136.
12  See Brand, Gerd: *Welt, Ich und Zeit*, Hague 1955.
13  GA I/4, p. 454.

## Life-World, Philosophy and the Other: Husserl and Fichte

There are two standpoints: the natural consciousness and the philosophical consciousness reflecting on and interpreting the former. Ordinary consciousness is described and explained by the philosopher, and the philosophical consciousness depends on and is rooted in the experience of ordinary consciousness. The claim that there are *two* series, each necessary and irreducible, is precisely the claim of transcendental idealism. As Fichte puts it, "The type of realism that presses itself upon all of us – including the most resolute idealist – when it comes to acting, i.e., the assumption that objects exist outside of and quite independently of us, is contained within idealism itself, and is explained and derived within idealism."[14]

This distinction between the standpoint of transcendental idealism and the standpoint of ordinary consciousness allegedly 'contained' within the former, raises the question of the relation between thought and being, between philosophical reflection and experience in the broadest sense. How does thought, i.e., reflection, go beyond itself? This question becomes especially urgent in a transcendental program that focuses not on objects in the world but on the conditions of possibility of experience. Assuming that this program is successful, does it yield anything more than an empty formalism? This issue becomes even more acute in regard to the problem of the other: is the transcendental, is *Ichheit*, inherently solipsistic? Husserl's nightmare was that phenomenology may vanquish garden variety Cartesian solipsism, only to discover that solipsism emerges again at the transcendental level. He insisted that transcendental solipsism is a misunderstanding and suggested a transcendental intersubjectivity.

In the Second Introduction Fichte characterizes the two standpoints as apparently opposite and contradictory: In an important note, he writes: "It is only in his own name [i.e., from the standpoint of philosophy] that the philosopher asserts that '*everything that exists for the I exists by means of the I*.'"[15] It is difficult to imagine a stronger or more ambiguous statement of idealism: what does "exists by means of the I" mean? Is it a metaphysical claim that the subject creates being? that all being is relative to the subject? an epistemological claim, to wit that we can know only what we can make? a transcendental claim that invokes the I as the condition of possibility of experience? All of the above? Whatever

---

14 IWL, p. 38n.
15 IWL, p. 38n.

it may mean, it is clear that the philosophical standpoint *inverts* the claim of ordinary consciousness. Fichte explains:

> The I that is explained within his philosophy however, asserts that 'just as truly as I exist and live at all, there also exists something outside of me, something that does not owe its existence to me.' Basing his account on the first principle of his philosophy, the philosopher explains how the I comes to make such an assertion. The philosopher occupies the standpoint of pure speculation, whereas the I itself occupies the standpoint of life.[16]

Fichte sharpens Husserl's paradox into an explicit opposition. How can these opposing claims —"everything for the I exists through the I", and "there exists something or someone outside of and independent of me" — be reconciled?

If the two standpoints are opposed, mutually contradictory, they cannot co-exist side by side, but rather appear to cancel each other out. Yet Fichte insists that "the standpoint of life is comprehensible only from the standpoint of speculation."[17] According to Fichte the apparent realism of ordinary consciousness "has some basis, since it forces itself upon us as a consequence of our own nature, but this is not a basis that is known and understandable [from within the standpoint of life]."[18] Experience in short, is not transparent or intelligible by itself. Like the dwellers in Plato's cave, ordinary consciousness does not understand itself; philosophy is necessary to comprehend it. For this comprehension philosophy must go beyond experience. It apparently leaves the cave. But if the philosophical comprehension of experience means to negate or invert it, then the philosophical standpoint would seem to be charging ordinary consciousness with *error*.[19] Philosophy then would not explain experience, so much as correct or displace it.

If this were what Fichte meant to suggest, his speculative or transcendental philosophy would be just one more theoretical science which downgrades the life-world as merely subjective, and finds it to be the "primordial error". Fichte and Husserl would thus part company.

However this is not what Fichte means. In a cryptic remark Fichte informs us that "The standpoint of speculation exists only in order to

---

16 IWL,. p. 38n.
17 IWL, p. 38n.
18 IWL. p. 38n.
19 Daniel Breazeale notes this issue surfaces in Fichte's earlier Jena writings. See "The Standpoint of Life and the Standpoint of Philosophy in the Jena *Wissenschaftslehre*" in: *Transzendentalphilosophie als System: Die Auseinandersetzung zwischen 1794 und 1806*, ed. Albert Mues, Hamburg 1989, pp. 81–104.

make the standpoint of life and science comprehensible. Idealism can never be a way of thinking; instead it is nothing more than speculation."[20] What is cryptic here is Fichte's suggestion that the standpoint of philosophical speculation is not a way of thinking but merely speculation. This suggests that philosophical speculation does not displace the life-world, but is somehow relative to and dependent on it. The philosopher, qua human being, inhabits the life-world and lives in the natural attitude. The philosophical standpoint is not a life-world standpoint, but a deliberately and artificially sustained one. Moreover, as an abstraction, it does not really leave the cave. Fichte maintains *both* that ordinary consciousness requires and needs philosophy for its comprehension, *and* that philosophy presupposes and depends in some sense on the life-world. The task of philosophy is phenomenological:

> Therefore it describes the entire way which the former [viz., ordinary consciousness] has taken, but in reverse order. And the *philosophical reflection, which can merely follow its subject, but prescribe to it no law,* necessarily takes the same direction.[21]

Here Fichte sounds a note astonishingly like Husserl's declaration that phenomenological explication does nothing but explicate the sense this world has for us all, prior to any philosophizing, a sense which philosophy can uncover but never alter. Philosophical reflection is a reconstruction in thought of the meaning of experience. It cannot displace the latter. Both standpoints are necessary.

But how can this be? This question cannot be answered from Fichte's introductions to *Wissenschaftslehre*. Instead we must turn to the *Wissenschaftslehre novo methodo* of 1796/9. These lectures are a new – but by

---

20 Fichte, Johann G.: "The Standpoint of Life", pp. 81–104.
21 GA I/2, p. 365; *Science of Knowledge*, trans. by Peter Heath and John Lachs, New York 1970, p. 199. *Wissenschaftslehre*, SW I, p. 223. Cf. Husserl, Edmund: "phenomenological explication does nothing but explicate the sense this world has for us all, prior to any philosophizing, and obviously gets solely from our experience – a sense which philosophy can uncover but never alter" *Cartesian Meditations*, p. 151. Cf. Fichte: "We shall see that in natural reflection, as opposed to the artificial reflection of transcendental philosophy, we are able, in virtue of its laws, to go back only so far as the understanding, and then always encounter in this something given to reflection [...] but we do not become conscious of the manner in which it arrived there. Hence our firm conviction of the reality of things outside us, and this without any contribution on our part, since we are unaware of the power that produces them." GA I/2, p.374; *Wissenschaftslehre*, SW I, p. 234; *The Science of Knowledge*, p. 208.

no means final – statement of Fichte's *Wissenschaftslehre*. This work aims at a new more complete and systematic presentation that incorporates Fichte's account of the *Aufforderung* in the 1795 *Grundlage des Naturrechts* and 1796 *System der Sittenlehre*.

### III. Wissenschaftslehre 1796/9: Foundations of Transcendental Philosophy

Fichte offers a programmatic clarification of the relation between ordinary consciousness and the transcendental standpoint of philosophy. He tells us that "by itself transcendental philosophy creates nothing [...] it has no desire to become a way of thinking that could be employed within life; instead it observes an [actual] I which embodies within life this system of thinking described by transcendental philosophy."[22] The sharp delineation of the transcendental standpoint from the standpoint of ordinary consciousness creates several problems: how is the philosopher as a human being within the ordinary standpoint, able to raise himself to the transcendental standpoint? This is the question concerning the motivation for going beyond ordinary consciousness, i.e., the possibility of philosophy itself. Second, the sharp delineation suggests that the two standpoints "are diametrically opposed to each other."[23] But this is not the case; Fichte expressly declares "these two viewpoints must not be absolutely opposed to each other [...] but must be united."[24] This is a stronger claim than he previously made, which was simply that both standpoints are necessary and not incompatible. Now he claims that they must be united.

How can this be? Fichte claims that even though they may say the same thing, the two have different objects and thus their words have a different sense. The idealist philosopher we are told, observes the way in which reason becomes determinate, individuated in an actual rational being. But

> the situation is different for the observed individual than it is for the philosopher. The individual is confronted with things, human beings etc., that are independent of him. But the idealist says, 'There are no things outside of me and present independently of me.' Though the two say opposite things, they

---

22 FTP, p. 472.
23 FTP, p. 472.
24 FTP, p. 473.

do not contradict each other [...]. When the idealist says 'outside of me,' he means 'outside of reason'; when the individual says the same thing, he means 'outside of my person'.[25]

This implies a revision of the earlier formulation, that everything for the I exists by means of the I. The earlier formulation undercuts not only the Kantian doctrine of the thing in itself, but also the thesis of ordinary consciousness concerning the life-world. Fichte's reformulation of the transcendental viewpoint is that there is nothing outside of *reason*. This is compatible with the ordinary consciousness thesis that there are persons. The claim that there are others outside of me qua person, does not mean that these others are outside of reason.[26] What are the implications of this revision for our issue?

This revision reflects both Fichte's thesis of the primacy of the practical, and Fichte's discussion of the *Aufforderung*, or summons. Fichte maintains that practical standpoint

> enables one to see why and to what extent the ordinary view is true and why one has to assume that a world exists. Speculations do not disturb the idealist [...] and do not cause him to commit errors [...]. One has not yet achieved a clear understanding, has not yet obtained the true philosophical view of things [...] so long as one continues to think and expect that daily life is something altogether different from life as it is characterized from the speculative standpoint.[27]

On the contrary, Fichte assures us, "the results of experience and speculation are always in harmony."[28] This is a statement of Fichte's faith; it is a promissory note. To determine whether Fichte's assurance and confidence on this point is justified, we must press on to a consideration of his views in more detail. I shall focus on an ambiguity in his account of the *Aufforderung* and freedom.

---

25 FTP, pp. 105–6.
26 Fichte's strategy here is not unlike Kant's in the third antinomy: the apparent contradiction can be removed by distinguishing different senses of the language and corresponding different senses of the object. The question however is what the spatial term 'outside' means, and whether it is even appropriate in transcendental philosophy.
27 FTP, p. 106.
28 FTP, p. 106.

## IV. Fichte's Account of the *Aufforderung* or *Summons*

The status and location of the *Aufforderung* in Fichte's *Wissenschaftslehre* is one of the most vexing questions. In his introduction to the English translation of *Grundlage des Naturrechts*, Frederick Neuhouser notes that Fichte identifies the relation of right as a necessary condition of self-consciousness, only to run into the problem that membership in a community based on right is not only a contingent decision, but one that might be decided negatively. In short, community might be optional. This creates the problem how an arbitrary, optional and contingent membership in a certain type of community could be a necessary condition of self-consciousness. Fichte subsequently revises his position: since right is grounded in recognition, and since recognition in turn presupposes the *Aufforderung*, it is the *Aufforderung*, not right, that is a necessary condition of self-consciousness.[29] While the concept of right is supposed to belong to Fichte's *Realphilosophie* of which the *Naturrecht* is part, the concept of *Aufforderung* seems to belong to the transcendental conditions of *Realphilosophie* (right). Before turning to our examination of Fichte's discussion of the *Aufforderung* in *Wissenschaftslehre novo methodo*, let us first recall Fichte's explicit phenomenological descriptions of intersubjectivity at the level of ordinary consciousness and the experiential aspect of being summoned to freedom.

Recall first of all his discussion of the face of the other in his lectures concerning the vocation of the scholar. This anticipates certain features of Levinas's discussion in *Totality and Infinity*. The difference is that Levinas asserts the ethical primacy of the other, while Fichte seems to maintain that self and other are equiprimordial. Second, consider Fichte's candid raising of the issue of intersubjectivity in his *Grundlage des Naturrechts* which he characterizes as "a vexing question for philosophy which as far as I know it has not yet anywhere resolved".[30] He elaborates:

> How do I know which particular object is a rational being? How do I know whether the protection afforded by [...] universal legislation befits only the white European, or perhaps also the black Negro; only the adult human being or perhaps also the child? And how do I know whether it might not even befit the loyal house-pet? As long as this question is not answered, that principle [of right] has no applicability or reality.[31]

---

29  Fichte, Johann G.: *Foundations of Natural Law*, trans. Michael Baur, Cambridge 2000, pp. xviii-xix.
30  Fichte, Johann G: *Foundations of Natural Law*, p. 75.
31  Fichte, Johann G.: *Foundations of Natural Law*, p. 75.

Further, Fichte observes that this question does not await some technical philosophical resolution, but is already decided by ordinary consciousness: "Surely there is no human being who, upon first seeing another human being" would not expect an

> immediate reciprocal communication. This is the case not through habituation and learning, but through nature and reason [...]. However, one should not think – and only a few have to be reminded of this – that the human being must first go through the long and difficult process of reasoning we have just carried out, in order to understand that a certain body outside him belongs to a being that is his equal. Such recognition [...] either is achieved instantaneously without one being aware of the reasons for it [...] or [it] does not occur at all.[32]

Philosophy does not produce the *Aufforderung* or create intersubjectivity. But it is supposed to make sense of it, comprehend it and its necessity genetically. The central problem is, How does consciousness transcend itself? "One can summarize the entire task of the *Wissenschaftslehre* in this single question: How does the I manage to go outside of itself?"[33] The *Aufforderung* by other may be crucial to the determination of this question.

The *Wissenschaftslehre novo methodo* continues the distinction between the two series, the ideal and the real, first distinguished in *Aenesidemus* and in the Introductions to *Wissenschaftslehre*. While Fichte assures us that both are compatible and both are necessary, in *novo methodo* he gives much less attention to ordinary consciousness than to the transcendental side. Again, the two series are contrasted: the transcendental-speculative according to which nothing is outside of *reason*; and ordinary consciousness according to which others are transcendent to and independent of me as *person*. The *Aufforderung* is a concept that is on the boundary between the two. This makes it both important and next to impossible to determine whether in a given passage Fichte is considering the transcendental or the empirical-phenomenal aspect of the issue. He makes a sharp distinction and yet has to transgress it repeatedly.

So here is a rough statement of how the two standpoints appear to be opposed, the inverse of each other, in spite of Fichte's assurances that they are compatible and merge. In the experiential-empirical aspect of the summons, the other – the summoner – takes priority over the one summoned. The summons in Fichte's description, "appears to come from a

---

32 Fichte, Johann G.: *Foundations of Natural Law*, pp. 75–76.
33 FTP p. 388.

rational being outside ourselves."[34] That is, the summons immediately implies the existence of the summoner as its condition. The summons to self-activity grants a certain relative priority to the other person. The other summons, poses a question, and I find myself questioned, i.e., summoned to act *freely*. Fichte describes the summons "from below" as follows:

> As the ground of the summons that occurs within me, I necessarily think of a free acting that actually occurs outside of me. This, which is a determining subject and also determinable, is an actual free being outside of me. This determining subject is necessarily free, since what is discovered in this case is supposed to be an instance of acting, which can be explained only with reference to a free intellect. *Ordinary human understanding immediately makes just this inference. It says, 'I am questioned; therefore a questioner must exist. Furthermore, it is entirely justified in saying this.*[35]

For ordinary consciousness, the summons implies the existence of the summoner. Fichte asserts that ordinary consciousness is entirely justified in this inference. Is this an inference? Or is it rather an immediate truth? Fichte does not explain.

However, when we turn to the transcendental standpoint, we discover that it inverts the ordinary consciousness standpoint. From the transcendental standpoint "all external influence is completely eliminated, for otherwise we would be dogmatists."[36] Here freedom has priority.[37] "The I is what acts upon itself, and by virtue of this self-directed activity, it is a willing subject."[38] Acting upon itself means that the I is self-reverting activity. This self-reversion means that the transcendental standpoint inverts ordinary consciousness. What the ordinary consciousness takes as a summons by other, must from the transcendental viewpoint be regarded as self-determination, the I acting upon itself, i.e., as auto-affection. Fichte seems to be thinking of the categorical imperative here, namely, as a summons to act by limiting one's activity. In the categorical imperative the I is autonomous, i.e., the I summons itself.

Further, from the transcendental point of view, freedom is described negatively as *not being determined*. Fichte refers to Kant: "Kant said (and so do we) that freedom, negatively defined, is the power to be first rather

---

34 FTP, p. 74.
35 FTP, p. 454. My italics.
36 FTP, p. 339.
37 The empirical will first arises from the pure will, and the pure will is the categorical imperative. FTP p. 293.
38 FTP, pp. 74; 422.

than the second member of a series. It can be positively described as the power to make an absolute beginning."[39] Pure freedom is radically indeterminate. It is the power to determine itself out of this radical indeterminacy; in this sense it must be or have the power to be first. Freedom is the power to make an absolute beginning. As transcendental, freedom is asymmetrically related to what it constitutes. Thus transcendental analysis inverts the relation between self and other present in the phenomenon of the summons. What is prior is the subject (will), not the other.

This inversion of ordinary consciousness constitutes an antinomy that can be stated as follows. According to ordinary consciousness, the consciousness of freedom originates through the summons to action. Freedom is experienced as being summoned to act. The summons means that my freedom cannot possibly be first, or absolutely self-originating. Individual freedom of persons presupposes not only others, but community. However, transcendentally viewed, freedom is the power to be first, to make an absolute beginning; freedom is radical autarchy. Nothing can be prior to freedom. Unless freedom were capable of self-origination, it would not be free. But if freedom is absolutely self-originating, how could such freedom possibly be compatible with, much less need or require an *Aufforderung*, a summons by another to act? If nothing can be prior to self-originating freedom, how could such radically indeterminate, self-originating freedom need, require or exist in community? For community would have to precede my freedom as its condition, and that is impossible because it would contradict freedom's indeterminacy.

*Both sides of this antinomy are necessary.* For *ordinary consciousness*, we are conscious of our freedom as not self-creating or as not the *causa sui*; we discover our freedom to be mediated by others: we are questioned, summoned to act. In this request, question or solicitation, we discover our freedom, to respond or not. The other who summons us renders us determinate; the other appears primary, and our freedom is not an unmotivated absolute self-generation, but a response to a request, a solicitation, a summons. In short, "The summons would contain within itself the *real ground* of a free decision [...] i.e., it would be the determining agency that intervenes between what is determinable and what is determinate [...]. *Something is posited in the summons which is not posited in mere determinability,*"[40] to wit the other as real ground of the summons.

---

39 FTP, p. 423.
40 FTP, p. 356. My italics.

On the other hand, the *transcendental analysis* focuses on the equally crucial point that the response to the other has to be our own, has to be self-generated, even if we refuse the summons. Unless our response to the summons were self-generated, it would be heteronomous, or an automatic response to an external stimulus. But the summons is not a merely external stimulus, rather it is a condition in which we are called forth to be self-generating and self-active in a moral sense. Transcendentally the summons appears to be like the categorical imperative. Autonomous self-determination requires both that we impose categorical imperatives on ourselves, and that we must ourselves be the real ground of our moral activity. Thus the summons is a situation in which we must be both passive and active: "Here we encounter 'determinate determinability,' freedom in combination with a passive state of being affected."[41]

How does Fichte propose to resolve this apparent antinomy? Like Husserl, Fichte affirms both sides of it. For example, in *Naturrecht* he claims that freedom has a divided ground, partly 'external' to the subject in the summons – the "real ground" – and partly 'internal' to the subject, i.e., the "ideal ground".[42] This division of real and ideal grounds implies an intersubjective mediation of freedom. What we might expect Fichte to do is to take up the problem of how the ideal ground and real ground of freedom can be correlated and reciprocally conditioning. That was Schelling's approach, in which Schelling flirted with the doctrine of pre-established harmony as a way of grounding and explaining the correlation.[43] This is a questionable metaphysical solution that probably undermines

---

41  FTP, p. 452.
42  This means that freedom or autonomy is a mediated one. Mediated autonomy means that *freedom has a divided ground*, partly in the subject and partly in the other: "The ground of the action of the subject lies immediately in the being outside of it, and in the subject itself. . . .Had that other being not acted and summoned the subject to activity, the subject would not have acted. Its action as such is conditioned by the action of that being outside of him". GNR §4, p. 41; FNR, p. 39.
43  Schelling, Friedrich W.J.: *System des Transzendentalen Idealismus*, Hamburg 1962; *System of Transcendental Idealism* (1800) trans. Peter Heath, Charlottesville 1978, pp. 155–175. Schelling identifies the issue quite clearly: "how [...] by pure negation, can anything positive be posited in such a way that I am obliged to intuit what is not my activity [...] as the activity of an intelligence outside me. The answer is [...] to will at all, I must will something determinate [...] but this is inconceivable unless already with my individuality [...] limiting points have been set to my free activity [...] by actions of intelligences outside of myself." pp. 166–167.

the very freedom it attempts to explain. It also obscures Fichte's discovery, namely that autonomy is not absolute, but mediated.

Another alternative would be to show that these grounds, although divided, are not finally self-sufficient, but are reciprocally mediating and co-determining. That effort would be consistent with Fichte's observation that "reciprocal interaction is the category of categories."[44] And it could make good on Fichte's claim that persons may be 'outside' each other without being 'outside of reason'. What might emerge would be an account of the interhuman or 'between', i.e., a mutual recognition where each party jointly and reciprocally plays the role of mediator to the other, and the role of extreme. The result could be a "syllogism of recognition" in which ideal and real grounds can neither be identified nor separated; that is, they must dialectically related and reciprocally mediating. This is the path that Hegel takes.

But Fichte does not, as far as I can see, pursue this path in the *novo methodo*. He raises the issue of correlation between ideal and real grounds, only to reject the very idea of correlation because it implies an inadequate conception of the unity of the I. The *Aufforderung* implies that something is posited in the I that is *not* posited in *mere determinability*. This implies some agency that intervenes in the I and serves as the mediator, the "awakener" of the ideal ground in the I. The apparently external basis of the *Aufforderung* and its contingency implies that the unity of the I is pieced together. Fichte believes that while such a view has "a certain amount of truth", it is inadequate[45] because it introduces an unacceptable contingency into the unity of the I. Instead, Fichte believes that the I must be grasped as the *unity* of synthesis and analysis.[46] To be sure, the original duplicity of the ego means that it cannot be sheer unity.[47]

---

44 FTP, p. 421.
45 FTP, p. 364 f.
46 FTP, p. 368.
47 FTP, p. 365. The text presents difficulties noted by Breazeale. K reads that the unification of the I is "first divided without being able to be united." H has "it is first divided for the possibility of a union. Radrazanni suggests that in K "ohne" is a mistranscription for "um", hence, K should read, "first divided in order to be able to be united". At issue is how serious the negation is. If negation means simply that division is the possibility of union, and union the possibility of division, the two are made symmetrical. But this leaves out the crucial idea of synthesis being the overcoming of a resistance that surely is Fichte's central emphasis in the primacy of the practical. So the "first divided without being able to be united" conveys precisely the idea of a resistance that must be overcome. To

Unity is not a given, rather it must be achieved. This means that "separation occurs in and through the unification, and unification occurs through the separation."⁴⁸

This is a promising beginning because it connects union and separation, necessity and contingency as necessary conditions and moments. But Fichte does not show how or why separation occurs, i.e., a one becomes a many and how the many resolve into the one. Nor does he take up the problem of the unity of necessity and contingency, union and separation within the I. Instead he demands unity and focuses on the *unity* of analysis and synthesis. As we will see, the term for this unity of synthesis and analysis is the *will*, i.e., practical reason. To anticipate, Fichte maintains the primacy of the will over the apparent "externality" of the *Aufforderung*, and demotes *Aufforderung* to the status of a *phenomenon*. The *Aufforderung* is reduced to being the sensible manifestation of the categorical imperative. Thus Fichte obscures his own important discovery of the *Aufforderung* to wit, that autonomy is mediated and achieved in union with other. The unity of the I, which is supposed to be a unity of self and other, of synthesis and analysis, turns out to be a subjective unity.

Fichte acknowledges a problem at this crucial step of his argument: "Haven't we [...] gone astray? We have analyzed the concept of a summons, but we arrived at a second concept [...]. We have discovered that what comes first is not the concept of the summons, but rather an act of willing. There is no moment at which consciousness first arises; consciousness is an act of willing."⁴⁹ How is it possible to move from Fichte's idealist concept of the will/categorical imperative to the intersubjective concept of the summons? Who summons who? Does another subject summons me? Or do I summon myself, as in the categorical imperative? Ordinary consciousness moves from the summons to the existence of the summoner, but from the transcendental standpoint the move is from willing oneself as a moral agent to the summons.⁵⁰ Fichte maintains the inferential process of ordinary consciousness is entirely justified. However, from the transcendental standpoint of the categorical impera-

---

suppress this difference collapses the *Ursprungliche Duplicitaet* of *Ichheit* into sheer identity.
48  FTP, p. 365.
49  FTP, p. 369.
50  Fichte refers to some version of the categorical imperative, which he does not hesitate to interpret theoretically.

tive, the other who summons the I to activity is displaced; the real ground of freedom collapses into the ideal, short-circuiting mediation. The I summons itself.[51] As we will see, Fichte himself says this.

Fichte asserts that the spirit of our philosophy is this: [there is] nothing outside of me, no alleged thing in itself can be the object of my consciousness. the only object for me is I myself.[52] Consequently, for reason, there is no limitation by other; *all limitation is self-limitation*, otherwise we have dogmatism, heteronomy. The original limitation of the will, or practical reason, is expressed by the categorical imperative, which sets for the will a moral task. This means that the limitation from which consciousness arises is not inflicted upon me; it is one which I have assigned to myself.[53] But according to Fichte the categorical imperative is only a first step in self-limitation; the imperative remains abstract and indeterminate, and is not yet actual because it lacks a determinate goal.

The moral task I have assigned to myself requires and includes individuation. In other words, practical self-determination involves a move from what is determinable to what is determinate.[54] In this move from the determinable to the determinate Fichte situates a transcendental argument for intersubjectivity. Transcendental intersubjectivity is a condition of individuation: "I cannot discover myself apart from similar beings outside of me[...] for I am an individual. It makes no sense to say 'I am an individual' unless others are thought of as well. Accordingly my experience begins with a realm of rational beings to which I myself belong; and everything else follows from this.."[55]

The practical imperative of moral self-consciousness originates with an act of self-selection from a mass of rational beings. Fichte apparently interprets Kant's *Faktum der Vernunft* as providing access not only to freedom, but to the noumenal realm, including a mass or community of rational beings as the condition of free self-limitation and individuation. In

---

51 It should be noted that on the very next page, he contradicts the above contention that the will, not the summons comes first, when he writes that "consciousness begins with consciousness of a summons." (FTP, p. 370). I don't know if this means that Fichte is careless, inconsistent, or simply that the text of the lecture manuscript is corrupt. Perhaps this inconsistency is a result of his distraction by the *Atheismusstreit*.
52 FTP, p. 332.
53 FTP, p. 342.
54 FTP, p. 351.
55 FTP, p. 304.

its practical activity reason issues categorical imperatives. The categorical imperative implies that reason is self-individuating. This implies that reason cannot be understood solipsistically or reduced to a merely first person egological standpoint such as in Husserl. According to Fichte, "individual reason cannot account for itself on the basis of itself alone. This is the most important result of our inquiry. No individual rational being can subsist for itself. It subsists only in the whole, by means of the whole, and as a portion of the whole."[56] Rational self-individuation implies others who are not me and from which I select myself. Reason therefore is in its primary practical activity a primordial mass of rational beings from which *both self and other* simultaneously distinguish and individuate themselves.

This is a transcendental argument that rational-moral self-limitation entails self-individuation. Individuation implies and presupposes other rational beings from which I select and individuate myself. The mass of rational beings clarifies Fichte's assertion that there is nothing outside of reason. Reason cannot be individual in a solipsistic sense as in Descartes; for Fichte reason is already social, communalized. Fichte even claims that the mass of rational beings precedes my free self-selection in the categorical imperative – to wit, it is the mass of rational beings from which I select myself. This mass of rational beings is the transcendental condition of possibility of my self-selection and rational/moral individuation inherent in the categorical imperative.

It is interesting that Fichte's transcendental argument for self-limitation reverses the direction of sense-transfer established by Husserl's analysis of pairing between ego and alter ego. As we have seen, Husserl's account is first-person: there is only one primordial ego; all others are appresented. Thus the transfer of sense is from the primordial first person ego to the alter ego, from the own to the alien. In contrast, Fichte in spite of all his talk about the *Ichheit*, is not committed to a first person account of the transcendental. He is committed only to an account of the rational will before which both empirical I and other are equivalent and reciprocal. Thus for Fichte, to say 'I am an individual,' makes no sense unless others are thought of as well. In other words, to say "mine" as Husserl does in the reduction to owness makes no sense unless saying "yours" also makes sense. For Fichte 'mine' and 'yours' are determinate, reciprocal concepts, and the mass or community of rational beings is a condition of

---

56 FTP, p. 352.

such determinacy, reciprocitiy and individuation. That is a stronger claim, and I would submit a more defensible claim than Husserl is able to make. But it requires the abandoning of the first person transcendental subject.

Note however that this claim that a mass of rational beings is the transcendental condition of self-individuation seems not only to resolve the intersubjective problem, but to suppress it. For if reason is already a transcendental intersubjectivity/community, it is difficult to see how solipsism could arise or be a problem – precisely because individuation is already determined as self-selection from this community/mass. Fichte endorses this when he remarks that "the sensible world is only a certain aspect or way of looking at what is intelligible."[57] For Fichte, individual and community are reciprocal concepts. If that is the case, there would be no intersubjective problem in Husserl's sense because the *Aufforderung* in which I am summoned by another would be grounded in transcendental intersubjectivity and reciprocity.

Nevertheless, it is far from clear that Fichte's significant differences from Husserl here make any difference in the final analysis, to wit, the question whether transcendental idealism means 'subjective idealism'. For Fichte's claim that reason is a mass of rational beings does *not* mean that the mass or community of rational beings (ends) is *present*. Rather it is *noumenal*, i.e., it is thought of or *inferred*. Fichte writes: "I do not perceive the reason and free will of others outside of me; this is something I only *infer* from appearances in the sensible world. Consequently these other rational beings belong not within the sensible world, but rather within the intelligible one, the world of *noumena*."[58] Fichte contends that

> rational beings *are merely thought of*. By means of thinking, I *project* them into the manifold of appearances in order to explain these appearances to myself [...]. I think of them in order to introduce unity into appearances and into my overall experience. Reason, freedom and rational beings: these therefore belong within the intelligible world, among the noumena.[59]

Are noumena projections? Postulates in Kant's sense? Apparently so.

With his admission that the community of rational beings is not intuited or discovered but rather inferred and/or projected, Fichte's claim that there *is* a community of rational beings seems to be called

---

57 FTP, p. 350.
58 FTP, p. 303. Italics mine.
59 FTP, p. 303 n BB. Italics mine.

into question, if not undermined. Such transcendental inference or projection seems questionable, and if questionable, then the possibility of solipsism emerges, this time on the transcendental level. How can community serve as the foundation of rational self-individuation if it is merely a projection of the rational subject? Of course Fichte could reply that such rational community may be a practically necessary assumption, like Kant's postulates of practical reason.[60] However, like Kant's postulates, its status remains unclear.[61] For the form of a postulate means that it is relative to a subject, and has no being beyond or independent of the postulating subjectivity. In Fichte, as in Kant, the *ontological status* of the *content* of the postulate/projection – the community of rational beings – remains unclear, as does its status as a foundation for individuation. The language of projection/postulation and the relativity of the postulate to the postulating subject reinstates in Fichte the limits of subjectivity upon which Husserl's account also suffers shipwreck. It deprives the subject of access to that independent mass of rational beings from which it selects itself in its individuation. Without the foundation provided by a mass of rational beings, there could be no individuation.

To be sure, Fichte wants to argue that the self-individuation of reason in practical activity and the *Aufforderung* to freedom are not only compatible, but merge. He strives valiantly to bring off this merger. According to Fichte, "The world of experience is erected upon the intelligible world. Both worlds – the intelligible thought world and the world of experience (discovered) – occur simultaneously; neither can exist without the other. These two worlds are reciprocally related to each other within the mind."[62] This means that individuation is a two step process, even if the two steps may be simultaneous instead of sequential. He maintains

---

60 Fichte writes: "I select myself from a mass of reason and freedom outside of me; thus it would appear as if this freedom outside of me were merely something thought of by me. This is not the case [...]. It is indeed true that a rational being outside us is only a noumenon, something thought of by us. Yet this is something I must infer only from the phenomena." FTP, p 448. But what justifies this transphenomenal inference? The claim that it is the body of the other that justifies this inference does not really help, because that seems to end in the fallacy of 4 terms, to wit, that the other is related to his body as I am related to mine, as Max Scheler pointed out. See *Nature and Forms of Sympathy*, trans. Peter Heath, Archon Books 1970, pp. 240–1.
61 Is it a concept of transcendental intersubjectivity? Is it a general Other? It seems that rational community is more like a general other that is a condition of possibility of individuation.
62 FTP, p. 305.

that individuation through the categorical imperative is only a first step towards individuation. That is, although I oblige myself to become a moral individual, my self-imposed categorical imperative remains indeterminate. The transcendental analysis of moral individuation as indeterminate points to the necessity of a complementary *Aufforderung* for its determinacy and actualization in the sensible world. The determinate *goal* of free activity is supposed to be supplied by the *Aufforderung*. In the summons I discover myself as a subject that ought to act.[63] The summons to free activity renders the "ought" [of the categorical imperative] sensible. The summons also renders freedom determinate by supplying a determinate goal:

> What is given me through the summons is a series of elements through which some goal is conditioned, and I am supposed to complete the series [...]. The other person initiates this series and proceeds to a certain point, and this is the point where I have to begin [...] he summons me only to carry it to its conclusion.[64]

The summons qualifies my determinability; it includes "the perception of myself as determined to act upon and in reciprocal interaction with other rational beings [...]. Here we encounter 'determinate determinability,' i.e., *freedom in combination with a passive state of being affected.*"[65] Thus the summons qualifies and completes the categorical imperative. The summons provides a determinate goal which it is my responsibility, not to *originate* absolutely, but to *continue* or *complete*.

Thus Fichte tries to show that freedom, while practically and morally self-originating, is also self-limiting, and that transcendental self-limitation coincides with the summons (i.e., limitation) by other. The summons connects the ordinary consciousness standpoint with the transcendental standpoint by connecting the body of a being outside of me with the concept of a rational being. I infer, he says, "the existence of a rational being outside of me from my own freely produced limitation, i.e., from the task of limiting myself."[66] However he fails to show how the *inferred* existence of a rational being outside of me can also be a *ground* of the task of self-limitation, of determinate determinability.

---

63  FTP, p. 450.
64  FTP, p. 455.
65  FTP, p. 452. My italics.
66  FTP, p. 458.

## V. Towards an Evaluation

Fichte contends that consciousness resembles a circle of conditions in which what is determinable within the ideal series and what is determinable within the real series must mesh and be determined by each other.[67] What is determinable in the ideal series is the realm of rational beings from which I select myself as an individual; what is determinable in the real series is the world within which I express myself as an individual.[68] The sensible realm is thus founded on the intelligible, and Fichte strives to show that the two merge. Fichte tries to show that moral self-limitation and limitation by the *Aufforderung* of the other coincide. Freedom in combination with a passive state of being affected is the decisive point and meaning of the *Aufforderung*.

But do self-limitation and limitation by other coincide? This is the very point at issue. The critical question is the place of the summons qua *intervention* by other in this circle. Does the unity of the I, the unity of *Ichheit*, include the real ground of the summons, such that there is nothing outside of reason? That is the transcendental requirement. If so, then the real ground of determinate determinability would be included in the ideal ground, i.e,. reason. But then Fichte's position appears to become one-sided: the other who summons me to responsible action would be displaced, for all limitation is self-limitation. So the I as rational will summons itself; the unity of *Ichheit* apparently excludes any other (external to reason) who summons. On the other hand, as Fichte also points out, the real ground of the summons is *not* included in the ideal ground, i.e., in *Ichheit*; the real ground of the summons "is not posited in mere determinability."[69] Consequently the summoner must in some sense be 'outside' *Ichheit* and thus 'outside of reason'. The summoning other would be external, and the unity of *Ichheit* would appear to be 'pieced together', i.e., a synthesis or a "We".

Fichte remains faithful to the transcendental requirement of autonomy: there is nothing outside of reason. This means that the sensible is founded on the intelligible or the noumenal. In Kantian language, what is first is not the summons but *willing*. As rational will the I summons itself. Fichte's transcendental account of the summons/categorical imperative appears to displace the summons – and summoner – by reduc-

---

67 FTP p. 446.
68 FTP p. 446n.
69 FTP, p. 356.

ing them to "phenomena" of the will. Fichte writes: "This summons to freedom is only the sensibilized form of the summons to act upon and interact with other rational beings. *Summoned by myself* to engage in acting, I find myself within a determinate sphere".[70] Here Fichte alters the form and meaning of the summons from 'summons by other' to 'summons by oneself'. Not only is the other displaced, Fichte states that I "attach" the determining subject to the summons.[71] Günter Zöller has observed that a realist interpretation of the solicitation or summons is implausible: "Yet the solicitation is not really an appeal issued from outside the individual but is the individual's 'clandestine' representation to itself of its own finite being under the form of the solicitation."[72] Zöller's reading of the summons not only seems correct, it appears authorized by Fichte's summary of the main points of the *novo methodo:* "this task of limiting oneself is a summons to engage in a free activity (for it does not appear to come from the individual; instead it appears to come from a rational being outside of us)."[73] This appearance is misleading. The other who summons me is a phenomenon; however transcendentally-practically considered, I summon myself. The intersubjective significance of the summons seems to be subordinate to the requirement of autonomy, to wit, the categorical imperative. The phenomenal 'other' appears superfluous.

If the other who summons me turns out to be myself as other, this would mean that Fichte fails to establish a correlation of the transcendental with the empirical, of philosophy and life-world. Instead he reduces the other to, or displaces the other by, the will, i.e., the *Aufforderung* by other is a phenomenal expression of the self-summons in categorical imperative. If this is correct, then Fichte fails to demonstrate his claimed harmony of the philosophical standpoint with ordinary consciousness. Contrary to Fichte's express declaration, ordinary consciousness would *not* be justified in its inference that the other summons me; rather it would be in error.

If so, then Fichte would have failed to achieve his systematic project in the *novo methodo.* The claimed harmony of the ideal and real series masks an asymmetrical subordination of real to ideal. That subordination may accord with the primacy of the practical and the requirement of a

---

70 FTP, p. 452nG. My italics.
71 FTP, p. 453.
72 Zöller, Günter: *Fichte's Transcendental Philosophy,* Cambridge 1998, p. 119.
73 FTP, p. 74.

certain sort of autonomy. But does such autonomous will exclude community or rather found it? Even if there were a noumenal community, it would still be asymmetrically related to empirical community which it founds. This asymmetry implies that, like Husserl, Fichte fails to make good on his claims that reciprocity is the category of categories and that autonomy is mediated. Rather, reciprocity is founded on and asymmetrically related to an original unity. In spite of Fichte's claims that there is an original duality within the I, and that there is nothing outside of reason, the unity of this original duplicity trumps, or rather defines, synthesis. The other, who by summoning me, co-determines my determinability, is ultimately subordinate to or excluded by the requirement of strict autonomy, to wit, that all limitation and determination must be self-limitation. Precisely because unity of the *Ichheit* trumps synthesis, the I does not become a we, and the unity of the I remains subjective.

# Self-Consciousness and Temporality: Fichte and Husserl

GARTH W. GREEN

Boston University

In this paper, I argue that Fichte's doctrine of self-consciousness prefigures Husserl's own. I argue further that this relation between Fichte and Husserl, on a theme of evident centrality to each – that of the role of temporality in the constitution of self-consciousness – can be understood fully only through the identification of a prior and problematic inheritance shared by both, that of Kant. I argue that Fichte's critical reception of Kant's doctrine of time as form of inner sense anticipates Husserl's own critique of Kant, and thus offers a key to understanding both the context for, and content of, Husserl's phenomenological investigations of the structure of inner time-consciousness. In previous work on Fichte, I have analyzed Kant's doctrine of time as form of inner sense, its problematic role in Kant's depiction of the form and dynamics of the acts of cognition and self-cognition, and Fichte's identification and critique thereof in the *Grundriss*.[1] I will here (1) summarize the most basic characteristics of Kant's doctrine, in order to (2) contextualize an exegesis of (a) an important instance of Fichte's early critique thereof, in the *Meditationen über Elementarphilosophie*, and (b) important instances of Husserl's critique thereof, particularly in *Zur Phänomenologie des inneren Zeitbewußtseins*.

I. An Unintended Antinomy: Kant's Doctrine of Inner Intuition

In the Preface to the first-Edition of the first *Critique*, Kant announced his intention to take up "that most difficult of tasks," the "self-critique of pure reason" (*Selbsterkenntnis der menschlichen Vernunft*, KrV Axi). This self-critique, as a *"tribunal,"* would "*adjudicate* the sources, scope, boun-

---

[1] See Green, Garth, "Fichte's Critique of Kant's Doctrine of Inner Sense", in: *Idealistic Studies* 37: 3 (December 2007), pp. 157–78.

daries, and limits" of cognition (KrV Axii). In the Preface to the second edition, Kant differentiated "positive" from "negative" aspects of this attempt to adjudicate the range of human cognition. Kant's self-critique of reason would assign the "limits" of possible or valid cognition, and would thus "differentiate reason's rightful claims from its groundless pretensions" (KrV Bxxiv-xxv).[2]

Kant thus set out an "architectonic of human cognition" (KrV A61, B86; KrV A268, B324) or *ars characteristica* of the cognitive faculty, the "internal structure of our knowledge." Kant began with that most basic distinction in function between intuition or sensibility and intellection or understanding. It is by means of sensibility that we are passively or receptively related to objects. It is "through sensibility [that] objects are given to us." It is instead only then and "through understanding [that] they are thought" (KrV B30). Only, Kant continues, "in the case of a unity between intuition and intellection, or sensibility and understanding, can an object be thought," or determined synthetically so as to result in an object of experience.

Three theses contained in Kant's exposition of the doctrine of intuition in the Transcendental Aesthetic – the principal element in the "internal structure of our knowledge" and the "Organon" for Kant's theoretical philosophy – are of primary importance to the thesis of this essay. First and most importantly, Kant exposes the *ideality thesis* (KrV Bxxvi): "we can have no cognition of any object except insofar as the object conforms to the character of our sensible intuition, i. e., an appearance." Second, Kant exposes the *priority thesis:* "the conditions under which alone the objects of human cognition are given *precede* the conditions under which these objects are thought" (KrV A16, B30). Kant insists that *"the manifold for the intuition must be given prior to any activity of the understanding, and independently of it"* (KrV B145). This intuitive manifold, Kant continues at KrV A78, B103, "in order to be turned into

---

2 For this standard distinction see, e. g., Reuter's (*Kants Theorie der Reflexionsbegriffe* (Konigshausen & Neumann, Wurzburg, 1989, pp. 12, 82), between a *positive Funktionsbestimmung* and a *polemische Intention*. Ewing suggests in his *Commentary* that the Critique may be said to have had two main aims: "(1) in the Aesthetic and the Analytic, to provide a philosophical basis for physical science" in outer sense and "(2) in the Dialectic, "to deny knowledge" by denying a philosophical basis to the "sciences" of rational psychology and rational theology as *Seelenlehren* in inner sense. The first aim Ewing conceives as "constructive," the second as "critical." Both, Ewing notes, are founded upon the Aesthetic's doctrine of intuition. See his *Commentary* (London, Methuen, 1950), p. 9.

a cognition, must then be *gone over, run through, taken up, and combined in a certain manner.*"³ We will return to this point below.

In the context of this essay, however, I would like to place particular emphasis on a third basic thesis, the *heterogeneity thesis*. Kant distinguishes two forms of intuition, and differentiates "outer intuition" from "inner intuition." Kant presents space as "the form of outer sense," while presenting time as "the form of inner sense." It is to this last *divisio*, within the doctrine of intuition, that I will direct attention throughout the remainder of this paper, first, as exposed by Kant, second, as criticized by Fichte, and finally, as criticized by Husserl.

Kant first exposes space as the form of outer sense, in which "we present objects as outside us, as one and all in space." Through the *Merkmale* or characteristics of spatial form – limit, boundary, and position [*Grenzen, Schraenken, Position*] – space is rendered articulate as a coordinate system: "only in space can I present the relations of objects as outside and alongside (*Erörterung*) one another, as distinct and in different empirical locations" (KrV A23, B37). Kant brings out the difference between time and space first by stating that time "does not pertain to any shape or position" (KrV A33, B50). Time "cannot be intuited outwardly, any more than space can be intuited as something within us" (KrV A23, B38). Indeed, *only* "in space, are shape (*Gestalt*), magnitude, and mutual relation determined or determinable" (KrV A22, B37). Importantly, "while space is the pure form for all outer appearances, it is also limited to only outer appearances."

By means of *inner sense*, Kant continues, "the mind intuits itself, its inner state." But Kant's exposition of the character and capacities of time as form of inner sense is not as clear and unequivocal as his exposition of spatial form. Here in the Aesthetic, Kant attributes two

---

3   This priority thesis may be seen as grounding two complementary theses Kant advances through the doctrine of intuition. First, the *individuality thesis*, which is often exposed alongside and even as the *immediacy thesis:* "intuition is that faculty by which cognition can refer to objects directly (*unmittelbar*) (KrV A19, B33), *in concreto* (immediately, as individuals) rather than *in abstracto* (derivatively, mediately, as universals). According to this thesis, the merely formal "concepts of the understanding" are, in the order of cognition or *ordo cognoscendi*, derivative, and are understood as "mediate (intellectual) representations on an immediate (intuitive) presentation" (ibid). From this individuality, or immediacy, thesis, the (2) *passivity thesis* can be seen to follow: according to this, we "have no concepts of understanding and hence no elements whatever for objectual cognition except insofar as an intuition can be given corresponding to these concepts" – as the material or content of the concept, *per modum recipientis* (ibid).

modes to time: succession (*Folge*) and simultaneity (*Zugleichsein*). In the Analytic, however, Kant will attempt to justify an "amplified" doctrine of time as form of inner sense, and attribute three "modes," to time: *Beharrlichkeit, Folge, Zugleichsein*, or permanence, succession, and simultaneity (KrV B219). However, in the negative argumentative context of the Refutation of Idealism, at KrV B291, Kant will assert that in the time of inner sense only a "*mere flux, chaos*" obtains, a temporal succession or series not constant but inconstant, or "vanishing and starting" (KrV B291).[4] While the aspatiality of time as form of inner sense could be seen as more significant (both in the context of Kant's argumentation and the reception thereof) than the equivocation regarding the constancy or inconstancy of time, both issues indicate apparently unresolved elements of Kant's *Sinnenlehre*.

By means of the assertion of the aspatiality of time as form of inner sense, Kant intends to establish the distinct *capacity of outer intuition* and the distinct *incapacity of inner sense*. The thesis of the aspatiality of inner sense, if more significant ultimately than that of the inconstancy of inner sense, is asserted in tandem with the inconstancy thesis to a common end, that of the incapacity of and in inner intuition. Kant's repeated assertions of (a) inconstancy – "within inner sense, only a "mere flux, chaos" of perpetual succession can appear (KrV A33, B49–50; KrV B291) – are, with the assertion of (b) aspatiality, to yield a claim to (c) *indeterminacy* rather than determinacy. In the negative argumentative context of the Paralogisms, for example, time, "the sole form of our inner intuition, has nothing abiding and therefore yields knowledge only of the succession of determinations," and, explicitly, "not of any object that can thereby be determined" (KrV A381).

---

4  De Vleeschauwer, too, worries that "Kant is inconsistent on the number of dimensions that one must attribute to time." He notes that "the one-dimensionality of time is sometimes (R 4071), but not always, affirmed. Indeed, on occasion, Kant affirms that time possesses two dimensions (R 3797), and, still more frequently, three dimensions (R 372)." While in critical or negative argumentative contexts, "the only mode Kant affirms is succession," in constructive or positive argumentative contexts, "there are three; succession, simultaneity, and permanence or duration" (211 n). Because of the centrality of the doctrine of time as form of inner sense, and the distinct uses to which it is put in the Analytic and Dialectic, De Vleeschauwer concludes, "*without hesitation, that this ambivalence is not an empty game, but a necessity, required by the most general lineaments of the critical philosophy*" (*La déduction transcendentale dans l'œuvre de Kant*, v. 3, p. 212). See also Guyer's discussion of Kant's equivocation on the modes of time in *Claims of Knowledge*, ibid, pp. 209–12.

In this way and on the basis of the general *doctrine of intuition*, Kant grounded the "remarkable fact" that "from mere categories," without a possible relation to intuition, "no synthetic propositions can be formed." On the more specific basis of the *doctrine of inner intuition*, however, as both inconstant and aspatial, Kant accounted for the "even more remarkable" fact that "we need not merely intuitions, but indeed always outer intuition" in order to form synthetic propositions. For "in order to give as [an object] something permanent," we require the stability and positionality of and in the manifold of outer sense, conditions that Kant has denied to inner intuition, its temporality, and the "groundless pretension" to a synthetic application thereof to a rational psychologist or rational theologian as *Seelenlehrer* (KrV B291).

However, Kant also relied upon an apparently variant construal of the character and capacities of inner intuition. He also asserted that it is only "by means of this [inner] intuition" as a "universal representation," an *Inbegriff aller Vorstellungen*, that we "encompass within" or take up "into our power of presentation all outer intuitions" (KrV A34, B51). In the Transcendental Analytic, and particularly in the first-edition Deduction, inner intuition fulfills a positive function of inscribing spatiality and its conditions within itself, as a "*totum* of representations."[5] Thus, Kant will assert that, formally, "all presentations, whether or not they have outer things as their objects, do yet as determinations of the mind belong

---

5   On inner sense as a *totum* of representations in the Aesthetic, see: "time is the formal a priori condition of all appearances universally," and "any progress of perception, no matter what the objects may be, whether appearances or pure intuitions," is to be understood as "nothing but an expansion of the determination of inner sense" (KrV A34, also KrV A210, B255). In the first-edition Deduction, the three syntheses "amplify" inner sense successively in order that it yield an *Inbegriff*; this required that heterogeneity be resolved into a *unity* across the forms of intuition, that the inconstant series of times in inner sense be resolved to a *continuity*, and that inner intuition yield the conditions for a conceptual or categorical synthesis determination, or *determinability*. The three syntheses transform the character and capacity of inner intuition (1) from an exclusion to a containment of spatiality in the first synthesis in order that conditions for "apprehension" be attributed to inner sense (KrV A99–100), (2) from a inconstant to a constant or continuous series within the temporality of inner sense in order that conditions for "reproduction" obtain within inner sense (KrV A101–02), and, on that basis, (3) from an indeterminate manifold to a conceptually determinable form of intuition, in order that the conditions for "recognition" obtain (KrV A103–10).

to our inner state, and as such are subject to the form of inner intuition and hence to the condition of time" (KrV B50).[6]

This necessary unity and interdependence between outer and inner perceptions, however, must again obtain within inner sense, for, as above, "regardless of the place of origin of our representations – whether they are produced through the influence of external things or inner causes – as modifications of the mind they belong to inner sense." Thus, "for their pertaining to inner sense, all cognitions must be subject ultimately to the formal condition of inner sense, to time." While evidently necessary, this inclusion of the conditions and contents of outer intuition within the form of inner sense is not self-evidently possible, on Kant's own terms, at least without "violating the character and limits of our sensibility," as determined by the heterogeneity thesis, to employ the phrase that Kant employed against Leibniz.[7]

Above, in exegeting the priority thesis – of intuition to intellection within the *ordo cognoscendi* –we read Kant's assertion that "the manifold for the intuition must be given prior to any activity of the understanding, and independently of it" (KrV B145). This prioritization implied a dy-

---

[6] Baumanns treats what is here termed the interdependence thesis as the "coordination" (*Koordination*) thesis, the independence or heterogeneity thesis as a "disjunction" (*Disjunktion*) thesis, and the dependence thesis as the "subsumption" (*Subsumption*) thesis. Baumanns denounces the "*Unklarheit über Koordination oder Subsumption des äußeren Sinnes*" to inner sense – even before what he terms the *Disjunktion* thesis is added in the Refutation of Idealism. See Baumanns, Peter: *Kants Philosophie der Erkenntnis: Durchgehender Kommentar zu den Hauptkapiteln der "Kritik der reinen Vernunft"*, Würzburg 1997, pp. 178–182. Baumanns (ibid) treats Kant's treatment of inner sense as universal representation, "*das Medium aller synthetischen Urteile,*" as an *Inbegriff*, "*darin alle unsere Vorstellungen enthalten sind,*" (KrV A155, B194) on p. 182 ff.

[7] Lachièze-Rey, in *L'idéalisme kantien* (Paris, Vrin, 1972), juxtaposes Kant's positive and negative claims regarding the determinability of inner intuition. Kant is recorded as asserting (1) a "*parallélisme entre l'object du sens externe et celui du sens interne*" (p. 155). Kant also (p. 2) "*nous présente souvent sa critique comme une demonstration de l'impossibilité de convertir la representation 'je pense' en intuition ou de la completer par une intuition*" (p. 189). (Lachièze-Rey reviews the relevant assertions of the heterogeneity thesis from the Paralogisms, and juxtaposes these to Kant's contrary assetions in the Analytic, on p. 96.) This "impossibility" must be retained, according to Lachièze-Rey, since the conditions required for a categorical determination of inner sense in a *Seelenlehre*, would obtain thereby. Reininger, indeed identified a "paralogism" in Kant's doctrine on the basis of the undecidability between these two equally necessary construals. See Reininger, *Kants Lehre vom inneren Sinn und seine Theorie der Erfahrung*, 1900, p. 150.

namics of the act of cognition (in which the object of intuition to which we are related passively is "taken up" into the understanding in order to be determined to objectivity by the pure concepts of the understanding) as well as a merely formal or static enumeration of the elements of cognition, in an architectonic of cognition. On this dynamic basis, Kant was able to determine that the understanding has laying before it a manifold of a priori sensibility, offered to it according to the principles of the Transcendental Aesthetic. By means of this primitive receptivity, the *materium dabile* of intuition, *in concreto*, as an individual, and in a relation of immediacy to the faculty of cognition, can be "offered to," given dynamically or transposed to, the understanding in order to be determined by the pure concepts – that same material for the pure concepts without which the activity of the understanding would be, simply, "empty."

Kant reasserts the priority thesis again at KrV A77, B102: "this [intuitive] manifold, in order to be turned into a cognition, must first be gone through, taken up, and combined in a certain manner." This imperative is founded on the principle, adduced above, that only the interdependence of intuition and intellection yields the conditions for an object of experience. However, without the capacity of inner intuition to contain within itself the *materium dabile* received by and in outer sense, the content of cognition cannot be transposed to the understanding, and the integrity of the act of cognition itself – as well as the transcendental determination of its possibility-conditions – is threatened. It is for this reason that "the mode in terms of which we likewise take up into our faculty of representations all outer intuitions" (KrV A34, B51) is a central rather than peripheral theme to the transcendental determination of the nature and limits of our cognition.[8]

This amplified construal of inner intuition and its role (whether rendered formally, as *Inbegriff,* or dynamically, as a principle for the transi-

---

[8] As Kant notes also at *Loses Blatt* B 12 (Ak XXIII, p. 19): "all appearances are nothing for us unless they are taken up into consciousness." Paton (*Kant's Metaphysics of Experience* (London: Allen and Unwin, 1976), v. II. p. 421), with reference to KrV A702, B730 as well, is especially attentive to this *ordo cognoscendi*. First, "the manifold must be originally be given to outer sense." It is only on being transposed through inner sense that we may be "aware of it before our minds." Only if so transposed is it "given to inner sense as well" (p. 421). Regarding this "*processus*," Nabert notes a "*les intuitions externes [...] doivent entrer dans le sens interne pour être soumises aux lois de l'entendement*" ("L'expérience interne chez Kant," in: *Revue de metaphysique et de morale* 31, 1924, pp. 205–268, p. 266).

tion from outer sense to the understanding) requires the representative *capacity* rather than representative *incapacity* of inner intuition. It will only be by means of the conditions required for a synthetic determination of inner sense as an *Inbegriff* that, "through these latter principles [of the possible presentations of inner sense], the principles of mathematics and general dynamics" as synthetic determinations of intuition by the understanding, "acquire one and all their possibility" (KrV A162, B202). Only if inner intuition can contain within itself an object originally given to outer sense can this *transitus* or *processus* – in the terms Kant will use to depict this aporia in the *Opus postumum*[9] – through the heterogenous manifold of inner sense and its pure temporality, wherein alone it could be presented to, or "gone over and run through (*Durchlaufen* and *Zusammennehmen*)" by the understanding. Kant will assert that it is, then, "in time, as form of inner sense" that "all cognitions must one and all be ordered, connected, and brought into relations" according to its formal character and conditions.[10]

Such an inclusion, however, may seem problematic, given Kant's claims that time as form of inner sense cannot include, on principle, but rather excludes, spatial form, its characteristics, and its capacities,

---

9  E.g., Ak XXII, p. 38.
10 The fundamental question animating such construals, of course, remains that of KrV A213, B260: "*wie in einem denkenden Subjekt überhaupt, äußere Anschauung, nämlich die des Raumes (einer Erfüllung desselben Gestalt und Bewegung) möglich sei.*" Baumanns (ibid) worries that the resolution to this question would require the "*Zusammenstimmung der inneren Erfahrung, der Selbsterfahrung der denkenden Natur mit der äußeren Erfahrung*" in an "*Innen-Außen-Union*" as would violate the heterogeneity thesis and the expressed limits of our (inner) sensibility (p. 686). Further, Baumanns recognizes that this integration risks introducing the conditions required for a "*körperlichecommercium*" (p. 686), which itself risks construing the "*denkende Ich [als] Korrelatum.*" Such a Korrelatum would implicitly contain the formal conditions necessary for the "*Möglichkeit der Objektivation des Seele*" (p. 685). But just as Baumanns can worry that inner intuition will be unable to perform its *positive* function, Benoist can worry that inner intuition will be unable to perform its negative function. Benoist (*Kant et les limites de la Synthèse: Le sujet sensible* (Paris, PUF, 1996) notes the ultimately critical or negative position of the first Critique doctrine of inner sense: "*dans la Dialectique,*" Kant will "*combattre [...] l'usage métaphysique c'est-à-dire ontologique*" of its manifold. Only this negative construal of inner sense will ground Kant's "*critique radicale du concept d'âme,*" which will thus be "*relégué au rang des illusions fondatrices de la métaphysique,*" precisely that of "*l'idée d'un sujet comme sujet donné*" (93).

from its manifold.¹¹ The contravening "exclusiveness" or heterogeneity thesis, then, that Kant would apply in the critique of *Seelenlehre* in the Paralogisms of Rational Psychology in the Transcendental Dialectic, can be seen clearly in two assertions regarding inner temporality: first, on its aspatiality, from KrV A381: "in us, there does not occur any relation of place, or motion, or shape, or any determination of space at all," and, second, regarding its inconstant and indeterminate temporal succession, from KrV B413: "in inner intuition we have nothing permanent at all." For this reason, Kant there asserts, inner intuition "yields absolutely no cognition," for if "an object is to be given, we must lay at a basis a permanent intuition."

Kant's competing thesis on the capacity of inner intuition – as dominant in the Analytic as the heterogeneity thesis is in the Dialectic – can be seen equally clearly at KrV A210, B255: "time is the formal a priori condition of all appearances universally," and "any progress of perception, no matter what the objects may be, whether appearances or pure intuitions," is to be understood as "nothing but an expansion of the determination of inner sense." In the tension between these two theses on the character of our self-cognition lies the aporia of inner sense. It is to Fichte's,¹² and thereafter Husserl's surprisingly similar identification of, and attempt to resolve, this tension that I would like now to turn.

---

11  Dieter Sturma, in *Kant über Selbstbewußtsein: Zum Zusammenhang von Erkenntniskritik und Theorie des Selbstbewußtseins* (Hildesheim, Georg Olms Verlag, 1985), first considers inner intuition, and *"die Form desselben a priori, die Zeit,"* in terms of the universality thesis: *"all mentalen Akte [...] als Modifikationen des Gemüts zum Inneren Sinne"* (p. 79). Sturma also notes, however, the equal salience of the heterogeneity thesis, and the resultant inability of inner intuition to inscribe spatial form and content. This *"aporetisch Theoriesituation"* results from the aspatial temporality of inner sense: *"Diese Strukturierung oder Formierung ist eine Bedingung der Möglichkeit der kognitiven Erfassung von gegenständen äußerer Reflexion"* (p. 81; see also pp. 90–92, 94–95). Sturma does not deny the *"intrikaten konzeptualen Problemen"* involved in this tension.

12  Baumanns (ibid) has placed *"Das Hauptproblem"* of *"die Bestimmung der Zeit als Anschauungsform"* (p. 148) as the context for (a) Kant's second edition Refutation of Idealism, (b) the *Übergang* and *Selbstsetzungslehre* of the *Opus postumum* (p. 147), and (c) Fichte's critique of Kant's "Zeittheorie" in the *Grundriß* of 1795 (p. 148) in ibid, IV. 4. *Transzendentaler Raum-Zeit-Idealismus und Evolutionstheorie der Erkenntnis*. Baumanns pushes forward his analysis of *"Zeitkonstitution"* in all of its complexity, through the (problematic) *Disjunktion* thesis (bewteen *"Das Ich in der Welt"* and *"Die Welt im Ich,"* see p. 152), noted above and termed herein the heterogeneity thesis (p. 150).

## II. Fichte: From Inner Intuition to Intellectual Intuition

Fichte's announcement of the need to defend Kantian philosophy from skeptical critique in his first publication, the *Aenesidemus Rezension*, is well-known.[13] But Fichte there defended Kant's philosophy only by means of a concession: "Kant has not traced the pure forms of intuition, space and time, to a unified principle, as he has done for the categories," in the manner required for a synthetic or intuited unity of cognition.[14] For this reason, Fichte was constrained to admit – in precisely the same terms that Husserl will use – that "much work is required, in order to bring the elements [of transcendental philosophy] into a well-integrated and unshakable whole."[15] Kant could not have secured the requirement for such a principle by means of an interdependence in intuition, Fichte suggests, "in accordance with his intention to sketch [the possibility conditions] for only [physical] science," the *Körperlehre* of outer sense, and instead assert the impossibility of the rational sciences of rational psychology and rational theology as *Seelenlehre*, or 'doctrines of the soul.'[16] Thus, Fichte claims that "the skeptical question concerns simply the question of a transition, or *Übergang*, from outer sense to inner sense, and reciprocally from inner sense to outer sense."[17] Fichte's intention, then – if not yet the meaning or significance of this intention – is made clear: "if inner intuition is made possible, then [skepticism] will be refuted," and the central intention of the critical philosophy ensured.[18] For this reason, Fichte suggests, "the thematic of the forms of sensibility is the most difficult to comprehend" as well as the most important.

---

13 On this theme, see the important articles of Breazeale: "Fichte's 'Aenesidemus Review' and the Transformation of German Idealism," *Review of Metaphysics* 35, 1982, pp. 785–821, and "Fichte on Skepticism," *Journal of the History of Philosophy* 29, pp. 427–453, 1991. See also Michael Baur, "The Role of Skepticism in the Emergence of Geman Idealism" *The Emergence of German Idealism*, Baur and Dahlstrom, eds. (Washington, D.C.: Catholic University of America Press, 1999), pp. 62–91.
14 SW I, p. 19.
15 Ibid, p. 25.
16 Ibid, p. 19.
17 Ibid, p. 15.
18 Fichte identifies "the decisive battle" already in the second paragraph of the Aenesidemus Review: it is not ultimately over Reinhold's *Elementarphilosophie* and its integrity, but instead "the most authoritative document of the new philosophy, the *Critique of Pure Reason*."

As the opening pages of Fichte's early *Grundriss des Eigenthümlichen der Wissenschaftslehre in Rücksicht das theoretische Vermögen*[19] also proclaim, Fichte intends to set out the manner in which the I can be "determined by the -I," passively related thereto, and "how and in what manner" the noematic correlate of that relation, the object of outer sense qua particular [*des Besonderen*] individuated in intuition, "can be thought, in its presence, within a rational being".[20] For Fichte, "Kant presupposed the [possibility that] a manifold [*ein Mannigfaltiges*]" of outer sense and its objects "can be absorbed into the unity of consciousness."[21] Fichte, instead, "must *prove*" — by means of a "deduction" — that a manifold — and a determinate object of intuition, *in concreto* — is given for possible (inner) experience."[22] Fichte thus identified as problematic the "absorption" of the object of outer sense into the faculty of cognition, and to this difficulty designated a "mediating intuition." This mediating intuition served primarily as an *Übergang:* it was "posited within ourselves" while yet "corresponding to something outside of us." The deduction of this adequation is "most important" for Fichte.[23] Indeed, it is "the basis of all the harmony which we assume to exist between things and our representations of them," between mind and world.[24]

---

19 SW I, pp. 331–411.
20 Ibid, p. 331.
21 Ibid, pp. 332–33.
22 Ibid, pp. 334–35.
23 SW I, pp. 375, 392.
24 Ibid, p. 377. The "basis for this [previously] only assumed harmony," then, as Fichte had already conceded in the *Aenesidemus Rezension*, was not secured by Kant. Only with the revision of the character and capacity of inner intuition was Fichte able "to show how the opposed terms are synthetically united and related to the I" (SW I, p. 348) and united within the sphere of inner intuition, "as posited within the I" (SW I, pp. 344, 350, 352, 355). In this way, "inner intuition (the intuition of the sensor) and outer intuition (the intuition of what is sensed)" are shown to be "one and the same," and each "impossible without the other" (SW I, p. 355). Only then can the -I or sphere and determinate objects of outer intuition be "*in* and *for* the I." Only then can each of these elements obtain in a *totum* of synthetic cognition, within an *Inbegriff aller Vorstellungen* capable of containing the determining subject and determined object together for the sake of synthetic cognition, both "activity and passivity, internally united in a unified state" (SW I, p. 369). Such interdependence is no less than "how things must be if any relationship and synthetic unity are to be [demonstrated to be] possible and necessary." Baumanns, in his treatment of the *Meditationen* (J.G. Fichte, *Kritische Gesamtdarstellung seiner Philosophie*, Karl Alber Verlag, München, 1990), treats this "*Selbstbeschränkung des Ichs*" on p. 43 ff. Baumanns

I have written elsewhere on the structure of, and development within, Fichte's *Grundriss*.[25] Here I will only indicate Fichte's own understanding of its task and accomplishment: "in the *Critique of Pure Reason*, Kant begins his reflections at a point at which time, space, and a [single, unitary] manifold of intuition are [assumed to be] already present in and for the I." In the *Grundriss*, instead: "we have now *deduced* these a priori," in their universality and necessity. Thus, "they are now [legitimately] present in the I." This deduction allows Fichte to claim that "we have now established the distinctive character of the theoretical part of the *Wissenschaftslehre*," But through this 'distinctive character' we may also establish the relation between Fichte's *Wissenschaftslehre* and Kant's doctrine of intuition and its role in the theoretical philosophy. For having committed to defending Kant's philosophy from skeptical critique, Fichte is now able to "take leave of our reader – who will find himself precisely at the point where Kant begins," with the doctrines of space and time as forms of intuition in the (now amended) Transcendental Aesthetic.[26] Thus one can see that the myth regarding Fichte's *Wissenschaftslehre* propagated by Kant in his famous *Open Letter* of 1799 and again in the *Opus postumum* regarding the *Wissenschaftslehre* as a "pure logic" is, however rhetorically successful, simply erroneous.[27] The task of Fichte's

---

    also treats of the characters of *Nacheinandersein* and *Zugleichsein* and their compatibility with "*Raumliche und Zeitliche Anschauungsformen*" (see p. 45 passim). However, Baumanns (in ibid, 2.2.3), identifies as relevant to this *Entgegensetzen des Nicht-Ichs im Ich* the "*Kategorie der Realität*" (p. 73), the "*Kategorie der Negation*" (p. 74), and the "*Kategorie der Limitation (Begrenzung, Bestimmung).*" Baumanns does not, however, acknowledge the intuitive rather than merely intellectual problem-context for Fichte's critique. This limits the effectiveness of his analysis, even when he treats of the "*grundcharakteristische*" of and in the "*Dialektik des Ichs [...] in der Spannung von Sich-Setzen und Entgegenstzung eines Nicht-Ichs.*" Even in this context, Baumanns continues to conceive of the *Einschrankung* at issue in this "*Urkonflikt der Ich-Setzung und Nicht-Ich-Setzung*" as not intuitive but intellective, implicative instead of the *Kategorien* of "*Negation, Limitation*, and *Wechselwirkung*" rather than *Limitation*, etc. as possible *Merkmale* of outer and inner intuition (p. 60). Baumanns has directed us, helpfully, to a central concept in Fichte's earliest philosophical work, but the problem-context for both the *Meditationen* and the *Grundriss* is not first a "conceptual," intellectual, categorial determination of "limit," but an intuitive determination thereof, and its role in Kant's theoretical philosophy.

25 "Fichte's Critique of Kant's Doctrine of Inner Sense," see note 1, above.
26 SW I, p. 411.
27 For the less well-known reference in the *Opus*, see Ak, XXI, p. 207: "a science of knowledge (*Wissenschaftslehre*) in general, in which one abstracts from its matter

propaedeutic *Grundriss* is to secure rather than abandon the Kantian doctrine of intuition and its passivity thesis, and to amend instead the heterogeneity thesis.

But this theme appears throughout Fichte's early writings, both published and unpublished. Fichte's *Meditationen ueber Elementarphilosophie*, for example, written in the winter of 1793, were intended neither for publication nor for purposes of instruction. Intended only for Fichte's personal use, the *Meditations* evince the priority and centrality of this problem-context to Fichte's early philosophy.[28] The *Meditations* announces itself in its first pages as an "elementary philosophy," which for the limited purpose of this essay can be understood simply as concerned with articulating "determinate processes in our mind" according to "the most fundamental, most general laws which one can find as obtaining in the mind."[29] In this exercise, "each proposition" of an elementary philosophy will obtain as the result of "an experimentation in inner intuition, accomplished according to [its] determinate laws," and accomplished "against the fallacious character of the accusations of Maimon" or in order that such skeptical critiques be rendered innocuous. Thus Fichte's first imperative: '*Schaue dein Ich an!*'

Fichte's intention, and "the end of the elementary philosophy" itself, is to deduce the manner in which this inner intuition "is compatible with the conviction in the existence of outer objects," as was already announced in the *Aenesidemus*. Indeed, this question still concerns for Fichte "the exigence of Aenesidemus,"[30] Fichte announces that "our ob-

---

    (the objects of knowledge) is pure logic, and [...] is, conceptually, to chase one's own tail."

28  *Meditationen ueber Elementarphilosophie*, GA II/3, pp. 21–177. This document yields for interpretation less the order of reasons Fichte will follow in his mature expositions of his philosophy, than his own order of discovery, and the problem-context for this discovery. The *Meditationen* are propaedeutic, critical, and charged with securing the conditions for the possibility for the definitive doctrinal *Wissenschaftslehren* still to be acheived. Importantly, Fichte will in 1800 indicate the authority of the *Meditationen* over the *Grundlage*, and claim indeed the context for his later thought as lying in and with the former rather than the latter (see GA III/4, p. 357; letter of 15 November 1800). For a more sustained account of the relation between Kant, Reinhold, and Fichte in the *Meditationen* than that attempted here, see Isabelle Thomas-Fogiel, *Critique de la représentation: Étude sur Fichte* (Paris, Vrin, 2000). I will here allow myself to rely on the exceptionally lucid analyses of ch. 1, pp. 19–33.

29  GA II/3, pp. 21, 23.

30  Ibid, p. 30.

jective lies in the comprehension of the nature of our receptivity," and, given the dynamics of cognition inherited from Kant, what could be thought as "common to time and to space."[31] This objective remains paramount in order that the conditions for the possibility for the *ordo cognoscendi* definitive of the act of synthetic cognition be demonstrated to the skeptic: "the task for a philosophy of the elements must be, then, to answer 'how is this possible,' or rather 'how can this be understood'? Precisely this is what the elementary philosophy is to understand." In fact, "the elementary philosophy as such concerns itself only with demonstrating the impossibility of all cognitive activity without such an intuition."

Opening the Second Main Division of the *Meditations*, Fichte asks repeatedly "what is inner intuition?"[32] He worries that "until now," and as inherited from Kant according to the letter of the heterogeneity thesis, "inner intuition and outer intuition" have been "deduced" as "contradicting," or as "negating" the other.[33] In the second principal division of the *Meditations*, Fichte insists that his own "deduction" will "still concern intuition, and here particularly inner intuition," in order to "be able to determine the necessary connection between inner sense and outer sense, by means of a third term."[34] The full complexity of this 'deduction,' which might seem to risk, in Fichte's own terms, "vain scruple" and "pedantry," need not detain us – neither the complete context nor content of this document can be made articulate in this brief article.[35] The task of Fichte's deduction, however, can and therefore should be made clear to demonstrate the manner in which "inner intuition integrates outer intuition, which is space, within its temporality." For only "in this way, inner intuition would be effectively deduced."[36] Only in this way, and "as a consequence," would one "have found the necessary connection between the two forms of sensibility."[37] For "if there is to be a synthesis, the necessary character of this *übertragung* must be demonstrated." It is precisely this interdependence that one must demonstrate, since "by this alone is cognition possible."[38]

---

31 Ibid, pp. 72–73.
32 Ibid, p. 74.
33 Ibid, pp. 82–83; for a similar critique of Kant see ibid, p. 91.
34 Ibid, p. 75.
35 Ibid, pp. 74 and 157.
36 Ibid, p. 83.
37 Ibid, p. 84; see also pp. 100–101.
38 Ibid, pp. 98–99.

Fichte opens the Third Main Division[39] with a review of the dynamic act of synthetic cognition. In this, the object of and in "outer sense," in terms of which we are "passive," is to "be affected by inner sense" or taken up into its own temporal manifold: "from this [transition] is generated intuition" as such. Such intuitions are only then "ordered by concepts in accordance with the synthetic unity of apperception." Such are "the operations that are effected upon the object of outer sense." The "intermediate power" or *medius terminus* that is inner sense, as a "*nexus*" is charged in particular with "ordering" and "determining the reality of these intuitions" in accordance with its own formal character.[40]

Inner intuition, then, "determines in the I [the] admissibility" conditions for any possible synthetic cognition. Any object determined in accordance with the principle of transcendental unity "must already and first be intuited" according to the laws of our sensibility.[41] This *ordo cognoscendi* requires that we begin transcendentally "not from a pure consciousness" as a logical consciousness "but from the possibility of empirical consciousness" in the doctrine of intuition. For this reason, too, the diversity or distinction between inner sense and outer sense "that must be integrated into a [single] consciousness."[42] The resolution to their "disparity" is "the highest task of philosophy" to attempt. For in this account of the dynamics of cognition, "the I gives to itself a -I as within the I." Regarding the priority thesis, of outer sense to inner sense, Fichte comments: "here then is the proof that without the representation of the -I, no consciousness of the I is possible." By this proof, "we have arrived at the same point as has Kant" on the necessary priority of a synthetic to an analytic unity of apperception, though through a demonstration rather than a problematic claim.[43]

---

39  Ibid, pp. 129–177.
40  Ibid, pp. 129, 134.
41  Ibid, p. 130.
42  Ibid, p. 131.
43  Ibid, p. 142. Only in this context of the requirements of sensible intuition does Fichte advance the concept of an intellectual intuition. To the determination of the possibility of synthetic cognition, Fichte advanced the necessity of the determinability of inner intuition as an *Inbegriff aller Vorstellungen* (as permanent, and limited, as containing spatial form within itself, etc.; see p. 122). Only thus can the *ordo cognoscendi* be determined transcendentally. By means of the determinacy of this inner intuitive manifold, further, the "I presents itself to itself as intuited, intellectually." Intellectual intuition is a species of intuition, the intention of which is not however sensible but is instead intellectual, the sphere of which lies not in outer sense but in inner sense. Intellectual intuition is proposed upon a

In spite of Fichte's remonstrance for his own "pedantry" or punctiliousness, cited above, the significance of these unpublished meditations even as revealed by our cursory review is not minor. Both for his identification of Kant's "ill-formed synthesis" of the relations and characters of inner and outer sense, and for his own amplification of the doctrine of intuition (a project taken up in the same terms by Husserl), the *Meditations* merits a thoroughgoing attention, one that scholars have yet to dedicate to the essay and that we have only begun to attempt herein.[44] Fichte herein develops not only a definitive transcendental (rather than skeptical or dogmatic) critique of Kant's critical philosophy, but equally, and constructively, the principle for both the *Anstoss* of his later theoretical, and the *Aufforderung* of his later practical, philosophy.[45] For our present purposes, however, it is less important to evaluate such projections than to identify the basic problem-context for, and content of, Fichte's early philosophical work. Fichte's first insight and philosophical contribution was occasioned by the skeptical challenge in the *Aenesidemus*, intimated in the *Meditationen,* and prosecuted in the *Grundriss*. But it is unintelligible in each case, a merely formal algebra, if we have not clarified the aporia that Fichte was attempting to resolve. The aporia of inner sense contextualizes

---

double exigence: Fichte notes that "Kant asserted that a concept without intuition is empty" and remarks for his own part that both "intuition and concept pertain to representation," which requires that "the I must be determined as both intuiting and as thinking" (p. 144). For this is required an intuition not merely sensible but, equally, intellectual. It is of significance to note that Fichte remarks that "strictly speaking, it is not the I as such but the relation of the -I to the representing I that must be thought" through an intellectual intuition. It is not first "the I thinking the I" as object of inner sense but "the I thinking the -I" as object of outer sense, and "as realized in intuition" that must first be attained (p. 151). Only thereafter does the self-relation of the I, as both subject and object and as ordered according to the intellectual (rather than intuitive) laws of identity, negation, and excluded middle, obtain for transcendental analysis. Fichte does not fail to note the implication of this advance with regard to Kant's own architectonic, and indeed his own prosecution of this late philosophy of religion: it is "here that one finds the reason for the Kantian attacks against the transcendent use of the forms of pure thought" in the critique of rational psychology and theology (p. 151, note). With Fichte, and "in our system, these [elements] are not contradictory and empty chimeras as they are in the *Critique of Pure Reason*, and must not be." For this theme one may now consult the magisterial analyses of Tilliette in *L'intuition intellectuelle de Kant à Hegel* (Paris, Vrin, 1995).

44 GA II/3, p.103.
45 See ibid, pp. 151 ff for Fichte's own assertion thereof.

the character of these early propaedeutic works, just as these early works contextualize the later *Wissenschaftslehren*, including those advanced after 1800.

## III. Husserl: From Inner Intuition to Eidetic Intuition

I would like now to argue, through a necessarily brief exegesis, that a series of Husserl's investigations into the structures of inner time-consciousness can be understood, both in terms of their context and their content, by means of the Fichtean critique of Kant's doctrine of inner intuition just elaborated. On this basis, I will suggest that the identification and clarification of Kant's doctrine of inner sense illuminates not only the relation between Kant and Fichte, and hence German Idealism, but also the relation between Kant and Husserl as well, and thus provides an important aid in understanding the development, and our inheritance, of $19^{th}$ and $20^{th}$ century European philosophy.

Already in his early *Phenomenology of the Consciousness of Internal Time* from 1905, Husserl had sought to provide "the fundamental founding of the doctrine of original time consciousness."[46] This required an investigation into both "the structures of sensibility" as such and a more sustained and "profound investigation into time-consciousness" itself. In §44, for example, entitled "Internal and External Perception," Husserl set out this order of his analysis in three stages: (1) "the appearance for consciousness of something external," (2) "the constituting consciousness in which the appearance of something external becomes constituted as something immanent," and (3) "the attentive awareness in consciousness to the appearance and its components as to *that which* appears, which implies an "immanent appearance of the external object."

This problem-context for – and hence significance of – Husserl's investigations is set out still more clearly in the *Analyses Concerning Passive and Active Synthesis* and its account of "the structure of lived experience" as both intuitive and intentional.[47] Just as Kant committed to "starting from the bottom upward" at KrV A120–121 in order to determine

---

46 HUA, X, p. 95.
47 Husserl, Edmund: *Analysen zur passive Synthesis*, in: Fleischer (ed.): *Husserliana* vol. XI, 1966; *Analyses Concerning Passive and Active Synthesis*, Collected Works IX, trans. By Anthony J. Steinbock (Kluwer 2001). See Introduction, Part 5. For the readers convenience, citations herein reference the section, German pagination, and then English pagination of this edition.

the order of the act of synthetic cognition, and just as Fichte in the *Grundriss* had traced the dynamics thereof from passive reception to the spontaneous determination of that which is thereby given in the *Grundriss*, Husserl's *Synthesis* lectures too "begin from below and ascend upward" (Introduction, Pt. 9). This Husserl will prosecute (within "the framework of the phenomenological reduction" as explicated in §26, of course) in order to accomplish the task of a "transcendental-phenomenological aesthetic," itself propaedeutic to a transcendental-phenomenological logic.[48]

Husserl invites his reader to "begin with any external perception." Normally, in a "natural attitude" or a "thematic basic attitude" we are "directed toward the external object," or "turned toward external things" (Introduction, Part 10). If we "turn to the sphere of our external experience," we may come to understand the manner in which "the world is given to us originally through external perceptions" (§§22–23) in what was termed the "process of acquisition" (§2). However, this "external experience" contains implicitly "a complex structure of consciousness that emerges in the nexus of consciousness and its motivations" in acts of apprehension (§23). On this basis, then, "let us turn back to the immanent sphere" in order to make explicit the hidden or invisible, intrinsic structures that make possible such experience of external objects (§24). External experience in this way "serves as a starting-point from which we must turn away in order to get hold of something new in our conscious lived-experience" (Introduction, Part 10). Even external perception "is an intentional lived-experience and has immanently, within itself, an intentional object as an inseparable sense" within the sphere of "immanent being" (ibid).

Thus Husserl will direct us through a three-fold process from "1. concrete lived-experience of perceiving, to 2. appearance," as evident within

---

[48] Husserl there "traces the constitution of sense through passive associative syntheses leading up to the constitution of the object as such through intellectual acts." This 'leading up' implies a movement from the perceptual to the conceptual or judicative, from an aesthetic to a doctrine of synthesis. This passage, then, will take us from "*Vorgegebenheit* [pregivenness]" to object formation "*Gegenstaendlichkeit*." In this passage or "*progressus*," our original passivity is recognized and retained as a "founding level of experience" the "subsoil" of life, and provides "the basic, essential conditions of the possibility of a subjectivity itself" (ibid, p. 163 ff). For discussion, and for manuscript references and secondary source treatments of Husserl's intention to revise phenomenologically the transcendental aesthetic, see pp. xli-xliii, and xxiii of the Translator's Introduction to the English Edition, ibid.

the immanent sphere, in light of a reflective change of perspective through which I grasp it and then judge it thematically, and 3. the intentional object as such," as an intellectual act (Introduction, Part 10). The aporia of inner sense, of course, concerns only the *mysterium minorum*, the *intuitive* problem represented by the relation between 1 and 2, which is merely propaedeutic to the *mysterium maiorum*, the purely *intellectual* problem represented in 3. Husserl in spite of this clarity does not claim that "phenomenology has already progressed so far that it would have neatly solved the genetic problems existing here."[49] He will claim, however, have the problem-context for such solutions clearly in view: phenomenology "is far enough along to be able to specify these problems and to sketch the method for their solution" (ibid).

Phenomenology is sufficiently developed to recognize the origin or source of these problems, most specifically in "Kant's system of transcendental syntheses in the transcendental deduction of the first edition of the *Critique*," in which the three syntheses led to the depiction of time as form of inner sense as an inclusive *Inbegriff* (§27, 125–26, 171). However, in specifying problems for resolution, Husserl first identifies the problem that Kant "unfortunately only had in mind there the [...] problem of the constitution of a spatial, worldly object," as Fichte had worried in the *Aenesidemus*, "of an object that transcends consciousness."[50] For Husserl, Kant's "question was only this; what kinds of syntheses must be carried out subjectively in order for things of *nature* to be able to appear, and thus a *nature* in general" (ibid)?

---

49 See §26; pp. 119, 164.
50 On this point, see ibid, pp. 275–76, 410. Husserl suggests that "it is of some historical interest here to recall Kant's brilliant insights, as expressed in his profound but obscure doctrine of the synthesis of productive imagination, in the first edition transcendental deduction." Thus, we may claim that the reception and critique of the doctrine of time as form of inner sense of Kant places phenomenology in a position already occupied by Fichte. The concern with the temporality of inner intuition is as central to the work of the early Fichte and to Husserl as the heterogeneity thesis is foreign. Husserl records literally hundreds of pages, as variations on this theme, to the effect that "external perceptions must arise in the immanent stream [of consciousness] and must arise from this continuously" in order that "internal time possess both a position and a duration for consciousness" (HUA XI, p. 234; and ibid, p. 292). A precise understanding of the horizon for Husserl's exertions can only be given in the doctrine of time as form of inner sense and the heterogeneity thesis of Kant. The implications for this rejection of the heterogeneity thesis, however, either by Husserl's successors or in Fichte's own later philosophy, has yet to be widely understood.

For Husserl, however, "lying deeper and essentially preceding this is the problem of the purely immanent, object-like formation and constitution of the inner world" as an immanent and intelligible world (§27, 125, 170). Husserl reasons – and here only an adumbration of Husserl's exposition even in these single sections can be attempted – that since "the spatial world is constituted through consciousness," it "can only be there for us as existing and can only be conceived at all by virtue of certain syntheses carried out in immanence."[51] Thus, the experience of a world "presupposes" a more fundamental "doctrine of the [...] universal synthetic forms of immanent constitution" (ibid, 126, 170).

The immanent syntheses Husserl would identify as a particular problem for transcendental-phenomenological analysis, then, are "most particularly, the syntheses concerning *the content of what is exterior to the [immanent] transcendental synthesis of temporality*" (ibid, 126, 170). Indeed, for Husserl, this problem possesses a most general rather than partial or derivative significance: "the phenomenological task, then, will be to seek precisely such syntheses" (ibid). For not only in external perception, but also and by means of a "*processus*" and "in immanent time-conscious-

---

51 The tracing of the "storied structure of constitution" as a "*progressus* of graduated levels" however is "only a beginning" (*Analysen*, §48, p. 219) This beginning reveals the proper character of inner intuition and its necessary function within the *ordo cognoscendi*. We have not yet addressed the thematics consequent upon the fulfillment of this necessary function, once the determinability of inner intuition is secured. This first problematic concerns the *transitus:* "what belongs essentially to something like physical nature?" in order then to see how something of this sort gives itself to consciousness. The consequent problematic concerns the manner in which, or "how it gets [constituted and] legitimated in consciousness [...] with respect to all its essential aspects [...] shaped according to *noesis* and *noema*" (ibid, p. 222). This latter is "the most radical problem of a transcendental logic, to understand how in the streaming egoic life that is the life of consciousness – this life itself can be constituted as a true being, as the ideal correlate of possible verification, as an ideal norm which according to essential laws lies *in* consciousness, and more precisely, in the self-givings belonging to it" (ibid, p. 255 ff). But the aesthetic-theme is a theme for logic propaedeutically; "so that later in its freedom the ego can seize hold of it and can make it manifest," in the 3rd moment indicated above. This problem leads Husserl to the higher problem of "the pure science of logos, the science of the essence of logos as logos, that is, of knowledge of knowledge" (HUA XXXI, pp. 256, 390). But this intellectual problem can only be addressed properly if preparatory (intuitive) analyses have already been accomplished. "Pure logic must yield essential insight into how consciousness as such contains sense, how within itself it makes objects present to consciousness, and then how it necessarily makes them present to consciousness as an objectlike formation" (§48, p. 222).

ness, a spatio-temporal world is given" as "contained within immanent time-consciousness" (ibid, 105, 155).[52] In this *Inbegriff* that is inner time-consciousness, the object of outer sense that is "structured externally" must be "structured immanently" (ibid, 111, 156) as determinable so as to yield "the identical *dabile*" (ibid, 110, 155) for both cognition and recognition.

Nonetheless, Husserl will advise that we "work within the limitations of the transcendental aesthetic."[53] Herein, "objects of possible perception have the necessary *Sinnesform* of time," while "objects of possible external perception also have the *Sinnesgestalt* of spatiality." But this basic Kantian thesis regarding our intuitive forms need only be expressed, according to Husserl, in order to evince "the incentive for pursuing the drawing of a parallel between temporal and spatial form still further." This parallel will be drawn in order that "the accomplishment of transcendence actually comes about in the immanence of lived-experiencing" (ibid, 303, 590), in order that, as Husserl so often repeated, "being and being-intended coincide,' and in order that we 'posit the immanent in connection with the

---

52 *Erste Philosophie*, (HUA VII, Erster Teil, [Haag, Nijhoff, 1956]), p. 276. For reasons of space, I will defer a full discussion of Husserl's *Erste Philosophie* (e. g., HUA VII, pp. 232–72). and *Erfahrung und Urteil : Untersuchen zur Genealogie der Logik* (Meiner, Hamburg, 1972), translated as *Experience and Judgment* (Northwestern University Press, Evanston, 1997), and their both clear and extended depictions of this theme. I would note in the latter the important series of reflections from §36 (entitled "The Passive (Temporal) Unity of Perception) to §38 ("The Necessary Connection, on the Basis of Time as the Form of Sensibility, between the Intentional Objects of all Perceptions and Positional Presentifications of an Ego"), to §41 ("The Problem of the Possibility of an Intuitive Unity between Objects of Perception and Objects of Imagination of one Ego"). These, taken together with §42 (both Parts A; "The Temporal Unity of all the Lived Experiences of an Ego," and C, The Intuitive Unification of the Intuitions of Perception and Imagination on the basis of Association, and the Broadest Concept of the Unity of Intuition") effectively reproduce the progressive series of determinations in Kant's first-Edition Deduction, by granting cumulatively to time (1) a spatio-temporal unity (§36), (2) a constancy to its purely successive flux (§37), and (3) a determinability to its manifold (§38–39, §§41–44, concluded in §64) in which inner intuition appears thoroughly determined as an *Inbegriff*. See also §64, Part A; "Immanent Time as the Form of Givenness of all Objectives in General"). Here, I can only indicate that this problem-context provides "the great theme of a more fully worked-out phenomenology of time-consciousness" (§38).
53 HUA XI, pp. 295, 581.

real world."⁵⁴ In this last statement, a more familiar and distinctly Husserlian vocabulary and theme begins to emerge, but only out of this less familiar, but evidently crucial, transcendental context.

I must indicate, however, an affectation. When Husserl in the same text claims that this "point of entry" will allow him to "open to a totally new domain of consciousness" which due to "the imperfections of prior research" had "never before been thought," he does so after and in a crucial respect in the same way as did Fichte (ibid, 283). This anticipation, or prefiguration, can be seen not only in the *mysterium minorum* of inner intuition, but in the *mysterium maiorum* of the self-alienation of consciousness. Husserl extends his analysis from the propaedeutic problem of inner intuition and its temporal form, to the consummating problem of the intellectual consciousness of consciousness. When Husserl elevates his analyses to the more widely reported problem of "the essence of logos as logos; that is, knowledge of knowledge," he again follows Fichte. When Husserl in that latter context names as a problem the *Ich-Spaltung* that is generated when "intellectual consciousness returns upon itself [*Ein sich zurueckbiegen*]" he again works within a thematic horizon opened up – though not for the first time – by Fichte. In other words, when Husserl discovers the *Ich-Spaltung*, he rediscovers Fichte's own "original insight."

I would suggest, then, that Husserl's claim to have "opened up a world that had never before been thought" should be amended in light of our analysis of both Kant's problematic doctrine of inner intuition and Fichte's anticipation of Husserl's critique. I would also suggest, then, that the unacknowledged importance of Fichte to the character and development of phenomenology can be appreciated on this basis. Perhaps it could be said that Fichte's influence over the founding and development of phenomenology is actual not in spite of, but instead to the degree to which, it was unrecognized, as Husserl set out on a path of thinking already taken by Fichte. This status as a precursor, even if only evident retrospectively and for a historiography, extends no less to Fichte's later philosophy of religion, which unexpectedly provides a model for an understanding of the development of phenomenology after Husserl in a way that Husserl's own does not. For the "turn to religion," taken in contemporary phenomenology repeats the themes of the later Fichte's work in the same way that Husserl repeated themes in the

---

54 For the former locution, see, for example, *Analyses on Passive Synthesis* Section 24. For the latter locution, see, for example, *Lectures on Inner Time-Consciousness*, Appendix, p. 136.

early Fichte's work. On this basis, one could say that the one hundred-year progress of phenomenology repeats at least in terms of this guiding theme the roughly twenty years of Fichte's written work. For these reasons – both for the *terminus ad quem* of its telos and for the *terminus a quo* of its origin – phenomenology may return to Fichte as well as to Husserl as a guide for its further research.[55]

---

[55] I examine, for example, Michel Henry's critique of Kant (in "*Le Concept d'ame a-t-il un sens?*," *Revue Philosophique de Louvain*, n. 81, 1966) and reception of Fichte (in *L'essence de la manifestation* [PUF, Paris, 1963]) in this light, and examine the significance of this "inheritance" or lineage for the philosophy and phenomenology of religion, in "Una fenomenologia trascendentale, Un'e epistemologia fichtiana: L'eredità fenomenologica di Fichte in Husserl y Henry," Metamorfosi del transcendentale. Percorsi filosofici tra Kant et Deleuze (Editrice Università di Padova, Padova, 2008), pp. 16–52.

# Body and Intersubjectivity: The Doctrine of Science and Husserl's *Cartesian Meditations*[1]

VIRGINIA LÓPEZ-DOMÍNGUEZ

Universidad Complutense de Madrid

The fifth *Cartesian Meditation* probably constitutes the best proof of the tremendous impact of Fichtean anthropology on Husserl. It brings into philosophy, now understood as a rigorous universal science[2], the idea that the constitution of the world rests upon a transcendental intersubjective community, to which one may accede phenomenologically through one's own body, conceived of as an originary sphere. Husserl's development of this theme is very similar to that laid out by Fichte in Paragraphs V and VI of his *Foundations of Natural Right*.

Husserl's interest in Fichtean anthropology was already apparent in Göttingen, where in 1915 he gave a seminar on *The Vocation of Man*. But it was the three lessons entitled "The ideal of man in Fichte", delivered in 1917 to soldiers returning from the battlefields and repeated one

---

1 This work belongs to the Research Project UCM 2005–930499: "La filosofía alemana contemporánea".
2 In its scientific pretensions, philosophy has two demands or requirements: that of grounding (it is a form of knowledge without suppositions) and that of systematisation (it postulates the total unity of knowledge). See Husserl, Edmund: *Logische Untersuchungen* I, HUA XVIII, §§ 4–11; and *Ideen zu einer reinen Phänomenologische Philosophie*, HUA III, Introduction pp. 3–9. These two characteristics mean that transcendental phenomenology constitutes a theory of science, which not only receives the Fichtean name of *Wissenschaftslehre* (see, e.g., Second Part of *Vorlesungen über Grundprobleme der Ethik* (1908–9), HUA XXVIII, § 7 a), p. 284 f.; *Formale Typen der Kultur in der Menschheitsentwicklung*, HUA XXVII, p. 83; *Cartesianische Meditationen*, HUA I, p. 181 or *Logische Untersuchungen* I, HUA XVIII, §§ 5–11), but also, as in Fichte, includes formal and ontological aspects. In the *Cartesian Meditations* Husserl calls this universal science of transcendental subjectivity "phenomenologico-transcendental idealism" (HUA I, § 62, p. 176) and in *Crisis* (HUA VI, § 73, p. 272 f.) he states that it is "a self-reflection of humanity, a self-reflection of reason".

year later,[3] which constituted a landmark in the development of phenomenological thought. The second of these lessons, "World's ethical order as the creative principle of the world",[4] signals the beginning of a transformation in phenomenological ethics, as it passes from an intuition of values to a "thematisation" of subjectivity as responsibility, after making an ethical reflection on culture. The circumstances of the War allowed Husserl to emphasise the exhaustion of European culture and the profound crisis of values it was undergoing, and to urge an ethico-political renewal of humanity.[5] Philosophy, with its ability to determine the meaning of

---

3   Concerning these lessons, Husserl wrote at the time to Adolf Grimme: "the religio-philosophical perspectives opened up to me by phenomenology show a surprising relation of proximity with the late theology of Fichte" (1918).
4   HUA XXV, p. 267 ff.
5   "What the war has revealed is mankind's indescribable misery, which is not only moral and religious but philosophical." Husserl's letter to William Hocking (3-7-1920), HUA XXVII, XII.
    "This war, the deepest and most universal sin of mankind in all its history, has laid bare all current ideas in their impotence and lack of authenticity… The present war, turned into a war of the people in the strictest and most awful sense of the word, has lost all its ethical sense"… "For the ethico-political renewal of mankind what becomes necessary is an art of the universal education of mankind, which would be sustained by the highest ethical ideals, clearly established, an art in the form of a powerful literary organisation to illustrate humanity and educate it by leading it along the path of truth", to Winthrop Bell (11-8-1920), HUA XXVII, p. XII.
    "Renewal is the general clamour of our troubled present, and this is so in every sphere of European culture. The war which has devastated it since 1914 and, since 1918, has limited itself to preferring, instead of military means of coercion, the "more elegant" ones of morally degrading spiritual torture and economic penury, has revealed the intimate lack of truth, the lack of meaning of this culture. Precisely this discovery means that the authentic impulsive force of European culture is exhausted". (I, 1. *Erneuerung: Ihr Problem und ihre Methode*, HUA XVII, p. 3.) [All translations are my own.]
    "What is needed is not only a doctrine of ethical principles, which is only and always formal, but a theoretical science of universal reach which will investigate the entire realm of the theoretically cognizable and which will lay it out in a multiplicity systematically woven together with particular sciences. What is needed, in short, is universal science placed under the direction of a life insomuch as it has to be concretely undertaken and it has to be achieved as far as possible to perfection […]. Rather than a mere individual ethics as formal doctrine of the principles of the rational life of man as an individual, what is needed above all is a social ethics whose maximally specific elaboration would make it possible for all individual actions to be submitted to concrete norms". (*Formale Typen der Kultur in der Menschheitsentwicklung* (1922/23), HUA XXVII, p. 87.)

life, was seen as a possible saving force capable of ethically transforming humanity by showing an individual that "in acting he is free, that is to say, a free citizen in a society destined to be free".[6] *Meditation* V should be placed within this context of the promotion of mutual understanding and respect for others, and transcendental otherness can be interpreted as a foundation of pluralistic ontology, i.e. as the basis of a world which, being valid for all, allows for multiple perspectives of configuration irreducible in its difference, that is, for a monadological community.

Like Husserl, Fichte considers "monadism" as a starting point in his explanation of intersubjectivity. His position is based on making a decision implied by one's choice of the first principle of philosophy. Given that such a decision is of an ethical nature, since it is an attempt to explain the world from the I or the thing, in the basic dilemma between freedom and determinism, it must necessarily be individual and untransferable. Such a decision conditions the methodology to be used, because the path to be followed will lead one to derive the other (the non-I) from a position of subjectivity, since the I is the only point of reference beyond all doubt in experience and, as in Descartes, constitutes an unquestionable starting point, both certain and reliable, and which, emptied of all empirical connotations, without pre-judgements, is, therefore, originary.

The main difference between the two authors is that in Husserl the act of freedom, of gratuity and spontaneity, from which philosophy begins and on which abstraction rests, is not sufficiently well highlighted, or not laid out in all its consequences. It comes across as nothing more than a theoretical choice in the cognitive effort to arrive in a radical manner at truth, i.e. at full, scientific truth. In Fichte, on the other hand, although one finds the same concern to transform philosophy into a science ensuring an indubitable and unconditioned starting point, emphasis is placed on the fact that choosing a first principle is an act of an ethical nature.[7] The founding character of practical action is made evident from the outset, and therefore also the idea that the aim of all philosophy is that of achieving a rational explanation of the social world. For the same reason, the deduction of intersubjectivity is first carried out in the realm of the foundation of principles of law and then incorporated into the *Doctrine of Science nova methodo* as another element in the sys-

---

6   Husserl, Edmund: *Fichtes Menschheitsideal* II: "Die sittliche Weltordnung als weltschaffendes Prinzip", HUA XXV, p. 279.
7   See Fichte, Johann G.: *Erst Einleitung in die Wissenschaftslehre*, GA I/4, §§ 3–5 and p. 204 f.

tem.[8] As a consequence, it is clear from the beginning that the system is at the service of the construction of political life, just as Fichte stated in the famous letter he sent to Baggesen in 1795.[9] This construction is achieved through law, understood as the only objective authority capable of regulating relations between subjects. In this way, Fichte follows the path laid out by Kant in his writings on philosophy of history, especially in "On Perpetual Peace."[10] However, the fact that social explanation should rest on a monadic basis points, from a philosophical consideration, to the metaphysical doctrine of Leibniz, and to its political application in the historical sketches of *Accesiones historicae* The latter work was the first well-grounded theoretical attempt to find harmony or consensus in a Protestant Germany which, locked within the dictates of its own inner heart and divided into a multitude of principalities, was then being torn apart by religious strife. The monadic starting point not only ensured individual freedom, which was strictly necessary in an ethical approach like that of Fichte, allowing one to conclude the inescapable responsibility of actions, but also served to uphold cultural and political differences between the distinct principalities as well as that between Germany itself and the unifying advances of France, underway ever since the end of the Thirty Years War.

Like Fichte, Husserl thinks that man, the individual, constitutes himself as an *Eigenheitsphäre*, but the conclusions derived from this same thesis are not identical in the two authors, precisely because the deduction of otherness is not contextualised in a juridico-political manner. Indeed, the term *Eigenheitsphäre* translates as "field of belonging", that which is di-

---

8   The first appearance of a reference to this theme is in a text on the French Revolution, i.e. in a context of the founding of political life, or rather of the foundation of the juridical order emanating from the Revolution. The second is in *Einige Vorlesungen über die Bestimmung des Gelehrten* (GA I/3, p. 34) and in the GWL, GA I/2, p. 337.
9   GA III/2, p.300. See also GA III/2, p. 298. "My system is the first *system of freedom*. Just as that nation [France] has broken the political chains of man, so mine, in theory, tears man from the chains of the thing in itself and its influence [...] and provides him with the strength to liberate himself also in praxis through the sublime animus which it transmits. My system arose during this nation's years of struggle for its freedom thanks to a previous inner struggle against old rooted prejudices. Seeing its strength has transmitted to me the energy I needed for it, and during the research and justification of the principles on which the French Revolution was built, the first principles of the system acquired clarity in me."
10  GNR, Einleitung, § III: "Ueber das Verhältnis der gegenwärtigen Theorie des Rechtes zu der Kantischen", GA I/3, p. 323 ff.

rectly linked to the intentional act, to the spontaneous activity of the I which spreads out as it leaves itself, in a reference which never comes to merge with an external object, leaving the activity reduced to its merely theoretical aspect. In Fichte, and even in Hegel, the free activity which realises itself through limitation, i.e. by providing itself with a determined sphere of manifestation proper to itself, belonging exclusively to it, refers to the phenomenon of appropriation which consciousnessess make of the world around them, such consciousnessess being understood as forces that can enter into litigation in their dispute for domination of the world. The theme of property, which was essentially that of landed property, since land was the source of wealth par excellence in contemporary Germany, constituted the basis of all legal regulation. The first act of appropriation, and the question of whether it was practised upon the body itself (as in Fichte) or on material goods (as in Hegel) respectively determined the socializable or private nature of property and the role played by the individual in the social and political whole.

For Husserl, on the other hand, the greatest concern was to avoid solipsism,[11] to explain the coherence and, above all, the universality of the experience of the I, although it has to be said that the result turns out to be the same as in Fichte: the body is the sphere of belonging of each consciousness and the means by which it becomes materially possible to relate to other concordant subjectivities, a relation which leads to the constitution of one's own subjectivity. It is clear that Husserl also sought to achieve a philosophy of "conciliation" which respected individuality, but the fact that the basic context of appearance of the alter ego is not related to the subject matter of property, but only to that of the constitution of the meaning of the world. This shows that his intention was to facilitate a renewal of the culture of humanity, still reeling from the consequences of the First World War, at a moment when the capability for social understanding had been lost, to a large extent because such capability had been assumed by the State and its institutions. The phenomenological message of holding to facts obliged philosophers to take the War and its after-effects into account and to recognise that it had become impossible to sustain the sort of trust Fichte illustrates in the ability of the

---

11 Husserl, Edmund: *Meditation* V, § 42. Cf. Lessons of 1910/11 on fundamental problems of Phenomenology (HUA XIII, pp. 11–195) and § 96 of *Formale und transzendentale Logik*, Epilogue, HUA V, p. 150; HUA VIII, p. 433 and Letter to Ingarden, p. 31. Fichte also responds to the objection of solipsism in ZwE, GA I/4, p. 4, passim, especially Para. I, p. 210, note.

State to promote internal and external concord, to make it materially possible to approach Kant's kingdom of ends and, consequently, happiness.

In the two authors, the characteristics acquired by the body are similar to one another, especially if one follows Fichte's description in the *Wissenschaftlehre nova methodo*. This work solves many of the difficulties and obscurities of previously attempted formulations of the Doctrine of Science. For example, the starting point of the system is no longer the pure I but the reciprocal relation between Ego and world,[12] so that the body plays a decisive role both in the link between theory and praxis and in the internal articulation of both fields. For it is presented as the necessary place for the constitution of the I and the consciousness, for the explanation of the finite being in general. It is for this reason that it is described, as in Husserl, as the system of sensibility.[13] It is a framework of sensations, of cross references, which are held fixed as a totality, despite the variation of its members and the appearance of new sensations. It represents the general framework within which these elements are woven together and because of which they acquire a meaning. Or, rather, it is literally "the possible sum of changes, according to their form, in complete abstraction from their contents". In sum, it constitutes the very determination of "alterability" (*Veränderlichkeit*) which makes it possible to perceive plurality and its concrete variations, an indispensable transcendental condition for the appearance of sensations in the consciousness.[14] The body is thus presented as an organism, even though it is not expressly recognised as such in this passage. It is seen as a whole that lives and becomes reality through its members but which in turn makes the existence of its parts possible by sustaining them in a totality which differentiates and generates itself.

With this new definition, the organic body comes closer to Husserl's characterisation of it and the reference to two different types of organs (inferior and superior) becomes unnecessary, as does the postulation of

---

12 WLnm-K (F. Meiner), p. 62. See § V passim and cfr. also WLnm-H, GA IV/2, p. 18 f. and Meiner, p. 12 f. Fichte had already used this opening in previous work, e.g. in ZwE, GA I/4, p. 186.
13 WLnm-K (F. Meiner), p. 120 and WLnm-H, GA IV/2, p. 68 / Husserl, Edmund: *Meditation* V, § 44, p. 160, §§ 52 and 54. For bodiliness and synaesthesis see Presas, Mario A.: "Corporalidad e historia en Husserl," in: *Revista Latinoamericana de Filosofía*, Buenos Aires, vol II, 2 (1976) pp. 167–177. For a German version, see "Leiblichkeit und Geschichte bei Husserl,", in: *Tijdscchrift voor Filosofie*, Lovaina 40/1 (1978) pp. 112–127.
14 WLnm, p. 68 and WLnm-H, GA IV/2, p. 118 and WLnm-K (F. Meiner), p. 90.

two different kinds of matter (brute and subtle),[15] distinctions which could only have metaphorical value after the discovery of the neuron and the research findings of early-twentieth-century atomic physics. Fichte's concern regarding this theme derives from the simple need to present the body as an instrument[16] acting efficiently on the Non-I and it serves to fill in the gap between theory and praxis or, more exactly, between the spiritual and material worlds. Yet this is a question which becomes secondary or irrelevant when posed in the directive context of the constitution of the meaning of the world by an intentional consciousness. At heart, these distinctions respond to the need to overcome dogmatic anthropological dualism, which recognised a soul separated from the body.

The *Doctrine of Science nova methodo* manages to overcome this dualism by referring only to an internal organ, the soul, and an external organ, the body, which constitute a unique I seen from two different viewpoints: "the soul emerges if I sensitize myself through the form of internal intuition, the body emerges through the "sensitization" of external and internal intuition at the same time."[17] In this sense, it cannot be said that the body is an instrument for the I, as if it were a tool exterior to it. For it is a starting point which we have constantly to overcome in order to undertake acts that transform the world and which, nevertheless, recaptures us again and again, given that we are irremissibly bound to it (*Gebundenheit*).[18] It constitutes, rather, our way of being installed in the world, a world, which the I has found upon acting and which is therefore primarily the place in which actions and their ends are carried out. In short, it is the way of adapting to a world set out teleologically from the beginning:

> What is my body but a certain perspective of my causality as intelligence? According to this my body would be a producing of concepts, because I am thought of as a body by a sensitive *thought* reaching out in space and transforming itself into matter.[19]

Man is a systematic unity where every characteristic is such with reference to all others. He is a moment in a primary unity lending coherence to all. And if such coherence comes about, this is because it constitutes a unity of meaning, a knot of significations. From that primary unity stems its

---

15 GNR, § 6.
16 GNR, § 6, GA I/3, p. 378. In the WLnm Fichte maintains this characterisation .
17 WLnm-K (F. Meiner), p. 171, cfr. p. 211 f. among others.
18 WLnm-K (F. Meiner), p. 120.
19 WLnm-K (F. Meiner), p. 197.

life principle and this principle is freedom, activity, self-possession and self-affirmation, which is lived and realised in each of its parts and actions. Every psyche belongs to a determined organism and vice versa, because the psyche is organic and the organism is psychic. This is the meaning of the body as "psychophysical unity" in Husserl.[20]

As a result, the reception of one's own organism is not comparable to that of any object. It can only be lived and felt from within in full identification with one's own I, which becomes transparent to itself. According to Fichte, this occurs because of a feeling (*Urgefühl*), which is the most primitive or originary of all.[21] The intuition of the I as an object is secondary and is based on an abstraction of the world in which the I has been spilt and on a turning of the consciousness upon itself, i.e. a free reflection:

> I intuit myself as a feeler whilst I feel as an intuiter of an object in space [...] the intuition of myself as an object comes later and is based on a reflection for freedom.[22]

Husserl was to call this primitive feeling the ""mundanising" apperception of myself" and explained that it reveals the "Ego in a reciprocal relation with the Non-I",[23] i.e. as in Fichte, it constitutes a synthesis in which the I and the Non-I come into contact for the first time, as spontaneity and receptivity relate. Because of this double belonging, the body allows the I to become conscious of itself as well as its surroundings.

Indeed, by presenting itself as the exterior side of interiority, the body places man in a physical world, where he acquires the function of spatial configurator, turning himself into an absolute place or axis from which all distances unfold, or, as Husserl puts it, into the "central here" of Nature.[24] The spatial regulation of the world thereby converges with the immanent configuration of lived experiences in time, the deduction of which Fichte had already undertaken in the *Foundations of the Entire Doc-*

---

20 "If I reduce myself as a man I obtain my organic body and my soul, that is to say myself as psychophysical unity and, in this unity, my personal I, which, in this organic body and by means of it acts upon the exterior world and suffers from the action of it," (Husserl, Edmund: *Meditations* V, § 44, p. 128. See also § 55, p. 153 and § 58, p. 161.) As can be seen from the cited text, Husserl also takes into account the physical character of the body, as an efficient receptor and instrument of actions in the world.
21 WLnm-H, GA IV/2, p. 118.
22 WLnm-K (F. Meiner), p. 120.
23 Husserl, Edmund: *Meditation* V, § 45.
24 Ibid., § p. 53. Cfr. WLnm-K (F. Meiner), p. 121.

*trine of Science*. This deduction refers to the constitution of representation initiated by the oscillatory motion carried out by the imagination when it comes up against the obstacle of sensation, or rather, to the feeling of limitation.[25] In this way, the body individualizes subjectivity, for it accords an nontransferable point of view, which would become incompatible with others if it did not also constitute – as Fichte thought – the immediate place of expression of freedom, of the tendency towards absolute affirmation,[26] which is a vehicle of the universal and consequently of moral law.[27] The admission that the rational being places itself in space as a being that tends practically, like a will,[28] forces one to transcend the mechanistic vision of the world configured from the body and to recognise that nature is the place where its aims are realised. In fact, Fichte was to propose Teleology as the final synthesis of the *Wissenschaftslehre nova methodo* – something he had previously rejected but now accepted as a scientific discipline whose object of study was the physical world understood as an analogon of freedom.[29] But in addition, the assumption of one's own body as the exclusive sphere of freedom not only opens up the individual to the relation with others, founding the idea of the juridical person, but also and at the same time represents access to the cultural world, because the work of culture begins with the care and elevation of sensibility.[30] All of this is possible because of bodily "ductility" (*Bildsamkeit*),[31] the body's ability to model itself according to its needs.

In the *Foundation of Natural Right* Fichte holds that man is born in a full state of non determination, being originally nothing. For, as abandoned by nature, he has practically no instincts to show him the path to follow.[32] This lack of determination and precariousness in the face of nature forces him, on the one hand, to place himself in the hands of the species and to create culture as a second nature to protect himself.

---

25  GWL, GA I/2, p. 360 f.
26  WLnm-K (F. Meiner), p. 120.
27  GWL, GA I/2, pp. 398 f., 404 f. and especially p. 432 ff. The body is the sum of determinability which considered sensibly shows itself as individuality, but thought of suprasensibly it appears as a moral law. WLnm-K, GA IV/2, p. 139.
28  WLnm-K, GA IV/2, p. 122. "The transcendental concept of the body is: it is my originary will considered in the form of external intuition", WLnm-K (F. Meiner), p. 160.
29  WLnm-K (F.Meiner), p. 238 ff.
30  Fichte, Johann G.: *Einige Vorlesungen über die Bestimmung des Gelehrten*, GA I/3, p. 31.
31  GA I/3, p. 383.
32  GA I/3, p. 379.

But, in addition, it allows him to transform his own body. For within it, there exist many options he may freely choose, even individually, employing for human functions, such as language, organs that in other species are pre-determined for natural functions like feeding. This capacity for self-formation also appears in Husserl, since for him the body constitutes the synthetic unity of an infinite system of potentialities or, as Fichte would put it, a whole with the capacity for "articulation towards the infinite".[33] However, the theme of bodily "ductility" does not acquire in the *Meditations* the importance it possesses in Fichte, due to a large extent to the fact that each philosopher was responding to a different cultural and scientific context. For his explanation of "ductility," Fichte makes use of suggestions deriving from the theory of evolution recently formulated in the First Part of *Ideas for the Philosophy of the History of Mankind*, which resulted in polemic between Herder and Kant on history. He adapts these suggestions to an anthropology which thinks of man as a cultural being, as in Kant, and not exclusively as the result of natural forces created by God, as in Herder. Seen in this way, bodily "ductility" is the effect of human freedom and for this reason allows one perfectly to distinguish the human organism from that of animals, transforming it into a place of recognition between rational beings, due mainly to the mouth and eyes.[34]

Of course, it might seem at first that this perspective does not fit well into phenomenological ways of thinking. Husserl does not allude directly to freedom or will in *Meditation V*, given the noumenical character of both ideas. But the fact is that when referring to the human body, he not only defines it as fields of sensation but as the only sphere in which "I command and govern in an immediate manner."[35] As a consequence, he also recognises, in that primordial world which is nature reduced to property, the presence of predicates that possess meaning from the psychophysical I, for example, those of value and work.[36] Only on the supposition that in the phenomenon of the world such meanings exist can access be gained to the sphere of culture, to the ""mundanities" (*Weltlichkeiten*) of superior degrees".[37] As in Fichte, it is

---

33 Husserl, Edmund: *Meditation V*, § 48, p. 136, See also §§ 44, 129, and § 46, passim / GNR, §§ V and VI, especially SW III, p. 60.
34 For this issue, see my article "Die Idee des Leibes im Jenaer System," in: *Fichte Studien* XVI, (1999), especially p. 282 f.
35 Husserl, Edmund: *Meditation V*, § 44, p. 128.
36 Ibid., § 44, 129.
37 Ibid., § 55.

values and aims, that is to say ideas, which configure the intelligible world. And they also have a bearing in the last instance on the constitution of the ambit of sensibility.[38] For the statement that the world of man is a cultural universe and not merely natural must constitute a strong thesis for a philosophy which, starting from the phenomenon, i.e. from the manifestation of things to man, attempts to reconstruct the genesis of all meaning. It is precisely in this theoretical context where otherness becomes a necessary element in the construction of general meaning, thus avoiding the objection of solipsism.

In keeping with the phenomenological method, Husserl sees the guiding thread of the constitutive theory of experience of the strange as the other experienced just as it is given directly to the consciousness with its ontico-noematic content. This means that there is no doubt that we experience that others truly are and that, moreover, they are objects of the world. Yet the problem is that they do not present themselves as mere natural things but as psycho-physical objects governing psychically in their corresponding natural organic bodies, i.e. as subjects for that world which I experience myself.[39] The question to be resolved is then, as in Fichte, that of explaining how the admission of other rational beings is produced, i.e. it is one of recognition (*Anerkennung*).[40] And the answer is similar in both authors: the explanation of the phenomenon of otherness is a complex process involving the body, but experience itself as produced in practice constitutes an immediate synthesis which according to Fichte

---

38 *Ueber den Grund unserer Glauben an einer göttlichen Weltregierung*, GA I/5, p. 353 f.; *Appellation an das Publicum gegen die Anklage des Atheismus*, GA I/5, p. 431; WLnm, GA IV/2, p. 125, among others.
39 Husserl, Edmund: *Meditation* V, § 43. In § 48 Husserl even uses Fichtean terminology: "The factum of the experience of the strange (Non-I) presents itself as the experience of an objective world and of others (Non-I in the form: other I)", p. 136.
40 In the *Vorlesungen über die Bestimmung des Gelehrten*, Fichte argues that philosophy, understood fundamentally as anthropology, as a theory of man, should answer certain questions, among which the first has to do with grounding natural law and consists in clarifying what authorises us to consider a part of the Non-I as ours and to assume it as our own body; the second is how we come to admit and recognise other rational beings as our like, when neither determination is immediately supplied in our self-consciousness. (GA I/3, p. 34). Incidentally, these issues had already been considered by Jacobi in the *Letters to M. Mendelssohn on the doctrine of Spinoza* (Werke IV, p. 211).

is not accessible "by custom or teaching but by nature and reason",[41] which Husserl, though without much conviction, called *Einfühlung*.[42]

For Husserl, the recognition of otherness corresponds to an embodied, "sensibilized" human subject, a member of an exterior world and capable of distinguishing itself from it. This Ego-monad is the true starting point, for it is in it that the intentionality occurs which is directed at the other through remission to itself. The stranger comes across as a reflection of oneself thanks to an analogizing or assimilating apperception, a type of mediated intentionality which, starting from the perception of the physical body of the other, transfers to it the organic character of my own body. This is an organicity I know perfectly, for it is I myself, as a psycho-physical being, who governs fully in it.[43] The association of facts implicit in this apperception is, therefore, indirect, for it evokes a similar appearance corresponding to the constitutive system of my organic body in space. Husserl thus calls this first intuition one of a "reminding" kind (*Erinnungs-Anschauung*).[44] As a consequence of this process, the meaning of the objective world is constituted against the background of the sphere of belonging of each, with the constitution of the alter ego or the You as the first step. This is a dual experience, termed coupling (*Paarung*),[45] through which another meaning is superimposed on the primordial world, conferring upon it objectivity and allowing at the same time the opening up of an infinite ambit, of other possible acts of creation of meaning which overlap with the first ones. An instance is the constitution of a community of monads which find themselves in a harmony established not metaphysically but phenomenologically.[46] This intermonadic community is eventually likened to humanity.[47]

---

41 GNR, GA I/3, p. 380.
42 Husserl had known Theodor Lipps' theory of the *Einfühlung* since 1905, possibly through Alexander Pfänder and Johannes Daubert, who had been disciples of Lipps. According to Iso Kern's Introduction to Husserl (*Zur Phänomenologie der Intersubjektivität*, en HUA, XIII, XXV), Husserl never accepted Lipps' theory and although he used the term *Einfühlung*, was unconvinced that it was correct. See, for example, *Erste Philosophie* (HUA VIII, p. 63), where the experience of the other through his/her bodiliness is defined as "experience through interpretation" and it is recognised that "this has recently been called *Einfühlung*, which is an inappropriate term". Cfr. HUA V, p. 109.
43 Husserl, Edmund: *Meditation* V, § 50.
44 Husserl, Edmund: *Meditation* V, § 53.
45 Husserl, Edmund: *Meditation* V, § 51.
46 Ibid., § 49. It is worth noting that for Husserl the originary self-appearance is purely passive (§ 55, p. 156). This coincides with Fichte, in the sense that it is

The "communalization" of the monads (*Vergemeinschaftung*) is the first form of objectivity, constituted by the common being of nature, of the organic body and of the psychophysical I of the stranger coupled with my own.[48] This common basis is what makes the *Einfühlung* of determinate contents of the superior psychic sphere possible. For these are found indicated through the body and its behaviour in the external world.[49] Given that all association is reciprocal, its comprehension reveals one's own emotional life in its similarity and difference with others.

Although this explanation seems to rely too heavily on theory of knowledge, it generally converges with that of Fichte. In fact, in the *Foundation of Natural Right* the relation with others is explained by reference to an external influence (*Einwirkung*), a remote action which does not assume the form of brute matter and is therefore termed appeal (*Aufforderung*). Although the presence of this external influence leads one to suppose from the outset the existence of a freedom outside the I, in fact this is finally resolved in the active formation by the subject of an image of the other.[50] In both cases, recognition begins with the appearance of the *alter* in the perceptive field of the I, when it places itself under its gaze and incorporates itself into that world which it has configured in identity with its body. But in addition, in neither case can the relation be reduced to a simple image. For the other appears before me as in person affecting my entire primordial world. It is therefore a dialectical relation which reverts to the first subject constituting it both as person and member of a community; in short, a relation between being and being, an existential determination which comes to complete self-recognition as a finite being, or, put another way, as an I in reciprocal relation with the Non-I or as a being open to the world. This mutual ontological determination, which becomes so obvious in the comparison with Husserl, allows one to reject out of hand the interpretation first ventured by Eduard von Hartmann, and developed by Martial Guéroult, which pointed to an alleged contradiction between the ideal phenomenalism and the transcendental realism which respectively characterise the Fichtean grounding of theoretical and practical fields. According to this inter-

---

produced in a feeling, which must then be actively elaborated through the imagination.
47   Ibid., § 58, p. 159.
48   Ibid., § 55.
49   Ibid., § 54.
50   Ibid., § VI.

pretation, theory is ruled by solipsism, since all reality is postulated by faith, having been produced by the empirical subject from private sensations and feelings. Yet in the second field, the demand for a moral postulate forces one to admit the existence of others as necessary, leading to altruism.[51] In response to this, it has to be said that in the *Foundation of Natural Right*, the starting point for the deduction of the body and of the other, is the unity of freedom and limitation, in other words, an ambit which comes before the separation between theory and praxis. In addition, the point of arrival and the sphere to be developed is that of natural law, which does not have anything to do with duty (*Sollen*) but with what is permitted (*Erlaubtsein*).[52] The deduction explicitly signals the function of the productive imagination, insomuch as it spatially configures the external ambit. But it also implies temporal configuration, insomuch as time is the general form of sensibility, for the body is at the same time the internal and external sensibilisation of the I, as it also occurs in Husserl.[53] As a result of all this, it has to be concluded that both the material community of which Fichte speaks and Husserl's later intermonadic version are situated in space and time and are thus historical, admitting change, though always within a transcendental horizon. It is this concession about difference in the heart of the community which makes a pluralistic ontology linked to the idea of harmony or dialogue possible, and which turns it into the adequate means, in the case of Husserl, for the required renewal of culture, and in that of Fichte, into the way of approaching the teleological community. This is the kingdom of ends, which, as an ideal, must necessarily place itself beyond all space and all time as a regulating goal of humanity.

---

51 Hartmann, Eduard von: *Geschichte der Metaphysik* II,. Leipzig, 1899–1900, p. 75 f. and Guéroult, Martial: *L'evolution et la structure de la Doctrine de la science* I, Paris, 1930, p. 339 f. As is explained by Pareyson, L.: *Fichte. Il sistema de la libertà*, Milano, 1976, 2ª ed. expanded, p. 397 ff., this line of interpretation gained widespread acceptance in 20th-century Italy because of its affinities with the philosophy of Gentile and Calogero. Cfr. GWL, GA I/2, p. 439 ff.
52 WLnm-K (F. Meiner), p. 145; WLnm-H, GA IV/2, p. 137.
53 Cfr. Husserl, Edmund: *Meditation* V, § 46 and §§ 55, 156.

III. Fichte and Heidegger

# Martin Heidegger Reads Fichte

JÜRGEN STOLZENBERG

Martin-Luther-Universität Halle-Wittenberg

The methodology in *Being and Time* was described by Martin Heidegger as "phenomenological".[1] Quoting Husserl, Heidegger summed up the motto of phenomenology as "Keep to the objects!"[2] Heidegger's exposition of the concept of phenomenology – "making the object visible on its own terms; showing what is shown exactly as the object shows itself"[3] – and to an even greater extent the explanation of the so-called "phenomenological concept of the phenomenon"[4] (according to this, the being of the existing is concealed and must first of all be indicated and represented with reference to its sense, its modifications and its derivatives) contain a piece of implicit criticism of Husserl's philosophy in spite of the acknowledgement of Husserl expressed in *Being and Time*.[5] This concerns in particular criticism of the concept of the "pure ego" which Husserl introduced in his *Ideen zu einer reinen Phänomenologie und phänomenologischen Philosophie* in 1913. Criticism of this concept – Husserl remained true to it even in his latest texts – had already inspired Heidegger's early outline of a "phenomenology of the self".[6] The theme of this is the factual, finite subject living in the world – what Heidegger, referring to these early lectures in *Being and Time*, called the "hermeneutics of facticity".[7] In such a study Husserl's "pure ego" is not to be expected. With regard to these discussions Heidegger's analysis of Fichte's philosophy and its idea of a pure ego and the corresponding statement "I am" in the summer semester of 1929 is of special significance.

---

1   Heidegger, Martin: *Sein und Zeit*, Tübingen 1927 ([16]1986), p. 27.
2   SuZ, ibid.
3   SuZ, p. 34.
4   SuZ, p. 35.
5   Cf. SuZ, p. 38, note.
6   GAH 58, p. 167.
7   SuZ, p. 72, note.

## I. "A new world"

"At the present moment I am lecturing on Fichte, Hegel and Schelling for the first time – and once more a new world opens up before me. It is the same old experience: other people cannot do your reading for you."[8] These are the words written by Heidegger to Karl Jaspers in a letter dated 25th June, 1929. How did Heidegger read Fichte? What kind of world opened up before him?

Heidegger, while examining Fichte, always had *Being and Time* before his eyes. When he says that at this time he perceived a whole new world, this does not mean that a new realm of thought was opened up to him, a rival, as it were, to his own convictions. It rather means that Heidegger became aware of the original quality of Fichte's philosophy in relation to his own theory in *Being and Time*. Heidegger's study of Fichte is seen to be an attempt to get the following two different things into a solid, rational relationship – congeniality and closeness on the one hand, distance and critique on the other. Here Heidegger's presentation of Fichte's philosophy takes on a certain systematic urgency through the discovery of discrepancies which themselves allow Fichte's individual conception to reveal itself. In Heidegger's view, however, the characteristics of this conception become limitations which must be surmounted and overcome in the direction of an analysis of existence (Dasein). Heidegger's reading of Fichte appears thus in a double hermeneutic perspective: We have here an attempt on Heidegger's part to give Fichte's view its own due precisely with the aim of emphasising and underlining the justness of his own claims.

In Heidegger's letter to Jaspers we cannot deny the tone of astonishment at all the things which became clear to him in the course of his work on the idealism lectures. Here, in relation to Fichte, we can point to the concept of the ego as "Tathandlung" (fact/act), Fichte's theory of thetic judgment and the grounding of the finite nature of the ego in the second and third principles. In addition we have Fichte's theory of imagination where the problem of the relationship between existence (Dasein) and

---

8   Martin Heidegger/Karl Jaspers: *Briefwechsel 1920–1963*, ed. Walter Biemel and Hans Saner, Frankfurt a. M., München, Zürich 1990, p. 123 (translation of quotations here and in the following by Kenneth Caskie).

temporality[9] in *Being and Time* is announced as it were in a "flicker of summer lightning"[10]. Strictly rejected, on the other hand, are the technical aspects of deduction and the system character of Fichte's *Doctrine of Scientific Knowledge*. Once the constraints of system have been laid aside and the content of Fichte's concept of "Tathandlung", the systematics of the principles and the theory of imagination have been grasped, Heidegger sees a perspective opening up which has its vanishing point in the conception of *Being and Time*. This is Heidegger's reading of Fichte.

What are we to make of this? Is Heidegger's interpretation of Fichte convincing? To put the question more precisely: Is Heidegger's interpretation of Fichte convincing *independently of* the assumed truth of the position adopted in *Being and Time?* Is there perhaps some "violation"[11] here at work – as Heidegger hiself admitted with regard to his Kant interpretation? Are we faced here in the last instance with "misconceptions and omissions"?[12]

## II. Being a self

Heidegger did not spare his audience. "The only possible way" he could see of gaining an adequate understanding of Fichte's topic and its problems was to "think through [the Doctrine of Scientific Knowledge)] *in toto* step by step".[13] And indeed Heidegger pursues Fichte's train of thought with an exactitude and perspicacity which impresses us and demands our respect. The first and decisive point is Heidegger's interpretation of the first principle of Fichte's Doctrine of Scientific Knowledge, the statement "I am".[14] This we can use as a model to present and evaluate the double hermeneutic perspective in which Heidegger read Fichte.

---

9 It is not possible here to give an analysis of Heidegger's interpretation of Fichte's theory of imagination, the background to which is given in Heidegger's interpretation of Kant (cf. GAH 28, pp. 163 ff.).
10 GAH 28, p. 170.
11 Cf. Heidegger's explanation in the preface to the 2nd edition of *Kant und das Problem der Metaphysik* (1950), here quoted according to the 5th enlarged edition, Frankfurt a. M. 1991, XVII.
12 Ibid.
13 GAH 28, p. 51.
14 For the following cf. GAH 28, pp. 55 ff.

First of all we have to bear the following points in mind. In §1 of the *Foundation of the Entire Doctrine of Scientific Knowledge*[15] Fichte introduces the statement "I am" in the course of a reflection on the conditions under which an unquestionable certainty exists that the statement "A is A" is a true statement. One of the essential steps in this reflection is Fichte's indication of the connection between the identity of A in the judgment "A is A" and the consciousness of the identity of the judging subject in its relationship to A both in subject and in predicate position, the latter being "united" in the judgment (the proximity to Kant's synthesis theory is quite evident here). This consciousness of the identity of the ego is expressed in the statement "I am I". Since the normal usage of the word "I" implies a relationship to something real, the consciousness of the identity of the judging subject directly implies the idea of its reality. This is expressed in the statement "I am."

The decisive step lies in Fichte's thesis that the statement "I am" is the expression of a "Tathandlung" (fact/act).[16] The argument for this thesis is derived by Fichte firstly from the status claim of the statement "I am" (we need not go into this more deeply here) to be the highest and unconditional condition of all judging; and secondly from the action-orientated interpretation of a judgment. Since judging is the expression of a mental activity and since the judgment "I am" is the highest and unconditional condition of all judging, there is at the basis of the judgment "I am" an action which has the sole function to produce the reality of that which is implied in the thought "I". In this way the reality of the ego can be described as an action which is in no way independent of the activity in the course of which it is realised and takes shape. This strictly functional connection of activity and action in the thought "I" is expressed by the concept "Tathandlung" (fact/act). Heidegger gives this careful consideration. He emphasises the peculiar manner of being which the ego has and which may be described (using Fichte's words) as "self-positing".[17] "The essence

---

15 GWL, pp. 255 ff. A detailed analytical reconstruction of the chain of thought in § 1 der Wissenschaftslehre may be found in the present author's "Fichtes Satz "Ich bin". Argumentanalytische Überlegungen zu Paragraph 1 der "Grundlage der gesamten Wissenschaftslehre" von 1794/95", in: *Fichte-Studien*, vol. 6, 1994, 1–34, cf. more recently: Ryue, Hisang: *Über Fichtes ersten Grundsatz "Ich bin". Kommentar zu dem § 1 der Grundlage der gesamten Wissenschaftslehre (1794/95)*, München 1999.
16 Cf. GA I/2, p. 259.
17 GAH 28, p. 65.

of being of this being of the character of the ego is self-positing."[18] This defines what Heidegger calls "a self". Being a self means being the basis of one's own reality.[19]

If one compares this presentation of Fichte's concept of the ego with Heidegger's commentaries on the modern theory of subjectivity, e.g. in the lectures on *The Fundamental Problems of Phenomenology* (1927)[20], one may be justified in speaking of a revision of his critical assessment in this respect. While in those lectures he talked of "an indifferent characterisaton of the subject as something present"[21], we must conclude that Heidegger has revised this thesis with regard to Fichte.

The real confrontation with Fichte, however, is to be found in what the editor calls a "parenthetical consideration of the 'I am'"[22]. This takes up Heidegger's discussion of the second and third principles of the Doctrine of Scientific Knowledge. The essential characteristics of these must now be presented.

### III. The finite quality of the ego

Here one may admire Heidegger's hermeneutic subtlety in using careful accentuation to make visible what according to Heidigger should be visible. This is the logically not deducible structure of the finite quality of the ego. Here, according to Heidegger, lies the real point within the systematics of the principles. More precisely, it is the partial indeducibility (conceded by Fichte) of the two other manners of action of the ego: the action of positing a non-ego in opposition in the second principle and the action of limiting in the third. As is well-known, it is Fichte's thesis that the second action *as action* is not deducible from the first principle. If, however, it is deployed – as is necessary when one takes as point of departure a different fact, the truth of the statement "-A not = A" and its analysis[23] –, then it must be understood as an act of opposing, where in the first action the self-positing of the ego is assumed. The necessity of a third action, however, is to be explained on the basis of the contradictory situation between the first and second principle; but this does not hold

---

18 Ibid.
19 Cf. GAH 28, p. 67.
20 Heidegger, Martin: *Die Grundprobleme der Phänomenologie*, GAH 24.
21 GAH 24, pp. 169 ff., pp. 191 ff.
22 GAH 24, pp. 108 ff.
23 Cf. GA I/2, p. 264 ff.

good for its content. The third action, the action of limitation, is due to what Fichte calls an unconditional "Machtspruch der Vernunft" (claim to power on the part of reason).[24] This may be understood as Fichte having recourse to the assumed repertoire of the mental activities of the ego, motivated by a desire to avoid contradiction; among these the action of limitation is to be found. Both manners of action, both the opposing and the limiting, provide the basis for the finite character of the ego. "The essence of positing – and so also of ego-ness – is finiteness"[25]. With these words Heidegger summarises his discussion of the three principles.

However, it is not so much the formal character of finiteness which Heidegger wishes to draw our attention to. What is of systematic importance for him is above all the significance which the action of opposing has for the ego. This lies in providing the structural possibility by means of which a horizon of a world is opened up for the ego. The concept of world, which Heidegger identifies as Fichte's concept of the non-ego, has thus its sense and meaning only in relation to the original positing function of the ego. In this, according to Heidegger, one must agree with Fichte: The sphere of the non-ego, the world, is merely a function of the ego and, to be more precise, of the finite ego.[26]. The second point in which one must agree with Fichte is the fact that the action which opens up the horizon of a world for the ego is not deducible from the concept of the self-positing ego. In actual fact, it has the same original quality as that concept.

This is true, too, of the third manner of action, the action of limitation. This concept cannot be logically deduced either, but is due – as Heidegger emphasises along with Fichte – to the above-mentioned "Machtspruch der Vernunft" (power claim of reason). And so in the end it becomes evident that the basic structure of the finiteness of the ego can by no means be deduced logically. It can only be shown to be a final condition, resistant to further analysis. This is the third point in which, according to Heidegger, one must agree with Fichte.

---

24 GA I/2, p. 268.
25 "Das Wesen des Setzens – damit der Ichheit – ist die Endlichkeit" (GAH 28, p. 91).
26 Cf. here Heidegger's comment: "The essence of the ego includes something like an opposing element as such; the ego as ego stands in relationship to the *contrasting thing*. This contrasting thing is not the non-ego being itself, but the horizon into which the ego *projects itself.* Projecting, however, as relating to." (GAH 28, p. 77; emphasis as in the original).

From this Heidegger derives a decisive thesis. This has to do with a number of problematic questions which are inherent to the system and which Fichte did not actually deal with separately; they lie concealed within the system itself and are, according to Heidegger, insurmountable. They have to do with the tension lying between the content itself, i.e. the uniform structure of the finiteness of the ego, and its presentation, which is necessarily influenced by the systematics of the principles. Heidegger's diagnosis is that Fichte is attempting here (in the form of the three principles) to put something in words "which is basically not conceivable as such". Heidegger goes on to say that this "becomes evident in the third principle."[27] This principle makes it clear that the finiteness of the ego and not the self-positing ego of the first principle is the true foundation of philosophy.

Here we may observe in Heidegger's Fichte interpretation a developing tendency towards nothing less than a revolution of the Fichtian idealist manner of thought.

Seeing that the Fichtian system of principles only leads to the ineducibility of the finite ego, Heidegger makes a strong plea for a representation of the uniform structure of the finiteness of the ego which renounces any claim to absolute certainty and ultimate grounding, and thus any claim to be an "absolute ideal of scientific knowledge".[28] The reason is, as he says, that this structure cannot possibly be made into something which has "absolute certainty and grounding"[29]. This naturally leads on to the methodical demand that the function of the self-positing ego must be deployed and represented in a way that makes it quite clear that it is situated, so to speak, at the centre of the facticity of the ego and its finiteness, i.e. something which can only be demonstrated descriptively and which does not lie outside this. It must be made clear that the construction of the finite ego in actual fact contains the reason by which an understanding of the function of the self-positing ego is possible. This is a reversal of the Fichtian idealistic manner of thought and it lies behind Heidegger's note: "The other way round: use the problem of the non-ego in order to understand what the search for ego-ness implies."[30] A remark of Heidegger's, given in an editor's appendix, goes in the same direction, openly using the language of *Being and Time*:

---

27 GAH 28, p. 91.
28 GAH 28, p. 92.
29 Ibid.
30 GAH 28, p. 78.

Power claim [...] here the I itself is infinite, only made finite! It should be the other way round: [...] this fact a problem in its *facticity!* i.e. being! [...] and correspondingly I qua *existence* [Dasein] and not of infinite nature, posited as such, towards finiteness, *but the other way round.*[31]

In Fichte's theory of the thetic judgment and in his use of the concept of freedom with regard to the ego Heidegger considers such a reversal as having more or less already taken place – the seemingly paradoxical point of Heidegger's Fichte interpretation. In order to demonstrate this Heidegger must, of course, "go beyound Fichte".[32] What does this mean?

## IV. Beyond Fichte

A thetic judgment according to Fichte is a judgment which does not follow the lines of the difference *genus* and *species* and for the truth of which no basis, either relational or differential, can be given. In the judgment "A bird is an animal"[33] the generic concept "animal" according to Fichte is the basis on which the concept "bird" rests and from which the truth of this judgment proceeds. The specific difference of the concepts for different animal species is of no account. In contrast to this Fichte calls the judgment "I am" a thetic judgment in which only the existence of the subject material is posited and in which, as Fichte himself puts it, "the position of the predicate is left vacant for the possible definition of the ego in the direction of the infinite".[34] To take up an expression of Gottlob Frege's, the judgment "I am", appears to be an unsaturated sentence radical which contains an unconditional existence statement. Its semantic function, however, is to give expression to the self-determination of the ego with reference to its different ways of relating to the world.

According to Fichte, this also holds good for the judgment "The human being is free".[35] In this judgment the concept of the human being is thought of by means of the concept of the self-determining subject. The direction of its determination makes up the manners in which it relates to the world both theoretically and practically. Since, however, the world cannot be entirely understood through theoretical laws of freedom

---

31  GAH 28, p. 246; emphasis as in the original.
32  GAH 28, p. 115.
33  GA I/2; p. 276.
34  GA I/2; p. 277.
35  Ibid.

and cannot be structured in every aspect according to practical laws of freedom, the judgment "The human being is free" is the expression of an idea and the position of the reason of the judgment is taken over by "a *task* for the reason".[36] This can be formulated in the postulate: "The human being should approximate to the (in fact) unattainable freedom towards the infinite."[37]

In these reflections "a deep insight into the whole"[38] is revealed to Heidegger. This whole is the fundamental constitution of the ego and its ontological status. This it the point where Heidegger sees the closest affinities to his own convictions. The first and systematically most significant aspect is the renunciation of the paradigm of "Vorhandenheit" (being present)[39] which has been achieved in Fichte's conception of the ego. Fichte's ego cannot be thought of along the lines of an existing substance which can be used as the object of predicative statements. The truth is that the existence of the ego is only the manner in which it determines and realises itself in a concrete fashion on each occasion. The existence of the ego is thus only a function of the act of self-determination which defines its essence. It is in keeping with this that the predicate "freedom" does not stand for some present characteristic which "viewed from nowhere" – Fichte calls this "any intelligence at all outwith itself"[40] – might be discovered in the ego. And thus it is possible to say that freedom is not a genuine descriptive predicate of the ego; it only names its manner of being. It is the manner in which the ego under the postulate of self-determination relates to itself and thereby to that which appears to it as "world". As is well-known, Heidegger attempts to give expression to this fact in *Being and Time* using the concept of the existential ("Existenzial"). This is the concept to which he refers (indirectly, at least) in our present context[41] and in which he evidently sees the greatest congruency with his own reflections. Fichte's remarks on the idea of the ego and on an infinite task of realising the quality of freedom under definite conditions in concrete relationships to the world allow Heidegger to speak with reference the ego of a definite task in which it absorbs itself and which, once realised, allows it to understand itself for the first time. This allows

---

36 Ibid.
37 Ibid.
38 GAH 28, p. 110.
39 Cf. GAH 28, pp. 111 ff.
40 GA I/2, p. 406.
41 GAH 28, p. 108.

Heidegger the liberty of taking Fichte's concept of the realisation of freedom as an infinite task and understanding it as an essential interpretative tool with regard to the constitution of the finite ego. According to Heidegger this can be formulated in the following way: The finiteness of the ego *sub specie* of its freedom is an expression of the openness and incompleteness of its existence, and this means for Heidegger that the ego can (and must) determine itself in different ways with regard to the way it desires to be, to live and thereby to understand itself. At this point Heidegger makes direct reference to what is developed in *Being and Time:* the finiteness of existence (Dasein) lies in incompleteness, and that means "*remaining suspended among possibilities* as such of the most individual existence potential."[42] Explaining this, Heidegger continues:

> Ego-being is open, i.e. the being-meaning of "I am" is *I stand amidst possibilities* which I can organise in this or that way; standing amidst them means the necessity of a 'choice in this directon or in that direction'. Openness of the ego means in the first instance: existence is *being potential.*[43]

This is the reversal in the manner of thinking between the doctrine of scientific knowledge and the doctrine of being as an ontology of existence (Dasein) which according to Heidegger is contained in the result of Fichte's commitment to the ineducibility of the finiteness of the ego on the one hand, and the conception of the thetic judgment "I am" together with the use of the concept of freedom of the ego, on the other. Through this reversal, as Heidegger presents it, the philosophy of Fichte is to be liberated from the dross of logical constructions which are foreign to the phenomenon and from the obsession with absolute certainty and grounding and so be brought to its own true form. This we have to see as the systematic highpoint of Heidegger's Fichte interpretation. At this point at the latest, however, we have to remember our original question: What objective opinion can we have about all this? Can we agree with Heidegger's Fichte interpretation? The question is urgent.

---

42 GAH 28, p. 114
43 Ibid. Cf. Heidegger's explanation: "Freedom or my being free is not a quality present in me; my being free lies on each occasion only in my freeing myself. This implies: Freedom, i.e. my being free, will never be found as a present quality, it is the initiator in determining existence potential and existence obligation. My being free is not given in me, it is laid upon me. This being laid upon me is precisely my specific being as I, i.e. as 'I act'." (GAH 28, p. 112).

## V. Heidegger's Fichte interpretation

There are several things to be said here. The first is admittedly trivial, but perhaps not without some significance. Fichte's Doctrine of Scientific Knowledge and Heidegger's Analysis of Existence deal with quite different subjects and problems. The subject of Fichte's Doctrine of Scientific Knowledge is the question of consciousness and the grounding of the possibility of object-orientated knowledge of a thing, this being derived from the relationship between consciousness and self-consciousness. Heidegger's subject, in contrast, is concrete human existence in the different ways of its self-interpretation. The result of this is that in the two theoretical contexts the same concepts are used for different objects. Fichte's pure ego is not the concrete individual human being in the manner of his existence but that aspect of the concrete human being which grasps itself only as the unconditional subject of all its cognitive achievements, 'quite empty of all content'. Furthermore, the finiteness of the ego in Fichte does not refer to the fundamental character of human existence in an original relationship to the world; it refers to the formal aspect of differentiating with regard to the mental fact "consciousness of something". Finally, the action of limiting describes only the subjective condition of the *determinatio* under which something can be represented at all as something which is defined in relation to a given area of predication, which is itself limited through the setting of a limit.

This difference, however, which was most certainly quite clear to Heidegger, is not the problematic point in Heidegger' interpretation of Fichte. Problematic is the way in which Heidegger *without further ado* takes Fichte's statements about the ego to be statements about each concrete human existence. This on its own is sufficient to explain how Heidegger could be of the opinion that Fichte's theory contains the foundations of a yet concealed theory of existence which could be liberated from distortions (foreign to the phenomenon) and from prejudices (due to the system) and so be brought to its own form. However, neither Heidegger's interpretation of Fichte's theory nor the opinion which he derives from it is correct. The reason for this lies in the undeniable differences in the subjects and the points under discussion. These differences require in each case a quite different discourse. They cannot be passed over in a pose of originality.[44]

---

44 Unfortunately we cannot deal here with the question what the correct systematic position is for a theory of the conditions of knowing within the framework of a

However, it does not follow from this that Heidegger' Fichte interpretation is a complete misconception and must be rejected. There is no reason to doubt the truth of Heidegger's words when he says that in the philosophy of Fichte a world was opened up to him and, indeed, a world which in its basic contours could appear quite familiar to him. If we make the attempt to take Heidegger's words seriously and try to name the objective reason for Heidegger's feeling of conviction or even astonishment at finding in Fichte's philosophy as it were a kindred spirit, then we will at least be able to say that both theories have at their centre an identical phenomenon and that both thinkers, each in his own way and with differing aims, tried to throw light on this. This is the phenomenon of autonomy or self-determination and a relationship to the world which is based on this. In both philosophies this relationship to the world is conceived in such a way that the subject is the constructor both of its relationship to the world and of the relationship to the self which is involved there. Fichte, in revealing this fundamental structure, strives to write the "pragmatic history of the human spirit"[45] as a 'history of self-consciousness'; Heidegger, in contrast, turns this fundamental relationship into the basis of a theory of the possibility of human self-interpretation in the form of sketches of existence under the conditions of a life which is aware of its finiteness. The reasons for this Fichte interpretation and Fichte transformation are manifold. For the most part they can be derived from Heidegger's interpretation of the course of the history of philosophy. Heidegger referred to them in the introduction to his lectures in connection with the relationship between metaphysics and anthropology and the contemporary theoretical situation; his purpose was to provide a basis for his project of writing the metaphysics of the finiteness of human existence.[46]

We do not have the space to go into this in detail here. With regard to the relationship between Heidegger and Fichte there is, however, yet another question of important systematic interest which must be solved. This question is put by Heidegger himself and he gives his own answer to it. Assuming one wishes to achieve a "radical interpretation of the subject"[47] (as Heidegger puts it in the above-mentioned lecture series of

---

    broad theory of personal conscious life, nor can we determine what systematic position a theory such as Heidegger's should occupy within this framework.
45  GA I/2, p. 365.
46  Cf. GAH 28, pp. 1–47, esp. 40 ff.
47  GAH 24, pp. 249.

1927), does the analysis of self-consciousness presuppose a correct understanding of the constitution of existence or not? Heidegger's position is clear. A correct understanding of the constitution of existence must precede the analysis of self-consciousness.[48] This position is clearly taken in Heidegger's Fichte interpretation and it is assumed in the thesis of the "reversal"[49] presented there. On this point hangs the justification of Heidegger's Fichte interpretation. Our concluding point is to show that in fact the reverse of the reversal thesis is true. Clear understanding of the constitution of existence presupposes the analysis of self-consciousness.

## VI. Existence (Dasein) and self-consciousness

A useful procedure here is to take as starting point the following explanation of Heidegger's. It is to be found in the context of his explanations of the Fichtian statement "I am". According to Heidegger the statement "I am" and the thesis of predicative openness contain the thought that "I, who am in such and such a condition, am only thus insofar as I have made such and such a choice with regard to my being."[50] To make a choice, however, does not just mean choosing from among possibilities, as Heidegger proceeds to demonstrate. It also means that on the part of the subject making the choice there is a consciousness present that it is itself the author or constructor of this decision. An original practical self-consciousness of this nature is characterised by the fact that the author of this decision knows itself to be different from all content or forms of self-interpretation for which it decides. It must therefore be

---

48 Cf. Heidegger's summary of the thoughts in the above-mentioned lecture: "From a correct understanding of the self-concept of existence we must reach the conclusion that the analysis of self-consciousness presupposes clear understanding of the structure of existence." (GAH 24, p. 249.).

49 With reference to Fichte's position we find the following: "The ego is self-consciousness in the sense that the character of consciousness supplants the character of ego-being and self-being and the opinion arises (among other things) that self-consciousness as consciousness offers the genuine possibility of determining the self-being of the self and of leading the search for this; in fact one must put the matter the other way round and ask in how far self-consciousness *belongs* to *the being* of the ego and in what manner must the character of *being* of this consciousness be structured in order that the *ego-being* may become visible in its totally different quality to any other type of being." (GAH 28, pp. 121 ff.; emphasis as in orig.).

50 GAH 28, p. 107.

given logical precedence before that which Heidegger in the passage quoted above calls "remaining suspended amidst the possibilities of the most individual existence potential". Thus clear understanding of the constitution of existence presupposes the analysis of self-consciousness.

Should we object that Heidegger's talk of 'deciding' or 'choosing' refers to an anonymous occurrence which is concealed to the subject and has already taken place, then it becomes impossible to see how it makes sense to speak of 'deciding' at all. Secondly, one must point to Heidegger's theory of the authenticity of existence in *Being and Time* to which he is evidently alluding when he speaks of 'deciding'. This can be read as Heidegger's answer to the "innermost and most secret question of existence itself",[51] as he himself puts it in his lectures on Fichte.

As is well-known, this is a *call of the conscience* which puts forward a demand for the free choice of one action among possibles and thus a demand for self-determination.[52] However, if the self is to be able to understand and relate to itself this call and demand for a free choice among actions and in the same way the demand for self-determination, then it must not only be able to stand apart from its primary and unreflected relationships to the world and from the models of self-interpretation and in this apartness relate itself to itself; in this relationship to itself it must also understand itself *positively* as a being which can make a choice on its own initiative, understand itself with relation to this decision and act constantly on the basis of this self-concept. It must be a self-consciousness of such a nature as is required for the understanding of the call and for Heidegger's conception of the authenticity of existence. Thus the fact is confirmed once more that clear understanding of the constitution of existence presupposes the analysis of self-consciousness. Other than by recourse to such a preceding consciousness of autonomy it would not be possible to see how the call to authentic and *most individual* existence po-

---

51  GAH 28, p. 133.
52  Heidegger's theory of conscience cannot be dealt with here at greater length. Cf. here Figal, Günter: *Martin Heidegger. Phänomenologie der Freiheit*, Frankfurt a. M. 1988 and the present author's "Martin Heidegger: Sein und Zeit", in: *Klassische Werke der Philosophie. Von Aristoteles bis Habermas*, ed. Reinhard Brandt and Thomas Sturm, pp. 257–284. For the following cf. also the present author's "Personalitas moralis. Zu Martin Heideggers Kritik von Kants Theorie des moralischen Bewusstseins", in: *Kant und die Berliner Aufklärung*. Akten des IX. Internationalen Kant-Kongresses, ed. by commission of the Kant-Gesellschaft e. V. by Volker Gerhardt, Rolf-Peter Horstmann und Ralph Schumacher, vol. V, Berlin/New York 2001, pp. 609–618.

tential, as Heidegger himself puts it, could be understood, adopted and made one's own. Where "the self is brought to itself through the call",[53] as Heidegger writes in *Being and Time*, it is not possible to speak of an anonymous or subconscious occurrence or an occurrence for an outside observer. It can only be an occurrence in which the self relates to itself in a conscious manner. Otherwise it would not be a self; it would be something which is for itself merely something present, and that is not the case.

At this point we must return to Fichte. What Heidegger's theory of the authenticity of existence really requires is Fichte's concept of an original practical self-consciousness, preceding all concrete relationships to the world and the models of self-interpretation. Having developed this in a fairly comparable context, i.e. in his theory of the demand for a free choice of and realisation of an individual life-plan, Fichte was the first to bring it into the modern theory of subjectivity. In Fichte's *Foundation of Natural Law* we find the following consideration. If the demand for free self-determination which, according to Fichte, proceeds from an *alter ego*, is really to be understood, then the challenged subject must – on its own part and quite independently of all concrete purposes – have at its disposal "a concept of freedom",[54] which it attributes to itself. Fichte understood this original practical self-consciousness as the basic principle of a theory of finite, concrete subjectivity.[55] It should be incorporated into Heidegger's concept of the authenticity of existence.

In the final analysis, the really paradoxical point of Heidegger's Fichte interpretation lies in the fact that Heidegger did not interpret the content of the Fichtian concept of the ego as it is to be found in the first paragraph of the early Doctrine of Scientific Knowledge at all. What Heidegger interpreted and discovered for himself was that original practical self-consciousness which is the basis of Fichte's theory of concrete subjectivity. At this point the world of Fichte was opened up for Heidegger.

---

53 SuZ, p. 273.
54 Fichte, Johann Gottlieb: *Grundlage des Naturrechts*, GA I/3, p. 345.
55 Cf. on this the present author's "Reiner Wille. Ein Grundbegriff der Philosophie Fichtes", in: *Revue Internationale de Philosophie*, vol. 206, pp. 617–639 and more recently Klotz, Christian: *Selbstbewusstsein und praktische Identität*, Frankfurt a. M. 2002.

# Fichte, Heidegger and the Concept of Facticity

M. JORGE DE CARVALHO

Universidade Nova de Lisboa

The concept of "Facticity" plays a key role both in Fichte's *Wissenschaftslehre* and in Heidegger's phenomenological hermeneutics – so much so that both philosophical undertakings regard themselves as radical attempts to tackle the question of facticity. But on the other hand they differ on what facticity is and how it can – and should – be dealt with. Our aim is to compare – or rather to grasp the link between – these two different approaches. No history of the concept of facticity can be written without this comparison. But besides their historical interest, the problems faced and posed by these two different approaches are ones no philosophy can safely ignore.

Our main concern is in the first place to outline Fichte's radical critique of facticity and in particular to highlight the following key points: a) his understanding of facticity (what is it that in fact constitutes facticity?); b) his understanding of its negative role (why is it a hindrance?) and c) his assumption that it is possible to overcome facticity or to make a total and radical change in the way we are subject to it.

One fundamental characteristic of facts is that they are *found* ("etwas Vorgefundenes").[1] They are, so to speak, "already there" and force us to watch or confront them. Facts are undeniable, unyielding, uncompromising. There is something about them that makes them absolute. Fichte speaks of an "absolut Vorhandenes" (of something "absolutely there").[2] Facts are indubitably given, they impose themselves, "inscribe" themselves irrevocably. They form that absolute manifestation (and are endowed with that particular kind of *indelibility*) that Fichte expresses by say-

---

1 See, for example, SB, SW II, p. 357, p. 398, and Schelling, 15. 11. 1800; GA III/4, p. 360; SS, SW IV, p. 13 f., p. 19; WL-1804-II, SW X, p. 111, p. 194, p. 424; PEr, GA II/9, p.51; WL-1805, GA II/9, p. 298; AzsL, SW V, p. 442; WL-Kö, GA II/ 10, p. 112 f., Nz1., GA II/10, p. 254; TdB-1811-12, GA IV/4, p. 137, p. 182 ff., ÜVLP, SW IX, p. 325; UI, p. 189, p. 192, p. 197, p. 208, p. 370.
2 See SB, SW II, p. 398.

ing: "Es ist, ist *nicht* nicht" ("it is, it is *not* not")³. On the other hand, facts "are *what* they are" – that is, they have their own shape, their own characteristics. "Things are the way they are" – they have a kind of absolute "thisness": the quality of being just how they are and not otherwise. This they impose upon us, so that we find ourselves confronted with the facts, that is, with the particular way they shape reality. Facticity means "Gebundenheit"/"Bindung"⁴. It means that we are *bound* or *constrained* – in other words, that we are caught or immersed in the particular shape of reality facts force upon us. In principle *it could be otherwise, but it isn't*. Reality as it were turned in a certain direction: "*as a matter of fact* "it is "like this" and not otherwise.⁵

That being said, it must be added that this brief account of facticity does not emphasize those facets that are more characteristic of Fichte's use of this concept. For Fichte, facticity does indeed mean something of this kind (not really altogether different from the usual meaning). And there is a very good reason for this: because in his view the characteristics we have stressed constitute the main features of normal consciousness: consciousness *finds* facts, understands itself as consciousness *of facts*, is caught or immersed in the particular shape of reality the facts force upon itself. In short: normal consciousness has the *form of facticity*.⁶ But here is where Fichte departs from the usual understanding. To begin with in his view facticity is first and foremost a trait of consciousness, a *form of consciousness*. To be sure, normal consciousness has the form of facticity precisely because it understands itself as a "picture" of facts, which exist by themselves and are themselves the core and source of facticity. But in the end

---

3  UI, p. 373.
4  See, for instance, GNR, SW III, p. 18; ErE, SW I, p. 423, VLM, GA IV/1, 206 f., SS-1798, SW IV, p.35; WL-1801, SW II, p. 18, p. 56, p. 57, p. 64, p. 90, p. 108, p. 119, p. 128 f., p. 148; PfGD, GA II/6, p. 355, p. 358 f., p. 363 f., TdB-1810, SW II, p. 552, p. 560, p. 568, p. 652, p. 688; ZAdWL, GA II/6, p. 57; WL-1805, GA II/9, p. 231; TdB-1811-12, GA IV/4, p. 135 ff., WL-1812, SW X, p. 318, p. 434; EVWL-1813, SW IX, p. 19; AzsL, SW V, p. 442.
5  The concept of "facticity" implies contingency: the fact appears against a background – the possibility of being otherwise. This background does not need to be explicit. And even when one assumes the existence of invariable laws, that these laws "are a fact" means that they are seen in the light of the possibility of being otherwise – a possibility they are supposed to exclude. See, for example, WL-1811, GA II/12, p. 165.
6  See, for instance, WL-1810, GA II/11, p. 329; WL-1811, GA II/12, p. 227; see also PfGD, GA II/6, p. 332.

all this is but a claim, an assumption, and, at best, a self-evident truth – that is a *trait belonging to consciousness.*[7] And the problem is: how does consciousness constitute facticity or how does it assume the form of facticity? What is this fundamental feature of normal consciousness – the *form of facticity* – composed of?[8] And in the final analysis what is it worth? Does it fulfill its own claims? What are we really dealing with when our consciousness has this form?

A complete examination of Fichte's answer to this question would require a detailed discussion beyond the scope of this paper. We must confine ourselves to a sketch of a few main points.

First of all, according to Fichte, facticity does not only mean that consciousness is consciousness of facts. For this feature cannot be separated from another characteristic trait of factical consciousness – one it usually remains completely or partially unaware of: factical consciousness is *finite*. It is restricted, confined. Finiteness, narrowness, and fragility characterize this form of consciousness. The question is: how and to what extent? And how does this fundamental characteristic of facticity determine and modify its nature?

Let us begin by considering the most obvious aspects – those Fichte develops along lines already belonging to the philosophical tradition. Factical consciousness is *empirical, historical* knowledge in the traditional sense (viz. *cognitio ex datis: a posteriori* knowledge).[9] This traditional concept refers to a certain mode of access characterized simultaneously by its "strength" and its narrowness. On the one hand, the content of factical

---

7   The current understanding of facts neglects the question of consciousness. Fichte's whole approach to facticity tries to correct this neglect. The rediscovery of consciousness (the rediscovery of facts as inseparable from consciousness – i.e. the rediscovery of the "whole thing" as a phenomenon of consciousness) is the starting point. See for example VLM 1797, GA IV/1, p. 179, p. 203 f., p. 234 f., WL 1804-II, p. 13, to Appia 23.6.1804, GA III/5, p. 244 ff., TdB-1810, SW II p. 560, p. 655, WL-1810, GA II/11, p. 511, p. 297 f., WL-1811, GA II/12, p. 143 f., p. 170, p. 198, EiP-1810/11 (Twesten), GA IV/4, p. 24 f., StL-1813, SW IV, p. 372 f., p. 376 f.

8   See for example WL-1811, p. 227; UI p. 280 f. Facticity is therefore the form of "reality" sc. of the "normal world" and the concept denotes the "whole of reality", of "everyday reality"– see for example WL-1805, GA II/9, p. 245: "die Facticität, d.h. die gesammte Wirklichkeit".

9   Fichte frequently uses these traditional philosophical concepts to designate the phenomenon of facticity. For the history of these concepts, see Seifert, Arno: *Cognitio historica. Die Geschichte als Namengeberin der frühzeitlichen Empirie*, Berlin 1976.

knowledge is *given* (and therein lies its strength). On the other hand factical knowledge is characterized precisely by its *dependence* on givenness: it must "wait and see" – it must wait until the facts give or manifest themselves. In other words: it is unable to *anticipate*, to know *beforehand*. The content of factical knowledge is a certain fact (*only that* fact, *nothing else*). And factical knowledge can only establish that something is, as long as it belongs to its sphere of givenness. Factical knowledge cannot establish that something *must* or *will* be (or, for that matter, that something *was* or *is*, if it remains beyond its sphere of givenness).[10] The concept of factical knowledge denotes, therefore, a fundamental feature of the phenomenon of givenness, as we know it: that the sphere of givenness is *radically finite*. It is split. It happens, so to speak, "in installments". It involves single appearances, each time within rather narrow bounds, and is absolutely unable to determine whatever lies beyond those bounds. This means on the one hand that it covers certain objects during a certain period of time, but leaves out other objects and other periods of time. But this is only a specific point and should not distract us from the fundamental problem. And the fundamental problem is that even if it manages to broaden its scope, this kind of knowledge still remains confined to a certain range of experience, or more precisely, it still remains unable to determine whether there is something *beyond its bounds* (and *a fortiori* unable to determine its content). So that it cannot preclude the possibility that with a continuation of experience viz. *from a a widened horizon* new perspectives could emerge and put what was previously observed *in a different light* – so much so that it turns out that it is *otherwise*.

This rough outline must suffice. But there is an important aspect we cannot leave unmentioned: Fichte's understanding of this problem does not consider only the spatiotemporally enclosed form of normal experience. He focuses on a *core* that may be present even in other forms of consciousness: there is a vulnerability in consciousness each time it is enclosed within certain bounds and *unable to determine* its *relationship to*

---

10  In other words: factical consciousness covers only a certain part of the realm of facts (not all of them, and indeed only a very *small* part). And factical consciousness is *a fortiori* absolutely unable to provide more than facts – "nicht etwa es muss, nothwendig, Princip: was alles hinausgeht über das Faktum; sondern nur so eben ists, ohne einen Grund (WL-1811, GA II/12, p. 263 – see, for instance, SS-1812, SW XI, p. 6). I. e.: factical consciousness does not provide insight into any form of genuine "Müßen" (which would cover the *whole* realm of corresponding facts, but from a higher point of view – so that *all* corresponding facts would result from a *necessary principle* and be *founded* upon it).

*what lies beyond* – that is, unable to determine whether it can be broadened ("erweitert") and how far the "Erweiterung" may change it. In other words, factical consciousness is structurally unable to exclude the possibility of being *narrow-angled*. It cannot determine *if* and *how* it is subject to change. And all forms of consciousness that present a *delimited sphere*, and have no insight into what remains "out of sight" (all forms of consciousness which are unable to exclude the possibility of being *narrow-angled and one-sided*) are factical, "provisional and historical" ("provisorisch und historisch") in this fundamental sense.[11]

But to get to the root of the problem, we must take into account Fichte's specific concept of facticity. Facticity is a liability not only because of the way the factical relates to that which remains "out of sight", but first and foremost because of the way it relates *to itself*. Let us consider this in a little more detail.

First it must be pointed out that factical consciousness *finds* its content, that is to say, that its content "posits" itself, "makes itself" ("sich selbst macht"[12]) in such a manner that it is already there (already "com-

---

11 To apply the formula of the WL-1804-II, SW X, p. 94. We cannot describe this problem in detail. But, as a rough indication, let us stress a few main aspects. First, what we are here dealing with is the reason why there can be no *partial knowledge* sc. why all *real* "Wissen" must exclude the possibility of leaving something out of sight (and of which it has no notion). In other words: real knowledge must be *"total"* (a knowledge of the absolute "whole"). Otherwise it is "provisional and historical" in this sense: unable to determine its relationship to what lies beyond – that is, unable to determine whether it can be broadened ("erweitert") and how far the "Erweiterung" may *change* it. Secondly, this brief outline of Fichte's concept of "historical knowledge" gives us a glimpse of the way he handles traditional concepts. Fichte adopts traditional concepts, but at the same time *transforms* their meaning. He reassesses the phenomena and problems they denote. With the result that he applies these concepts to forms of knowledge, contents, etc. philosophical tradition did not associate with these concepts. The most obvious instance of this is the way he characterizes *logic* and *geometry/mathematics* (which traditionally were seen as paramount examples of *a priori* – i.e. non factical – insight) as forms of merely *factical* knowledge. See for instance WL 1804-II, SW X, p. 112, PEr, GA II/9, p. 55 f; LEr, GA II/9, p. 109, p. 128, p. 132, ÜVLP, SW IX p. 322, p. 325, p. 327, p. 329). Thirdly, this brief analysis gives us a glimpse of another fundamental feature of Fichte's concept of facticity and the factical (and notably of the *finitude* which is part and parcel of facticity): it is not simple; it comprises different components, so that a form of knowledge may be free from some of them, and still be factical because it is flawed on account of the others.

12 See PfGD, GA II/6, p. 356; ÜVLP, SW IX, pp. 122–123; TdB-1810, SW II, pp. 548, 673; LEr, GA II/9, p. 95, p. 102 f., p. 163; WL-1805, GA II/9, p.

plete" and "ready", or, as Fichte says, already a "factum factum et consummatum"[13]) when it comes to notice. In other words, factical consciousness finds itself driven by its content, always already "possessed" by it. The content of factical consciousness is therefore something "objective", "extraneous" – it "builds itself" – consciousness does not build it ("etwas Objektives, Fremdes, sich selbst Construirendes, aber nicht von ihr Construirtes").[14] And factical apprehension or factical evidence ("Evidenz") passively "accepts", "receives" this self-constituted content. Fichte speaks of a "leidendes Sich Hingeben an dieses sich selbst durch sich machendes Bild"[15]: factical consciousness is affected by its content in such a way that it submits, "yields", "gives itself" to it (or rather: *has already* submitted, "yielded", "given itself" to it).

But, as Fichte himself stresses, this sounds paradoxical. For the strength of factical knowledge (and indeed of any knowledge, of every kind of evidence) seems to lie precisely in this: that it comes *thurathen* (*from without*), that it proves to be *irresistible, compelling* – so irresistible and compelling that it *forces* us to *accept* it. How could it be otherwise? Why does Fichte view this as a deficiency or source of weakness?[16]

A closer glance shows that this phenomenon of compulsion is far from providing effective control of the facts or realities that factical knowledge is supposed to grasp. For the most cogent evidence is not the same as the thing presented in it. One can perfectly occur without the other. Evidence is a trait of consciousness, something that happens

---

284; Sd1 A1808, GA II/11, p. 195, p. 199, p. 202 f., p. 204; WL-1811, GA II/12, p. 198, p. 232 f., p. 248; UI, p. 340.
13 WL-1805, GA II/9, p. 253, p. 255 f., p. 269, p. 271.
14 WL-1804-II, SW X, p. 110: "Aller faktischen Evidenz, sei es auch die absolute, bleibt etwas Objektives, Fremdes, sich selbst Construirendes, aber nicht von ihr Construirtes, daher innerlich Unerforschtes übrig, das die ermattete, und an ihrer Kraft verzweifelnde Spekulation wohl unerforschlich nennt." See also WL-1812, SW X, p. 397, p. 399.
15 WL-1812, SW X, p. 320. See also LEr, GA II/9, p. 93, p. 95, p. 102 f., p. 163; MEr, GA II/9, p. 163, p. 165; WL-1805, GA II/9, p. 284; WL-1810, GA II/11, p. 315, TdB-1810, SW II, p. 548; WL-1812, SW IX, p. 421 f; UI, p. 340.
16 See, for example, LEr, GA II/9, p. 93 "Halte ich hier einen Augenblick an. Ich kann mir einen Empiriker denken, der wenn er mich so sprechen hörte, in diesem Bilde sich selbst mit Vergnügen anerkennte, meinte, ich hätte da was ganz vortrefliches geschildert, und gar nicht begriffe, was ich dagegen haben könnte [...]. Ein vollkommener ganz u. durchaus getroffener Abdruk der Dinge zu seyn, wie sie in sich sind, das sey ja etwas vortrefliches; was man denn höheres haben könne".

to it. And it can happen for reasons other than the real existence of the thing presented in it (and indeed so much so, that the real situation in which a given self-evident consciousness arises can be something which is completely different from its content and of which it has absolutely no idea). In other words: this kind of evidence is characterized by the fact that it finds itself installed ("niedergesetzt")[17] in certain contents, but provides no insight into its own origin ("Grund"). The whole thing is settled (all major "decisions" have already been taken) "behind the curtain".[18] Only an insight into the origin of evidence could enable us to ascertain its real value. But the problem is that this origin remains *inaccessible*, completely *out of sight* and *beyond control*. It constitutes something like a blind spot in the field of factical consciousness, a *punctum caecum* – and indeed one *upon which everything depends*. This is what Fichte seems to have in mind when he describes the content of factical consciousness as something *extrinsic, extraneous*, that builds *itself* – and we can see how this feature does indeed undermine this kind of evident knowledge, so that it is evident knowledge *with feet of clay*.

We should not be misled by the fact that Fichte speaks of a "Hingabe" of the passive role of apprehension, which submits itself to the self-made extrinsic content that forces itself upon it. "Etwas Objektives, Fremdes, sich selbst Construirendes" means here: something factical consciousness does not grasp, something remaining out of sight and not under its control. It is *extrinsic* or *extraneous* only in *this* sense. Perhaps it is something existing by itself and adequately portrayed by the content of factical consciousness; perhaps it is something existing by itself but very different from that content; perhaps it is nothing of the sort and does not exist by itself (or has nothing to do with our understanding of existence by itself); perhaps it is something pertaining to factical consciousness itself but of which it has absolutely no notion. The problem of factical knowledge is precisely that it provides no solid basis for choosing between these different possibilities. It is caught up in its self-constituted content, tied to it, and it has no access to the realm of its own origin, where these questions could be settled. And when Fichte speaks of a passive apprehension viz. of a "leidendes Sich Hingeben", we must keep in mind that this

---

17 ÜVdLzP, SW IX, p. 123, StL-1813, SW IX, p. 371.
18 In the *Metaphysik Erlangen*, (GA II/9, p. 164), Fichte cites the well-known verse of Horace's *Satires* (II, Vii, 82): "ducimur ut nervis alienis [mobile lignum]". Factical consciousness is "anheim gegeben jener unbekannten Gewalt" (*ibid.*, 165), like a puppet pulled by *alien, unknown* strings.

means only an *immanent relation* within the sphere of factical consciousness: namely that it submits itself *to its self-constituted content*. The "leidendes Sich Hingeben" is the exact opposite of what it pretends to be. For factical knowledge understands this "Hingabe" (and the cogency of its content) as if they could have only one meaning which is sufficient to determine its own origin, i.e.: as if consciousness were, to apply Bacon's words, "veluti dictante mundo conscriptum".[19] In other words, factical consciousness understands itself as if it were absolutely transparent – and as if the content ("das Vorgefundene") were the very origin of the whole thing (of the phenomenon of consciousness in which it appears). But in fact this assumption is ill-founded. To sum up: the illusion of transparency inherent in factical consciousness masks the unsolved problem of its origin, leaves it, as it were, in a blind angle and makes factical consciousness even more opaque and closed than it would be if it were aware of that problem.[20]

---

19 Bacon, Francis: *De sapientia veterum*, 6.
20 To sum up: the concept of "Hingabe" is not univocal. On the one hand it denotes the purely immanent relationship to the self-constituted content of factical consciousness. On the other hand it denotes the relationship of consciousness to an independent object, existing "by itself", "in itself" (or the relationship of consciousness to its own content, conceived of *as an independent object*, existing *by itself, in itself* – that is precisely the way the immanent "Hingabe" understands itself in everyday consciousness). This is why the same Fichte who over and over again stresses the role played by the "Hingabe" as a basic constituent of facticity can write (LEr, GA II/9, 102): "Wir anerkennen gar keine Dinge, u. drum auch kein Hingeben. In wiefern der Betaster in jener Beobachtung h=g. gleichfalls erhascht, ist er gar nicht, wie er meint, dem Dinge, sondern er ist dem *Denken hingegeben* wirklich, u. wahrhaftig, u. sein Produkt; nur tritt dasselbe in ihm nicht heraus als Denken, in seinem wahren Wesen". See also Nz1, GA II/10, p. 253. That the content comes "from without" can also be understood in different ways. On the one hand it can mean that it comes from a thing existing *in and by itself* (the content of factical consciousness conceived of as a thing existing in and by itself – so that consciousness gives access to its own *terminus a quo, knows* its origin. On the other hand it can mean the mere fact that consciousness finds its content, "receiving" it and having no insight into the way it has constituted itself, so that its origin remains *undisclosed, beyond the sphere of consciousness*. In this case the *terminus a quo* is completely *indeterminate* and *unknown*; consciousness has no access to it. The point is to keep these different senses apart and to show that the fact that consciousness is characterized by a "Hingabe" and plays a receptive, passive role in the one sense does not mean that it is also characterized by a "Hingabe" and that its contents come "*thurathen*" in the other sense. It is characteristic of factical consciousness that it does not distinguish between these different senses – and its whole understanding of itself relies on this *confusion*.

These rough indications should make one thing clear: factical consciousness as such has an *indeterminate value*. The only sure thing about it is that it is the view *that happens to present itself*. And factical knowledge is structurally unable to determine *why*, that is to say, to establish what really is happening while it cannot help but accept and follow the content that forces itself upon it. In other words: factical consciousness is factical mainly in this particular sense (not so much because it presents facts – that is no doubt its claim, but it is uncertain whether this claim is sound – but because it is the consciousness *one happens to find oneself in*). Since it has no insight into its own origin and its value remains completely *indeterminate*, factical consciousness (whether it is aware of it or not), is rootless, *anchorless* and drifts about in the unknown. Fichte emphasizes this by saying that factical consciousness is *unfounded* or *groundless* ("grundlos").[21] This does not mean it has absolutely no grounds, but only that it does not *know* its grounds and can invoke absolutely no grounds or fundaments in support of its claims. In the final analysis factical consciousness relies only *on itself*. And this is precisely the point Fichte stresses when he says that factical consciousness rests *on seeing alone*, "auf die Aussage des blossen Sehens", "auf den Credit des Sehens oder Anschauens"[22], and that this makes factical knowledge fundamentally vulnerable.

But a further point requires a more precise mention. Though fraught with all these problems, factical consciousness could at least form an open field within whose limits everything was absolutely transparent and clear. But that is not the way it is, far from it.

According to Fichte, one of the main features of factical consciousness is precisely that it includes secret, subsurface, or unconscious components, so that it remains *unaware of its true composition*. In other words, factical consciousness also includes *inexplicit* notions, conceptions or representations; and its content ("das Vorgefundene") is composed not

---

21 WL-1812, SW X, p. 399: "Zusatz: Es geht hieraus hervor der oft eingeschärfte Charakter des faktischen Seins, daß es gesehen wird, als seiend schlechtweg, ohne andern Grund: auf die Aussage des bloßen Sehens. Das Sehen desselben ist nämlich ein durchaus grundloses, und die Form der Grundlosigkeit ist ihm wesentlich. – Erst die Reflexion würde den Grund auffinden." See also ÜVLP, SW IX, p. 324, p. 363 f; EVWL-1813, SW IX, p. 11 f.
22 WL-1812, SW X, p. 319, p. 320, p. 399, p. 424; TdB-1810, SW II, p. 689, TdB-1811/12, GA IV/4, p. 90, p. 183 f; TdB-1813, SW IX, p. 456, p. 549 f; ÜVLP, SW IX, p. 267, SS-1812, SW XI, p. 18, WL-1804-II, SW X, p. 215, p. 222.

only of explicit, but of *implicit* elements. Subsurface representations and their correlates (subsurface determinations) are part and parcel of factical consciousness. They are involved in the constitution of the "Vorgefundenes" and without them it would look very different. But factical consciousness has no insight into this connection. Although it is composed of these very same implicit conceptions and determinations, it has absolutely no idea of them. Fichte speaks therefore of "*hidden* factors"[23], of an *underlying, presupposed, invisible* comprehension ("*vorausgesetztes*", "*unsichtbar bleibendes Verstehen*"[24]), or of a *tacit, hidden* consciousness ("*schweigendes Bewusstsein*"[25]). Here we cannot go into detail. Let it suffice to say that in this case "hidden" does not mean something beyond the sphere of factical consciousness, but something *belonging* to it, and *intervening* in it. What Fichte has in mind is that peculiar kind of *inexplicit presence* or unconscious supposition (that is, unconscious *taking into account*) he often alludes to when he maintains that factical perception is an *enthymeme* sc. a syllogism based on hidden premises.[26] In other

---

23   WL-1813, SW X, p. 23, p. 346; see also TdB-1811-12, GA IV/4, p. 133, p. 134 ff., p. 137, p. 144, p. 148, p. 151, p. 159.
24   ÜVLP, SW IX, p. 285. See also WL-Kö, GA II/10, p. 112, WL-1810, GA II/11, p. 313 f., p. 336 f, p. 343; WL-1813, SW X, p. 31; UI, p. 280 (and p. 413).
25   APR, SW II, p. 515. Elsewhere Fichte speaks of a "verborgene Potenz" (WL-1810, GA II/11, p. 314) and of "verborgen bleibende Akte des Lebens" (Sd1 A1808, GA II/11, p. 193 f.). See also WL-1805, GA II/ 9, p. 186 f.
26   See EVWL, SW IX, p. 16 f., p. 86, p. 90, ÜVLP, SW IX, p. 285f6, p. 330, p. 367, PEr, GA II/ 9, p. 56; WL-1810, GA II/ 11, p. 313 f., p. 336 f., WL-1811, GA II/12, p. 154, TdB-1811/12, GA IV/4, p. 134 f.; UI, p. 139, p. 154, p. 378, p. 383. In other words: The content of factical consciousness is borne by what Fichte calls an "unvermerkter Tun" (LEr, GA II/9, 132 f.): "Man treibt es eben, u. hats, ohne es zu wissen" (WL-1804-I, GA II/7, p. 97, cf. p. 107). See also WL-1811, GA II/12, p. 227, where Fichte speaks of "die im Fakto sich verbergende Sichvollziehung": "Die Wahrnehmung giebt nur das Faktum, das Resultat der Thätigkeit, weil sie nur dessen Reflex ist: die That selbst verbirgt sich ihr nothwendig, weil diese keinen Reflex hat." In the WL-1804-I (GA II/7, p. 88), he expresses the gist of the matter thus: "In allem gewöhnlichen Denken sind dunkle Voraussetzungen. Wir streben hinauf zur Thesis absque hypothesi, zur reinen Klarheit". That is: in factical consciousness there is absolutely *no* "*thesis*" without "*hypothesis*" (viz. without *hidden* premises). A "thesis absque hypothesi" is still to be attained. And it can only be attained – if at all – as the final result of the *Wissenschaftslehre*. But factical consciousness *seems* to be a simple "thesis" (a "thesis absque hypothesi") – i. e., it is not aware of the "hypothesis" (sc. of the multiple "hypotheses") on which it relies. And this produces a *semblance of transparency* ("Klarheit") which gives a final touch to its *lack of* "*Klarheit*" or *opacity*.

words: factical consciousness sees more than it is aware of seeing. It would not grasp those very things it is aware of, it would not understand them the way it does, if it did not include this *unnoticed* form of *sight*. But on the other hand this means factical consciousness lacks "Wissen vom Wissen" ("Verstehen vom Verstehen") – that is, it has a defective knowledge (a defective comprehension) of itself.[27] Factical consciousness finds itself "installed" as it were in a *result*; it is composed of several basic factical assumptions, out of which arises this outcome ("das Vorgefundene"). But it has eyes only for the outcome and is not aware of the interplay of immanent elements (that is, of constituent elements of factical consciousness) which lead to (and support) this result. Or, as Fichte says in the *Propädeutik Erlangen*, factical consciousness catches sight only of the "secondhand", and forgets the "firsthand".[28] In short: far from

---

27 See, for instance, ÜVLP, SW IX, 342, "Das Verstehen, durch welches das Ich ist, ist, habe ich gesagt, und zeigt sich an seinem Resultate: es wird aber nicht etwa selbst verstanden, und darin besteht eben das Wesen des faktischen Wissens, daß dies Verstehen des Ich nicht verstanden werde." For the concepts of "Wissen vom Wissen", "Verstehen des Verstehens", see, for example, WL-1813, SW X, p. 11, p. 58, p. 80, ÜVLP, SW IX, p. 330. In the WL-1813, SW X, p. 5, Fichte speaks of "subjective knowledge" ("subjektives Wissen"): factical consciousness (sc. "common knowledge") lacks "subjective knowledge" – it "weiß eben allenthalben in letzter Instanz, ist aber nicht seiner sich bewußt" (*ibid.*). Due to this defective knowledge (or defective comprehension) of itself, factical consciousness constitutes what Fichte calls a "sich nicht_begreifendes Wissen" (WL-1804-I, GA II/7, p. 10, p. 114), "das nicht zu sich gekommene, unsichtbare Wissen" (TdB-1811-12, GA IV, 4, p. 161), "ein sich nicht verstehender Verstand" (UI, 330, cf.p. 332, p. 442). In short: facticity means "Nichtverstand", "Nichtverständniß" (*UI*, p. 336, p. 442), not because "Verstand" (intellect sc. understanding) does not play any role in it, but because it remains hidden from itself, and factical consciousness does not understand itself. See also VLM 1797, GA IV/1, p. 196 f., SS, SW IV, p. 31, StL-1813, SW IV, p. 371.

28 PEr, GA II/9, 51 f. (cf. ÜVLP, SW IX, p. 320). That is: What comes into sight has an essentially *composite* nature. But this composite nature and the structural elements involved in it *do not come into sight*. This is what Fichte means when he speaks of "Konkrescenz": "In der Wirklichkeit u. Unmittelbarkeit des Wißens verschwindet eben die Zusammensetzung, durch Konkrescenz."(WL-1810, GA II/11, p. 315). In other words: Factical consciousness gives the impression that it is something simple (not composite) – a simple and direct apprehension of its content. But it is, after all, composite. That it seems to be a simple and direct apprehension is but the consequence of the concealment ("Verborgenheit") of its true nature. As Fichte puts it: "Eben durch diese Verborgenheit wird er zu dem einfach erscheinenden Zustande des Wissens" (WL-1810, GA II/11, p. 314). See also WL-1804-II, SW X, p. 136, p. 397, p. 399, p. 440; WL-1805, GA II/9, p.

being transparent to itself, factical consciousness is *opaque* and *elliptical* in this other sense, namely because to a large extent it simply *ignores* (that is: *eludes*) *itself*.

But there is more. Factical consciousness could be fraught with all these difficulties and still constitute a realm where everything was absolutely *intelligible*. But according to Fichte this is by no means the case. To be sure, factical consciousness can give the impression of being totally comprehensible. But Fichte points out that there are what he calls *hiatuses*, gaps ("Hiatus in der Continuität des Ersehens")[29]. In other words, there is no continuity in insight or intelligence ("Continuität der Einsicht"/"Gediegenheit der Einsicht").[30] Or, more precisely: even if there are things factical consciousness finds difficult to understand, there is, at any rate, a compact cluster of trivial, commonplace determinations which seem fully comprehensible. With regard to these determinations, the thread of understanding runs continuously, without any break. But this is precisely what Fichte denies. He points out that even our understanding of commonplace determinations does not withstand critical scrutiny. They may seem self-evident, but as a matter of fact prove to be obscure and abstruse. So that where intelligibility seems to be perfect, there are in fact *lacunae*. And this holds both for the explicit elements of factical consciousness (the "secondhand" conceptions and contents it is aware of) and for its subsurface, "firsthand" components (*tacit* conceptions and their correlate determinations).[31]

---

235, p. 244, p. 265; WL-1810, GA II/11, p. 311; WL-1811, GA II/12, p. 154, p. 195, p. 218, p. 223; WL-1812, SW X, p. 436, p. 440; ÜVLP, SW IX, p. 324.
29  WL-1805, GA II, p. 9, p. 222.
30  See ZAdWL, GA II/6, p. 57ss.; WL-1804-I, GA II/7, p. 129 f.; WL-1804-II, SW X , p. 93, p. 260, p. 300; WL-1804-III, GA II/7, p. 303, p. 310; Principien, GA II/7, p. 431, p. 441, p. 461, p. 463, p. 468; WL-1805, GA II/9, p. 180 f., p. 187, p. 207. Factical consciousness is characterized by what Fichte calls "Abbrechen des Intelligierens" (see WL-1804-II, SW X, p. 200) – or, as Fichte puts it in Zur Ausarbeitung der Wissenschaftslehre (GA II/6, p. 60): "das Bewußtseyn" "reißt ab".
31  We cannot go into detail. But it must be stressed that Fichte's concept of *hiatus* does not concern only his attempt to attain non-factical, "genetical" insight. To be sure, the process of overcoming facticity implies the gradual detection and elimination of hiatuses (which may to some extent be related to determinations or concepts which emerge only as a result of this process). But these gaps constitute a structural feature of factical consciousness – and the hiatuses that must be dealt with in order to overcome facticity are a *residue* of this fundamental feature of facticity. Nor does the concept of hiatus apply only to certain special determi-

But this is still not enough to characterize the kind of imperfection Fichte seems to have in mind. The concept of *hiatus* is likely to give rise to a misunderstanding we must try to avoid. For it could suggest that these problems concerning the intelligibility of commonplace determinations occur *only here and there* (in such a way that the gaps are surrounded by sound and perfectly intelligible determinations and that in the end these are the *rule, not the exception* in the realm of factical consciousness). Fichte, on the contrary, seems to have something different in mind. According to him, the gaps, the breaks in intelligibility concern the *fundamental* determinations – those relied on by the whole understanding factical consciousness has of itself, of its object, of their status, of the relationship between consciousness and its object, of the relationship between the different moments of consciousness, and of the relationship between the different moments of represented objects. And this means: according to Fichte, the lacunae concern precisely those determinations, which are to be found *in each and every moment* of factical consciousness *without exception* (and indeed so that each moment of factical consciousness relies not only on one, but on several determinations of this kind and therefore comprises *multiple* gaps in intelligibility).[32]

---

nations. It has to do with a fundamental epistemic problem: whether the determinations, structural elements sc. the forms of "sense" which compose the objects presented to us (and on which their presentation relies) are *thoroughly understandable* – whether the thread of understanding runs continuously, without any break, or whether it "breaks" (so that there are *gaps* or *lacunae* in intelligibility). Moreover, the problem posed by Fichte considers the possibility of *apparent* intelligibility – the hiatuses may be masked by "connectors", which do not provide real understanding (real continuity), but nevertheless manage to hide the gaping spaces, the ruptures of the thread. More precisely, the hiatuses may be masked by hollow viz. pseudo-intelligible concepts. In other words: Fichte points out that factical consciousness is characterized by *defective acuity*. Due to this *defective acuity* it does not become aware that the determinations or concepts on which it relies are *not thoroughly understandable* (viz. that factical consciousness is unable to provide *thorough understanding* of them). The voids, the ruptures of the thread remain undetected – and this creates an *illusion of thorough intelligibility* (sc. *pseudo-continuity* of the thread).

32 The hiatuses do indeed concern the *synthesis*, i.e. the *nexus*, the *connection* between the different elements of the manifold. But this does not mean that they have to do with only *some* (namely with the *connecting*, not with the *connected*) elements of consciousness sc. of its content. Synthesis, as Fichte conceives it, is not *added to pre-synthetic, simple elements*. In this regard Fichte follows in Kant's footsteps: consciousness (and everything in it) is *originally, intrinsically synthetic* (see, for example, ÜVLP, SW IX, p. 113 ff.). The model of independent, "sim-

In other words, what proves to be obscure and abstruse is nothing less than the whole set of fundamental, "transcendental" structures which constitute the *form of representation* in the Kantian sense – or rather the way these fundamental, "transcendental" structures are commonly understood. The gaps Fichte points out in the intelligibility of factical consciousness undermine, so to speak, its *whole* "tissue". They leave nothing intact. And factical consciousness is characterized precisely by the *pervasive* presence of *gaps* or *hiatuses* in intelligibility. It may seem to be totally intelligible and clear, but only before it comes under critical scrutiny: its apparent intelligibility derives precisely from the fact that this kind of consciousness takes its fundamental determinations for granted and is not inclined to scrutinize itself. When it does, it proves unable to elucidate its own fundamental categories. In other words, it proves to be obscure and abstruse *to the core, through and through*.

---

ple" elements which precede the synthesis is fraught with problems. To begin with, it simply ignores the "hidden factors" of consciousness (the *underlying, presupposed, invisible* comprehension). In other words: what appears to be simple is in fact already involved in (and *borne* by) a tacit, hidden *synthetic* consciousness, which makes it possible and from which it is absolutely inseparable. On the other hand, the apparently "simple" elements lack the intelligibility with which they seem to be endowed: the whole model positively bristles with pseudo-intelligibility – with *gaps* viz. with determinations which cannot be thoroughly understood. See, for instance, the analysis of the illusion of "simple" "Sein" and of the interdependency of "being" and "consciousness" (as moments of the *originally synthetic* "Wissen") in the WL-1804-II (SW X, p. 95 f., p. 98). To summarize: the synthetic structure of consciousness has to do with *intrinsic interdependency* – the peculiar structure he describes, for instance, in the *Propädeutik Erlangen* (GA II/ 9, p. 51): "indem ja keines von beiden sich gründlich verstehen läßt, ohne das andere. Beide nicht an sich erstes, sondern nur Glieder des Verhältnisses …u. dies, das Verhältniß, hier das absolute[.]" Determinations cannot be isolated, because they are *intrinsically synthetic*. And, if the gaps in intelligibility have to do with *synthesis*, this is only a further consequence of this fundamental feature of consciousness (sc. of the whole realm in which we find ourselves): that *synthesis* is the very "stuff" it is made of. If we consider, for example, "consciousness" and "being", we find ourselves unable to understand the "transition" from "being" to "consciousness" or from "consciousness" to "being". But that does not mean we have a perfect understanding of "consciousness" or of "being" as such (as "simple" elements) and only find the transition from one to the other difficult to understand. That we are unable to understand the transition is due to the fact that we do not understand the "simple elements" ("consciousness" and "being") either – which, as a matter of fact, are so intrinsically interdependent that our notion of the one always implies some notion of the other.

All this evinces that there is a considerable difference between the features of factical consciousness that are highlighted by Fichte and the way factical consciousness understands itself. According to Fichte, it is characteristic of factical consciousness to misunderstand itself. Fichte repeatedly highlights what he describes as the "Aufgehen" of factical consciousness in its content[33]. Factical consciousness is completely *absorbed* in its content; it is *"taken up"* with it; it *"gets carried away"* with it. He also says that factical consciousness is "durchaus in sich versunken" – that it is *lost* in itself [34]. He speaks of "Selbstvergessen" and points out that factical consciousness forgets itself.[35] This too constitutes an important feature of this kind of consciousness. We cannot look into it here, but what we have just seen enables us to understand the fundamental connections. It must be kept in mind that the content in which factical consciousness remains absorbed (the content in which it is *lost* and which makes it *forget* itself) is no other than the content in which it finds itself installed, the content of which it is immediately aware – the "secondhand" result of which we have spoken. As long as it remains absorbed in it, factical consciousness loses track of its own composition (of all its subsurface components). As long as it remains absorbed in it, factical consciousness does not realize that it is fraught with difficulties, and that the categories upon which it relies are ultimately obscure and unintelligible. As long as it remains absorbed in it, factical consciousness forgets that it is rootless, has no insight into its origin, and therefore drifts about in the unknown. The conjunction of these two characteristic features is central to factical consciousness as Fichte understands it: on the

---

33 See NaR, GA II/5, p. 460, p. 466; WL-1804-I, GA II/7, p. 174, p. 177 ff., p. 185 f.; WL-1804-II, SW X, p. 128, p. 220; WL-1804-III, GA II/7, p. 332; NdSdV, GA II/9, p. 13; WL-1810, GA II/12, p. 210, p. 218, p. 224 f., p. 226 f., p. 228 f., p. 232, p. 236, p. 245 ff., p. 260, p. 269, p. 275 f., . 289, p. 315; WLaU, SW II, p. 702; TdB-1810, SW II, p. 548; Nz1, GA II/10, p. 226; Sd1 A1808, GA II/11, p. 193, p. 210; WL-1811, GA II/12, p. 156, p. 214, p. 218, p. 226 ff., p. 245, p. 260, p. 275 f., p. 289, p. 297; WL-1812, SW X, p. 318 f., p. 325, p. 340 f., p. 407; EVWL, SW IX, p. 29, ÜVLP, SW IX, p. 184, p. 212; Sd1 A1808, GA II/ 11, p. 193, p. 197, p. 202, p. 210; EiP-1810/11(Twesten), GA IV/4, p. 25; TdB-1811/12, GA IV/4, p. 125, p. 132 f., p. 160; WL-1813, SW X, p. 16, p. 28; TdB-1813, SW IX, p. 555, StL-1813, SW IV, p. 371 f.
34 See, for example, WL-1812, SW X, p. 318; PEr, GA II/ 9, p. 45; WL-1811, GA II/12, p. 227.
35 PfGD, GA II/7, p. 330; PEr, GA II/9, p. 46; Sd1 A1808, GA II/11, p. 196, p. 202 f.; Nz1, GA II/10, p. 226.

one hand it is tainted with imperfections that jeopardize its value, so that it is *unoriented,* and in this sense *lost ("verloren")*; on the other hand, it forgets where it stands and loses sight of its own "lostness" (and indeed so much so that it feels oriented and "in control").

The concept of facticity Fichte shaped and used emphasizes, then, all these aspects related to the radical *finitude* or *imperfection of consciousness.* If one does not take this into account, one simply misses the point. For Fichte, facticity is diametrically opposed to the meaning the word would have if it were derived from our usual understanding of "facts": a clear-cut situation, in which one at least knows *what is going on* – what one is dealing with. For Fichte, facticity signifies mainly *the fact of bounded, imperfect consciousness,* which , for the previously mentioned reasons, is ultimately *unable to determine what is going on,* and does not know "where it is". Factical consciousness may (and indeed *tends* to) give the impression of being perfectly efficient. But this does not alter (it only *masks*) its imperfection. The radical imperfection and "lostness" ("Verlorenheit") of factical consciousness does not cease or diminish because one is not aware of it. On the contrary: unawareness only aggravates the fault. In short, the contrast with our usual understanding is so marked, that for Fichte facticity means primarily *the fact of opaqueness concerning the facts:* that there is an undeniable fact of consciousness, that this consciousness claims to know what is going on, but in truth does not live up to this claim and is indeed, despite all its apparent determinateness, *indeterminate and void* – so that it lacks all qualifications to provide real *knowledge* or *understanding* of the situation in which we find ourselves.

In the *Einleitungsvorlesungen in die WL 1813* Fichte expresses all this by speaking of "[…] jenes nicht lebendige und helle, sondern dunkle und träumende Bewußtsein": a "consciousness which is not lively (vivid) and clear, but dark (opaque) and dream-like".[36]

But this is not all. There are still other crucial aspects which should not be left unconsidered even in a brief outline like this.

To begin with, Fichte emphasizes that the "Hingabe" (the passive apprehension, which submits itself to the self-constituted *extrinsic* content) is not only fundamental for the characteristics of the kind of consciousness with which we usually are endowed, but also for the characteristic features of the "self" which submits and gives itself to the self-constituted extrinsic content. In other words, factical consciousness is characterized

---

36  EVWL, SW IX, p. 44.

by the fact that consciousness is consciousness *for itself* and *of itself* – that there is a "self" which is part and parcel of it – and indeed so that it lies in the heart of consciousness. Now, Fichte emphasizes that the "Hingabe" entails a particular *shape* for the "self". The one submitting, giving himself to the extrinsic-content has his own being fashioned by the thing to which he gives himself. To apply the words of the *WL 1812*, it has the form of a "Gemachtwerden zu Etwas" ("To-be-shaped-into-something").[37] The "self" of factical consciousness follows whatever forces itself upon it. It takes shape according to it, and is but a *repercussion*, an "*echo*" of the factical content. In short, it is what the extrinsic content of factical consciousness *makes of it*. So that the *root*, the *core* of its own being lies *outside*, and the "self" has no "content", no determination of its own (except, of course, for the fact that consciousness is always consciousness *for* and *of* it).[38]

In other words: it is the self that is *absorbed* in the factical content – it is the self that is "*taken up*" and "*gets carried away*" with it; it is the self that is *lost* in this content, so that it *forgets* itself. Factical consciousness is, then, characterized by this peculiar kind of alienation ("*Fortreissen/Entfremden*").[39] And facticity is not only a *form of consciousness*, for this form of consciousness means after all a *form of the self*: namely, that form of the self in which it is *alienated from itself*, snatched away, as it were, by the factical contents that force themselves upon it.

But there is more: the self takes the shape of whatever forces itself upon it. But what forces itself upon it is of a very peculiar nature: for, as we have seen, factical contents are characterized by the way they de-

---

37  WL-1812, SW X, p. 320, see also p. 421 f. and PfGD GA II/6, p. 356.
38  In the *Logik Erlangen*, GA II/7, p. 93, Fichte gives a direct and compact version of all this: "In der Empirie giebt nun dieser Lichtzustand im Menschen sich der durch sich selbst bestimmten Beschaffenheit der Dinge leidend hin, – durchaus u. total leidend – er ist daher, u. wird nichts mehr, und durchaus nichts weiter, als das, was der Gegenstand in dieser seiner Anschauung aus ihm macht: ausdrückend, bloß ihr Machen u. Seyn; ihr blosses Nachbild u. Abdruck, nichts ausser ihnen, sondern lediglich ihre formale Wiederholung; u. zweimahl Setzung. (..) Die innere Wurzel seines Seyns ist ausser ihm selber: er ist daher nichts an sich." In the PfGD, GA II/6, p. 365, Fichte compares this form of the self with the residual form of existence in the Greek Hades, the netherworld abode of the shades: on the one hand there is a "self" (something radically different from the complete absence of the "self"); but on the other hand the self is *debilitated, deprived of strength and vitality, oblivious* – in short: it is but a *powerless shadow of itself*. See also TdB-1811-12, GA IV/4, p. 154 f.
39  See UI, p. 139; Nz1, GA II/10, p. 270.

pend on subsurface, unconscious components, by the fact that they are fraught with unintelligibility, by their fragility viz. by the fact that they provide no insight into their origin and have therefore an indeterminate value. Moreover, factical contents are characterized by the way they conceal all this and cover the tracks of their own "lostness" (that is, by their "double-faultinesss" which is due to the fact that they are faulty but not even adequately understood to be faulty, so that they manage to give the impression of being perfectly sound). But precisely *this* – that is, this "double-lostness" – is the shape the self takes when it is "seized", "snatched away" by factical contents. Facticity means, then, that *form of the self* in which it is alienated from itself and *lost in nothing less than this peculiar kind of "double-lostness"*.

But all this is not sufficient to characterize Fichte's understanding of facticity. For he emphasizes that facticity, as we have described it, is ambivalent, amphibolic. On the one hand, it is characterized by its inertness. As Fichte puts it, it has the following form: "so ist's und damit gut".[40] Facticity binds to itself and is not easily moved or disturbed. But on the other hand, it is constituted in such a way as to provide opportunity for change. In other words: facticity comprises what Fichte calls "Reflexibilität".[41] Enchaining though it may be, ultimately it does not preclude the possibility of escape. On the contrary: it provides all *necessary* and *sufficient* conditions for it. For the very same presentation that is tainted by all the limiting characteristics we have described constitutes at the same time a possible *starting point* for *reflection* – viz. for reappraisal and critical evaluation of factical consciousness and for the exploration of new ways of conceiving things. In short: the factical point of view can break away, drag itself away ("Losreißen"/"Losreißung") from factical consciousness and trigger the development of other forms of consciousness.[42] And

---

40 WL-1812, SW X, p. 424, X 358; TdB1811–12, GA IV/4, p. 143, p. 147, p. 159, p. 165, p. 179; ÜdVLzP, SW IX, p. 141, p. 212, p. 304, p. 324, p. 358, p. 364, p. 379, p. 392; TdB-1813, SW IX, p. 430, p. 482, p. 492; EVWL, SW IX, p, 11 f.; WL 1813, SW X, p. 10, p. 34, p. 48, p. 84; UI, p. 327, p. 442; AzsL, SW V, p. 442; StL-1813, SW IV, p. 377.
41 See, for example, WL-1812, SW X, p. 378, p. 382, p. 385 ff., p. 388 f., p. 398 f., p. 404, p. 421; WL-1813, SW X, p. 6, p. 25, p. 46, p. 56 f., p. 69, p. 81; ÜdVLzP, SW IX, p. 296; TdB-1813, SW IX, p. 543 f., p. 545 f., p. 573, DdWL, SW II, p. 75.
42 See, for example, WL-1812, SW X, p. 326, p. 432; EidWL-1813, SW IX, p. 14; ÜVLP, SW IX, p. 399; Sd1 A1808, GA II/11, p. 199, p. 212; WL-1811, GA II/12, p. 229; EiP-1810/11, p. 25; TdB-1811-12, GA IV/4, p. 138 f., p. 156, p. 160 f., p. 185 f., p. 188; StL-1813, SW IV, p. 372; UI, p. 280 f., p. 327, p. 346 f.

this too constitutes a fundamental feature of facticity as Fichte understands it.

We cannot go into detail and analyze the roots of this ambivalence. Nor can we dwell upon the question of how Fichte explores this possibility of stepping beyond facticity and of overcoming its limitations.

Let it suffice to say that, on the whole, his work goes far beyond the pursuit of a certain degree of improvement in some aspects of factical consciousness. To be sure, Fichte is well aware of the fact that transformations intended to overcome facticity may result in new forms of factical consciousness (which differ considerably from the ones they replace, but are still nothing more than factical consciousness). And he is, no doubt, mindful of the fact that overcoming facticity would require complete elimination of all the faults we have spoken of – and indeed nothing less than a radically new mode of being. But the problem he tries to deal with is nonetheless the problem of a *thorough eradication* ("Austilgung") of facticity.[43] In other words: Fichte poses this problem and leaves no stone unturned in his effort to explore possible solutions. It need not be established here whether what he has in mind is a total elimination of facticity "überhaupt", or rather an attempt to achieve the highest possible level of depuration of it (so that there would, after all, be a residue of facticity[44], but this residue could be anticipated and understood *a priori*, by means of an "Ableitung der Unableitbarkeit" viz. a "Construction der Unconstruierbarkeit", in a completely *non-factical grasp* of facticity).[45]

---

43 WL-1804, SW X, p. 195; he says "absolute Vernichtung aller Facticität" in *Die Prinzipien der Gottes-Sitten- u. Rechtslehre*, GA II/7, p. 354; and in the Propädeutik Erlangen., GA II/9, p. 54: "Ich sage: alle Facticität kann genetisch werden."
44 DdWL SW II, p. 135; ÜVLP, SW IX, p. 173 f, p. 217 f., p. 313 ff., p. 318 f.; WL-1804, SW X, p. 133, p. 260; WL-1812, SW X, p. 318, p. 339 f.
45 See for example ÜVLP, SW IX, p. 216 f, p. 300 f, p. 319. That is: what Fichte has in mind is not a simple residue – a brute fact or a realm of brute facts: something *merely found* and absolutely *beyond comprehension*. In all likelihood, he has in mind a *very peculiar kind of residue* – one which can be *grasped, foreseen, deduced a priori* (in such a way that, although it resists comprehension, its incomprehensibility turns out to be totally comprehensible – see for instance WL-1805, GA II/8, p. 225). There are passages in his writings where Fichte points out that the insight provided by his *Wissenschaftslehre* sheds light on the *form*, and only on the *form* of consciousness (that is: not on its *matter*) – see, for example, ÜVLP, SW IX, p. 173 f.). But it must be kept in mind that his concept of facticity and indeed his whole endeavor suggest something *toto caelo* different from a mere elucidation of the "form" of consciousness (which leaves a residue of totally unknown reality) in the Kantian sense. In other words: Overcoming facticity

Be that as it may, there are two things worth noting: first, that Fichte's discussion of facticity poses this problem and that his concern is precisely to overcome facticity, in order to obtain real knowledge ("Wissen") – the knowledge factical consciousness does not provide; and in the second place, that Fichte's attempt to overcome facticity does not only mean that he tries to break away from it. For in truth this attempt opens up new perspectives on understanding facticity.

In other words: one cannot have a clear-cut idea of factical consciousness, as Fichte understands it, *from within*.[46] In a certain sense, facticity can be seen only "from without" – that is, once the grip of the factical content weakens and the "Aufgehen", the absorption in it, is no longer complete. From the very beginning, Fichte's critical survey of factical consciousness supposes some form of *breach* in facticity (namely a form of breach that does not prevent the insight into the faults of factical consciousness from being again a variety of factical consciousness).[47] But on the other hand the successive steps of the philosophical investigation Fichte carries out in his attempt to overcome factical consciousness provide several reappraisals of facticity and important developments in the understanding of its nature. In short: Fichte's concept of facticity is *multilayered* and undergoes a chain of metamorphoses. And what I have hitherto outlined is but the starting point of his whole analysis.

Now, it is far beyond the scope of this paper to examine all these developments. But we cannot leave out a crucial aspect – for even a brief outline like this would be misleading if it failed to take this aspect into account.

As we have pointed out before, Fichte's analysis of facticity emphasizes that the immediate content of factical consciousness is an *extrinsic, self-constituted* content, a "factum factum et consummatum", that forces itself

---

(viz. a *Wissenschaftslehre* in the Fichtean sense) can only be achieved if the "residue" ("matter" – or whatever remains opaque, incomprehensible) is *part and parcel of the a priori form* and can be *mastered* ("tamed" as it were) by the *a priori insight* into the form of consciousness.

46  See WL-1804, SW X, p. 111 f.: "Es scheint, die absolute Fakticität konnte nur von demjenigen entdeckt werden, der über alle Fakticität sich erhob, wie ich sie denn in der That erst nach der Entdeckung des wahren innern Princips der W.-L. entdeckt und stets den Gebrauch von ihr gemacht habe, den ich hier mache, die Zuhörer von derselben aus in die Genesis zu leiten".

47  In other words: from the very beginning Fichte's critical survey of facticity deviates from the understanding factical consciousness has of itself – an understanding which is part and parcel of facticity in the full sense of the word.

upon consciousness, so that factical consciousness has no insight into its own origin. We have also pointed out that the self "of factical consciousness has the form of a "Gemachtwerden zu Etwas". In other words, the factical "self" is completely immersed, absorbed in the factical content – it "gives itself away" to it and is, as Fichte says, but an "echo" of it. All this seems to mean that the self plays only a purely passive role: the self comes, so to speak, "in tow", when everything has already been settled by the unknown origin of factical consciousness. And this in turn seems to mean that the facticity of the self is but a corollary, an epiphenomenon. But Fichte points out that these basic features of factical consciousness do not rule out the possibility for the "self" of playing still another (and this time a *determining*) role.

Factical consciousness has no insight into its origin. So it follows that it cannot exclude, among others, the possibility that the "self" is involved in the unknown "Sich-selbst-Machen" of the factical content. And, on the other hand, factical consciousness has no insight into its own composition viz. no insight into its own components. On the contrary, it is characterized by "Undurchsichtigkeit", that is by the fact that it is everything but transparent to itself. And this holds likewise for the "self". In other words, factical consciousness does not know its own "self" well enough to be able to exclude the possibility of it being, after all, covertly involved in the constitution of the "factical content" (of the "factum factum et consummatum") that forces itself upon it.

Now, this is the very possibility Fichte explores in his attempt to overcome factical consciousness. He maintains that the "extrinsic", self-made content that forces itself upon factical consciousness is anything but extrinsic to consciousness and to the sphere of the self. It is, no doubt, extrinsic to factical consciousness, insofar as factical consciousness has no insight into its origin. But this only means that it is extrinsic to its restricted "angle of vision" (so that from the point of view of factical consciousness it comes "from without"). For it can be extrinsic to factical consciousness without being extrinsic to consciousness "überhaupt" or to that peculiar form of reality that surfaces in the factical self. In other words: factical consciousness *eludes* itself and *ignores* itself, the factical self *eludes* itself and *ignores* itself – and, according to Fichte, the unknown correlate of this ignorance (the realm of consciousness, the realm of the self, that factical consciousness proves unable to grasp) constitutes the very root of factical consciousness, the origin it is unable to determine.

It must be kept in mind that the unknown form of consciousness and the unknown form of the self Fichte tries to unveil, and which according to him constitute the very origin of factical consciousness, *differ* both from the factical content and from the factical self (that is, from the whole range of categories factical consciousness is used to, and on which it relies). The point is: Fichte's account of facticity (and indeed his whole philosophical endeavor) rests upon this *difference* and explores this possibility: that there are more things than are dreamt of in factical consciousness; that it is possible to escape the "either/or" of factical categories; and that factical consciousness is but a part of something of which it has absolutely no idea, and can be understood only in the context of it;[48] that this something other than factical consciousness, of which it is a part, is nothing other than "consciousness" and "self" – that very consciousness, that very self that factical consciousness proves unable to grasp. In summary, it can be said that, according to Fichte, this primal element of which factical consciousness is a part – the origin of its "Gemachtwerden" – is a form of consciousness (of life) and of self, that differs radically from anything factical consciousness conceives.[49]

---

48 This is made particularly explicit, for example, in the TdB-1811, SW II, p. 619, where Fichte points out that our normal understanding absolutizes certain categories viz. the opposition between them, and does not realize that the whole horizon of these absolutized categories (or oppositions) has, so to speak, blind angles, and is in fact far from being exhaustive. An "ausgedehnterer Gesichtskreis" reveals new, undreamt-of possibilities and abrogates the "tertium non datur" of common understanding. Fichte emphasizes that his categories – and in particular his category of "Leben" – are rooted in such an "ausgedehnterer Gesichtskreis" and are not to be mistaken for common categories.

49 The key to Fichte's whole endeavor lies in breaking the spell of factical categories and in particular of the category of "object" sc. objectivity (the tendency to understand everything as an "object" – or, as he also puts it, as a form of "Seyn"). More precisely, the key to Fichte's whole endeavor lies in the discovery of the peculiarity of the "NichtObjekte, was Du Wissen nennen kannst." (PEr, GA II/9, p. 50). This is what the fundamental category of "life" ("Leben") is all about. And one simply misses the point, if one understands life as just another form of "object" (or of "Seyn"). Cf., for instance, *WL-Kö*, GA II/10, p. 118: "Seyn. GrundIrrtum: – Dadurch nun, daß man ein anderes Wort, = Leben, an die Stelle sezt, ist der Irrtum nicht gehoben, wenn man dieses wieder zu einem *Seyn* macht […] Z. B. so nun etwa jemand fragte: *Leben* was ist das? so ware klar, daß er zu einem lebendigen Denken nicht gekommen sey. –. Es ist kein *was*, kein zweimahl zu setzendes, durch einen Beisatz zu bestimmendes. –." But on the other hand, it is not only a matter of discovering the "not-object". The discovery of the "not-object" paves the way for the discovery of the role it plays in the constitution of the object – and indeed so that the latter is but a "moment" in the realm of the former, and must be "reintegrated" or "reincorporated" in it. In other words: the illusion of the independent, "absolute" character of the object viz.

Fichte maintains that without this primal element there is simply no room for factical contents. Factical contents do not subsist by themselves, in themselves. They can only take place in the framework of a self-centered form of consciousness: *in the course of its relation to itself*, as *moments* of this relationship. In short, the self of which factical consciousness is not aware plays a decisive role in the constitution of the "factum factum et consummatum" which forces itself upon factical consciousness. And on the other hand, it is also the source of that peculiar form of self which is a characteristic feature of factical consciousness (the self which *"gets carried away"* with the factical content and is *lost* in it). Or, to put it more precisely: it is the self-centered consciousness of which factical consciousness is not aware that constitutes the "extrinsic" content which forces itself upon the factical self and makes of it an "echo", an "alienated" self.

We are now in a position to understand the peculiarity of Fichte's concept of facticity and the full extent to which it departs from the current understanding of facts and "facticity". According to Fichte, when all is said and done, facticity is *primarily* a *feature of the self* (or of something which is not a *caput mortuum* and corresponds to the very self that factical consciousness proves unable to grasp). The current concept of fact and facticity reflects the understanding facticity has of itself: facts are "by themselves", "in themselves". And the self is factical, because it finds itself confronted with the facts – with an "absolut Vorhandenes" – with facts existing "in themselves", "by themselves". According to this view, facticity of the self is, so to speak, but a by-product. But according to Fichte, it is more like "the other way around". The whole realm of this "absolut Vorhandenes" viz. of the factical content pertains to a self-centered consciousness and is constituted, generated by the Self (N.B. by the self-centered consciousness of which factical consciousness is not aware and which differs from any factical category). In other words: facticity is *primarily, not secondarily* (*"abgeleiteterweise"*), *facticity of the self*. To understand facticity (the whole realm of facticity: facticity as the

---

of "Seyn" must be broken. See, for instance, *ibid.*: "Grammatische Bestimmung Vita, vivere, esse, essential. – Das Leben ist[,] weset, active, u. virtualiter: *u. das ist ist eben als Leben zu denken.* [/] ein verbum activum, nicht neutrum. – Man kann das Leben eben nur *leben*[.][...] Wie sind Substantiva möglich? GrundIrrthum: ausgehen vom Substantivum: Wahrheit, ausgehen vom verbum activum." Cf., for instance, TdB-1811, SW II, p. 654; TdB-1811-12, GA IV/4, p. 141. The peculiarity of Fichte's approach is reflected in this "grammatical reform": the noun ceases to be the determining factor – the determining factor is the verb; and it is the *verbum activum*, not the *neutrum* that plays the decisive role.

form of usual consciousness and as the form of the usual "world") is to be able to grasp the primal element of this self-centered consciousness and to understand how it becomes factical consciousness – i.e. how it "poses" the content of factical consciousness, in which the factical self is lost.

But we cannot go into this any further and analyze how Fichte tried to establish this concept of facticity and conceived the possibility of a "genetical" insight ("genetische Evidenz") into the constitution of factical consciousness. Instead, let it suffice to focus on the *research questions* raised by the fundamental aspects we have mentioned.

Fichte draws our attention to this: our whole understanding of facts as something "absolut Vorhandenes" and of consciousness as pure transparency is ill-founded. It makes us blind to the very thing it pretends to clarify. It makes us forget what is *happening* in the coming-into-sight of facts, that facts *pertain* to this peculiar kind of "happening" or "event" – to "life", as we call it – which embraces facts and consciousness as inseparable components of this primal unity. It makes us forget that the concepts of "subject" and "object", "consciousness" and "facts", are fraught with difficulties, that these concepts do not provide an adequate understanding of "life", the "primal unity" – and that this "primal unity" is, instead, the key to understanding what the concepts of "subject" and "object", "facts" and "consciousness" stand for. At the same time Fichte draws our attention to the fact that this primal unity of "life" must be analyzed *in itself*. For it is not derivative (it is the very origin of everything we are aware of), and we are far from knowing what it is, and what it consists of – in short: it still *remains to be determined*. And on the other hand, Fichte also draws our attention to this: that our understanding of the apprehension of facts as a *straightforward, simple* apprehension (and of facts as the "plain" thing that is grasped by means of this simple apprehension) is ill-founded; it makes us blind to the very thing it pretends to clarify; for it makes us forget that what we call "facts" results from a complicated interweaving of elements in the realm of "life", the "primal unity"; it makes us forget that "factical contents" result from a "Hingabe" and a certain understanding of its meaning; it makes us forget that "facts" result from an "Aufgehen" and "Versunkenheit" – an "absorption", a state of being "lost" in them; it makes us forget that facts "result" from underlying suppositions and from their concealment; it makes us forget that "facts" are made of unintelligible determinations and of our unawareness of this; last but not least, it makes us forget that "facts" are inseparable from that peculiar kind of element that surfaces in the factical self, from its relation to itself and from the peculiar kind of "tension" that arises from it – so that in the end the "absolut Vorhandene", instead of being "absolut vorhanden," is but a *derivative* component within the framework of that primal element, the unity of life, that still remains to be determined.[50]

Now, this brief outline, no matter how rough and oversimplified, enables us to understand the fundamental link between Fichte's and Heidegger's concepts of facticity. Our task is not to track down the origin of Heidegger's concept of facticity and to ascertain whether Fichte did or did not play a direct or indirect role in its genesis.[51] We are just trying to highlight the fundamental affinity of approach between them – that they do have a common denominator in this regard. Or, to put it more precisely: we are trying to point out that Fichte's and Heidegger's concepts of facticity both constitute a watershed in the history of the concept – and that up to a certain point they move in the same direction. But on the other hand we are also mindful that resemblances, as Plato puts it in the *Sophist*, are a slippery thing.[52] And we are trying to isolate the fundamental difference between Fichte's and Heidegger's concepts of facticity – the dividing line, as it were, between them.

To begin with, it must be kept in mind that Heidegger's concept of facticity is not a minor or inconsequential aspect of his phenomenology. On the contrary: it is so central to his philosophical agenda that for a while he used it to define his whole research project: what we now know as Heidegger's "existential-temporal analytic of Dasein" was originally conceived as a "hermeneutics of facticity". And on the other hand some fundamental steps of the philosophical analysis Heidegger's concept of facticity is designed to express coincide to a large extent with Fichte's

---

50 It must be kept in mind that our remarks concerning Fichte's view of the primal unity, "life", give only a *glimpse* of his project and of his exploration of this primal unity. Our remarks highlight the *terminus a quo*, the starting point, not the *terminus ad quem* of his philosophical investigation. In other words, we have tried to depict the crossroad, as it were, and the way he goes – not the whole road, which may be (and in fact is) full of surprises and turns in unexpected directions.
51 For the "genealogy" of Heidegger's concept of facticity, see, for example, Tietjen, Hartmut: "Philosophie und Faktizität", in: *Heidegger-Studies* 2 (1986), pp. 11–40; Kisiel, Theodore: "Das Entstehen des Begriffsfeldes 'Faktizität' im Frühwerk Heideggers", in: *Dilthey-Jahrbuch* 4 (1986–87), pp. 91–119; Jamme, Christian: "Heideggers frühe Begründung der Hermeneutik", *ibidem*, pp. 72–90; Kisiel, Theodore: *The Genesis of Being and Time*. Berkeley 1993, p. 19 f., p. 23, p. 26 ff., p. 30 f, p. 34 f., p. 116, p. 136 f., p. 496 f.
52 *Sophist* 231a.8 ff.

radical reappraisal of our usual understanding of facts viz. of the "form of facticity".

To put it in terms we have been using, Heidegger as well emphasizes that our whole understanding of facts as something "absolut Vorhandenes" and of consciousness as pure transparency is ill-founded. It makes us blind to the very thing it pretends to clarify; it makes us forget what is *happening* in the coming-into-sight of facts, that facts *pertain* to this peculiar kind of "happening" or "event" – to "life", as we call it – which embraces facts and consciousness as inseparable components of this primal unity.[53] Heidegger as well points out that the usual under-

---

53 See, for example, GAH 58, p. 145: "Leben *nicht Objekt*, ist aber auch nicht philosophisch erfaßt durch Verankerung im *Subjekt*, durch ichliche Betrachtungsweisen. Objektivierung und Subjektivierung sind Theoretisierungsweisen. Auch immanente Reflexion geht auf objektivierte *Transzendenzen*."This point goes largely unrecognized and unconsidered, but Heidegger's Analytic presupposes a kind of "Rückgang auf das Subjekt", and constitutes a reappraisal of what Husserl calls intentionality and its problems. To be sure, Heidegger distances himself from the Husserlian form of "Rückgang auf das Subjekt". But this only means he distances himself from the "schlechte "Subjektvität" (GAH 27, p. 115) of the Descartes-Husserl tradition (viz. the "theroretical" subject). The point is that the "Rückgang auf das Subjekt" can be carried out in such a way that it simply misses the peculiarity of the "subject" (of that which is not an object, or rather of the *primal unity*) and its *unique mode of being.* To unveil this unique mode of being is the central issue of Heidegger's existential-temporal Analytic. In other words: the problem of intentionality (vz. of "constitution") should not make us forget Heidegger's critique of the "schlechte Subjektivität", but his critique of the "schlechte Subjektivität" should not make us forget that in his view some kind of "Rückgang auf das Subjekt" is essential and necessary – and that his problem is precisely: how to avoid missing the original mode of being of the primal unity. For Heidegger's "Rückgang auf das Subjekt", see for example: GAH 59, p. 133 f, p. 137 ff.; GAH 20, p. 18, p. 200 f.; GAH 24, p. 103 f., p. 155 f, p. 172, p. 219 f, p. 249, p. 318, p. 444; GAH 25, p. 101, p. 106, p. 397; GAH 26, p. 19 ff.; GAH 26, p. 19, p. 110, p. 189; GAH 27, p. 11 f, p. 72 f., p. 118 f., p. 313 f.; KPM, p. 206; GAH 31, p. 121 f, p. 127; GAH 32, p. 196 f.; VWG, GAH 9, p. 161 f.; HUA IX, p. 601 f. For his concept of "life" as the primal unity and the problem of grasping its unique mode of being, cf. GAH 58, p. 17 f., p. 29 f., p. 33 ff., p. 54, p. 58, p. 59 ff., p. 66 f., p. 68 f., p. 76 ff, p. 79, p. 96 f, p. 144 f., p. 155 ff, p. 171 ff, p. 185 f, p. 197 f., p. 227, p. 230 f., p. 236; GAH 59, p. 18 f., p. 88, p. 172 f., p. 175 f.; GAH 60, p. 10 ff.; AKJ, GAH 9, p. 14 f., p. 34 f.; GAH 61, p. 2, p. 37, p. 81 f., p. 84 ff., p. 89 ff., p. 94 ff., p. 107, p. 117, p. 119 ff, p. 123 f, p. 151, p. 168, p. 174 ff., p. 189; GAH 62, p. 17, p. 47 f., p. 174 f., p. 269, p. 305, p. 317, p. 335; PIA, GAH 62, p. 351 f., p. 397; GAH 63, p. 85 f., p. 102 f.; GAH 17, p. 112, p. 274 f., p. 320 f., BwJ, p. 26 f. In the middle of the 1920 s Heidegger changed his vocabulary, and "Dasein" be-

standing makes us forget that the concepts of "subject" and "object", "consciousness" and "facts", are fraught with difficulties, that these concepts do not provide an adequate understanding of "life", the "primal unity" – that this "primal unity" is, instead, the key to understanding what the concepts of "subject" and "object", "facts" and "consciousness" stand for. Heidegger as well draws our attention to the fact that this primal unity of "life" must be analyzed *in itself.* For it is not derivative (it is the very origin of everything we are aware of), and we are far from knowing what it is, and what it consists of – in short: it still *remains to be determined.* In other words, Heidegger maintains that the tendency to forget what we usually call the "subject" must be counteracted, that the problem of intentionality and of the "self" must be posed, but that we cannot rely on the categories of usual understanding, because they suffer from a restricted "angle of vision" and seem unable to grasp their objects. According to him, a radical reappraisal of "subjectivity", selfhood and objectivity (that is a radical reappraisal of the whole "thing" – the thing we usually call "life") proves indispensable – and this is what the "hermeneutics of facticity" is all about. But there is more: Heidegger as well draws our attention to this: that our understanding of the apprehension of facts as a *straightforward, simple* apprehension (and of facts as the "plain" thing that is grasped by means of this simple apprehension) is ill-founded.[54] It makes us blind to the very thing it pretends to clarify. For it makes us forget that what we call "facts" results from a complicated interweaving of elements in the realm of "life" viz. in the "primal unity". It makes us forget that "facts" result from an "Aufgehen"[55] (an "absorption", a

---

    came the term for the primal unity (viz. for the result of the rectified form of "Rückgang auf das Subjekt"). But his fundamental problem did not change.

54  See, for example, GAH 61, p. 149 ff.; GAH 63, p. 75; GAH 64, p. 41, p. 43, p. 51; GAH 17, p. 38, p. 298; GAH 18, p. 279 f.; GAH 19, p. 642; GAH 20, p. 81 f, p. 258, p. 264, p. 266 f.; GAH 21, p. 145 ff.; GAH 27, p. 76 f.; VWG 28 (131); GAH 32, p. 101 f.

55  See, for instance, GAH 58, p. 33, p. 49, p. 108 f, p. 112 f., p. 115, p. 117 f., p. 124 f., p. 16, p. 108, p. 2, p. 180, p. 217, p. 255; GAH 60, p. 200, p. 227 f., p. 239 f.; GAH 61, p. 90, p. 194, p. 103, p. 123, p. 132, p. 412; GAH 62, p. 17; PIA, p. 355 ff., p. 359 ff., p. 362, p. 366; GAH 63, p. 103, p. 112; GAH 17, p. 84; GAH 18, p. 108; GAH 20, p. 137, p. 250, p. 267 f., p. 286, p. 289, p. 329, p. 336, p. 339, p. 350 f., p. 352 f, p. 407, p. 420; GAH 21, p. 156 f., p. 230 f.; GAH 22, p. 8; GAH 24, p. 250, p. 463; GAH 26, p. 174; GAH 27, p. 135, p. 148, p. 333 ff., p. 357, p. 359; SuZ, p. 51, p. 54, p. 71 f., p. 75 f., p. 111, p. 113, p. 125, p. 129 f., p. 167, p. 172, p. 175 f, p. 184, p. 189, p. 192, p.

state of being "lost" in them), that this absorption, this "Verfallen an die Welt" ("falling prey to the world") gives evidence of life's "downfall", "decadence" ("Ruinanz"/ "Verfallen"[56]) – that life viz. the primal unity is *falling away from itself* : has become alien and blind to itself, and can be "restored" only by means of a countermovement ("Gegenruinanz"[57]). The illusion of simple, straightforward apprehension makes us forget that facts "result" from *underlying suppositions* and from their concealment, that they rely on what Heidegger calls tacit forms of "vorgängige Hinblicknahme"[58], which from the outset provide the understanding of their mode of being – and that the whole set of tacit suppositions that sustain our understanding of each "content" or "fact" is very extensive and complex. In other words, it makes us forget that our awareness of things has subsurface components (that it is composed not only of *explicit, thematic*, but of *inexplicit, unthematic* elements[59]) – so that when Fichte

---

203, p. 222, p. 224 f., p. 252, p. 270, p. 315, p. 322, p. 354 f., p. 369, p. 389; GAH 29/30, p. 153, p. 513; ZS p. 205 f., p. 256,

56 Cf. GAH 60, p. 15 f., p. 51, p. 102, p. 113, p. 128, p. 164, p. 197, p. 200, p. 205 f., p. 219 f., p. 228, p. 235, p. 237, p. 240, p. 244 f., p. 252 f., p. 259, p. 264, p. 268 f., pp. 298 f.; AKJ, GAH 9, p. 34; GAH 61, p. 2, p. 39, p. 103, p. 120 f., p. 125, p. 127, p. 131 ff., p. 139 ff., p. 142, p. 143 ff., p. 147 f., p. 149 ff., p. 153 f., p. 178, p. 184, p. 186; GAH 62, p. 37 f., p. 41, p. 48, p. 56 ff., p. 69, p. 74 f, p. 93, p. 95, p. 106, p. 226, p. 260, p. 269, p. 277 f., p. 280, p. 299; PIA, GAH 62, p. 350 f., p. 355 ff., p. 366; GAH 63, p. 109; GAH 64, p. 43, p. 50 f., p. 54, p. 56; GAH 64, p. 41 ff., p. 49 ff, p. 66; GAH 17, p. 83 f.; GAH 20, p. 336, p. 348, p. 376 ff., p. 384, p. 387 ff., p. 390, p. 404 f, p. 416, p. 421; GAH 21, p. 213, p. 230 ff.; SuZ, p. 4, p. 116, p. 175 ff., p. 179 ff., p. 221, p. 348; GAH 24, p. 227 f, p. 243 f., p. 384, p. 410 f.; GAH 26, p. 174; GAH 27, p. 207; KPM, p. 228 f.

57 That is what he calls a "Gegenbewegung gegen das verfallende Sorgen", a "Gegenbewegung gegen die Verfallstendenz" (PIA, GAH 62, pp. 360–361) – see also GAH 61, p. 132, p. 152 f., p. 160, p. 176, p. 178, p. 183; GAH 62, p. 37, p. 40, p. 52; GAH 63, p. 109, and SuZ, p. 222.

58 GAH 20, p. 64; GAH 21, p. 208 f., p. 274 ff, p. 277, p. 282, p. 287 f., p. 307 f., p. 318 f., p. 338, p. 345 f., p. 377, p. 339, p. 284 f., p. 345 f.; SuZ, p. 8, p. 31, p. 75 f., p. 86; GAH 24, p. 13 f., p. 72, p. 99, p. 103, p. 424, p. 432, p. 446, p. 451; GAH 25, p. 22, p. 23 f., p. 27, p. 45 f., pp. 125–129, p. 149, p. 150 f., p. 154, p. 231 f.; GAH 26, p. 16, p. 117, pp. 184–5; GAH 27, p. 203 ff.; GAH 29/30, p. 514, p. 524 ff.; KPM, p. 11 ff, p. 67; VWG, GAH 9, p. 131 f., p. 138 f., p. 158 f., p. 168; GAH 45, pp. 61–67, 74, p. 83 ff, p. 93, p. 200 ff.,

59 For Heidegger's phenomenology of the unthematic (*unausdrücklich, unabgehoben, unthematisch*) see, for example, GAH 58, p. 218 f.; GAH 61, p. 89, p. 93, p. 95, p. 98, p. 104 f., p. 134; GAH 62, p. 68, p. 78, p. 87, p. 92, p. 126, p. 137 f, p. 230, p. 269, p. 271, p. 291, p. 298, p. 300, p. 306;, PIA,

speaks of "*hidden* factors", of *underlying, presupposed, invisible* comprehension ("*vorausgesetztes*", "*unsichtbar bleibendes Verstehen*"), of opaqueness ("Undurchsichtigkeit") and of the lack of "Verstehen vom Verstehen", everything he says could be endorsed by Heidegger. The illusion of simple, straightforward apprehension makes us forget that "facts" are made of unintelligible determinations and of our unawareness of this – in other words, it makes us forget that trivial, commonplace determinations, which seem absolutely self-evident and fully comprehensible (and indeed fundamental determinations, on which our understanding of everything relies) do not withstand critical scrutiny and are fraught with what Heidegger calls "Fraglichkeit".[60] Last but not least, the illusion of simple, straightforward apprehension makes us forget that "facts" are in-

---

GAH 62, p. 354 f.; GAH 63, p. 31, p. 98; GAH 17, p. 82; GAH 18, p. 271 f., p. 304, p. 357, p. 374 f., p. 376 f.; GAH 19, p. 96, p. 182 f.; GAH 20, p. 65, p. 70, p. 250 ff., p. 265 ff., p. 281, p. 289, p. 349, p. 351; GAH 21, p. 104, p. 145, p. 154, p. 187, p. 275 f., p. 277 ff, p. 286, p. 288, p. 294, p. 345 ff, p. 383 ff., p. 399 ff., p. 404 f., p. 412; SuZ, p. 17, p. 31, p. 35, p. 74 f., p. 76, p. 83, p. 86, p. 112, p. 145, p. 324, p. 356, p. 364, p. 406, p. 408 f., p. 414 f.; GAH 24, p. 392, p. 439 f, p. 448, p. 453; GAH 25, p. 22 f., p. 128, p. 154, p. 172, p. 231; GAH 26, p. 259 f.; GAH 29/30, p. 505, p. 519; GAH 31, p. 40 ff.; PT, GAH 9, p. 50; KPM, p. 118 f., p. 139 f.

60 The concept of Fraglichkeit stresses, on the one hand, that self-evident trivial, commonplace determinations are fraught with difficulty: "Es besteht in Dasein selbst die Möglichkeit, daß es sich in einem Verstehen bewegt, das nur so aussieht wie ein Verstehen und keins ist. Dieses eigentümliche Scheinverstehen beherrscht das Dasein in weitem Ausmaß. "(GAH 20, p. 358). Cf, for example, GAH 56/57, p. 19; GAH 58, p. 31, p. 36, p. 43; GAH 61, p. 151 f., p. 174; GAH 17, p. 76; GAH 19, p. 7, p. 13, p. 16, p. 22 ff., p. 24, p. 55, p. 128, p. 153, p. 219, p. 358, p. 368 f., p. 371 ff., p. 376 ff, p. 435 f., p. 466 f.,p. 492 ff., p. 495, p. 520, p. 524, p. 534, p. 579, p. 630; GAH 20, p. 62, p. 189, p. 193 f., p. 202, p. 205, p. 253, p. 268, p. 296 f., p. 299 f., p. 353, p. 358, p. 372, p. 389, p. 415; GAH 21, p. 198, p. 288; SuZ, p. 4; GAH 24, p. 18 f., p. 72 ff., p. 80, p. 324 f., p. 371 f.; GAH 25, p. 310; GAH 26, p. 6; GAH 27, p. 50, p. 217, p. 222 f.; GAH 28, p. 44 f., p. 292 f.; GAH 29/30, p. 219, p. 258, p. 399, p. 490, p. 516; GAH 31, p. 143; KPM, p. 220 f, p. 226; BwJ, p. 70 f. But Heidegger's concept of *Fraglichkeit* stresses another aspect: it means *persistent* difficulty – not the kind of problem, which once posed, can be ultimately solved, but one which does not disappear, for all answers are fraught with difficulties and raise new questions. For Heidegger's concept of *Fraglichkeit* see, for example, GAH 58, p. 36, p. 42, p. 173; GAH 61, p. 2, p. 34, p. 37, p. 56, p. 93, p. 150 ff., p. 174 ff., p. 190, p. 195, p. 197; GAH 62, p. 37, p. 283; PIA, GAH 62, p. 348 ff.; GAH 63, p. 17; GAH 17, p. 76 f.; GAH 21, p. 23 f.; GAH 25, p. 2; GAH 26, p. 14; GAH 27, p. 200; GAH 29/30, p. 28 ff., p. 31 ff, p. 36, p. 84, p. 244 ff, p. 255; GAH 31, p. 116, p. 130, p. 143; GAH 32, p. 51, p. 56.

separable from that peculiar kind of element that surfaces in the factical self (:"selfhood"), from its relation to itself and from the peculiar kind of "tension" that arises from it – so that in the end the "absolut Vorhandene", instead of being "absolut vorhanden," is but a *derivative* component within the framework of that primal element, the unity of life, that still remains to be determined.

To be sure, Heidegger does not use the concept of facticity in the same way as Fichte. For Fichte facticity denotes the sphere of what we usually call facts, but in such a way that he changes our whole understanding of its nature. When he speaks of facticity, what he has in mind is the exact opposite of our usual understanding: factical consciousness (and the whole sphere of facts) is a "product" of "life" – the dreamlike product in which "life" is so absorbed that it "forgets" itself and becomes unaware of the role it plays in its constitution. For Heidegger, the concept of facticity does not refer primarily to the sphere of facts. But on the other hand, it denotes precisely what the absorption in "facts" makes us forget: the primal unity of life viz. a fundamental feature of this primal element. Moreover, according to him, the whole sphere of facts stems from this primal element, belongs to it, happens only insofar as it happens (and bears, as it were, its imprint). But that is not all: Heidegger's concept of facticity stresses a fundamental feature of "life": it is finite, "historical" – its "thrownness" ("Geworfenheit") and "Jeweiligkeit" and that it always happens in a certain "how" ("Wie") "des Sichhabens" and "des Sichnichthabens" – in a certain way of "having" ("possessing") and "not having" ("not possessing") itself.[61]. We cannot unravel these

---

61 For "Geworfenheit" see: GAH 25, p. 24, p. 85; GAH 26, p. 13, p. 174, p. 268, p. 278; GAH 27, p. 147, p. 328 f., p. 330 ff., p. 334, p. 338 f, p. 357 f.; SuZ, p. 134 ff., p. 144 f., p. 175 ff., p. 221, p. 276, p. 284 f., p. 297, p. 325 f., p. 328, p. 339 f., p. 348; KPM, p. 205 f., p. 221, p. 228, p. 261; GAH 3, p. 267; WiM?, GAH 9, p. 117; GAH p. 31, p. 181; for "Jeweiligkeit", see GAH 63, p. 7, p. 29, p. 48, p. 87, p. 95; GAH 64, p. 45 f., p. 111 f., p. 113, p. 115; GAH 17, p. 250, p. 288 f.; GAH 18, p. 32, p. 180, p. 186, p. 195, p. 246, p. 350 f.; GAH 19, p. 156; GAH 20, p. 205 f., p. 207 f., p. 325; GAH 28, p. 260, p. 267. What Heidegger calls "factical life" is constituted in such a way that it *always* possesses itself. It could not be without somehow possessing itself (without being somehow *aware* of itself). But, on the other hand, this does not mean that it must be *transparent* to itself – on the contrary: "life" is at the same time characterized by *eluding* itself viz. *not possessing* itself. In short: factical life always *possesses and does not possess* itself. Or, more precisely, it always possesses and does not possess itself *in a certain "how"* ("Wie"): *a certain way of possessing and not possessing itself.* Heidegger writes (GAH 64, p. 117): "Die Grundkategorie dieses Seienden ist das Wie".

concepts here. But we must keep in mind that they are designed to articulate the unique facticity of the "sum".[62] In other words, they state that the "sum" is a fact, but in a way that differs radically from the facticity of a "Vorgang", a "Vorhandenes", or a fact in the usual sense.[63] Having said this, we must also keep in mind that when Heidegger speaks of the facticity of the "sum" he certainly want to stress the unique way in which the "sum" is a fact, but that on the other hand he also wants to point out that the "sum" *finds* itself, that it is radically *bound*, that it is not transparent to itself, that it is far from understanding itself. In other words, like Fichte's, Heidegger's concept of facticity denotes *the finite*. But this time it is not only everyday consciousness or certain forms of knowledge, but the very fact of the "sum" in the core of life (the primal unity) that is factical. And this in such a way that there is absolutely no possibility of an "Austilgung der Fackticität" – of overcoming this radical facticity. Last but not least, we must also keep in mind that according to Heidegger, facts, in the *usual* sense, do not only bear the imprint of the primal element, life. They are what they are because of *life's facticity* – they bear the imprint of that fundamental feature of the primal element: *its* facticity.

In other words: The unique facticity and the finitude of the "sum" is in the end what Heidegger has in mind when he speaks of facticity.[64] But

---

This applies here as well. For the fundamental phenomenon of life's possession and lack of possession of itself, cf. GAH 58, p. 157 ff., p. 246 ff., p. 250 ff., p. 253 ff., p. 257 ff.; GAH 60, p. 15 f., p. 103, p. 105, p. 185, p. 187 f., p. 190 f., p. 227 f., p. 240 f., p. 243 f., p. 246, p. 252, p. 254, p. 263; AKJ, GAH 9, p. 31 f., p. 34; GAH 61, p. 18, p. 88, p. 106 f., p. 132, p. 137, p. 148, p. 171 f.; PIA, GAH 62, p. 360; GAH 63, p. 48 f., p. 50 f., p. 64 f.; GAH 64, p. 114; GAH 17, p. 249 f., p. 255, p. 278, p. 286 f.; GAH 18, p. 246 ff., p. 250, p. 270 f., p. 362 f.; GAH 20, p. 354, p. 405; GAH p. 21, p. 230 f.; GAH 24, p. 225, p. 227, p. 243.

62 For the "sum" ("bin"), its unique character and decisive role, see for instance GAH 60, p. 91 f., p. 192 f., p. 212 f., p. 238; AKJ, GAH 9, p. 5, p. 10, p. 19 ff., p. 29 ff., p. 35; GAH 61, pp. 172–177; GAH 64, p. 111 f., p. 113; GAH 17, p. 240 f., p. 243 f., p. 249 ff., p. 287 f.; GAH 20, p. 210, p. 296, p. 433, p. 437 f., p. 440; GAH 17, p. 247 ff.; GAH 21, p. 331 f.; SuZ, p. 46, p. 211; GAH 24, p. 220, p. 392; GAH 27, p. 118 f.; GAH 28, p. 106 f., p. 108 ff.; GAH 29/30, p. 30, p. 84; BwL, p. 29 f.

63 See, for instance, GAH 62, p. 355, p. 356 f., p. 358; GAH 20, p. 402 f.; GAH 21, p. 233; SuZ, p. 56, p. 179, p. 276.

64 The facticity of the "sum" is unique for various reasons. As Heidegger puts it (BwJ, p. 26 f.): "Es gibt Gegenstände, die man nicht hat, sondern 'ist'; und zwar noch solche, deren 'Was' lediglich ruht in dem 'Daß sie sind'". Cf. GAH 62, p. 180 f. There is a considerable difference between a fact one merely *observes*

and the fact *one is* (the *fact of oneself:* the fact that only is insofar as there is a "sum" generating and *assuming* that fact – *being itself the fact in question*). But, on the other hand, Heidegger stresses that in the particular case of the "sum" the fact does not possess a "Wesen" (an essence, a "quiddity") which can be grasped and understood irrespective of whether that "quiddity" is or is not. The "content" of the "sum" presupposes the fact (that there really is someone being *oneself* – actually caught in being oneself). In other words: the *content* of the "sum" is rooted in the fact, *emerges from it* and can be really *witnessed only by the fact itself.* Which brings us to a further key feature of the facticity of the "sum", namely: the fact of the "sum" is a peculiar kind of fact which *relates to itself* (and only is *by relating to itself*). And its relation to itself is again a most peculiar kind of relation: "Ich bin es" ("I am it", GAH 64, p. 43). What Heidegger calls facticity (the facticity of the "sum") has to do with this fundamental phenomenon that pervades our being: "mea res agitur" ("it is about me" – "I am it", viz. the "Grunderfahrung des "ich bin", in der es radikal und rein um mich selbst geht", AKJ, GAH 9, p. 29, cf. GAH 27, p. 325 f., p. 331). Facticity denotes the unique constitution of the "mea res agitur" and of that kind of being which only is insofar as it relates to itself in the form of the "mea res agitur". This being finds itself being itself (the central *contingent* fact of the "I am it" – "it is about me"). But, on the other hand, to be caught in being oneself, to be "tied" to it, means to be caught in the *concrete situation* in which the self finds itself – that is, in a certain combination of circumstances and facts (in a certain "state of affairs" of the self). See for instance *SuZ*, p. 56: "Der Begriff Faktizität beschließt in sich: das In-der-Weltsein eines "innerweltlichen" Seienden, so zwar, daß sich dieses Seiende verstehen kann als in einem "Geschick" verhaftet mit dem Sein des Seienden, das ihm innerhalb seiner eigenen Welt begegnet." Cf. also GAH 27, p. 325 f. Facts in the latter sense do not exist apart from the "mea res agitur" ("I am it" – "it is about me") and the fundamental facticity of the "sum". They are, as it were, an *extension* of that fundamental facticity. So that facts, in this sense, always have a peculiar constitution – a constitution which can be articulated as follows:

[Facticity of the "sum" ( the facts viz. the concrete situation in which the "*sum*" finds itself) ]

In short, the "I am it" ("it is about me") – this central *fact* – is the root of everything in the "existential monad". The point cannot be overemphasised that the root of everything in the existential monad (that is, for each one of us: the root of everything *überhaupt*) is simply a *fact*. In other words: the *lumen naturale* that lights up the existential monad is only a "nacktes Dass" – *a bare fact* viz. something *utterly* opaque and *utterly contingent.* This means: the "sum" has *no root*, only the absolute fact of itself. It is *groundless* ("grundlos"). It is incapable of accounting for its own being, steeped in what Heidegger calls (GAH 27, p. 340) the "Dunkelheit" and "Ohnmacht seiner Herkunft" (the "obscurity and powerlessness of its origin"). The "sum" is *anchorless, left entirely to itself,* perpetually *threatened* by the *possibility of annihilation, beleaguered* as it were by *nothingness.* In short: the "sum", the very core of the existential monad, is totally *adrift* in its own absolute facticity. For Heidegger's concept of "facticity" see GAH 58, p. 171, p. 173; GAH 59, p. 19, p. 37, p. 83 ff., p. 87, p. 174; GAH 60, p. 9, p.

this unique facticity of the "sum" is anything but a trait of a component of "life" among many others (and so that the sense in which these other components of "life" are "a fact" has nothing to do with the facticity of the "sum"). The opposite is true: the facticity of the "sum" is, according to Heidegger, the primal facticity, the origin of all forms of facticity. And that is precisely the point I wanted to stress: 1) For Heidegger, as for Fichte, facticity is *primarily, not secondarily* ("*abgeleiteterweise*"), *facticity of the self.* 2) But for Heidegger facticity is not a *moment* of the self or of life: it pertains to the very core and root of it. So that even the most accomplished "Gegenruinanz" remains caught in facticity.[65]

But I must conclude. And it is now time to shed some light on the dividing line between Fichte's and Heidegger's concepts of facticity. Let us consider the problem from Heidegger's perspective. From the very beginning, Heidegger's critique of the "absolut Vorhandene" points out that our whole understanding suffers from the *primacy* of what he calls "kognitives In-sein" ("cognitive being-in")[66] and the manner of being of the thing "already there in advance" – that is of "Vorhandenheit" (pure "presence", "on-handness").[67] He shows that the former is not the primary

---

93 f., p. 116 f., p. 118 f., p. 138, p. 145, p. 213, p. 215 f., p. 220, p. 230 f., pp. 241–244, p. 252, p. 253 ff., p. 263, p. 265, p. 280, p. 283, p. 298 f.; AKJ, GAH 9, p. 22, p. 29 ff., p. 32; GAH 61, p. 70, p. 76 f., p. 87 f., p. 97, p. 99 ff., p. 114 f, p. 117 f., p. 124, p. 139 f., p. 159 ff., p. 168, p. 176 f., p. 183 f., p. 187, p. 195; GAH 62, p. 27, p. 50, p. 113, p. 150, p. 176, p. 180 f., p. 181, p. 211 f., p. 226 f., p. 275 f, p. 277 f., p. 289 f.; PIA, GAH 62, p. 346, p. 351, p. 356, p. 357; GAH 63, p. 3, p. 7, p. 14 ff., p. 21, p. 26, p. 29, p. 65, p. 105, p. 109; GAH 17, p. 35, p. 106, p. 288 f.; GAH 20, p. 208, p. 304, p. 402 f., p. 408 f.; GAH 21, p. 213, p. 233, p. 409, p. 414; SuZ, p. 56, p. 145, p. 179, p. 180 f., p. 191 f., p. 221 f., p. 276, p. 284 f., p. 328, p. 348; GAH 24, p. 217 f., p. 399; GAH 26, p. 142, p. 198, p. 268; GAH 27, p. 279, pp. 325–326, p. 331 f., p. 338 f., p. 340 f.; GAH 28, p. 145 f., p. 259; GAH 31, p. 273, p. 283, p. 285, p. 291 f.; BwJ, p. 26 f.; BwL, p. 28, p. 29, p. 30, p. 31, p. 36 f., p. 38.
65 Cf. SuZ, p. 192: "Existieren ist immer faktisches. Existenzialität ist wesenhaft durch Faktizität bestimmt."
66 See, for example, GAH 62, p. 20, p. 28, p. 53, p. 58 ff., p. 63, p. 66 ff., p. 72, p. 74, p. 85 ff., p. 92 ff., p. 105, p. 107, p. 108, p. 115, p. 117, p. 126, p. 157, p. 165, p. 167, p. 180 f., p. 183, p. 192, p. 198 f., p. 207 f., p. 226 f., p. 239, p. 250 f., p. 253 f., p. 269, p. 271, p. 280 ff., p. 300, p. 307; PIA p. 352 ff., p. 358; GAH 17, p. 82 ff., p. 115, p. 123, p. 125, p. 269, p. 271; GAH 20, pp. 215–226, ff.; GAH 21, p. 153 ff.; SuZ, p. 59 ff.,
67 For *Vorhandenheit*, cf. GAH 56/57, p. 98; GAH 58, p. 50 ff., pp. 69–70, pp. 122–127, p. 152; AKJ, GAH 9, p. 21, p. 22, p. 31; GAH 62, p. 81 f., p.

mode of "being-in" and that the latter is not the primary manner of being. According to him, the primary mode of *being-in* is *pre-cognitive* (pre-theoretical).[68] It is inextricably intertwined with the existential character of "life" and with the existential forms of sense, which ultimately depend on the basic existential categories Heidegger calls "Existenzialien" (existentials).[69] And the primary manner of being is "Zuhandenheit" ("ready-to-handness").[70] It is characterized by "Bedeutsamkeit", *signifi-*

---

144, p. 201, p. 233, p. 240 ff., p. 257 f., p. 285 f, p. 319; GAH 63, p. 93, p. 95, p. 97; GAH 64, p. 19 f., p. 21 ff., p. 37 f.; GAH 20, p. 48 ff., p. 212, p. 255 f., p. 258, p. 263 ff., p. 269 f., p. 271 f., p. 289; GAH 21, p. 63, p. 76, p. 143, pp. 155–159, pp. 186–191, p. 314 f.; SuZ, p. 7, p. 42, p. 45, p. 48 ff., p. 54 ff., p. 70 ff., p. 75, p. 83, p. 88, p. 96 f., p. 98 ff., p. 114, p. 118, p. 130, p. 147, p. 153, p. 158 ff., p. 179, p. 183, p. 203 ff., p. 211 f., p. 224 f., p. 230, p. 238, p. 241, p. 283, p. 304, p. 316, p. 318, p. 362, p. 364, p. 389; GAH 24, p. 32, p. 36, p. 52, p. 92, p. 94 f., p. 153, p. 168 f., p. 209 ff., p. 236, p. 249, p. 410, p. 414, p. 416, p. 438 f., p. 445, p. 448; GAH 25, p. 19, p. 44, p. 145, p. 160, p. 200, p. 204; GAH 27, p. 71, p. 75 f., p. 82 ff, p. 94 f., p. 101, p. 111 f., p. 121, p. 158, p. 184, p. 208 f., p. 343; GAH 29/30, p. 398 f, p. 401 ff, p. 422 f., p. 498 ff.; VWG, GAH 9, p. 140; GAH 31, p. 50 f., p. 56, p. 155, p. 192, p. 197, p. 199 f., p. 213, p. 219.

68  Cf. GAH 56/57, p. 70 ff., p. 73 f., p. 85 ff., p. 88 ff.; GAH 58, p. 120 ff.; GAH 62, p. 20, p. 28, p. 53, p. 58 ff., p. 63, p. 66 ff., p. 72, p. 74, p. 85 ff., p. 92 ff., p. 105, p. 107, p. 108, p. 115, p. 117, p. 126, p. 157, p. 165, p. 167, p. 180 f., p. 183, p. 192, p. 198 f., p. 207 f., p. 226 f., p. 239, p. 250 f., p. 253 f., p. 269, p. 271, p. 280 ff., p. 300, p. 307; PIA, GAH 62, p. 352 ff., p. 358; GAH 63, p. 100 ff., p. 112; GAH 64, p. 19 f., p. 66 f.; GAH 20, p. 215 ff., 226 ff., 231 ff., 263–269, 379, GAH 21, 143 ff., SuZ, 59 ff., 89 ff., GAH 24, 153 f., 232, 239, 412 ff., GAH 27, 317 ff.

69  Cf. GAH 61, p. 2, p. 26, p. 55, p. 79, p. 88, pp. 98–99, p. 117, p. 124, p. 135, p. 148, p. 175, p. 185 f.; GAH 62, p. 298 f.; GAH 63, p. 16, p. 35, p. 43 f., p. 51, p. 66; GAH 17, p. 110 f., p. 116; GAH 20, p. 313; GAH 21, p. 402 f.; GAH 25, p. 377; SuZ, p. 44 f., p. 54; GAH 28, p. 108, p. 242.

70  For *Zuhandenheit*, cf. GAH 56/57, p. 70 ff., p. 84 ff., p. 98; GAH 58, p. 116 f., p. 120 f.; GAH 62, p. 57, p. 59 f., p. 63, p. 77 f., p. 83, p. 89, p. 93, p. 105, p. 107, p. 116 ff., p. 125, p. 129, p. 144, p. 147, p. 149, p. 165, p. 183, p. 188, p. 198 f., p. 253, p. 271, p. 277, p. 300, p. 306 f., p. 317; PIA, GAH 62, p. 352 f.; GAH 63, p. 86 f., p. 88 f., p. 90 ff., p. 93 f.; GAH 64, p. 22 f., p. 30 ff., p. 36 f.; GAH 20, p. 250, p. 252 ff., p. 257 f., p. 259 f., p. 263 ff, p. 269 ff., p. 272, p. 278 ff.; GAH 21, p. 104, pp. 143–153, p. 154ss., p. 158, p. 207; SuZ, p. 69 ff., p. 72 ff., p. 76 ff., p. 83 ff., p. 95 ff., p. 102 f., p. 104 ff., p. 110 ff., p. 117 ff., p. 144, p. 148 ff., p. 157 f., p. 164, p. 172, p. 183, p. 201, p. 211, p. 230, p. 297 f., p. 352 ff., p. 356 ff., p. 364, p. 388 ff.; GAH 24, p. 410, p. 412 ff., p. 416, p. 429 ff., p. 432 ff., p. 438 f., p. 442 f., p. 459 f.; GAH 27, p. 71, p. 75 ff., p. 82 f., p. 111 f., p. 184 f., p. 192 f., p. 208 f.; GAH 29/30, p. 498 ff.; GAH 31, p. 50 f.

*cance* (and indeed in such a way that significance is not a *trait* of the ready-to-hand, but its very *nature* – and that the phenomenon of *significance* presupposes the *existential* character of "life" and the *existential* forms of sense and would not be possible without them).[71] Heidegger's attempt to overcome the shortcomings of our usual understanding of life, consciousness, self and objects begins with the discovery of the *derivative* character of "pure presence" and cognition.[72] In other words, it begins as an attempt to counteract the tendency of cognitive in-being and "Vorhandenheit" to creep into our understanding of everything we examine and to dominate all our explicit views. In short, Heidegger's whole endeavor has its starting-point in this attempt to rediscover what lies *beyond* pure presence and cognitive in-being. From the very beginning the words "factical life" and "facticity" are associated with this attempt and indicate precisely what lies beyond cognitive being-in and pure presence – the iceberg the latter mask and of which they are but the tip. But it must be kept in mind that, when he speaks of the derivative character of cognition and pure presence, Heidegger does not only mean that cognition and pure presence "come later". They could be derivative in this sense and still constitute the correct approach viz. the real form of "reality". What he means is that pure presence and cognitive in-being are what he calls "deficient modi".[73] In the end, the existential neutrality of cogni-

---

71 For "Bedeutsamkeit", see GAH 58, p. 102 ff., p. 106 ff., p. 111 f, p. 124 f, p. 190, p. 197 f., p. 216 f., p. 218 ff., p. 231; GAH 59, p. 81 f., p. 84, p. 182 f.; GAH 60, p. 13 ff., p. 16, p. 116 f., p. 136 f., p. 197, p. 206 f., p. 214 f., p. 217 f., p. 226 f., p. 242, p. 248, p. 252 ff., p. 255 s., p. 258 f., p. 263; AKJ, GAH 9, p. 30; GAH 61, p. 90 ff., p. 119; GAH 62, p. 94, p. 223, p. 225, p. 250 f., p. 301, p. 353 f; GAH 63, p. 85 ff., p. 93 ff., p. 96 ff., p. 101, p. 111 f.; GAH 64, p. 22 f., p. 65 ff.; GAH 18, p. 300, p. 302, p. 314, p. 370, p. 378 f., p. 387; GAH 20, p. 272 f. p. 274 f., p. 278, p. 285 ff., p. 292, p. 359; GAH 21, p. 144, p. 146 ff, p. 150 f.; SuZ, p. 83 ff., p. 123, p. 142 ff., p. 297, p. 364.
72 See footnote 68.
73 SuZ 20, p. 57, p. 73, p. 104, p. 120 f., p. 121, p. 123 f, p. 336, p. 355. As "deficient modi", cognition and pure presence differ from "*pre-cognitive* being-in" and "ready-to-handness", but in such a way that they result from a modification thereof and always presuppose the original "modi". To be sure, cognition and pure presence may appear to be autonomous and the opposite of "*pre-cognitive* being-in" and "ready-to-handness". But Heidegger points out that these *derived modi* can only occur in the *medium* of "*pre-cognitive* being-in" and "ready-to-handness". Cognition and pure presence result from *Entlebnis/Entlebung* (cf. GAH 56/57, p. 73 f., p. 88 ff., p. 96 f., p. 100, p. 112, p. 207, p. 209, p. 211; GAH 58, p. 75, p. 77 f., p. 232; AKJ, GAH 9, p. 18, p. 33, p. 37 f.;

tion and the "pure there" is but an optical illusion (a new form of "transcendental illusion", as he puts it in *Grundbegriffe der Metaphysik*).[74] "Cognition" and "pure presence" arise out of an *existential* foundation. And they blind us not only to the other manners of being and modes of being-in, but also to their *own constitution*, in so far as they too are rooted in the existential core of life, which is, as Heidegger puts it, the real "Ursprung" in the neo-Kantian sense.[75] But on the other hand it must be kept in mind that the overcoming of this "transcendental illusion" and the discovery of the existential core cannot be attained once and for all – the "transcendental illusion" reenacts itself again and again, and it can "worm its way" into the very attempt to eliminate it.[76] Furthermore, according to Heidegger, the project of *knowledge* is in itself fraught with a tendency towards this transcendental illusion and towards making us lose sight of the existential core. In other words, the project of knowledge makes us, as he puts it, "einstellungsmässig" blind.[77]

---

GAH 61, p. 91) or *Entweltlichung* (cf. GAH 20, p. 227, p. 249, p. 265 f., p. 300 f, p. 308, p. 314, p. 381; SuZ, p. 65, p. 75, p. 112 f.; GAH 62, p. 82, p. 354). But *Entlebung* and *Entweltlichung* are *transformed "Erleben" and transformed "Welt"*. Or, as Kant says about the parts of space (Refl. 4425), they can only exist *abstrahendo a caeteris* (in this case, "Erleben, Welt , *"pre-cognitive* being-in" and "ready-to-handness") –: they cannot exist independently, *removendo caetera* (for these are their source and "medium"). See also GAH 59, p. 37.

74 GAH 29/30, p. 422 f.
75 GAH 56/57, p. 95 ff, p. 185; GAH 58, p. 1 ff., p. 11, p. 22, p. 25 ff., p. 30, p. 38, p. 55, p. 81 ff., p. 85 f, p. 136 f., p. 139, p. 147 f., p. 168, p. 171, p. 173 f., p. 203, p. 262; GAH 58, p. 96, p. 136; GAH 21, p. 271; GAH 25, p. 211; GAH 29/30, p. 485 f.
76 See for example GAH 61, p. 153.
77 Cf. GAH 60, p. 17: " Das "Subjekt" ist, besonders in *Fichtes* Behandlung des Sachproblems, eine neue Form der Gegenständlichkeit gegenüber den anderen "Objekten". Doch liegt auch hier, im Ausgang Fichtes von Kants praktischer Philosophie und unter Benutzung Kantischer Vorgriffe, eine im Grunde genommen einstellungshafte Tendenz vor." For Heidegger's phenomenology of the "theoretische Einstellung" and for his critique of the optical illusions generated by it, see, for example, GAH 56/57, p. 87 ff., p. 95 ff., p. 112 ff, p. 207, p. 210 ff.; GAH 58, p. 23, p. 46 ff., p. 50 ff., p. 65 ff., p. 69 ff., p. 75 ff., p. 110 ff., p. 114 ff., p. 120 ff., p. 126 f., p. 137, p. 209 ff., p. 218 ff., p. 221 f., p. 223 f., p. 243 ff.; GAH 59, p. 60 f., p. 63 f., p. 140 ff., p. 144, p. 151, p. 170; GAH 60, p. 14 ff., p. 48, p. 51, p. 58 f, p. 62 ff., p. 88 f., p. 110 ff., p. 168, p. 194, p. 225 f, p. 245; AKJ, GAH 9, p. 21 f., p. 23 f., p. 34 f.; GAH 61, p. 153, p. 159; GAH 62, p. 27, p. 40 f., p. 66, p. 81 f., p. 111 f., p.115, p. 119, p. 178, p. 222 f., p. 271, p. 275, p. 278, p. 282 f., p. 297 ff, p. 301, p. 309;

And here we reach the dividing line (actually not the dividing line, but a first glimpse of one side of a fragment of it). To be sure, Fichte's attempt to unveil the primal unity of life has much in common with Heidegger's. And for Heidegger Fichte goes no doubt in the right direction when he tries to unveil life, the primal unity, or when he draws attention to the role played by action in the constitution of objects. But Fichte's philosophical agenda is guided by the project to overcome facticity in the Fichtean sense and to attain *real* (i.e. *absolute*) *knowledge*. According to Heidegger, this makes him fall prey to the "transcendental illusion" of cognitive in-being, so that he loses sight of the existential core and of the radically finite character (that is, of the facticity, in Heidegger's sense) of the very life he tries to unveil.[78] Whether Heidegger's critique is sound or not (and whether the same accusation could be made against him) remains, of course, a matter of dispute. To say nothing of the objections

---

PIA, GAH 62, p. 353 ff., p. 358, p. 387 ff.; GAH 63, p. 52 ff.; GAH 17, p. 60, p. 62 f., p. 71 f., p. 81, p. 84 f., p. 87, p. 89, p. 92 f., p. 100 f, p. 104 f., p. 106 f., p. 114, p. 116 f., p. 119 f., p. 122 ff., p. 126 ff., p. 130 f., p. 194 f., p. 197, p. 221, p. 266, p. 271, p. 273, p. 277 f., p. 280, p. 288 f., p. 302 f., p. 304 f., p. 311, p. 317 ff.; GAH 20, p. 162, p. 254, p. 380 f.; GAH 21, p. 153 ff.; GAH 24, p. 250 f., p. 455 ff.; GAH 25, p. 25 ff.; GAH 27, p. 156 f., p. 159, p. 160 ff., p. 167 ff., p. 179 f., p. 182, p. 184, p. 192 f., p. 194 f., p. 196 f., p. 198 ff., p. 211 ff., p. 221 ff. It goes without saying that our remarks about Heidegger are still more limited and sketchy than our presentation of Fichte – they highlight the *terminus a quo,* the starting point, not the *terminus ad quem* of his philosophical investigation. In other words, we have tried to depict the crossroad, as it were, and the way he goes – not the whole road, which may be (and in fact is) full of surprises and turns in unexpected directions.

78 This is why Heidegger's appraisal of Fichte in GAH 28 is double-edged. On the one hand, Heidegger stresses the possibility of interpreting the *Grundlage der gesammten Wissenschaftslehre* as an outline of fundamental insights of his own analysis of *Dasein* (see the interpretation of Fichte's "Grundsätze", GAH 28, 52 ff., 239 ff., 247 ff., 283 ff., of the "Grundlage des theoretischen Wisens", GAH 28, 141 ff., 300 ff., and of the "Grundlage der Wissenschaft des Praktischen", GAH 28, 172 ff., 329 ff.). On the other hand, Heidegger points out that Fichte's concern for *certainty* and his attempt to build a *system* of knowledge distract him from examining fundamental problems and prevent him from exploring the paths which lead to the existential-temporal analysis of *Dasein* (see GAH 28, 30 f., 46, 50, 57, 74, 80, 91, 97, 101, 104, 119, 121, 125 f., 139, 145, 166, 170 f., 175, 183, 243 f., 247, 262, 295, 302, 307, 329, 334, and the analysis of the "Sorge um erkannte Erkenntnis" in GAH 17). For Heidegger, as far as philosophical insight into the nature of our existence is concerned, the idea of absolute truth is an "einschläferndes Opiat", a "soporific opiate", as he puts it in GAH 61, 163 f.

Heidegger's phenomenology may raise when considered from the Fichtean point of view. But I have only tried to adumbrate the problem.

# Overcoming the Priority of the Subject: Fichte and Heidegger on Indeterminate Feeling and the Horizon of World and Self-Knowledge

SHARIN N. ELKHOLY

University of Houston-Downtown

To the discriminating ear, the essential thoughts of Fichte and Heidegger appear far apart indeed. While both were concerned with the fundamental structure of the self and the self's understanding of its world, their conclusions could not, at first glance, be more different. Fichte is notoriously known as a subjective idealist who reduces the essence and existence of the world, along with everything in the world, to the activity, demands and understanding of the self. "The Source of all reality is the self, for this is what is immediately and absolutely posited."[1] "Everything posited in the self is reality: and all reality that exists is posited in the self."[2]

On the other hand, Heidegger makes his mark precisely by doing away with the primacy of the subject. The self does not exist apart from the world; rather, the world is a constitutive element of the being of Da-sein. Indeed, Heidegger reconceptualizes the self as inconceivable apart from its being-in-the-world and with others and does away with the notion of a self-sufficient and isolated subject once and for all. "As something factual, the understanding self-projection of Da-sein is always already together with a discovered world."[3] "Through disclosedness this being [Da-sein] is 'there' for itself together with the Da-sein of the world."[4] Nevertheless, while Heidegger asserts the equiprimordiality of the world and Da-sein he continues to fall victim to interpreters who ac-

---

1 Fichte, Johann G.: *The Science of Knowledge*, trans. and ed. Peter Heath and John Lachs, Cambridge 1982, p. 129.
2 Fichte, Johann G.: *The Science of Knowledge*, p. 132.
3 Heidegger, Martin: *Being and Time*, trans. Joan Stambaugh, Albany 1996, p. 194/181. The first number refers to the original German pagination, the second number to the translated English pagination.
4 Heidegger, Martin: *Being and Time*, p. 132/125.

cuse him of setting forth a too subjectivist model of Da-sein. It was not until the so called "turn" that he apparently made with his lecture "On the Essence of Truth," that the charge of egoism was dropped. *Being and Time*, regrettably, continues to be read as a metaphysical text that tries, but ultimately fails, to escape from under the cloud of subjectivism.

I aim to free both Fichte and Heidegger from the charge of egoism and subjectivism directed primarily toward their earlier work by highlighting the irreducibility of the ground of knowledge to the knowing subject in each thinker's thought. My comparison of Fichte and Heidegger occurs at a number of points. I show that for both, the world is the horizon from which all understanding arises. Secondly, the self is inseparable from its world and is inconceivable outside of its relations in the world. And finally, that the world is constituted by an indeterminate mode of feeling – in the case of Fichte the horizon of the world is projected as an infinite striving, while for Heidegger the horizon is revealed or disclosed by *Angst* as the boundless nothing. Characterized by the unlimitedness of the infinite striving of the Fichtean Absolute I or the unbounded nothingness of *Angst*, the world cannot strictly be said to be a determination of consciousness or of the self; in fact, as unlimited the world is beyond the activity and comprehension of the self. It is on the basis of this fundamental point that I aim to put both thinkers in dialogue with each other and venture to show the similarity of thought in Fichte and Heidegger.

This paper begins with a discussion of Fichte's model of the self from *The Science of Knowledge* (*Wissenschaftslehre*) of 1794 where I highlight Fichte's use of an infinite horizon as the ground of all understanding to show how his model of the self eludes the charge of subjectivism. Following this section I focus on *Being and Time* (1927) and discuss Heidegger's construction of the self or Da-sein in relation to *Angst* and show how Being, or the world, is beyond the control of the self. I also suggest that Heidegger's characterization and use of the nothing, as the ground of all beings, is very similar to that of Fichte's Absolute I and may indeed be inspired by Fichte's first principle. In the conclusion I briefly point out one major difference between Fichte and Heidegger with regard to their conception of finitude.

## I. On Fichte and the Infinite Horizon of the Absolute I

At the ground of all consciousness, Fichte places the "infinite self" or Absolute I, which is described as pure activity: "the *pure activity* of the self alone, and the *pure self alone*, are infinite."[5] The infinite here refers to the self's "unbounded," "unconditioned," and "undetermined" absolute activity.[6] By nature, this self must posit (or project) itself into the world, as it is the "the source of all reality."[7] And similar to Heidegger's notion of Dasein as being-in-the-world, Fichte's self can know itself only in its engagement with the world and subsequent reflection upon this engagement. For purposes of discussion, Fichte divides the self's activity into two opposing activities: a "self-reverting" one that contains within it the principle of inward reflection; and an "infinitely outreaching activity," or striving, which makes both reflection and creative outward activity possible.[8] The self's inward and outward activities are united by the self's primordial "demand" that it "encompass all reality and exhaust the infinite"[9] – an endless task that the self strives to fulfill through its productive activity in the world and its subjective reflection upon this activity.

Initially, the two directions of the self are indistinguishable and the self is unconscious. Thus to fulfill its demand, the self's infinite activity must encounter a limit: "If the self did not bound itself, it would not be infinite"[10]. A limit to the self occasions the self to go outside of itself, since it must, by nature, act to transcend this limit; a limit to the self also forces the self's activity back upon itself, thereby making self-reflection possible. As the infinite self or Absolute I is pure, self-reverting activity, "the self can never limit itself."[11] Hence, the limit that occasions both the self's outward activity and its subsequent self-reflection must be external to the self, an object, which Fichte terms a "not-self:" "Without an external prime mover it [the self] would never have acted, and since its existence consists solely in acting, it would never have existed either."[12] Herein lies the dependency of the self upon something external to

---

5 Fichte, Johann G.: *The Science of Knowledge*, p. 226.
6 Fichte, Johann G.: *The Science of Knowledge*, p. 117.
7 Fichte, Johann G.: *The Science of Knowledge*, p. 129.
8 Fichte, Johann G.: *The Science of Knowledge*, p. 193.
9 Fichte, Johann G.: *The Science of Knowledge*, p. 244.
10 Fichte, Johann G.: *The Science of Knowledge*, p. 192.
11 Fichte, Johann G.: *The Science of Knowledge*, p. 249.
12 Fichte, Johann G.: *The Science of Knowledge*, p. 246.

the self, an object, the not-I arising from the self's encounter with the world.

Nevertheless, the object that limits the self and occasions self-reflection is not entirely independent of the self, for it would not exist for the self were the self not equipped with the ability to "leave itself open" to the influence of an object, which it does by transferring its energy to it.[13] Consequently, the object that initially limits the self is also the occasion for the self to limit itself: "No Thou (object), no I (subject): no I, no Thou."[14] Here a significant question arises: Does the opening for the object occur for Fichte within the finite or the infinite self? This question is significant, for if the opening is made by the finite self then Fichte is indeed a subjective idealist. However, if, as I hope to show, the opening for objects occurs within the infinite self, then what determines the object is not the self but rather the indeterminate horizon of feeling. From within which the object shows itself in a manner similar to Heidegger's notion of the nothing that characterizes Being and is disclosed in *Angst*. I will return to this matter below.

At this point, however, the self is in "conflict" with itself, as it must be limited and limit itself so to act in the world and become knowledgeable and aware of the world and itself. Yet it must also continue to act until it exhausts the infinite, as this is what the self does by virtue of being a self. The "striving" toward the unknown, or the self's infinite striving, which is the practical counterpart to the theoretical infinitely outreaching activity of the self, is felt from out of this conflict. This infinite striving, which is inseparable from Fichte's principle of the imagination, is the driving force of Fichte's theory of subjectivity and it is the basis upon which I will argue against the absolute idealism of the Fichtean self.

The Absolute self is infinite with respect to its activity and to its demand to know itself as infinite through its productive activity in the world. However the self's infinite activity ceases to be infinite in reflection, "for as soon as we reflect upon it, it necessarily becomes finite."[15] Consequently, if the self is to strive towards its infinitude, there must be something within the self that drives it to transcend itself, or to overcome its finitude in reflection. This something is what Fichte calls a "longing," which conditions the self's activity and turns it into a "striv-

---

13  Fichte, Johann G.: *The Science of Knowledge*, p. 239.
14  Fichte, Johann G.: *The Science of Knowledge*, p. 173.
15  Fichte, Johann G.: *The Science of Knowledge*, p. 237.

ing" "for something totally unknown."[16] Through this striving the self transcends its finitude – the self limited in reflection – by projecting beyond the limiting object and the self limited in reflection an infinite boundary, or unknown horizon. This infinite boundary, which is the projection of the infinitude of the self's striving is the functional equivalent of Heidegger's notion of the nothing characterized by *Angst*. Like the nothing, the infinite boundary that is projected by the striving of the self is pre-reflective and indeterminate. It serves as the ground of reflection and thus is distinct from, while also inseparable from the finite self. And like Heidegger's nothing, the infinite, as the source and ground of all knowledge, is manifest only in relation to the self mediated by the self's activity in the world.

Already we see that there is a "reciprocity" between the finite self (limited in reflection) and the infinitely striving self. This reciprocity is made possible by "the wonderful power of productive imagination," a faculty that Fichte claims supports the "entire mechanism of the mind."[17] The imagination turns the "conflict" within the self into a "self-reproducing" conflict through the dialectic that it produces between the infinite and the finite self: It "wavers in the middle between determination and non-determination, between finite and infinite."[18] The imagination allows for a "reciprocity" between the subject and the object, holding them together and wavering between them in an "interplay" so that they can be synthesized in reflection.[19] However, the imagination does not simply bring the object into a unity with the subject, but has the more significant task of positing the infinite beyond the object that is fixed in reflection.

The infinite, which is a projection of the Absolute self's striving serves to circumscribe the limits of the object taken up into reflection and further prompts the finite self to transcend itself. The self transcends itself by actively striving beyond the self that is limited in reflection toward some unknown horizon that the imagination projects into the world *beyond* the real object, so on *ad infinitum*. This unknown horizon issues from the self yet can not be said to belong to the self qua individual, as it is infinite and completely indeterminate – it is a product of the Absolute self's infinite striving. The infinite serves as the horizon from

---

16 Fichte, Johann G.: *The Science of Knowledge*, p. 265.
17 Fichte, Johann G.: *The Science of Knowledge*, p. 188.
18 Fichte, Johann G.: *The Science of Knowledge*, p. 194.
19 Fichte, Johann G.: *The Science of Knowledge*, p. 151.

which self knowledge and world knowledge arise, but it itself is never known cognitively. Rather, it is the fold within which all knowledge of the world and self is derived. As infinite, it itself is beyond the grasp of the understanding. It is with respect to highlighting the indeterminacy of the horizon from out of which world and self knowledge arise that I now turn to Heidegger who, I suggest, seems to adopt a variation of Fichte's principle of the Absolute I as his (un) grounding principle of Being.

## II. On Heidegger and the Unbounded Horizon of the Nothing

Like Fichte, who hopes to point the way toward individual freedom and responsibility through his philosophy of Idealism, Heidegger too aims to liberate the individual or Da-sein for its authentic existence through his work. "Initially and for the most part," Heidegger never tires of saying, "the self is lost in the they" living an inauthentic life in comporting itself to Being understood in the mode of objective presence.[20] As is well known, the move from inauthenticity, from Da-sein's rootedness in the world of the "they", to authenticity happens in the mode of existence called Being-toward-death. But the occasion for this move is not the fact that Da-sein is going to die, but rather *Angst*.[21] Indeed, it is by virtue of one's relation to *Angst* that Heidegger classifies individuals as either authentic or inauthentic. Inauthenticity, he argues, results from the sublimating of the *Angst* that accompanies an authentic being-toward-death into a busyness with the matters that are closest at hand. "Everyday taking care of things makes definite for itself the indefiniteness of certain death by interposing before it those manageable urgencies and possibilities of

---

20 Heidegger, Martin: *Being and Time*, p. 384/351.
21 At the heart of the subjectivist reading of Da-sein is the misunderstanding of Heidegger's notion of being-toward-death where death is understood as the end of one's factical existence. The existential notion of death interpreted as the end of life leads to a notion of finitude whereby the limits of Da-sein's being and its projects are squarely rooted in the self. This understanding of death and finitude lends itself to the existentialist interpretations of Da-sein in *Being and Time* perhaps best summed up by Olafson in his book on Existentialism. "Underlying all these conceptions of self-choice is the profound Heideggerian conception of man as the being that founds his own being." Olafson, Frederick A.: *Principles and Persons: An Ethical Interpretation of Existentialism*, Baltimore 1967, p. 172.

the everyday matters nearest to us."[22] "In this entangled being together with [...], the flight from uncanniness makes itself known, that is, the flight *from* its ownmost being-toward-death."[23]

Yet, despite inauthentic Da-sein's flight from death, *Angst* nevertheless persists and remains constant by disclosing Da-sein's being-toward-death. The mood of *Angst* frees Da-sein from the hold of the they and for its authentic possibilities. "Uncanniness pursues Da-sein and threatens its self-forgetful lostness."[24] " In *Angst*, Da-sein finds itself faced with the nothingness of the possible impossibility of its existence."[25] Thus, Heidegger concludes, "Being-toward-death is essentially *Angst*."[26] But to understand Da-sein's mode of being in *Angst* one must understand the characterization of the world in being-toward-death and how this world differs from the everyday world of inauthentic Da-sein.

Through an elaborate discussion of various modes of referential relationships that things have to each other, Heidegger shows that the world serves to ground all knowledge, beings and relations, although it itself can never be objectively thematized. "World itself is not an innerworldly being, and yet it determines innerwordly beings to such an extent that they can only be encountered and discovered and show themselves in their being because 'there is' world."[27] In Da-sein's concernful taking care of things the world shows itself, unthematically, together with what matters to Da-sein. The world of the engineer, for example, gives meaning and shape to the tools that Da-sein operates with in the accomplishment of its tasks as an engineer. In turn, these tools point us toward the world of the engineer.

However, in being-toward-death Da-sein is disclosed in and by the nothing of *Angst* and thereby loses its relation to innerworldly beings. In the uncanniness of the mood of *Angst* Da-sein finds itself disengaged from others and from its everyday concerns because the world that gives to it meaning and structures its everyday associations with things has lost all significance. "Nothing of that which is at hand and objectively present within the world, functions as what *Angst* is anxious about. The totality of relevance discovered within the world of things at hand and objectively

---

22 Heidegger, Martin: *Being and Time*, p. 258/239.
23 Heidegger, Martin: *Being and Time*, p. 252/233
24 Heidegger, Martin: *Being and Time*, p. 277/256.
25 Heidegger, Martin: *Being and Time*, p. 266/245.
26 Heidegger, Martin: *Being and Time*, p. 266/245.
27 Heidegger, Martin: *Being and Time*, pp. 72/67–68.

present is completely without importance."²⁸ *Angst* thus works to clear Da-sein of its inauthentic associations with the everyday world and its affairs and to open Da-sein up to other possibilities on the basis of a different and more authentic relation to the world. Specifically, what Heidegger uses *Angst* to reveal when all of Da-sein's relations to things in the world disappear is the world as such; that is, the world as the ground of possibilities freed of all referential relations. "Being anxious discloses, primordially and directly, the world as world."²⁹

> The utter insignificance which makes itself known in the nothing and nowhere does not signify the absence of world, but means that innerworldly beings in themselves are so completely unimportant that, on the basis of this *insignificance* of what is innerworldly, the world is all that obtrudes itself in its worldliness.³⁰

But what I want to highlight here is that by using *Angst* to reveal the meaning of the world as such, Heidegger appears to break from his phenomenological method of deriving the meaning of the world from the things and relational structures that constitute the world. In the mood of *Angst* the world has lost all significance and possibilities have lost all meaning. Consequently, the world disclosed in *Angst* cannot be understood on the basis of the possibilities that it gives rise to, for in this disclosure there are no possibilities, there is only nothing. Moreover, stripped of all meaning, the world disclosed as such, cannot serve to ground possibilities – and this is because Heidegger posits the world not as prior to the possibilities that it gives rise to, but as an equiprimoridial part of the being of Da-sein by and through which it understands its possibilities and its own self in its relation to possibilities. "World is already discovered beforehand together with everything encountered, although not thematically."³¹

But the meaning of the world is not all that is lost in *Angst*. With the loss of the world, Da-sein loses its relation to its own self as well. This is because Heidegger defines Da-sein strictly in terms of its existence: in its activities in the world and in its relation to its possibilities. "Da-sein *is* always its possibility."³² "As long as it is, Da-sein always has understood

---

28 Heidegger, Martin: *Being and Time*, p. 186/174.
29 Heidegger, Martin: *Being and Time*, p. 187/175.
30 Heidegger, Martin: *Being and Time*, p. 187/175.
31 Heidegger, Martin: *Being and Time*, p. 83/77.
32 Heidegger, Martin: *Being and Time*, p. 42/40.

itself and will understand itself in terms of possibilities."[33] However, in the disclosedness of *Angst* Da-sein is not in relation to any possibilities at all because the world that gives to it meaning and grounds its possibilities has lost all significance. And as Da-sein is only what it projects upon, with the loss of all possibilities Da-sein too is lost. Indeed, what Heidegger characterizes as distinctive about *Angst* is that that which it is about, the world as such, is equally that which it is for, Da-sein's being-in-the-world as such.[34] This is what makes *Angst* ideal for disclosing Da-sein in its totality.[35] Nevertheless, the totality disclosed in *Angst* is, however, one between the world and Da-sein in and as the nothing.

It is this identity of the world and Da-sein characterizd by the nothing that I want to suggest is the same in both form and function to Fichte's infinite I. Because the totality of the world and Da-sein are disclosed in an identity characterized by nothing, there is no distance between Da-sein and the world, and thus no standpoint from which Da-sein may stand to act or to reflect. This is why Heidegger repeatedly states that being-toward-death is "non-relational."[36] In the attunement of *Angst* Da-sein is not in a relation to itself. Concomitantly, Da-sein is not in a relation to the world either – or therefore – a relation that may show itself only on the basis of possibilities that Da-sein projects upon. Thus in being-toward-death there is no world and there is no self, there is only the nothing of *Angst*. This identity of the world and Da-sein disclosed in the nothing, Heidegger posits as the ground of possibilities in general. "The nothingness before which *Angst* brings us reveals the nullity that determines Da-sein in its *ground*, which itself is as thrownness into death."[37]

> What oppresses us is not this or that, nor is it everything objectively present together as a sum, but the *possibility* of things at hand in general, that is, the world itself.[38]

Unless Heidegger intends to put forth a metaphysical account of the meaning of the world we appear to have caught Heidegger with his pants down. Read in light of Fichte's principle of the Absolute I, however, Heidegger's positing of the nothing as a ground begins to make more

---

33 Heidegger, Martin: *Being and Time*, p. 42/40; p. 145/136.
34 Heidegger, Martin: *Being and Time*, p. 187/175.
35 Heidegger, Martin: *Being and Time*, p. 188/176.
36 Heidegger, Martin: *Being and Time*, p. 259/240; p. 266/249; p. 307/283.
37 Heidegger, Martin: *Being and Time*, p. 308/285.
38 Heidegger, Martin: *Being and Time*, p. 187/175.

sense.[39] For both Fichte and Heidegger the ground of meaning is disclosed through an indeterminate feeling or mood; in Fichte's case the feeling of the Absolute I's striving; in Heidegger's case the mood of *Angst*.

As with Fichte's Absolute I characterized as infinite, Heidegger's nothing is unbounded and without limits. Also as with Fichte's notion of the Absolute, which is posited as the ground of all reality and of the self, the nothing is for Heidegger the authentic ground of Being and of Da-sein that first reveals itself in being-toward-death. Because the nothing is unbounded, it cannot, strictly speaking, be said to be the creation of the self or within the self's control, as I have argued above with respect to Fichte's Absolute I. The basis of all experience for both of these thinkers thus lies outside the self; specifically, in the relationship between the indeterminate horizon (world) that the nothing and the infinite project and the objects that the understanding or self encounters in the world on the basis of a mood, for Heidegger, and feeling, for Fichte. Therefore just as with Fichte's Absolute I, which is dependent upon a not-I for its activity in the world and subsequent self and world understanding, Heidegger's nothing is also dependent upon possibilities found in the world, for without possibilities there would be no Da-sein and no world to speak of, only nothing.

Because projecting upon possibilities belongs to Da-sein in the mode of understanding and because understanding is always attuned, possibilities are always framed by attunement. "As essentially attuned, Da-sein

---

39 Beginning with "What is Metaphysics" Heidegger explicitly deems the nothing to be a ground. There he says that *Angst* discloses the nothing and that in the nothing the concealment of Being finds its place. "Being held out into the nothing – as Da-sein is – on the ground of concealed anxiety makes the human being the lieutenant of the nothing." Trans. David Farrell Krell, Ed. William McNeil, In: *Pathmarks*, Cambridge 1998, p. 93. See also "Postscript to 'What is Metaphysics.'"
But the characterization of Being by nothingness and its relation to Da-sein can also be found in Heidegger's later writings, for example, "The Thing," a lecture given at the Bayerischen Academy of fine arts on June 6, 1950. What constitutes the essence of "mortals" in this lecture is that they die. "Death is the shrine of the Nothing, that is, of that which in every respect is never something that merely exists, but which nevertheless presences, even as the mystery of Being itself." Trans. Albert Hofstader, In: *Poetry, Language, Thought*, New York 1971, p. 178. One may also turn to the lecture "Time and Being" (1962) where Heidegger makes reference to the relation of humans to the nothing through his use of the terms "absence" and "denying and witholding" in his discussion of Time. Trans. Joan Stambaugh, In: *On Time and Being*, Chicago and London 2002.

has always already got itself into definite possibilities."[40] In the attunement of *Angst*, however, no possibilities lie before Dasein, only possibility as such. But in order for *Angst*, i.e., the nothing, to show itself as a ground there must be possibilities. Only by way of possibilities can the unbounded or groundless nothing of *Angst* become something: the ground of a world. And only by virtue of what it grounds, i.e., possibilities, can the world show itself as a ground in and through the *circumscribing of possibilities*. This manner of understanding the meaning of the world is in strict accord with Heidegger's phenomenological account of the meaning of the everyday world of Da-sein. The meaning of the world is structured by referential relations together with the possibitlities that are understood by Da-sein. But how do possibilities arise out of nothing?

In another similarity between Fichte and Heidegger, Heidegger's Dasein also encompasses a demand, but in Heidegger's case this demand is issued by conscience. Conscience demands that Da-seins act authentically in the world. Conscience, heard authentically only in the mood of *Angst*, summons the self "to its potentiality-of-being-a-self, and thus calls Dasein forth to its possibilities."[41] It is on the basis of being called forth to possibilities that Heidegger introduces a difference within the nothing that issues forth activity and self reflection. This difference unfolds as a distinction in directionality that finally gets characterized as temporality in a relation of the future to the past that unfolds in the present.[42] Through the mediation of possibilities, the nothing gets differentiated into the temporal ecstases of the future (being-toward-death) and having-been (being-guilty). Thus without possibilities there can be no temporality, no Da-sein and no world – only the undifferentiated nothing.

But what is essential to keep in mind is that the ground that, in Heidegger's language, "gives" to Da-sein its possibilities, is a groundless ground characterized by the nothing of *Angst*. This ground is boundless and is dependent upon possibilities in order to show itself. Therefore it cannot properly be said to determine these possibilities in any way. Rather, like Fichte's Absolute I, the nothing serves as the indeterminate horizon from within which possibilities arise. The horizon circumscribes the understanding but is itself never grasped thematically, nor is it itself a possibility. As such, Heidegger's Da-sein cannot be said to promote egoism,

---

40 Heidegger, Martin: *Being and Time*, p. 134/135.
41 Heidegger, Martin: *Being and Time*, p. 274/253.
42 Heidegger, Martin: *Being and Time*, p. 326/300.

as the horizon characterized by the nothing is beyond the control and knowledge belonging to the self. For both Heidegger and Fichte the horizon that gives meaning to all beings, including the self, is opened up by an indeterminate mood or feeling, respectively, that lies outside of a reflexivity identifying a specific or particular self.

## III. Conclusion

In Angst the world is disclosed as such, or as possibility in general. On the basis of this nothing, Da-sein comes to actualize its possibilities in an authentic manner through its resolute choices that occur within the ecstatic unfolding of Da-sein's temporality. But we asked: How is it that the nothing may come to be something, that is, the ground of all beings? Stated differently, how does the purely negative concept of the Nothing – revealed in *Angst* – get transformed into a positive grounding concept?

Like the Absolute I, which is infinite, the nothing has no boundaries. In order for the nothing to show itself as the ground of beings, it, like Fichte's Absolute Self, is dependent upon something outside of the self. Fichte calls that which allows the infinitely striving self to be active and to know itself, albeit only partly as a finite self, the not-I. Similarly for Heidegger it is only by virtue of the possibilities that it grounds that the nothing, which he posits as the ground of all beings, Da-sein and the world, is disclosed. In Da-sein's projection upon possibilities the self and the world arise together with the possibilities that are projected upon. Yet, for both Fichte and Heidegger, the ground itself is beyond comprehension. This is because the ground is characterized by an indeterminate feeling that has no boundaries prior to the possibilities that it gives rise to through the activity of the self in the world. Thus, the nothing, the Absolute, function as the horizon of all understanding but are beyond the thematic grasp of the self's understanding. Here questions arise concerning the construction of a shared horizon and the relation of the self to others on the basis of a shared attunement or a mood. But I only introduce this question here.[43]

---

43 In *Heidegger and a Metaphysics of Feeling: Angst and the Finitude of Being*, I argue that Mitda-sein, or the intersubjective self of Da-sein, is prior to the discovery of an individual self, which is rooted in a community grounded in a shared attunement to possibilities. (Continuum International Publishing Group, 2008).

Yet there does seem to be one radical difference between these thinkers with respect to finitude. In Fichte's case the infinite striving of the self ceases to be infinite with the death of the individual. Finitude belongs to the finite self alone, by virtue of the fact that it is limited by objects arising within the fold of the infinite self. While for Heidegger, Da-sein is always to exist as finite, but significantly, its finitude is inseparable from the determination of the nothing as a ground of possibilities understood in tandem with Heidegger's notion of truth or *aletheia* and the finitude of Being. Moreover, unlike Fichte's infinitely striving self, which is characterized by endless activity and subsequent reflection upon this activity, the boundless character of Heidegger's nothing promotes not activity, but rather a unique form of passivity. Positing the nothing as the ground of beings, Heidegger aims to promote a model whereby subjects do not impress themselves upon the world but rather allow the world to release to them the possibilities that are to be projected upon in a manner he calls "letting be." Thus for Heidegger, finitude belongs to Being; that is, to the ground of Da-sein's possibilities or the limits that this ground establishes by circumscribing Da-sein's understanding or relation to possibilities. Whereas for Fichte, finitude remains squarely within the self. This difference can be most clearly fleshed out by comparing the difference in transcendence between each of these thinkers and the way in which Fichte's notion of dialectic has no place in Heidegger's model of letting be. But that is a topic for a different paper.

# IV. Fichte, Sartre and Others

# How to Make an Existentialist?
# In Search of a Shortcut from Fichte to Sartre

DANIEL BREAZEALE

University of Kentucky, Lexington

The aim of the following remarks is, first of all, to call attention to some of the more striking similarities between two "systems of freedom," that of the early Fichte and that of the early Sartre. How similar are these two philosophies, really? Does Fichte deserve to be called in some sense a "proto-existentialist"? And if not, what might it take to transform him into one?

The history of philosophy is, of course, a cumulative affair, and every great philosophical system, Sartre's included, is intimately related to those that preceded it. Thus one would expect there would be room for a discussion of Fichte's *Wissenschaftslehre* in a comprehensive account of the origins of Sartrean existentialism, though such a discussion would presumably occupy less space in such an account than the portions devoted to, say, Descartes, Hegel, Husserl, and Heidegger.

But I am really not interested in the actual genesis of Sartre's views nor in the direct or indirect *influence* of Fichte upon *Being and Nothingness*. And, in fact, the evidence for any such influence is very meager. We know, for example, that in October of 1926, while he was a third-year student at the École Normale Superieure, Sartre checked out from the library French translations of three of Fichte's earlier works – the *Foundations of the Entire Wissenschaftslehre*, *Some Lectures Concerning the Scholar's Vocation*, and *The Vocation of Man* – and that he kept them for five months. What we do *not* know is if he actually *read* any or all of these volumes nor, if he did, what he thought about what he read.[1] Nor do

---

1   This was reported by Ronald Hayman in his *Writing Against: A Biography of Sartre*, London 1986, p. 55, and subsequently confirmed by Dorothea Wildenberg from archival sources in Paris. Sartre checked out the books on October 26, 1926 and returned them March 29, 1926. See Wildenburg, Dorothea: *Ist der Existentialismus ein Idealismus? Transzendentalphilosophische Analyse der Selbstbewußtseinstheorie des frühen Sartre aus der Perspektive der Wissenschaftslehre Fichtes*, Amsterdam 2003, p. 3n.

the few, passing references to Fichte in Sartre's own writings – one in *The Psychology of the Imagination*, another in *Search for a Method*, and two in the posthumously published *Notebooks for an Ethics* – offer much insight concerning his knowledge of Fichte's works. Instead, they reflect the conventional, received view of Fichte as a subjective idealist who maintains that the Not-I is created by the I as an arena for its own activity[2], or as something to be fully "assimilated to" or "digested by" the I.[3] If some of Fichte's ideas nevertheless seem to anticipate some of Sartre's, this is not necessarily evidence of any *influence* of the former upon the latter.

The point of the present enterprise is to see if a comparative study or these two systems might illuminate certain features of both the *Wissenschaftslehre* and Sartrean existentialism which might otherwise go unnoticed. That such a comparative study can illuminate Sartre's philosophy can certainly not be denied, at least not by anyone who has read Dorothea Wildenburg's massive dissertation, *Ist der Existentialismus ein Idealismus? Transzendentalphilosophische Analyse der Selbstbewußtseinstheorie des frühen Sartre aus der Perspektive der Wissenschaftslehre Fichtes*.[4] No one interested in this topic can ignore Wildenburg's work, which persuasively demonstrates – in meticulous detail – the many ways in which Sartre's account of "human reality" resembles Fichte's account of the I in his Jena writings. Wildenburg argues that, Sartre's insistence to the contrary notwithstanding, his version of existentialism incorporates many elements associated with transcendental idealism and that focusing upon the idealistic aspects of his philosophy reveals important features of the same that would otherwise be obscured. I fully concur with this conclusion, but my own interest on this occasion is less in understanding Sartre "in the light of Fichte" than in understanding the *Wissenschaftslehre* "in the light of existentialism." This is the meaning of my subtitle, inasmuch as what I am

---

2   See *The Psychology of Imagination*, trans. Bernard Frechtman, New York 1948, p. 155. See too Sartre, Jean Paul: *Search for a Method*, trans. Hazel E. Barnes, New York 1963, pp. 4–5, where, in the context of a discussion of how philosophical systems are related to actual instances of knowledge, Sartre writes: "reduced to its simplest expression, the philosophical object will remain in 'the objective mind' in the form of a regulative Idea, pointing to an infinite task. Thus, in France, one speaks of 'the Kantian Idea' or in Germany of 'Fichte's *Weltanschauung*."
3   Sartre, Jean Paul: *Notebooks for an Ethics*, trans. David Pellauer, Chicago 1992, p. 498. There is another reference to Fichte in this same text (p. 63), but it occurs in a quotation from Jean Hyppolite's *Genesis and Structure of Hegel's Phenomenology*, in which Hyppolite stresses the similarities between the dialectics of Fichte, Schelling, and Hegel.
4   Wildenburg, Dorothea: *Ist der Existentialismus ein Idealismus?* Amsterdam 2003.

trying to do in this paper is to assess the plausibility of any proposed "shortcut from Fichte to Sartre."

Though such a project might appear arbitrary or quixotic, I consider it to be an indirect contribution to the ongoing controversy concerning the "unity" and "development" of the *Wissenschaftslehre*. There is, of course, no gainsaying the historical fact that Fichte's own thought developed in precisely the manner than it did; and it can be easily demonstrated that even the most dramatic changes and alterations in the course of Fichte's development are all presaged by and rooted in the earlier stages of the same. With the inestimable advantage of hindsight, one can see how the seeds of even the final versions of the *Wissenschaftslehre* are already present in the notes Fichte wrote in Zurich during the winter of 1793/94. But it is wrong to conclude from this that the particular way in which Fichte's philosophy *did* develop is the only way in which it *could have* developed, or that the only way in which the various systematic ambiguities and tensions implicit in the Jena *Wissenschaftslehre can be* resolved is the particular way that Fichte himself actually *did* resolve them in the Berlin, Erlangen, and Königsberg versions of the same. One can surely admit the internal *coherence* or *continuity* in the actual historical development of the *Wissenschaftslehre* without claiming any *necessity* for the same.

I view Fichte's intellectual development as traversing a series of "crossroads," from each of which a limited number of divergent routes lead forward in different directions. Pursing this metaphor, the present paper might be thought of as an attempt to explore one of the many "roads not taken" by Fichte himself and to calculate the advantages of moving in such a direction as well as the costs and dangers that may lie along that path.

Whether or not there is anything to be gained from such an experiment is not something that can be decided in advance. Therefore, I invite you to travel along this "shortcut" with me for half an hour or so. Along the way, we will touch on numerous points of comparison between Fichte's philosophy and Sartre's, including their status as "systems of freedom," their unapologetic reliance upon extra-philosophical evidence and foundations, their fearless employment to *ad hominem* modes of argumentation, their strategy of beginning with the I or the *cogito*, their account of the complex interrelationship between the I and the Not-I (or between the for-itself and the in-itself), their analysis of the relationship between original or pre-reflexive consciousness and actual consciousness, their recognition of the necessary finitude of the latter, their explication of the intimate relationship between actual consciousness and temporality, their joint commitment to the primacy of practical reason, and, finally, their similar conclusions concerning the final end or ultimate project of human beings as such.

Lengthy as it is, this list by no means exhausts the possible points of comparison between Fichte and Sartre. I regret, for example, that there will not be time to analyze the fascinating similarities and differences between their accounts of the primordial presence of the "other" to the self and of the ways in which Fichte's understanding of this presence as an *Aufforderung* or "summons" to limit one's own freedom anticipates and yet goes beyond Sartre's account of one's "shame" in the presence of the other.[5] Another topic I wish I had time to explore is the importance of the *human body* for our two philosophers, both of whom recognize embodiment to be a transcendental condition for the very possibility of actual self-hood. Another point well worth exploring might be how Fichte and Sartre each arrive, albeit by very different routes, at what one might call an "ethics of total responsibility," according to which there are no morally neutral acts.

It would also be interesting to explore the similarities between Fichte's and Sartre's understanding of their own activities as philosophers and the relationship of the same to their vocations not just as human beings, but as human beings powerfully engaged in the events and history of their own times. Indeed, it would be hard if not impossible to find two major philosophers who less fit the image of the "ivory tower intellectual" than these two men, both of whom devoted themselves to affecting the great events of their time. Of Sartre, no less than Fichte, one could say what Forberg said of the latter: "he really intends for his philosophy to have an effect upon the world!"[6] Is there not some relationship between

---

[5] On this topic, see Fleischer, Margot: "Das ursprüngliche Verhältnis zum Anderen bei Sartre ('Der Blick') und die unverzichtbare Gegenposition Fichtes," in: Baum, Manfred und Hammacher, Klaus (ed.): *Transzendenz und Existenz. Idealistische Grundlage und moderne Perspektiven des transzendentalen Gedankens. Wolfgang Janke zum 70. Geburtstag*, Amsterdam 2001.

[6] Forberg, Friedrich Karl: *Fragmente aus meinen Papieren*, Jena 1796, p. 63. For more on this point, see Rockmore, Tom: "Fichte et Sartre, ou Sartre fichtéen?," in: Radrizzani, Ives (ed.): *Fichte et la France*, Vol. 1, Paris 1997, p. 225: "Ce sont deux philosophes que dérangent, que sortent des 'sentiers battus.' Is sont les deux tout sauf calme. Fichte et Sartre se disputent à tour de rôle avec tout le monde et adoptent généralement des attitudes sans compromis. […] De l'extérieur de l'Université, ils exercent tous deux une influence considérable sur la philosophie de leur moment historique."

the fact that Fichte and Sartre were so thoroughly and uncompromisingly *engaged* as human beings in some of the more momentous social and political struggles of their time and the fact that both of them propounded a philosophy of endless striving and practical, worldly engagement? To paraphrase Fichte's famous observation in the *First Introduction to the Wissenschaftslehre*, are the similarities in their philosophies ultimately grounded in similarities in their characters? Fascinating questions, I believe; but ones I will not be pursuing on this occasion.

I. Two Systems of Freedom: Duty and Anxiety as "Facts of Reason"

One of the most obvious similarity between Fichte and Sartre is that both prided themselves on having constructed a systematic philosophy of human freedom. If Fichte boasted that the *Wissenschaftslehre* was "the first system of freedom,"[7] *Being and Nothingness* might well be described as "the last system" of the same. (And, yes, I agree with Alan Renaut, that Sartre is not only an important systematic philosopher, but perhaps the last major representative of this dying species.[8]) And indeed, Sartre himself explicitly maintained that the sole "dogma" of his philosophy is simply "the affirmation of human freedom."[9] In striking contrast to all of those thinkers willing to engage in a theoretical dispute about "freedom vs. determinism," both of these philosophers treat freedom *not* as something to be justified or defended by philosophical argument, but rather, as the proper *starting point* for any adequate philosophical system. The reality of freedom is not something that can be *demonstrated*; instead, it is something that is and can only be *directly experienced* by every human being.

To be sure, Fichte and Sartre offer dramatically different descriptions of our original, pre-philosophical experience of freedom. For Fichte, as for Kant, this lies in our awareness of our moral responsibility, that is to say, in our *duty* to be the autonomous authors of our own acts. For

---

7 Fichte to Baggesen [Draft], April-May 1795 (GA III/2, p. 300). In: EPW, p. 385. See too Fichte's comment in his June 17, 1798 letter to Friedrich David Gräter, June 17, 1798 (GA III/3, p. 125): "[The *Wissenschaftslehre*] is the system of freedom, and it makes itself absolutely free."
8 Renaut, Alain: *Sartre, le dernier philosophe*, Paris 1993.
9 Sartre, Jean Paul : "La processus historique," *La Gazette de Lausanne*, February 8, 1947; as quoted by Fillesdal, Dagfinn: "Sartre on Freedom," in: Schilpp, Paul Arthur (ed.): *The Philosophy of Jean-Paul Sartre*, La Salle, IL 1981, p. 292.

Sartre, in contrast (and following not Kant but Kierkegaard and Heidegger), the practical confirmation of our freedom lies not in our awareness of moral duty, but rather in our experience of *anxiety* ( *l'angoisse*),[10] For the Kantian "fact of reason" Sartre substitutes our anxious awareness of ourselves as "having the character of an unjustifiable fact."[11] Such an awareness is not simply *accompanied* by anxiety; it *is* anxiety, a state "in which freedom is anxious before itself inasmuch as it is solicited and bound by nothing"[12] Like duty, anxiety involves an immediate recognition of our unavoidable *responsibility* to determine our own freedom, and thereby to determine ourselves and our world. This is the existentialist version of the Kantian "fact of reason." Freedom is something to which transcendental philosophy must always *appeal*, but which it cannot *justify* – except insofar as such an appeal is "justified" retrospectively by the system that can be constructed thereupon.

## II. The ad hominem "Argument" for Freedom

It is always possible, of course, for any individual either to *deny* these experiences of freedom, or, while admitting them, to *interpret* them as illusory phenomena or products of social conditioning. And no one can be *argued out* of such a position. This is something that both Fichte and Sartre grasp with equal clarity: namely, that a robust awareness of one's own freedom must be the starting point of any systematic philosophy capable of embracing human reality in its totality. True to the logic of their positions, both emphasize the element of *choice* that is inextricably involved in this and every other philosophical starting point. And they also agree in characterizing this same "choice" in heavily value-laden terms, as grounded in and revelatory of one's basic character.[13] Though no amount

---

10 "It is in anxiety that man gets his consciousness of his freedom," writes Sartre in *Being and Nothingness: A Phenomenological Essay on Ontology*, trans. Hazel Barnes, New York 1992, p. 65 (translation modified).
11 BN, p. 128.
12 Ibid., p. 73 (translation modified).
13 According to J. Douglass Rabb this explicit recognition of the connection between character and philosophy is perhaps the prime instance of certain "unmistakable Existentialist elements" in Fichte's writings. See Rabb: "Marxism, Existentialism, and Fichte's Idealism," in: Hammacher, Klaus (ed.): *Der transzendentale Gedanke: Die gegenwärtige Darstellung der Philosophie Fichtes*, Hamburg 1981, p. 483.

of argument can prevent some people from choosing to deny their own freedom and preferring, in Fichte's memorable phrase, "to consider themselves a chunk of lava on the moon rather than an I ,"[14] such a choice can never be condoned by a "philosopher of freedom."

Though one certainly *may* deny one's freedom as well as that of others in this manner, one *ought not* do so. Accordingly, Fichte describes "dogmatists" (that is, those who deny or explain away their awareness of their own freedom) as suffering either from an incomplete moral education or simply from a morally defective character,[15] whereas Sartre, with somewhat less delicacy, describes those who deny their own freedom and that of others as "cowards" *(lâches)* and "bastards" *(salauds)*."[16] Rarely in the history of philosophy have such *ad hominem* arguments been invoked as frankly and as effectively as by Fichte and Sartre.

Instead of wasting their energy trying to dispute with bastards and chunks of rock, Sartre and Fichte instead offer explanations of *why* someone might deny human freedom in this way. (Here I refer you to Fichte's typology of the stages of moral development and to Sartre's familiar account of "bad faith.")

### III. Starting with the I: Two Philosophies of the Subject

To say that philosophy must start with freedom means, for both Fichte and Sartre, that it must start with the sole locus of freedom: that is with the I, with the self, with self-consciousness, with the for-itself. As Sartre puts it in *Existentialism is a Humanism,* "our point of departure is indeed the subjectivity of the individual and that for strictly philosophical reasons." Note that, as is also true in the case of the *Wissenschaftslehre, Being and Nothingness* does not commence with "individuality" or "the

---

14 Fichte, Johann G.: "Foundations of the Entire Science of Knowledge," in: *The Science of Knowledge*, trans. Peter Heath and John Lachs, Cambridge 1982, p. 162n. (GA I/2, p. 326n.) (translation modified).
15 See, for example, the First Introduction to the "Attempt at a New Presentation of the *Wissenschaftslehre*" in: IWL, p. 20: "Someone whose character is naturally slack or who has been enervated and twisted by spiritual servitude, scholarly self-indulgence, and vanity will never be able to raise himself to the level of idealism" (GA I/4, 195).
16 Sartre, Jean Paul: *Existentialism is a Humanism*, trans. Philip Mairet, in: rev. ed., Kaufmann Walter (ed.): *Existentialism from Dostoevsky to Sartre*, Cleveland 1975, p. 366 (translation modified).

individual" but rather with the sheer "subjectivity" of the same, that is, with the *for itself* as a universal act or structure. We begin with subjectivity, according to Sartre,

> because we seek to base our teaching upon the truth and not upon a collection of fine theories, full of hope but lacking real foundations. At the point of departure there cannot be any other truth than this, *I think, therefore I am*, which is the absolute truth of consciousness as it attains to itself. Every theory which begins with man, outside of this moment of self-attainment, thereby suppresses the truth, for outside of the Cartesian *cogito,* all objects are no more than probable, and any doctrine of probabilities which is not attached to a truth will crumble into nothing. In order to define the probable one must possess the true. Before there can be any truth whatever, then, there must be an absolute truth, and there is such a truth which is simple, easily attained, and within the reach of everybody; it consists of one's immediate sense of one's self.[17]

Nothing else possesses "apodictic certainty,"[18] according to Sartre, but the immediate presence of the I to itself that is expressed by the "I think." For the same reason, the Jena *Wissenschaftslehre*, particularly in its definitive formulation *nova methodo* commences with the self-evident proposition that the I *setzt sich selbst schlechthin* or "simply posits itself." For both Fichte and Sartre, freedom *is* self-consciousness and self-consciousness *is* freedom. This, of course, is why contemporary critics of Sartre, as of Fichte, felt justified in characterizing – and rejecting – each of them as "subjective" thinkers.[19] Though there is surely some merit in this characterization, it is also – as shall see – profoundly misleading.

---

17 Ibid., pp. 360–61 (translation modified). "In truth the *cogito* must be our point of departure" (p. 120). "In a word the sole point of departure is the interiority of the *cogito*" (p. 329).
18 Ibid., p. 329.
19 Hegel's and Schelling's criticisms of Fichte's "subjective idealism," are familiar. Less familiar, perhaps, are the similar criticisms of Sartre by, for example, Theodor Adorno, who interprets *Being and Nothingness* as the subjective "counterpole" to Heidegger's *Being and Time* and criticizes Sartre for "reifying the subject" (*Negative Dialectics*, trans. E. B. Ashton, New York 1973, p. 123). "Despite his extreme nominalism, Sartre's philosophy in its most effective phase was organized according to the old idealist category of the free act of the subject. To existentialism, as to Fichte, any objectivity is a matter of indifference" (Adorno, p. 50). See too Herbert Speigelberg's caustic verdict that "Sartre's insistence on freedom may at first appear not only extreme but dogmatic, reminding one of Fichte" (*The Phenomenological Movement*, 2nd ed., The Hague 1965, Vol II, p. 485).

Neither Fichte nor Sartre thought of himself as a "subjectivist" – a point Fichte sometimes tried to make by contrasting his own Critical idealism or "real-idealism" with both dogmatic or purely subjective idealism and dogmatic realism, and which Sartre tried to make by subtitling his magnum opus "an essay in phenomenology ontology" and likewise characterizing his own position as "beyond realism and idealism"[20] But let us now dig a bit deeper and consider the dialectic of I and Not-I in Fichte and Sartre.

## IV. Dialectic of the I and the Not-I

Not only do Fichte and Sartre adopt similar philosophical starting-points, they also share the same proximate *goal:* to examine and – insofar as possible – to make intelligible the situation of a free and responsible self-conscious agent in an un-free and un-self-conscious natural world – to explain (or, if you prefer, to describe) why and how a free being finds and *must* find itself in an unfree environment, or, if you prefer, to explain why freedom must be *finite* and *limited*, if it is exist at all. Their *strategy* for pursing this investigation of the relationship between the I and the Not-I, or between the for-itself and the in-itself, is also similar, inasmuch as both insist that such an investigation must *begin* with the former and proceed to the latter, thereby indicating, in Fichtean language, how and why the I necessarily "posits" (*setzt*) a system of representations accompanied by a feeling of necessity, that is world that is Not-I, or, in Sartre's language (derived, of course, from Brentano and Husserl), how and why the for-itself necessarily "intends" an object other than itself.[21]

While recognizing that mundane consciousness always refers beyond itself, toward an object "intended" as "transphenomenal" or "Not-I," Fichte and Sartre also agree that this same world that consciousness opposes to itself and its freedom is one that exists only *for* that same conscious subject. Despite its alien appearance, the world in question, as Fichte constantly reminds us, is always *our* world and exists only *for* consciousness. Indeed, one of the fundamental lessons of transcendental idealism is precisely this: no matter how much this conclusion may seem to

---

20  BN, p. 26 (translation modified).
21  Alain Renaut, in his excellent book on Sartre, calls explicit attention to the manner in which Fichte's analysis of consciousness anticipates the account of intentionality developed by Brentano and Husserl and appropriated by Sartre. See Renaut, Alain: *Sartre, le dernier philosophe,* pp. 92 and 178.

conflict with the evidence of ordinary experience, "all consciousness is determined by self-consciousness; i.e., everything that occurs within consciousness has its foundation in the conditions that make self-consciousness possible – that is to say, is given and is produced thereby and possesses no foundation whatsoever outside of self-consciousness."[22] Or, as Sartre puts it: "The world is human." "By nature, it is *mine* in so far as it is the correlative in-itself of nothingness."[23]

Does this mean Sartre is an "idealist" of some variety? The answer to this question, I believe, must be a qualified "yes." (Anyone with lingering doubts on this score is referred to Wildenburg's dissertation. Adorno made a similar point many years ago, but, unlike Wildenburg, he did not mean it as a compliment!"[24]) To be sure, Sartre always styled himself an implacable and hard-headed foe of idealism in all its varieties, including the Kantian, but he invariably understood "idealism" in a one-sidedly Berkleyean way.

On closer examination, the vaunted "realism" that Sartre finds implicit in his analysis of the intentionality of consciousness and which is enshrined in the so-called "ontological proof" at the end of the introduction to *Being and Nothingness* is by no means incompatible with Fichte's transcendental explication of the objectivity of experience. Indeed, Sartre's explicit denial notwithstanding,[25] his "ontological proof" of the reality of the in-itself actually recalls Kant's "refutation of idealism," and, like the latter, is quite compatible with the recognition that an "objective world" exists only for the conscious subject. For all of his emphasis upon the sheer "being" and "contingency" of the in-itself, and despite his infamous "nausea" before a world that is simply "too much" or *de trop*, Sartre was never a transcendental realist or "dogmatist" in the Kantian and Fichtean sense of those terms. This, I think, should be clear to any careful reader of *Being and Nothingness*, and it was also clear to Sartre himself in 1939 when he was working out the basic plan for *Being and Nothingness* in the December 7 entry in his "War Dairy," where he explicitly describes his project as uncovering "the transcendental structure of human reality."[26]

---

22  Fichte, Johann G.: "Second Introduction to the *Wissenschaftslehre*," in: IWL, p. 62.
23  BN, p. 297 and 157.
24  Adorno, Theodor: *Negative Dialectics*, pp. 50–51.
25  See BN, p. 23.
26  Sartre, Jean-Paul: *War Diaries, November 1939 – March 1940*, trans. Quinton Hoare, New York 1984, p. 110.

This, of course, is not to claim the Sartrean existentialism should be interpreted as transcendental idealism in the full-fledged Fichtean sense of the term, for it does not include any genetic account of the a priori "constitution" of experience and of the objects of the same. Though *The Transcendence of the Ego* still betrays a certain lingering sympathy toward Husserl's theory of the spontaneous a priori constitution of objects, there is little trace of this in Sartre's later works, in which he is generally content to treat the in-itself as simply "given" in a more or less fully-constituted form[27] – though, to be sure, it is "given" in this way only *for* the for-itself and only within the horizon of the latter's projects.

For Fichte, as for Sartre, the recognition that the objects of experience exist only for the subject of experience does not imply that the "being" of the latter is the same as that of the former. On the contrary, it makes it all the more important to distinguish as carefully as possible between the being of the I and that of the Not-I or between being-for-itself and being-in-itself. Moreover, our two philosophers make this distinction in a similar way: namely, by ascribing "being," in the full and proper sense of the term, only to objects. For Fichte, "being" is not an original predicate of pure subjectivity, which must always be characterized first of all in terms of its spontaneity and activity. The I must therefore be originally understood not as a special kind of thing or substance, but as an *agent*. As Fichte puts it, "self-consciousness is possible only in the way we have indicated: I am only active."[28] Similar considerations underlie

---

27 "Subjectivity is powerless to constitute the objective" (Sartre, Jean Paul: *Existentialism is a Humanism*, p. 24). In addition to the famous description of the chestnut tree in *Nausea*, see the description of perceiving a sheet of paper, with which Sartre's first book on the imagination begins: "I look at this sheet of paper lying on my desk. I perceive its shape, its color, it position. These various qualities have traits in common. To begin with, they present themselves as beings whose existence in no way depends on my whim, as beings of which I can only take note. They exist *for me*, but they are not myself. [....] This inert shape, which must be observed and learned about bit by bit, is what we call a 'thing'" (Sartre, Jean Paul: *Imagination: A Psychological Critique*, trans. Forest Williams, Ann Arbor 1962, p. 1).

Nevertheless, *Being and Nothingness* does contain many hints of a more robust idealism: e.g., in the remark that, "human-reality is the being which causes a place to come to objects" (BN, p. 370) – a remark that might be compared with Fichte's account, in § 10 of his 1796–99 lectures on *Wissenschaftslehre nova methodo*, of the determination of spatial location by the I. See WLnm, pp. 234–49.

28 First Introduction to the "Attempt at a New Presentation of the *Wissenschaftslehre*" in: IWL, p. 50.

Sartre's description of the for-itself as, literally, *nothing*. Unlike so many other would-be "philosophers of freedom," Fichte and Sartre clearly grasp the full implications of a robust concept of freely active subjectivity: namely, that the I cannot be produced by anything outside of itself; indeed, it cannot be understand as *anything* at all prior to its own active self-construction, which is why it can only be described metaphorically as an "original upsurging" (*surgissement originell*) or fact/act (*Tathandlung*).

Few if any thinkers in the history of philosophy have made a more radical distinction between the spontaneity of the I and the being of the world. Sartre would certainly endorse the Fichtean dictum that "this strict, sharp distinction between the pure self and everything that is not the self is the truly characteristic feature of humanity,"[29] and Fichte, who seems to have appreciated paradoxical philosophical formulas just as much as Sartre, would, I think, have been pleased to characterize the being of the I as "nothingness."

As we have already noted, critics of both Fichte and Sartre have seized upon this radical opposition between the I and the Not-I, the for itself and the in-itself, as evidence of an objectionably "subjective" or "anthropocentric" worldview and a concomitantly defective understanding of man's relationship to nature. One critic has even cited this similarity as evidence of their shared "nihilism" – which, I suppose, is even worse than their shared idealism, unless Jacobi was right after all, and these are just two names for the same thing![30] In any case, it is true that Fichte and Sartre remain resolute opponents not only of "philosophical naturalism," but also of all efforts by philosophers to understand human beings in purely "naturalistic" terms. Instead, they both subscribe to a transcen-

---

29 "On Stimulating and Increasing the Pure Interest in Truth," in: EPW, p. 228. The American translators of Sartre's *Transcendence of the Ego* write that "almost the entire novelty of Sartre's major work [i.e., *Being and Nothingness*] consists in the radical distinction between consciousness and absolutely everything else, that is between intentionality and the non-intentional" (*The Transcendence of the Ego*, translated and with an introduction by Forrest Williams and Robert Kirkpatrick, New York 1962, p. 22). Fichte, however, preceded Sartre by a century and a half in making a similar – and equally radical – distinction between the two.
30 See Hübner, Kurt: "Fichte, Sartre und der Nihilismus," in: *Zeitschrift für philosophische Forschung* 10 (1956), pp. 40–43.

dental humanism[31] that is perhaps best captured in the credo attributed to that great American philosopher, Woody Allen: "I am two with nature."

## V. The Theoretical Allusiveness of Original Self-Consciousness

Fichte and Sartre further agree that pure spontaneity, original freedom, the pure I, "consciousness of consciousness" – call it what you will – is something of which we can never be directly conscious.[32] According to Fichte, the original self-positing of the I, the action that makes consciousness possible in the first place "cannot itself occur within consciousness."[33] And Sartre concurs: every effort to become directly acquainted with non-reflective or pre-reflective consciousness succeeds only in thematizing it and turning it into an object (namely, a transcendent "ego") for a reflecting subject.

The philosopher can therefore become acquainted with his systematic starting point, the pure I or original self-consciousness, only *indirectly*, since as Sartre puts it, "the ego never appears, in fact, except when one is not looking at it."[34] Fichte is somewhat less coy in arguing that we freely *postulate* the necessity of original consciousness by reflecting upon ordinary reflective consciousness and abstracting from the objects of the same. We thus arrive, via a process of creative, reflective abstraction and inference, at the concept of the pure I.[35] And Sartre seems to have something similar in mind when he interprets the philosopher's consciousness of the pre-reflexive cogito as a product of the *epoché*. Hence it is only within the context of a transcendental investigation of the conditions for ordinary, reflective consciousness or, alternately, within the context of a phenomenologically clarified hermeneutic description and

---

31 For a penetrating discussion of the important differences between Fichtean Sartrean "humanism," see the concluding section of Renaut, Alain: *Sartre, la dernier philosophe*.
32 See Fichte, Johann G.: "Outline of the Distinctive Character of the Wissenschaftslehre with Respect to the Theoretical Faculty," in: EPW, p 176: "the I itself never becomes conscious of this act, nor could it ever become conscious of it." See too Sartre, Jean Paul: *Transcendence of the Ego*, pp. 40–41.
33 WLnm, p. 84.
34 Sartre, Jean Paul: *Transcendence of the Ego*, p. 88.
35 See IWL, pp. 45–49 and pp. 106–18, as well as § 1 of WLnm.

interpretation of the human condition that we discover – or better, posit – the concept of pure, pre-reflective, non-thetic consciousness.

Even Sartre's use of the expression "being-for-itself" to designate the pre-reflectively self-referential dimension of consciousness is anticipated by Fichte's description of "the I" or "the intellect": "Everything included within the intellect exists *for* the intellect, and the intellect is *for itself* everything that it is,"[36] though Sartre's own employment of this term is presumably derived from Hegel via Kojéve and Hyppolite. What matters is not what name we give to this concept – "*Tathandlung*," "*reines Ich*," "*intellectuelle Anschauung*," "*conscience de premier degrée*," "*consience irréfléchi*," "*conscience non-thétique*," "*conscience non-positionelle*," or "*le pour-soi*"– but rather that we recognize that the term in question designates an immediate consciousness of consciousness, which never appears within but is always presupposed by ordinary consciousness.

I am well aware that there is nothing particularly original about my claim here. The many striking resemblances between Fichte's account of "original self-consciousness" and Sartre's account of "pre-reflexive" or "non-positional" self-consciousness have been noted and discussed by several commentators, including Dorothea Wildenburg, Kurt Hübner, Frederick Neuhouser, and Tom Rockmore, all of whom have called attention to the many striking parallels between Fichte's revolutionary challenge to the so-called "reflective model of consciousness" and Sartre's account of the relationship between ordinary, "thetic" or "positional" consciousness and the pre-reflective *cogito*.[37] Despite the obvious differences between Sartre's more purely "descriptive" methodology and Fichte's method of regressive analysis and imaginative construction, both philosophers maintain that ordinary object-consciousness, including reflective self-consciousness, always presupposes and is implicitly accompanied by a very different kind of "original" or "non-positional" consciousness, an impersonal self-consciousness that is not characterized by the subject-object structure of ordinary consciousness[38]; for only on this assumption can I

---

36 First Introduction to the "Attempt at a New Presentation of the *Wissenschaftslehre*," in: IWL, p. 21.
37 See Wildenburg, Dorothea: *Ist der Existenzialismus ein Idealismus?* pp. 322–56; Hübner, Kurt: "Fichte, Sartre und der Nihilismus," pp. 29–35; Neuhouser, Frederick: *Fichte's Theory of Subjectivity*, Cambridge 1990, pp. 72–89 and p. 170; and Rockmore, Tom: "Fichte et Sartre, ou Sartre fichtéen?" pp. 221–45.
38 Though it is certainly implicit in the 1794/95 *Foundations of the Entire Wissenschaftslehre*, this revolutionary new theory of consciousness is fully articulated only in Fichte's lectures on *Wissenschaftslehre nova methodo* and in the published

account for my unquestioned confidence that "my experience" is indeed "*mine*."[39]

Once again, it is important to emphasize that what guarantees the *reality* of this postulated pure and spontaneous subjectivity is, for both Fichte and Sartre, no philosophical or theoretical operation whatsoever, that is to say, no argument or inference of any kind, but rather our direct, *practical* awareness (or "real intuition") of our own freedom and responsibility – whether in the guise of a conscientious apprehension of our moral duties or in that of "an anxiety which imposes itself upon us and which we cannot avoid; it is both a pure event of transcendental origin and an ever possible accident of our daily life."[40] Without a direct, lived experience of freedom, neither system would have more than hypothetical validity.

## VI. Differences regarding the Relationship of Pure to Empirical Consciousness

Despite the many striking similarities between Fichte's and Sartre's accounts of original self-consciousness and of its relationship to ordinary object-consciousness, only a few of which have been mentioned here,[41] there are also significant and glaringly obvious *differences* between the two. Fichte, for example, provides a systematic, genetic deduction of *why* and *how* finite object-consciousness arises and must arise from pure self-consciousness and is thereby a condition necessary for the possibility of the former; whereas Sartre, in keeping with his more narrowly "phenomenological" method, is usually content simply to distinguish these two types of consciousness and to describe the relationship between

---

portions of the *Attempt at a New Presentation of the Wissenschaftslehre*. In Sartre's case, it is already fully developed in *The Transcendence of the Ego* and then elaborated in *Being and Nothingness*.

39 "[Sartre's] concept de la conscience pré-thétique reprend très précisement le concept d'intuition intellectuelle fichtéen" (Rockmore, Tom : " Fichte et Sartre, ou Sartre fichtéen ? ", p. 241).

40 Sartre, Jean Paul: *Transcendence of the Ego*, p. 103 (translation modified). Compare this with Fichte's well-known reference, in section 5 of "Second Introduction to the *Wissenschaftslehre*" to our "actual" intellectual intuition of the moral law (see SS, p. 50 and section 5 of "Second Introduction to the *Wissenschaftslehre*", in: IWL, pp. 48–50).

41 For a detailed examination of these similarities, see Wildenburg, Dorothea: *Ist der Existenzialismus ein Idealismus?* Chs. 1–3.

them.[42] Thus he explicitly denies any *necessary* relationship between the pure *cogito* and the reflectively apprehended "I," and maintains that "one can even suppose a consciousness performing a pure reflective act which delivers consciousness to itself as a non-personal spontaneity."[43] Unfortunately, as Sartre is quick to add, "this phenomenological reduction is never perfect," and thus we never actually obtain to such a postulated pure consciousness of the pre-reflective *cogito*. (The parallel with Fichte's comments on the "intellectual intuition" of the pure I and the "fictional" character of the same is striking.[44]) Thus, for both Fichte and Sartre, actual consciousness always involves the subject/object polarity, the exception to this being, for Fichte, the "real" self-intuition of one's own freedom that is involved in moral self-determination and for Sartre the equally "real" immediate consciousness of one's freedom that surges up and overwhelms us in the form of anxiety.

Similarly puzzling is Sartre's assertion that unreflected consciousness "has the ontological priority over the reflected consciousness, because the unreflected consciousness does not need to be reflected in order to exist, and because reflection presupposes the intervention of a second-degree consciousness."[45] Fichte, in contrast, by virtue of his adoption of a *genetic* method of inquiry, is able to show that the I, in order to posit itself *as an I, must* be limited and *must* oppose itself to itself. In doing this he demonstrates that "second degree consciousness" is as much a condition necessary for the possibility of "original consciousness" as the latter is a condition for the former. (This, in any case, is how I interpret the Jena system; I doubt that this would be an apt interpretation of the later *Wissenschaftslehren*.) Moreover, since original or pre-reflexive consciousness is posited by the philosopher purely for the purposes of explaining ordinary object-consciousness, it is extremely difficult to imagine how the former might "exist" apart from the latter.

---

42 See Neuhouser, Frederick: *Fichte's Theory of Subjectivity*, pp. 85n and 89n.
43 Sartre, Jean Paul: *Transcendence of the Ego*, p. 73.
44 On this point, see Breazeale, "Fichte's Philosophical Fictions," in: Breazeale, Daniel/Rockmore, Tom (ed.): *New Essays on Fichte's Later Jena Wissenschaftslehre*, Evanston, IL 2002, pp. 175–208.
45 Sartre, Jean Paul: *Transcendence of the Ego*, p. 58.

## VII. Philosophies of the Divided Self and the Primacy of Practical Reason

When one combines a philosophy of radical freedom with an analysis of consciousness similar to that developed by Fichte and Sartre the result is likely to be what I propose to call a "philosophy of the divided self." And this is precisely how I would characterize both Sartrean existentialism and the early *Wissenschaftslehre*. As we have seen, both Fichte and Sartre paint a portrait of consciousness that distinguishes sharply not only between the I and the Not-I, the for-itself and the in-itself, but also between the freedom and the facticity of the I itself, or between the pure and the finite I. And, of course, each of these thinkers thought it was essential to integrate his account of our practical, pre-theoretical grasp of freedom into the larger theoretical edifice of his philosophical account of consciousness. Indeed, this is the whole point of both exercises, at least as I understand them: *not to heal the division within the self, but rather to explain its necessity* and to show that facticity does not necessarily trump freedom, any more than freedom is incompatible with facticity.

The key to their common strategy for dealing with the problem of the divided self lies in the fact that for neither Fichte nor for Sartre is *cognition* the sole or even the fundamental function of the self; instead, they both understand consciousness, first and foremost, in *practical* terms: first of all, in the sense that intentionality or reference to objects is to be understood as an *act* of the I,[46] and second, in the sense that the I encounters a world in the first place only insofar as it freely projects determinate and self-determined *goals* – that is, a future – for itself.

It is only because the I encounters the world in the context of its own free projection of specific goals that this world possesses any "meaning" for it at all. And only insofar as the world possesses such practical "meaning" can it subsequently become an object of purely theoretical interest. As Sartre puts it, "reflective consciousness can be properly called a moral consciousness since it cannot arise without at the same time disclosing values."[47] This is also Fichte's view, which is most explicitly developed in the *Wissenschaftslehre nova methodo*, where he abandons his earlier, un-

---

46  This point is emphasized with special clarity by Renaut, when he observes: "Et ce sur le terrain même qu'une telle representation de la subjectivité comme activité libre devait nécessairement conduire à privilégier dans l'édifice philosophique, à savoir le terrain de la philosophie pratique, plus particulièrement: celui de la morale" (Renaut, Alain: *Sartre, le dernier philosophe*, p. 149).

47  BN, p. 146.

successful attempt to treat theoretical reason in abstraction from practical reason. Though Fichte emphasizes that both theoretical and practical elements are necessarily involved in every moment of consciousness, it still remains true that both the "origin" and the "end" of consciousness have to be conceived in purely practical terms of radical self-assertion and endless striving. One immediate implication of these strategies is that, for both Fichte and Sartre, there can be no "value-neutral" facts; instead, we always encounter the world and ourselves only within the context or "horizon" of the particular values or projects that we have already posited.[48] There is therefore no "facticity," no "situation," no "world" for us apart from our free projection of values and our striving to realize them.

## VIII. The Finitude of the Self

The converse of the preceding principle holds as well: namely, that there can be no real freedom apart from some particular situation and the determinate limits this places upon the I. According to Fichte, the spontaneously self-active subject originally arises by simply positing its own unlimited freedom, or, as Sartre might put it, by trying to preserve its own "nothingness" and avoid reification. But it immediately discovers that it can actually posit its own free efficacy *for itself* – which it must do in order to become an *actual* I – only insofar as it also finds its infinite freedom to be thwarted and limited and then strives endlessly to overcome or to expand these limits.

Though a philosophical analysis of consciousness must, for reasons already explained, *begin* with a description of the absolutely self-positing I, this same analysis soon reveals that, in the very act of positing itself, the pure spontaneity in question becomes limited and finite. It is limited, moreover, not by its own free action, but by something else, by something radically *other* – whether the latter is understood as the in-itself, the Not-I, or simply as the original determinate nature of the empirical (that is, the *actual*) I itself, as revealed to it through the passive medium of feeling.

---

48 The parallels between Fichte and Sartre on this point are stressed by Renaut, who describes Sartre has having made an effort " à recentrer la philosophie du sujet du côté du *sujet pratique*" (Renaut, Alain: *Sartre, le dernier philosophe,* pp. 148 and 192–94).

*Actual* freedom, therefore, is and must always be the freedom of a *finite individual human being*.⁴⁹

## IX. The Circuit of Selfhood

We have now arrived at one of the most significant similarities between Fichte and Sartre: namely, their joint recognition and insistence that finitude, contingency, and limitation (in short, *la force des choses*) are not *simply obstacles* to human freedom, but are, at the same time, *essential conditions for the possibility of the same*. The opposition of the world – whether this is understood, following Fichte's doctrine of the "check" or *Anstoß*, as an original limitation of the I itself, in the form of "feeling,"⁵⁰ or, following Sartre, as the sheer "facticity" of the for-itself – has to recognized by the philosopher (if not by the practical agent) as an *enabling condition* for the very possibility of freedom. Thus the Fichtean thesis, "Freedom is nothing without constraint, and vice versa,"⁵¹ is echoed in Sartre's formulation of what he calls "the paradox of freedom," namely: "there is freedom only in a *situation*, and there is a situation only through freedom. Human-reality everywhere encounters resistance and obstacles which it has not created, but these resistances and obstacles have meaning only in and through the free choice which human-reality *is*."⁵² Or, as Sartre put it in a letter to Simone de Beauvoir, written just prior to the drafting

---

49 "Thus, from its first arising, consciousness by the pure nihilating movement of reflection, makes itself *personal;* for what confers personal existence on a being is not the possession of an Ego – which is only the *sign* of the personality – but it is the fact that the being exists for itself as a presence to itself" (BN, pp. 156–57). For Fichte's clearest statement of this point see the first sections of the *Foundations of Natural Right* and *System of Ethics*.
50 See Breazeale, Daniel: "Check or Checkmate? On the Finitude of the Fichtean Self," in: Ameriks, Karl/Sturma, Dieter (ed.): *The Modern Subject: Conceptions of the Self in Classical German Philosophy*, Albany 1995, pp. 87–114.
51 WLnm, p. 219. L. Ph. Richard has also observed that this shared recognition of the necessity of limits for the possibility of freedom is, along with their doctrine of reciprocal recognition, one of the main links between Fichtean idealism and twentieth-century existentialism. See Richard, "La philosophie de Fichte et l'existentialisme," in: *Proceedings of the Tenth International Congress of Philosophy, Amsterdam, August 11–18, 1948*, Amsterdam 1949, pp. 1174–76.
52 BN, p. 629. "Thus the world by nature is *mine* in so far as it is the correlative in-itself of nothingness; that is, of the necessary obstacle beyond which I find myself as that which I am in the form of 'having to be it'" (*Being and Nothingness*, p. 157).

of *Being and Nothingness*, "human reality is neither a fact nor a value, but rather the relationship of a fact to a value."[53]

Both the Fichtean *Wissenschaftslehre* and Sartrean existentialism may therefore be characterized as philosophies of the "engaged self," inasmuch as the very distinction between freedom and determinism can arise only for a self that is "engaged" with the world.[54] Sartre's "ontological proof" that "consciousness is *supported* by a being which is not itself"[55] plays the same role within his system that Fichte's demonstration that the I cannot posit itself (and hence, cannot actually *be an I* at all) unless "there emerges in it a disparity, and hence something alien"[56] plays in the early *Wissenschaftslehre*. The point in both cases is to highlight a certain reciprocity between the for-itself and the in-itself, between the spontaneous self-activity and the original determinacy of the I, a reciprocity that is essential *both* for the possibility of theoretical consciousness *and* for the possibility of free action. Fichte and Sartre even employ similar metaphors to capture this idea, with the former referring to the "circuit of selfness" (*Circuite d'ipséité*) and the latter to the "circuit of the I's function" (*Kreislauf der Funktionen des Ich*).[57]

## X. The Limits of Transcendental Explanation

Let us now direct our attention to certain similar *conclusions* drawn by Fichte and Sartre from their descriptions of the finitely free, divided self. Later on, we will examine the very different ways they *respond to and interpret* these same conclusions.

The existing I, according to Fichte, simultaneously affirms its absolute freedom (or pure I-hood) and recognizes its determinate limitations. *Both*, after all, are conditions for the possibility of any actual conscious-

---

53 Sartre to Simone de Beauvoir, December 9, 1939, in : Sartre, *Oevres romanesques*, Paris 1981, p. 1899.
54 "Consequently the resistance which freedom reveals in the existent, far from being a danger to freedom, results only in enabling it to arise as freedom. There can be a free for- itself only as engaged in a resisting world. Outside of this engagement the notions of freedom, of determinism, of necessity lose all meaning" (BN, p. 621).
55 Ibid., p. 23.
56 "Foundations of the Entire Science of Knowledge," p. 233 (GA I/2, p. 400).
57 BN, pp. 155–58 and "Foundations of the Entire Science of Knowledge," p. 258 (GA I/2, p. 423).

ness whatsoever and have now, or so Fichte claims, been demonstrated to be such by means a complete genetic account of the transcendental conditions for the possibility of original self-positing. But neither of these extremes – neither the original freedom nor the original determinacy of the I – can be further "explained" by transcendental philosophy. The finite I simply *finds itself* to be free, or rather, to be obliged to act in a certain way – namely, according to the highest principle of morality). Similarly, it simply *finds itself* to be this particular, determinate individual in this particular time and place. These, according to Fichte, constitute the two "incomprehensible boundaries" within which any philosophical explication of human freedom is confined.[58] That I am the individual that I am, in the world in which I find myself: this is simply a "contingent fact."[59]

Sartre too stresses the sheer *contingency* and *inexplicability* – and hence "absurdity" – of the human condition and observes that, "in our own apprehension of ourselves we appear to ourselves as having the character of an unjustifiable fact."[60] Furthermore, not only is the original facticity of the for-itself "unjustifiable" (that is, incapable of being derived from anything higher), but so are the various free choices we are "condemned" to have to make and through which we, in turn, "make ourselves": hence the *anxiety* with which freedom is apprehended. Despite its claim to radical freedom, the for-itself is not the ground of its own being as a for-itself, and neither is the Fichtean I. Both simply find themselves to be free in a situation for which they are nevertheless responsible, trapped within inscrutable boundaries, living embodiments of the paradox of freedom.

## XI. Temporality and the Problem of the Pure Will

Another striking similarity between our two philosophers lies in their accounts of *temporality*, and, more specifically, in their profoundly *practical* accounts of the origins and meaning of the same. For Fichte, time is no longer to be understood primarily as a passive a priori form of sensible intuition, but instead as a schema of free acting, which can, in turn, be

---

58 "On the Basis of Our Belief in a Divine Governance of the World," IWL, p. 149 (GA I/5, p. 353).
59 SS, p. 220.
60 BN, p. 128.

explicated only with reference to the agent's past, present, and future.[61] So too for Sartre, "temporality is only a tool of vision,"[62] through which the for-itself views its own facticity (the past), its presence to the in-itself (present), and the projected self that it is striving to become (the future). Though Fichte's theory of temporality as the schema of acting (which is developed most fully in § 13 of his lectures on *Wissenschaftslehre nova methodo*) remains undeveloped in comparison with Sartre's extended discussion of ecstatic temporality in the second chapter of Part Two of *Being and Nothingness*, both accounts stress the intimate connection between the freely efficacious self-activity of the I and the temporality of the same.

This similarity, however, should not be allowed to obscure a major *difference* between Fichte's and Sartre's theories of time. Though both accounts stress the essential temporality of the finite self, which cannot act unless it temporalizes itself, Fichte, unlike Sartre, nevertheless claims that the "true" or "intelligible" I lies altogether outside of time, which he compares to a "colored glass" or "prism"[63] through which the I views its own intelligible action through the empirical medium of the sensible world. "Consciousness itself," Fichte claims,

> is simply not in any time at all, and only {what is in} time has a beginning and an end. Time as a whole is merely a certain way of looking at things, one that arises when we start with what we take to be a first act of willing and then connect this act with another, [preceding one,] which is supposed to explain it, and with another, subsequent one, which is supposed to follow from it.[64]

On this point I must confess my sympathy with critics such as Peter Rohs,[65] for whom such remarks about the relationship of consciousness to time point to a fundamental ambiguity or tension within the Jena *Wissenschaftslehre*, one that might be formulated as the tension between the claim that the only *real* or *actual* I is the finite, temporal, human agent and the competing claim that my true self is a noumenal or intelligible

---

61 See WLnm, p. 224: "Time originates solely within the I, in the concept of substantiality that is applied to the I when the I employs its power of imagination to run through the various possibilities of action. Insofar as the object is simply an object for the acting I, the object as extended over time along with the I itself."
62 BN, p. 281.
63 WLnm, pp. 366–67; GA IV/2, p. 187.
64 WLnm, p. 359.
65 See Rohs, Peter: "Über die Zeit als Mittelglied zwischen dem Intelligiblen und dem Sinnlichen," in: *Fichte-Studien* 6 (1994), pp. 95–116, and *Johann Gottlieb Fichte*, München 1991, pp. 77–82.

member of the "kingdom of ends," determined as such by a predeliberative determination of the pure will.

One way, therefore, to contemplate the possibility of a shortcut from the *Wissenschaftslehre* to existentialism would be to eliminate this tension by denying this controversial claim concerning the timeless, true self, even though Fichte himself, in his post-Jena lectures, seems to have proceeded in precisely the opposite direction: namely, towards an ever more robust (and, in my opinion, transcendent rather than transcendental) theory of the Absolute. In this sense, Sartre's resolutely this-worldly account of freedom might represent something of a "road not taken" by Fichte himself, though it is a road clearly anticipated by certain features of the early *Wissenschaftslehre*.

## XII. Man's Final End or Fundamental Project

Actions, of course, presuppose ends or goals, something to be accomplished thereby. A theory of finite human freedom is thus a theory of human striving, and it therefore comes as no surprise that before Fichte adopted the name "*Wissenschaftslehre*" for his new system, he referred to it on at least one occasion as a *StrebungsPhilosophie* or "philosophy of striving."[66] But beyond the particular goals of particular actions, one can always inquire if there is some larger or final goal of *all* our actions. According to both Sartre and Fichte, the answer to this question is "yes." Any freely acting individual's various choices and projects may all be interpreted as efforts on that individual's part to achieve a larger "fundamental project" or "final end," one common to and shared by all finite agents: namely, to overcome, once and for all, the various internal divisions that, as we have seen, characterize the Fichtean and Sartrean self.

Moreover, our two philosophers offer remarkably similar accounts of this "fundamental project." According to Fichte, the goal of all striving on the part of the finite individual is to attain absolute self-identity, to obliterate the gap between I and Not-I, to heal the fractured self not by rejecting the demands of the pure will, but rather, by subordinating the Not-I and the empirical I to the infinite demands of the pure I, by finally transforming, to modify a Nietzschean formula, "all that is" into "thus I

---

66 "Eigne Meditationen über ElmentarPhilosophie/Practische Philosophie," GA II/3, p. 265.

have willed it." The final aim of every finite human being is, in short, nothing less than the "self-sufficiency" of reason as such.⁶⁷

According to Sartre, the fundamental project of the for-itself is to overcome its own contingency, to provide itself with the "foundation" it lacks, with a genuine "being" of its own, thereby becoming a "free thing," an "in-itself-for-itself," or, more succinctly, "God."⁶⁸ Fichte, too, on some occasions, described the final end of all human striving in similar terms, declaring for instance, in his *Lectures on the Scholar's Vocation*, that man "will risk anything to pluck the apple of knowledge, for the drive to be equal to God is ineradicably implanted in him."⁶⁹ "Man's final end is to subordinate to himself all that is irrational, to master it freely and according to his own laws. This is a final end that is completely unachievable and must always remain so – so long, that is, as man is to remain man and is not supposed to become God."⁷⁰

To this Sartre might respond by saying, granted, we cannot assume that we will ever succeed in becoming God; but the Fichtean I's striving for complete sufficiency as an I is precisely its striving to *become* God.

---

67 "The ultimate goal is the self-sufficiency of reason as such and thus not the self-sufficiency of one ration, insofar as the latter is an individual rational being" (Fichte, SS, p. 220). See too "Some Lectures concerning the Scholar's Vocation," in: EPW, p. 150 (GA I/4, p. 31): "Man's ultimate and supreme goal is complete harmony with himself and – so that he can be in harmony with himself – the harmony of all external things with his own necessary, practical concepts of them (i.e., with those concepts which determine how things ought to be)."
68 "The fundamental value which presides over this project is exactly the in-itself-for-itself; that is, the ideal of a consciousness which would be the foundation of its own being-in-itself by the pure consciousness which it would have of itself. It is this indeed which can be called God. Thus the best way to conceive of the fundamental project of human reality is to say that man is the being whose project it is to be God [...]. To be man means to reach toward being God. Or, if you prefer, man fundamentally is the desire to be God" (BN, pp. 723–24).
69 Fichte, Johann G.: "Some Lectures Concerning the Scholar's Vocation," in: EPW, p. 183 (GA I/3, p. 66).
70 Fichte, Johann G.: "Some Lectures Concerning the Scholar's Vocation," in: EPW, p. 152 (GA I/3, p. 32).

## XIII. Endless Striving

Fichte and Sartre agree on this fundamental point: human beings are always striving for a final end that can never – even in principle – be achieved, for if it were to be achieved then the conditions necessary for the possibility of actual freedom and real self-consciousness, that is, the dialectic of freedom and facticity, original self-assertion and original limitation, would be destroyed. "Human reality" is therefore described by Sartre as "a perpetual surpassing toward a coincidence with itself which is never given."[71] Fichte, in *The System of Ethics,* uses different language to make exactly the same point:

> The pure drive aims at absolute independence; an action is suitable to the pure drive if it is also directed toward absolute independence, i.e., if it lies *in a series, through the continuation of which the I would have to become independent.* [...] however, the I can never become independent so long as it is supposed to be an I. Consequently, the final end of a rational being necessarily lies in infinity; it is certainly not an end that can be achieved, but it is one to which a rational being, in consequence of its spiritual nature, is supposed to draw ceaselessly nearer and nearer.[72]

To be sure, there is also an important difference between Sartre's conclusion and Fichte's, inasmuch as the latter insists that even if our final end is unobtainable in principle, we can nevertheless draw ever closer to or "approximate it." For Sartre, in contrast, that idea that by dint of free acting we could even become "more like God" is patently absurd. Let us therefore conclude our comparison of these two thinkers by looking more closely at this difference.

---

71 BN, p. 139.
72 SS, p. 142 (GA I/5, pp. 140–41). See too the following passage from "Some Lectures Concerning the Scholar's Vocation,": "It is part of the concept of man that his ultimate goal be unobtainable and that his path thereto be infinitely long. Thus it is not man's vocation to reach his goal. But he can and he should draw nearer to it, and his true vocation qua *man*, that is, insofar as he is a rational but finite, a sensuous but free being, lies in *endless approximation to this goal*" (EWP, p. 152 [GA I/3, p. 32]).

## XIV. To Despair or to Rejoice, That is the Question

No sooner does one reflect upon the similarities between Fichte's and Sartre's conceptions of the final end of human striving than one must also be struck by the dramatically different ways in which they *interpret* and *respond* to this conclusion. To judge by the infamous final pages of *Being and Nothingness*, recognition of our final goal would appear to be a formula for despair, inasmuch as it reveals that "man loses himself in order that God may by born. But the idea of God is contradictory and we lose ourselves in vain. Man is a useless passion."[73] Our lot as humans is therefore a profoundly unhappy one.

> The being of human reality is suffering, because it rises in being as perpetually haunted by a totality which it is without being able to be it, precisely because it could not attain the in-itself without losing itself as for-itself. Human reality therefore is by nature an unhappy consciousness with no possibility of surpassing its unhappy state.[74]

How dramatically different is Fichte's response to what is basically the same realization of the unachievability and even incoherence of our final end! Instead of lamenting our unhappy lot, he instead exhorts us to "rejoice over the prospect of the immense field that is ours to cultivate! Let us rejoice because we feel our own strength and because the task is endless!"[75] And, following Kant, Fichte also treats the infinite character of our moral responsibility as grounds for a practical postulate concerning personal immortality, as well as an indirect argument for positulating a moral world-order or divine author of the same.[76]

Despite this last postulate, there are good reasons to think that Fichte actually agrees with Sartre regarding the "contradictory" character of the concept of God as the final object of human striving, at least if this is understood in Sartrean terms as the in-itself-for-itself, a freedom that is at the same time the foundation of its own being: an infinite self-consciousness. For Fichte, no less than Sartre, shows us that actual freedom and consciousness can be ascribed only to finite selves, and thus the idea of God's self-consciousness (and hence of divine freedom) is, as he explicitly remarks in § 5 of the *Foundations of the Entire Wissenschaftslehre*,

---

73  BN, p. 784.
74  Ibid., p. 140.
75  Fichte, Johann G.: "Some Lectures Concerning the Scholar's Vocation," in: EPW, p. 184 (GA I/3, p. 68).
76  See, above all, Book III of *The Vocation of Man*.

quite "inexplicable and inconceivable to any finite reason."[77] But since transcendental philosophy deals only with what is included within "the circle of consciousness," i.e., only with what is indeed conceivable by finite reason, there seems very little difference between saying, with Fichte, that such an idea is "inconceivable" or, with Sartre, that it is "impossible."

For Fichte, however, the recognition of such a theoretical impossibly does not justify Sartrean despair about the human condition. On the contrary, it simply means that we need to distinguish sharply between this concept of our infinite final end and the various finite ends of determinate moral actions. The latter *can* be accomplished, and such an accomplishment *does* make a difference. One may well raise theoretical quibbles concerning Fichte's description of such finite accomplishments as bringing us "closer" to our infinite final end, but the goal of the former is not to make us and our world *perfect*, but only *better*; not to make the finite I one with the pure I, nor to assimilate the Not-I completely to the formal demands of the I, but simply to make the finite I less dependent upon the Not-I and more self-sufficient than it was before.[78] In other words, the goal of free action is to become every more free, to extend continually what another student of Fichte, namely, Karl Marx, called "the sphere of freedom" and to diminish "the sphere of necessity."

Is *this* an impossible or self-contradictory goal? Surely not, nor is Sartre justified in concluding, as he at times appears to conclude, that because our fundamental project is impossible then all of our lesser ones must inevitably fail as well. Fichte's reply, in the *System of Ethics,* to those who object to his talk of drawing ever closer to an infinite (or impossible) goal thus apply as well to Sartre's dramatic conclusion that man is a useless passion and perpetual failure, inasmuch as he can never accomplish his fundamental project of becoming God.

> In expressing such scruples, it seems as though one is talking about infinity as a thing in itself. *I* draw nearer to it *for myself.* I can, however, never grasp infinity; hence I always have before my eyes some *determinate* goal, to which I can undoubtedly draw nearer, even though, after I have achieved this determinate goal, my goal might well be extended that much farther as a result of the perfecting of my whole being, as well as of my own insight, which I have achieved through this process. In this *general* regard, therefore, I never

---

77  GWL, p. 242 (GA I/2, p. 407).
78  On this point see § 12 of SS, where Fichte explicitly contrasts the infinite final end of pure reason as such (the aim of the "pure drive" of the I) with the finite, determinate ends of concrete moral action (the aims of the "ethical drive" of the I).

draw nearer to the infinite. – My goal lies in infinity, because my dependence is infinite. Yet I never grasp my dependence in its infinity, but only with respect to some determinate range; and within this domain I can undoubtedly render myself more free.[79]

## XV. Explaining the Difference: The Critical Role of the Pure Will

What are we to make of this difference? Does it simply reflect a "temperamental" difference between two very different individuals, or perhaps some larger difference between the eras and places in which these two individuals lived and wrote, one gripped by the spirit of Revolutionary optimism and the other burdened by the pessimism and resignation of an occupied land and a defeated people? Or is there instead some more substantial, systematic or internal difference between the *Wissenschaftslehre* and Sartrean existentialism that might explain this striking difference concerning the implications of a philosophy of endless striving? I believe that there is such a doctrinal difference, and by identifying it I hope to shed some more light upon the issue that here concerns me and, ultimately, to indicate precisely why Fichte cannot be considered a proto-existentialist – as well as what might have to be *altered* in his early system in order to transform him into one.

The difference in question has to do with the character of that *pure willing* or the original spontaneity of the I, with which both systems begin. Whereas Sartre understands original freedom simply as the ungrounded and ungroundable demand that one determine oneself in one way or another in a particular situation, Fichte maintains that the pure will that precedes and conditions all of my individual choices possesses a distinctive determinacy of its own: namely, it is a moral, or at least a proto-moral will, and what it wills is its own self-sufficiency or autonomy, which is the ultimate end of all determinate moral action.[80] Thus he writes, "we have now postulated a kind of willing that does not pre-

---

79 SS, pp. 142–43
80 Immediately after his deduction of the original determinate pure will, as the only way to resolve the viciously circular relationship between theoretical and practical reason, which threatens to undermine his entire theory of consciousness in the Halle transcript of the *Wissenschaftslehre nova methodo*, Fichte remarks: "To *will* something is thus a *categorical*, unconditioned demand – what is willed appears as an *absolute postulate* of actuality; it demands only this *being* and none other" (GA IV/2, p. 114).

suppose cognition of an object, but which carries its object within itself and which is not based upon any act of deliberation."[81] Such an "ought, or determinate, pure willing is something objective." It is something that is discovered by or given to us, and "consequently, this pure act of willing does not first originate through an act of thinking; it [simply] is, and its must exist in advance of all thinking. "[82]

Indeed, the supreme and perhaps most audacious speculative claim of the *Wissenschaftslehre nova methodo* (the consequences of which are explicated in detail in the *System of Ethics*) is precisely this: that only reference to the original determinacy of the pure will can allow us to cut the Gordian knot presented by the circular relation between human cognition on the one hand and finite projection of goals for free action on the other; for only by positing the original, predeliberative self-determination of the pure will and hence determination of the finite will can the unstable reciprocal relation between the theoretical and practical drives or powers of the I be resolved. Only by appealing to the "highest synthesis" contained in this "pure will" can we explain our own "original determinacy," both as human beings in general and as individuals.[83] Without this final synthesis, Fichte believed that his entire account of the genesis of experience from the postulate of original self-consciousness would be incomplete and therefore unstable. In the end, the claim of the Jena *Wissenschaftslehre* is this: finite selfhood, concrete freedom, actual self-consciousness, and real cognition of the world are all possible only because "the pure will is the categorical imperative,"[84] which is simply another name for that "pure will that I ought to have in time."[85]

> Answer to the question, Who am I? {I am the person I make of myself; my determinacy depends upon my free decision, which follows from the task of limiting oneself.} But who ought I to be? {This lies in my individuality.} But

---

81 WLnm, pp. 192–93.
82 WLnm, p. 299 (GA, IV/2, p. 139).
83 "This determinacy of the pure will is the explanatory ground of all consciousness" (WLnm, p. 306). For a helpful and detailed analysis of Fichte's extremely difficult (and rather problematic) but also extremely important concept of the "Bestimmtheit des reinen Willes," see Stolzenberg, Jürgen: "Reiner Wille: ein Grundbegriff der Philosophie Fichtes," in: *Revue Internationale de Philosophie* 52 (1998), pp. 617–39; Pt. IV of Zöller, Günther: *Fichte's Transcendental Philosophy: The Original Duplicity of Intelligence and Will*, Cambridge 1998; and Zöller, "Einheit und Differenz von Fichtes Theorie des Wollens," in: *Philosophisches Jahrbuch* 106 (1999), pp. 430–40.
84 WLnm, p. 293.
85 WLnm, p. 337.

individuality is not determined by any being; it is determined by a law: what I should be is something that is prescribed for all time. {This... is the ethical law.} The pure will is limited: this pure will is not human understanding, for it is certainly not extended in space; it is spontaneity and can be limited only by itself. Therefore, to say that the pure will is limited is to say that a law of willing (an ethical law) is contained within my being as a whole.[86]

According to the *Wissenschaftslehre*, therefore, our original freedom should not be understood, as it is by Sartre, as something *absurd*, as "a monstrous spontaneity."[87] Self-consciousness arises not from a non-thetic grasp of our own sheer nothingness, but from a living awareness of a determinate concept of our concrete moral vocation, a awareness that appears in the form of a categorical imperative to determine our own freedom in this particular context in accordance with the universal demands of pure willing (the moral law).

Perhaps Fichte's most explicit affirmation of this point occurs in a passage from the *System of Ethics*, in which he certainly seems to anticipate what is perhaps the fundamental thesis of twentieth-century existentialism:

> In order for something to be thought of as free, you required it to determine *itself* and not be determined from outside or even by its own nature. What does this "*itself*" mean? Some duality is obviously being thought in this case. What is free is supposed to be before it is determined; it is supposed to have an existence independent of its determinacy. This is why a thing cannot be thought of as determining itself, since it does not exist prior to its nature (i.e., the total sum of its determinations). As was just said, something that is supposed to determine *itself* would, in a certain respect, have to be before it is, before it has properties and any nature at all. This can be thought only under our presupposition, under which, however, it can be thought very easily. As an intellect with a concept of its own real being, what is free precedes its real being, and the former [that is, the intellect] contains the ground of the latter [that is, its own real being]. The concept of a certain being precedes this being, and the latter depends upon the former.[88]

---

86 WLnm, p. 337–38.
87 Sartre, Jean Paul: *Transcendence of the Ego*, p. 99.
88 SS, p. 40. Frederick Neuhouser, who also calls attention to the resemblance between this claim and twentieth century existentialism, proposes an ingenious interpretation of Fichte's notion of free self-determination, an interpretation that avoids the extremes of arbitrariness and heteronomy. Yet Neuhouser entirely ignores Fichte's concept of pure willing and instead interprets Fichte's position in the context of Charles Taylor's "weaker" notion of substantial self-determination. Though Neuhouser's challenge to a purely existentialist interpretation of Fichtean self-determination is justified, his alternative interpretation is unpersuasive.

## XVI. Existence Precedes Essence

So where does this leave us? To what extent is the philosophy presented in the Jena *Wissenschaftslehre* compatible with and even an anticipation of twentieth century existentialism, and particularly the radical, Sartrean variant of the same? If the essence of the latter position is supposed to be encapsulated in the familiar formula that in the case of human beings – and human beings alone – "existence precedes essence,"[89] then a strong case might be made for the claim that Fichte is, on this point anyway, clearly a forerunner of Sartre. Just as strongly as Sartre, Fichte also stresses that it is up to us to determine our own freedom and hence our own nature as free individuals.

> The *Wissenschaftslehre*, after all, maintains that "Freedom or (what is the same thing) the immediate action of the I is, as such, the point where ideality and reality are united. The *I* is free inasmuch as it posits itself as free or sets itself free [*sich befreit*]. It posits or sets itself free inasmuch as it is free. Determination and being are one; the acting subject and that which is acted upon are one. Precisely insofar as the I determines itself to act, it acts in this [very] act of determination; and insofar as it acts, it determines itself."[90]
> 
> All animals are complete and finished; the human is only intimated and projected [*nur angedeutet, und entworfen*] [...] Every animal *is* what it is: only the human being is originally nothing at all. He must become what he is to be: and since he is to be a being for himself, he must become this through himself. Nature completed all of her works; only from the human being did she withdraw her hand, and precisely by doing so, she gave him over to himself. Formability [*Bildsamkeit*], as such, is the character of humanity.[91]

---

Indeed, it forces him to reject the central Fichtean concept of "infinite striving" as incompatible with the proposed, "weaker" concept of self-determination. See Neuhouser, Frederick: *Fichte's Theory of Subjectivity*, pp. 155–66.

89 "What [the existentialists] have in common is simply the fact that they believe that *existence* comes before *essence* – or, if you will, that we must begin with the subjective." "Man is nothing else what he makes of himself. That is the first principle of existentialism" (Sartre, Jean Paul: *Existentialism is a Humanism*, pp. 348 and 349).

90 "Outline of the Distinctive Character of the Wissenschaftsleher with Respect to the Theoretical Faculty," in EPW, p. 276 [GA I/3, p. 176].

91 *Foundations of Natural Right*, trans. Michael Baur, Cambridge 2000, p. 74 [GA I/3, p. 379]. As Fichte says later in the same text, "if the human being is an animal, then he is an *incomplete* animal, and for that very reason he is not an animal" (p. 76; GA I/3, p. 381). To this he adds, a few pages later, "and it is precisely because of this incompleteness than the human being is capable of such formability" (p. 78 [GA I/3, p. 383]).

## XVII. Why Fichte is Not an Existentialist

Despite the many striking similarities between Fichte and Sartre, what finally keeps Fichte from being called an "existentialist" is precisely his refusal to stop with this description of the self-determination of the finite I. Instead, even in the Jena period, he insists on connecting the self-determination of the concretely free moral agent with that mysterious act of determination by means of which the pure will determines the original character of finite individuals, who are then able to become aware of themselves not only as this or that individual, but also – and more truly – as the pure will itself, which is something I grasp only insofar as I conceive of myself as an instrument or "tool of the moral law."[92] This is, if you well, the speculative truth behind the real, everyday intuition of freedom in the form of moral obligation.

Fichte's remarkable and profoundly original claim is that we could not be self-conscious individuals at all, that we could not be finitely free agents, unless we also are and originally were something *more* than this. And that we *are* more than finite individuals is precisely what we realize when we recognize the moral law. Only in knowing my *duty* do I really know *who, or rather what, I truly am.*

In section 13 of the *Wissenschaftslehre nova methodo* Fichte elucidates the relationship between the finite, conscious, temporal agent and the pure and infinite, timeless and, presumably, unconscious will as follows:

> How is the movement of transition of my pure willing from its determinability to determinacy related {to consciousness}? This is a transition that occurs without any help from us, for we ourselves first come into being by means of our movement. (I appear to myself as determined to determine myself in one way or another.) The Idea that we ourselves originate within time is contained in this. The I here appears to itself as determined to have to determine itself in just the way it does determine itself, and the movement of transition is here thought of not as free, but rather as necessary. It is something discovered. This determinacy, which constitutes my basic character, consists in the fact that I am determined to determine myself in a certain way. For this reason, it only assigns me the task of acting in a certain way; it assigns me an "ought." Man's determinate nature or "vocation" is not something he gives to himself; instead, it is that through which a human being is a human being.[93]

---

92  See SS, pp. 225, 244, 248, 258, 267, and 296.
93  WLnm, p. 300.

Thus, even though Fichte unquestionably anticipates Sartre in denying that human beings possess a "nature" or "being" that determines their freedom, he does not conclude from this that the I is simply "nothing." Though the *use* we make of our freedom is determined by nothing outside of ourselves, we our nevertheless guided in its use by a task or an ought, by a law that is given to us along with our original determinacy. However free we are to do and to become whatever we freely will, we are not the authors of this law nor the producers of this original determinacy.

## XVIII. The Shortcut

How then can Fichte be most quickly and easily transformed into an existentialist? The short answer is as follows: by rejecting the categorical imperative and the account of the pure will based thereupon; by denying that, as a matter of fact, we find ourselves to be bound by the universal moral law in the manner that Fichte, following Kant, seems to have taken for granted; and thus by challenging the legitimacy of appealing to this particular "fact of reason." Deprived of this "real intellectual intuition" of moral duty, the *Wissenschaftslehre* no longer has a warrant for seeking its highest synthesis in the pure will and is left instead with a truncated transcendental account of human, all-too-human freedom and self-consciousness – a "pragmatic history of the human mind," if you will. Such a theory, shorn of its ambitious extensions into the quasi-transcendent domain of the pure will, would in certain important respects – including the ones I have catalogued in this paper, as well as others I have not discussed – closely resemble Sartre's account of human reality in *Being and Nothingness* and might therefore deserve to be called at least "proto-existentialist."

But why might one think that such a drastic revision of Fichte's system is actually called for? Why? Because "we" – or at least many of us at this point in human history – no longer profess to believe in the "rational fact" of an objectively binding, timelessly universal moral law. Whether with regret or relief, many contemporary students of the *Wissenschaftslehre* will conclude that the concept of the "determinacy of the pure will" simply cannot be made intelligible without appealing to problematic moral assumptions or falling back upon untenable theological presuppositions and prejudices. If a person in this situation still wishes to defend an uncompromising doctrine of human freedom, then he or she cannot do so by postulating freedom as a condition for dutiful action; such a person may therefore well be attracted instead to Sartre's existentialist system of freedom, with its roots in anxiety – which might well seem to be a more viable contemporary candidate as a "fact of reason" – and its willingness to recognize the basic absurdity of the human condition as such, and, more specifically, the absurdity of freedom itself.

For such a person, Nietzsche's announcement of the "death of God" and the deflationary genealogy of morals which he inaugurated stand as an insurmountable barrier to all attempts, Fichte's included, to construct a fundamentally *moral* account of the foundations of free self-consciousness. Perhaps, then, something resembling Sartrean existentialism really is the best that can be salvaged from Fichte's early philosophy at this late date, and perhaps we have a formula for our shortcut from Fichte to Sartre: "the Jena *Wissenschaftslehre* minus the moral law = existentialism"?

## XIX. The Road Not Taken

A very different reason for questioning Fichte's doctrine of the pure will and subjecting the early *Wissenschaftslehre* to the drastic surgery this would entail is because even a diligent and well-disposed reader might conclude that Fichte's sincere effort to go beyond the immanent realm of finite selfhood and to ground the latter on an elaborate account of the timeless pure will and its relationship to the embodied individual agent is, strictly speaking, *incompatible with the transcendental "spirit" of his own enterprise.* Such a conclusion is, in my opinion, certainly hard to avoid in the case of the some, if not all, of the later versions of the *Wissenschaftslehre.* But I believe it also applies to central portions of the crowing achievements of Fichte's Jena period, the *Wissenschaftslehre nova methodo* and *System of Ethics.* And if it is indeed the case that to talk about the "pre-deliberative self-determination of the pure, infinite will" is to make a fateful step outside that "circle of consciousness," within which, according to Fichte himself, transcendental philosophy must scrupulously confine itself, then perhaps one could make a good philosophical case for revising the early *Wissenschaftslehre* in a manner that brings in somewhat closer to twentieth century existentialism.

In such a case, one would be motivated not by problematic culturally based assumptions about the death of God and self-overcoming of our highest values, but rather *by considerations internal to Fichte's own transcendental project.* After all, the most effective criticism of any philosophical system, Fichte's included, is not *external* but *internal*; and what I am here suggesting is that a rigorous internal critique and revision of the Jena *Wissenschaftslehre* does not *necessarily* have to lead in the direction of the full-fledged philosophy of the absolute that Fichte himself actually developed after leaving Jena. It *might* lead in that direction, of course, but I am not convinced that it *must*.

Perhaps such a critical reassessment will leave us instead with a theory of selfhood that is less ambitious than Fichte's own, but also more truly critical and transcendental: with a genetic account of the conditions necessary for the possibility of self-consciousness, but one that recognizes the *limits* of transcendental or philosophical explanation and is willing to confess its ignorance concerning what might or might not lie on the far side of those "inscrutable boundaries" within which transcendental philosophy shows us to be constantly confined – *even as philosophers.*

A system that could survive such a critical winnowing might be called "minimal Fichteanism" or "Fichte Lite" or "*Wissenschaftslehre* degree zero." To be sure, it would still include many of the early *Wissenschaftslehre*'s most original and familiar doctrines, including the clear recognition of the extra-philosophical foundations of philosophy in human life, the lucid analysis of the interplay between theoretical and practical reason in the constitution of self-consciousness, the innovative transcendental deduction of the necessity of the social dimension of self-consciousness, and the insistence that the only actual self is the finite, temporal one. It would still be a philosophy of endless striving, but it would relinquish any claims to being a doctrine of the absolute.

Though this kind of minimal Fichteanism is clearly a "road not taken" by Fichte himself, I believe that there are nevertheless good reasons for taking it. One of those reasons is the one we considered in the previous section: namely, the widespread reluctance of contemporary readers to endorse the kind of extravagant moral rigorism that rests everything upon the "fact" of (moral) reason. That by itself, of course, is not a sufficient reason for stripping Fichte's early philosophy of the doctrine of the pure will, no more than the denial of human freedom by the "dogmatists" of his own era was a good reason for him to mitigate has own insistence upon the same. Maybe we moderns are just *wrong* on this point? If so, *we* will certainly be unable to understand and be convinced by the *Wissenschaftslehre*, but that may just be a fact about us and our age – more specifically, about our moral corruption – and not a criticism of Fichte. I am fairly confident that this is how Fichte himself would reply to any suggested "short cut" to Sartre.

That is why it is so important to base one's criticisms of Fichte on considerations internal to his own philosophy. Everyone, after all, is supposed to "think the *Wissenschaftslehre* for himself," in order to think it at all. After three decades of trying to do just this, I find that in order to maintain the integrity of his system as both a "system of human freedom" and a transcendental examination of the conditions for selfhood, I am sometimes forced to reject some of what were clearly Fichte's own most cherished doctrines – most notably, his doctrine of the original determination of the pure will.

In the end, the only serious way to test my proposal for a "Fichteanism degree zero" is to *make the experiment for oneself* in order to determine if one really can succeed in constructing an adequate "pragmatic history of the human mind" without grounding it upon a theory of the pure will. Anyone foolhardy enough to accept such a challenge would, I suggest, find a rich source of inspiration and plenty of help in *Being and Nothingness*.

# Consciousness. A Comparison between Fichte and the Young Sartre in a Bio-Political Perspective

GAETANO RAMETTA

Università degli Studi di Padova

I. Foucault on Biopolitics

In the middle of the 1970 s, Michel Foucault formulated a new paradigm for the interpretation of political power. He advanced the concepts of "bio-politics" and "bio-power", in order to better understand the transformations that had occurred in the relationship between State and society, between politics and economics. He attempted to explain this concept especially in the last chapter of *La volonté de savoir* (1976) and in the last *Cours* of his lessons at *College de France* in winter 1976, published under the title *"Il faut défendre la société"* (1997).

In Foucault's view, a radical change has been effected between the 19th and the 20th centuries in the nature and constitution of political power. The political theory of natural right, of course, centered around the idea of "sovereignty", which consisted in the faculty of "*killing* and letting *live*". The concept of sovereignty designated the political unity of a Commonwealth. The political unity was concentrated in the State as the representative of the common will of the people. The power of the State was a fundamentally *negative* one. It consisted especially in the legitimate exercise of a right to punish whomever disobeyed the law, and thereby violated the established order of the society.

Since the French revolution, the sovereignty of the State can be understood to be progressively increasingly supported by a complex of disciplines, such as medicine and statistics. These disciplines, according to Foucault, gradually transform the aim and structure of political power. The power aims no more at simply creating the *negative* conditions, inside which men are let to live. His function becomes instead the *positive* promotion and implementation of *life*.

With regard to the prior, negative conception of sovereignty, we have a complete reversal in the relationship between power, on the one hand, and life and death, on the other. Power is no longer centered around a complex of differentiated institutions, determined as the "State"; it no longer signifies the monopoly in the exercise of legitimate violence, in order to punish, and in the extreme case to give *death* to guilty citizens. Power becomes a multiplicity of *positive practices*, a set of *strategies* which are *productive* in order to determine and constitute social relations between human beings. Its aim is to "defend society", not merely negatively, but in such a way that the conditions for an increasing expansion of *life* can be devoloped. And the life in question is not only that of the society as a whole, but also and especially the life of each single member within it.

Foucault describes this complex process of transformations with the concept of "bio-power", which in his view denotes the irreversible crisis of the old paradigm of State sovereignity. The formula of bio-power is no more, as in the prior political paradigm: "kill and let live", but rather: "*make* anyone *live* and *let* him *die*". "Bio-politics" signifies a multiplicity of practical strategies, through which state agencies, medical institutions, and reasearch centers co-operate in the realization and development of this new kind of control and production of life.

## II. Agamben on Deleuze

Along with the publication of Foucault's *Cours* at *College de France*, many thinkers have concentrated on the problem of bio-politics. Giorgio Agamben is undoubtedly among the most acute and original ones. I would like to mention two of his books: *Homo sacer* (1995, 2005[2]) and *Stato di eccezione* [*State of Exception*] (2003). Many of his most significant essays have also recently been collected in the Italian edition entitled *La potenza del pensiero* [*The Power of Thinking*].

The last of these essays, *L'immanenza assoluta* [*Absolute Immanence*][1], is particularly important for us. It was the first article which drew attention – already in 1996 – on the short text written by Gilles Deleuze in the year of his death (1995), which is entitled *L'immanence: une vie....*[2]

In order to articulate his theory of "absolute immanence", Deleuze makes reference to authors whose focus is the idea of *consciousness*. The relationship between the concept of consciousness and the concept of

---

1   Agamben, Giorgio: "L'immanenza assoluta," in : *La potenza del pensiero*,Vicenza 2005, pp. 377–404.
2   *Philosophie* 47 (1995), pp. 3–7.

life, I will argue, will allow us to understand the importance of Fichte's theory for contemporary philosophical thinking.

Deleuze sees life as an impersonal kind of creative becoming. I will focus here on the manner in which Deleuze's interpretation of Fichte's theory of life is developed through his reading of, and reference to, the young Sartre and his phenomenological essay *La transcendance de l'Ego*. I will also suggest that the themes Deleuze underlines (e.g. the relationship between the impersonal becoming of life and the problem of consciousness within the "transcendental field") also raise doubts about Deleuze's own attempt to answer the question of a new theory of life.

With regard to Fichte, Deleuze mentions two passages. The first one is from the *Second Introduction to the WL* of 1797, and the second one is from the *Guide to the Life of Bliss* of 1806. Surprisingly, Agamben does not even mention Fichte in the constellation of authors, which he considers important for Deleuze. At the end of his essay, he tries to show the existence of two main lines in Western philosophical tradition. The first is centered around the idea of "Transcendence", and moves from Kant to Levinas-Derrida, who are connected by Husserl. The second is centered around the idea of "Immanence", and moves from Spinoza-Nietzsche to Foucault and, obviously, Deleuze himself, who has dedicated important studies to each of them.

According to Agamben, both traditions are in radical opposition with each other. But the situation is complicated by the fact that Agamben identifies an important crossing-point, which connects and divides the two traditions in question. This point is represented by Heidegger. He is the author who tries to unify the transcendental and phenomenological tradition (Kant to Husserl) with the tradition of "Immanence" (Spinoza to Nietzsche). From Heidegger onwards, both lines separate again in two different directions: in the second half of the 20$^{th}$ century, the line of "Transcendence" is represented by Levinas and Derrida; the line of "Immanence" by Foucault and Deleuze.

If we consider this interpretation, it is not difficult to understand why Agamben does not even mention Fichte. He is undoubtely one of the main representatives of the transcendental tradition. For this reason, in Agamben's model, he should be placed inside the line of "Transcendence". But Deleuze identifies Fichte as a philosopher of absolute immanence. This would strikingly contradict Agamben's scheme. The solution appears to consist in simply ignoring Fichte and the Doctrine of science in order to understand the position of Deleuze and his conception of the "*immanence absolue.*"

*Mutatis mutandis*, the same question arises with regard to Sartre. If we look at the title of Sartre's second book on the imagination (*L'imaginaire. Psychologie phénoménologique de l'imagination*),[3] we can place his juvenile work under the aegis of Husserlian Phenomenology. We do not have to discuss here if Sartre's concept of phenomenology is fully consistent with Husserl's original conception of it. One could, and perhaps one *should* be perplexed about the way Sartre places "psychology" next to "phenomenology". But here we come across the same problem we discussed before concerning Agamben's interpretation of Fichte's thought.

According to Agamben, the phenomenological tradition is placed on the side of transcendance. It crosses the line of immanence only in Heidegger: starting from Heidegger, phenomenology takes to the road of transcendence again, which culminates in the philosophy of Derrida and Levinas.

Now, just as we have seen in the case of Fichte, a question arises about the meaning and position of Sartre, with particular regard to his first essay entitled *La transcendance de l'Ego*.[4] Deleuze refers to this essay with special emphasis, because here the young Sartre fomulates the concept of an "impersonal transcendental field", which, according to Deleuze, comes near to his own theory of the absolute immanence of life as an impersonal process of creative becoming. If it were true that the phenomenological tradition from Husserl onwards is on the side of transcendance, and therefore in opposition to Deleuze (with the only and partial exception of Heidegger), one could hardly understand why Deleuze chooses such a representative of this tradition, as the young Sartre was, to illustrate his own theory of immanence. As in the case of Fichte, Agamben's solution is not to mention the young Sartre at all.

### III. Deleuze on Fichte and Sartre

In order to understand the connection between Fichte and Sartre, I believe we have to go back to Deleuze's text. In fact, to return to Deleuze will draw attention to the meaning that the transcendental tradition (represented by Fichte) and the phenomenological tradition (represented by Sartre) still have with regard to the present situation of philosophy in general and to the question of biopolitics in particular. I shall also try to high-

---

3  Paris 1940 (1986²).
4  First edition in *Recherches Philosophiques*, 1936; reprinted Paris 1996.

light the fact that in a certain way the theory of consciousness and imagination, as it is conceived by Fichte and by Sartre, is more convincing than Agamben's interpretation of Deleuze, and maybe more advanced than the theory of Deleuze himself.

With regard to Fichte, Deleuze shows how the German thinker supersedes the theory of the 'I' as a first, absolutely unconditional Principle, and how already in the *Second Introduction* he formulates an impersonal theory of life, which finds its mature formulation in the Berlin period. In this context, he underlines the fact that the idea of the "Absolute" coincides with a concept of life as an impersonal becoming. With respect to that, the meaning of the 'I' changes as well. It is no longer the transcendental foundation upon which life is grounded, but only the temporary shape or *Gestalt* through which life comes to appearing.

I think that in this way Deleuze catches the core of Fichte's late conception. In fact, the so-called "second" Fichte presents a theory of the Absolute as a "compenetration between being and life",[5] within which not only the personal and merely individual dimension of subjective existence, but also the critical concept of the subject as "transcendental apperception", that is, as the universal and necessary condition of all and every experience, is exceeded and acquires a relative meaning only.

This theory does not mean that the consciousness becomes something accessory or even superfluous. In WL-1804-II, for example, absolute life is conceived as "*esse in mero actu*". In deleuzian terms, we could translate this as "pure or absolute virtuality". In fact, this conception is reached only through the self-conscious practice of philosophical reflection. It is only *through* the activity of thinking that life can reveal itself as actual, impersonal becoming. It is only through the self-reflection of consciousness which takes its form in thinking that philosophy can conceive of itself as a creative and free expression of life's impersonal becoming.

In WL-1807, we find a very clear expression of this. Fichte states that absolute life cannot be understood as a noun or a substantive. This could tacitly lead us to conceive life as a substance, as a kind of immovable *hypokeimenon* or transcendent *Summum Ens*. So Fichte plays with the ambiguity of the German word *Leben*, stressing the fact that this term should have to be understood not as a noun, but rather as a verb, that is, as an expression of the activity of becoming.

---

5  Fichte, Johann Gottlieb: *Die Wissenschaftslehre. 2. Vortrag im Jahre 1804*, edited by Reinhard Lauth, Hamburg 1986, p. 151.

But at this point Fichte puts the following question: how do we have to understand this verb? Do we have to understand it under a personal mode? Fichte's answer is straightforward: life as a process of living cannot be understood as the activity of any "person". It cannot be conceived of as an activity, which proceeds from someone or something other than, or external to, life itself. Therefore it cannot be conceived of either as an "I" (first person) or as an "*Es*" (third person). Fichte says that it should rather be conceived as an "infinitive", that is as an impersonal becoming of indefinite duration and unending creation. In this meaning, life is relative to nothing other than itself as "*esse in mero actu*" and pure virtuality.

Now this is perfectly consistent with the concept of "absolute immanence" in the sense of Deleuze. With "absolute immanence", in fact, Deleuze means a process which is not *relative* to something else, but whose immanence relates to nothing other than itself. Therefore he indifferently speaks of "*immanence absolue*" or of "*immanence pure*". There is no substance or subject *with respect to which* the immanence of life qualifies itself. Immanence is neither a subject, nor an object, nor a predicate inherent to either or both.

But exactly through this point of similarity we can state the radical "*difference*" which separates the position of Fichte from that of Deleuze. For Fichte, we cannot conceive "life" as a verbal "infinitive" *without consciousness*. In other terms, we cannot put consciousness aside from the process, we cannot abstract from it. Consciousness is essential to life in its appearing. In Fichte's terminology, consciousness is the "Through" (*Durch*) of life's appearance.

From my point of view, it is extremely important to stress the fact that the presence of consciousness does not necessarily imply the position of any "transcendence" at all. On the contrary, Fichte shows how without consciousness life would be impossible in its appearing, that is, how life would cease to be life at all. Without consciousness, in fact, we should reestablish a metaphysical separation between the *what* and the *how* of the appearance. And in the last analysis, it would be indifferent to formulate this separation as one between the Substance and its modes, or as one between a Subject and his actions. In either way, we would introduce transcendence inside the life. Pure immanence would be broken into a substratum, on the one hand, and into its predicates, on the other hand.

On the contrary, it is this relationship between impersonal life and the dimension of consciousness that Deleuze seems to criticize. It is not true that Deleuze wants to delete consciousness *sic et simpliciter*. Rather, he wants to eliminate *reflection* from consciousness. This explains the difference between him and Fichte. For Fichte, freedom as creation is possible only by virtue of the reflexivity of consciousness. It is only through reflection that the 'I' becomes a self-conscious subject. Without reflection, the Self could not posit itself "as" a self, and so no emergence of freedom could be possible from the impersonal becoming of life.

For Deleuze, life must affirm itself not simply against consciousness, but rather against the reflexivity from which the subject raises. This explains why he stresses the meaning of a literary text such as *Our Mutual Friend* by Dickens, where we find the idea of a *minimum* of consciousness and of a *maximum* of impersonality in the experience of life. And that is the crucial point: in criticizing reflection as the condition for the constitution of self-consciousness, Deleuze tries to eliminate the "self" from "consciousness", in order to conceive an absolutely impersonal experience of the impersonal and indefinite becoming of life.

But we have to ask: does this represent a consistent position? I do not think so, because Deleuze, on the one hand, must stress the co-extensivity of consciousness and "transcendental field", without which his own idea of life would break; on the other hand, he must separate from consciousness the idea of the "self", which the concept of consciousness necessarily implies as a structural possibility and condition for freedom and creation.

## IV. Sartre's Transcendental Field

The young Sartre can help us bringing our discourse further. As we have already said, Deleuze draws his attention on the essay *La transcendance de l'Ego*, and he correctly shows that the crucial concept of this text is represented by the idea of an "impersonal transcendental field". Sartre demonstrates that this impersonal dimension has a structural priority prior to the "I" as a personal subject, which he calls an "*Ego*". *Ego* is the concrete unity of "*Je*" and "*Moi*", which can be separated from each other only at an analytical level. With *Je*, Sartre means the 'I' as a subject of action; with *Moi*, he means the 'I' as a substratum of psychological "states" (such as anger, fear, and alike) and of psychological "qualities" (such as being angry, fearful, and alike).

Now, for us it is particularly important that Sartre identifies the transcendental field with what he calls "non-positional consciousness". In this way, he can incorporate the impersonal dimension of life inside the sphere of consciousness. Besides, he provides the conceptual instruments required to avoid confusion between personal and impersonal dimensions, showing at the same time the way for unifying them with each other.

In other words, we have to avoid the confusion between the concept of consciousness and the concept of the "I" (that is, the *Ego* as unity of *Je* and *Moi*). In order to avoid this confusion, it is enough to apply the distinction between positional and non-positional consciousness. Positional consciousness means an "intentional" structure, which is oriented towards what is "other" than itself. In this meaning, "consciousness" always refers to something *other* than itself.

Now, if intentionality constitutes the immediate life of consciousness, this implies that immediate consciousness is characterized by a fundamental *nothing* of being. Being is always an object of reference, that is, external to and other than non-positional consciousness. From this conviction, Sartre will develop the famous distinction of *L'être et le néant* between consciousness as "for-itself" or "nothing", and being as "in-itself" and fullness.

At this moment, the "I" as personal being has not yet arisen. Non-positional consciousness is still anonymous and impersonal, without any "I" as a centre of actions, states or qualities. The I arises only by virtue of *reflection*. When the intentionality of consciousness orients itself itself *as* non-positional consciousness, then the impersonal transcendental field transforms into a personal subject, which separates from other sujects and the world of objects.

But there is more than this. The birth of the *Ego* implies also the objectifying reification of non-positional consciousness as an impersonal field of experience. In this way, we obtain the ordinary "psychological" subject, which can be the "object" of so-called human sciences such as psychology, psychiatry, psychoanalysis, and so on.

If we expand Sartre's analysis concerning the social field, we can show the critical potential of his position. When we forget that the "I" as a personal subject arises as a "fiction" from the activity of reflection, then we necessarily transform it into a "natural" object, into a "thing in itself". It no longer appears as an artifice resulting from reflection, but simply as a "given" substratum for actions, qualities and states.

But in this way the I becomes not only "owner" of states and actions, but also owner of his body. The body can appear as an "organism", that is, as a clearly-defined totality. Life is no longer an impersonal field of changing experience, but becomes something established with respect to a "subject" as simply an "object". And this is valid both for the interior life of the "Ego" and for the external life of "nature".

Nonetheless, reflection can separate from the transcendental field only insofar as it *imagines* its artificial products *as things*. It is subject to an idea of consciousness, according to which imagination constitutes a world of interior objects. Sartre criticizes this conception in books on imagination, which are published in 1936[6] and in 1940. He says that the image is external with respect to consciousness, but that externality has nothing to do with the reality of objects in the world. The externality of the image, in fact, is the externality of an "unreal".

In this way, Sartre criticizes the objectivities, which result from reflection, *when reflection does not reflect once again upon itself*. When reflection reflects upon itself, it cannot only be subtracted as positional consciousness from the transcendental field as an impersonal, non-positional consciousness. It can also understand that its products are not anything "given", but are products of its own power of creation. In this way, it can conceive of itself not simply as external to the transcendental field, but rather as an *essential articulation of the transcendental field itself*.

## V. Fichte's Transcendental Concept of Life

We can explain this by stating that the activity of thinking is in its own actual exercising *a non-positional expression of the life of consciousness*. Once again, we can find an example of this position in Fichte's WL-1804-II. In the 15th conference, he says:

> *Wir leben*, eben unmittelbar im Lebensakte selber; wir sind daher das Eine ungetheilte Sein selber, in sich, von sich, durch sich, das schlechthin nicht herausgehen kann zur Zweiheit.[7]

And then:

> Wir stützen uns daher hier *gar nicht auf eine empirische Wahrnehmung* unseres Lebens, welche als eine Modifikation des Bewußtseins durchaus abzuweisen wäre; sondern auf die genetische Einsicht des Lebens und Ich, aus der Construction des Einen Seins, und umgekehrt.[8]

For Fichte, the activity of thinking is not a "modification of the empirical consciousness", but rather a non-positional experience of philosophical

---

6 Sartre, Jean-Paul: *L'imagination*, Paris 1936; reprinted in the series "Quadrige", Paris 1994.
7 WL-1804-II, p. 152.
8 WL-1804-II, p. 153.

inquiry. This experience implies the formation of a community of human beings ("*Wir*"), who share the same interest for transcendental truth, which is not achievable once and for all, but has the same "infinite" character as the process of the appearing of absolute life. In this appearing, life maintains its absolutely indivisible character, which is immanent in us. The immanence of life in us does not indicate any such relation as inherence between predicates and their subject, but it is one and the same thing with the process of life itself. "We" are immediately life, and life is immediately one with ourselves. Life as "act" (cf. *supra*, first quotation) does not result from the activity of the "I", because in this case we do not have any separation yet. Life remains one and undivided, and it is just in this oneness with itself that it affirms its impersonal character. And the impersonal character of life is not anything different from the activity of "our" thinking. On the contrary, in our thinking "we" express and realize the unity between the common absolute life and ourselves.

In this way, Fichte underlines the fact that thinking does not properly express any special *relation to* life. In Sartre's terminology of Sartre (drawn on by Deleuze), we do not as yet have a position of *transcendance.* We are and remain inside the "impersonal transcendental field" of absolute life. On this point, I think that Fichte's position has the same meaning as Sartre's. For Sartre, too, the logical circle among non-positional consciousness, reflection and the reinstauration of a non-positional consciousness at the level of reflection itself *implies only a temporary exit from the transcendental field.* The life-in-common of impersonal thinking does not mean the ceasing of being self-conscious at all, if we understand this being self-conscious in its non-positional meaning. Whatever has non-positional character is impersonal, but this impersonality does not imply that it must be not conscious at all. On the contrary, one could ascribe to the very *lack of reflection* proper to common-sense consciousness one's believing in the "I" and the "free will" as the principle and foundation of one's life and actions.

Fichte and Sartre give us the possibility of conceiving a *transcendental* concept of life. That is, a concept of life from a *philosophical* point of view, which is different from the strictly biological one. I would like to say that this concept is characterized by spontaneity and unceasing becoming, on the one hand, and by the dialectical circle of non-positional and positional levels of consciousness, on the other hand. Now, this circle necessarily implies that life in consciousness takes a specifically *unreal* character.

The transcendental and phenomenological traditions combine this aspect with the simply biological dimension of life. From the point of view of both Fichte and Sartre, the compenetration of positional and non-positional attitudes constitutes the specific character of consciousness as a living process of experience, which is at the same time subjective *and* impersonal. As we have seen, the circular and "infinitive" movement of self-reflection does not imply the dimension of any "person" as an individual subject, but rather constitutes an undeniable articulation of the "plan of immanence" *in the very sense in which this concept is elaborated by Deleuze himself.*

The fact that the life of consciousness is characterized by the dimension of the *unreal*, as the young Sartre masterfully demonstrated, implies that the "transcendental field" is in principle unaccessible to so-called biopolitical power. It is only when consciousness is eliminated in its "unreality", when it is transformed into a "thing in itself", that the "transcendental field" becomes subjected to the technological control of neural and biological sciences. But, then, it is not "consciousness" properly which can be dominated. Rather it is consciousness *negated* as such, that is, thinking and imagination, which have been reduced to natural "objects" and real "things", and which, as a domain of the "unreal", do not exist any more.

On the contrary, the logical circularity between consciousness, reflection and the Self, revealed by Fichte for the first time in all the complexity of its structure, is the way the common and absolute life appears and realizes itself as *"esse in mero actu"*, and at the same time as exceeding in principle the possibility of domination from biopolitical power. Biopolitical power can operate only by naturalizing consciousness, that is, by reducing consciousness to something objectively "given" in front of a subject. But this implies a contradiction in the self-definition of biopolitical power itself. By reducing consciousness to a simply biological function of life, it must in fact *kill* consciousness in the specific character of its *properly "unreal"* life. That is, we have to re-establish a dimension of power, which contradicts the particular aim of its bio-political dimension, which is – as we have seen at the beginning of this paper –*"make anyone live and let him die"*. With regard to consciousness, it seems that power has the need to *reduce and cancel the fact that consciousness exceeds in principle – that is, by virtue of its self-reflexivity – any "natural" dimension of the "real" world.* But in order to do this, bio-power has to fall back to a *prior and more primitive* stage in its historical development, that is, to the old concept of sovereignty conceived as the faculty of *"killing and letting live"*.

If we cancel the dialectical implication between consciousness and reflection, between non-positional and positional levels inside the consciousness, we cancel the specific character which *life assumes within consciousness*. This is, in my opinion, the philosphical limit of the otherwise rich and stimulating interpretation of Fichte and Sartre by Deleuze. It is not simply, as Agamben states, that Deleuze wants to cancel consciousness *tout court* from what he calls the "plan of immanence". As we have seen, he rather tries to separate consciousness from self-reflection. In his opinion, the exclusion of self-reflection from consciousness makes it possibile to realize a perfect co-extensivity between consciousness and anonymous "transcendental field".

But the question is: what is the price he must pay? On the one hand, in order to find the possibility of an impersonal experience of life, Deleuze must look for any kind of extreme experience, such as Riderhood's agony in Dickens' novel *Out Mutual Friend*; on the other hand, by reducing consciousness to simple biological survival, he risks going against his own philosophical position. Aiming at deleting self-reflection from consciousness, he must reabsorb consciousness in the biological dimension of natural life. But it is exactly this merely "biological" life, which results as a product and abstraction from the development of "life-sciences" and biopolitical power connected with each other. "Life" as an unqualified biological event means an abstraction, which reifies life in order to make it subject to the grip of techno-sciences. And so, destroying the circle between non-positional and positional consciousness implies the elimination of thinking as a kind of experience, which is different from simply "natural" life. Therefore it implies the impossibility of saving any dimension of resistance to the expansion and efficiency of biopolitical power.

## VI. Differences between Fichte and Sartre

I would like to conclude with a last observation about the relationship between Fichte and Sartre. In this paper, I have insisted on the similarity of their position. In fact, both articulate a non-substantial theory of consciousness; and both insert their theory of consciousness in a wider phenomenological theory of world-appearance. But there is a fundamental difference between these two positions, and it concerns the meaning and character of philosophy itself. In Fichte, philosophy acquires its scientific status only by means of realizing a *system*. This concept of philosophy as a systematic exposition of the structures of consciousness and appearance remains unvaried along the whole course of Fichte's activity. There are, obviously, important changes in the role of the "I" and the scope of philosophical theory. In Jena, the doctrine of science is mainly a theory of the finite consciousness; in Berlin, it becomes an original kind of transcendental ontology of being and appearance. As we have already said, the "I" loses the meaning of being the first unconditional principle of philosophy, and this role is assumed by absolute life as an impersonal *"esse in mero actu"*. In spite of that, the idea of a systematic construction remains an essential character of the philosophical inquiry, without which it could not realize itself as "science" properly.

For Sartre in his phenomenological period, philosophy renounces any claim on systematic construction. According to Husserl's appeal *"zu den Sachen selbst"*, he concentrates on the rigourous *description* of limited fields of the appearance. Philosophy as a *"strenge Wissenschaft"* has nothing to do with the two main aspects of Fichte's concept of system. On the one hand, it is no longer a systematic construction in the sense of a *logically unfolding demonstration*, in which each stage of the process must be justified from his antecedent. On the other hand, no longer aims at the character of *completeness*.

In Fichte, the mono-directional movement was corrected and integrated by its opposite, that is, the *circularity* of the whole process, through which philosophy must demonstrate that it has *exhausted* all that should be derived. In the Berlin period, too, he maintains that a logically unfolding demonstration and its completeness are the main characters of philosophy as a systematic science. But here, according to the wider modification of his theory, we have a radical change in the *meaning* that philosophy as a system has in its relationship with life. Philosophy must be a system, and in order to be a system, it must logically deduce its consequences, and it must deduce *all and every* transcendental condition in order to explain the structures of consciousness and world-appearance. But its aim is not limited to itself. At the culmination of its process as a system, philosophy must reunify itself with life and become "Wisdom" (*Weisheit*). As Fichte says in WL-1807,[9] philosophy must "subtract" (*abziehen*) itself from real life. It must become a way of life, in which the transcendental vision (*Einsicht*) compenetrates and transfigures the way of acting and feeling on the part of each single subject. In spite of that, it remains

---

9   On this subject, see my article "Einleitende Bemerkungen über die Wissenschaftslehre von 1807," in: *Fichte-Studien* 26 (2006), pp. 33–61.

true that philosophy *qua talis* remains and must remain a system centered around the principles we have already indicated.

For Sartre, on the contrary, philosophy as a phenomenological description of appearances refuses to be an activity of deductive construction. Once it is free from the constraints of logical deduction, philosophy can also free itself from the obligation of realizing *completeness* in the form of wholeness and totality. Rather, it must concentrate on *partial sections* of experience, whose analysis is in principle open and unending.

Any construction alters phenomena in their own being. Philosophers do not have to build a system in order to subtract their concepts from life. Instead of doing this, they should draw attention from the start to phenomena just so as they present themselves in their purity.

We do not have to discuss here if this is really possible. Assuming that it really is possible, philosophy can liberate itself not only form the artificial constructions of traditional metaphysics and of natural sciences, but also from the "unreflected" presuppositions of ordinary consciousness. And this is just what the young Sartre shows in his early works on the *Ego* and the imagination. Applying Husserl's phenomenological-transcendental *epoché*, he can dismantle the reifying constructions of consciousness as a natural "object" – that is, in Fichte's terminology, as a *caput mortuum* and a *Ding an sich*. We have tried to show the important meaning that this program can assume in the contemporary philosophical debate.

# Fichte and Levinas. The Theory of Meaning and the Advent of the Infinite

Isabelle Thomas-Fogiel

Université Paris 1 Panthéon-Sorbonne

## I. Introduction

There are many points of contact and comparable elements in Fichte's philosophy and today's phenomenology. Most notable among them is that Fichte was the first to use the word "phenomenology" in a positive sense. Lambert, who first introduced this word into philosophy in 1764, defined phenomenology as the science of illusion and considered it as strictly preparatory to the unveiling of truth. This is the meaning retained by Kant when, in his letter to Lambert, he toyed with the idea of calling "phenomenology" the *Critique of Pure Reason*[1]. This negative sense has even left its trace in Hegel's *Phenomenology of Spirit* since this text is an account of the illusions of consciousness. Fichte differs from these philosophers and defines phenomenology positively as the science of appearing (*Erscheinungslehre*). Appearing (*Erscheinen*) never is the mere appearance of illusion (*Schein*). The phenomenon is not "fake" but the truth; it is this appearance beyond which nothing is conceivable, whether it be a thing in itself, a deeper world, or transcendence. Phenomenology, which completes the theory of truth[2], was conceived as a "return" to the appearing, or, in other words as a description of the field of the appearing. In this respect, one may assert that the criticism Husserl aims at Descartes[3] doesn't apply to Fichte, who "thematized" philosophy along this double line : the foundation of principles (the theory of truth) and the description of what appears (phenomenology). With Fichte as

---

1  See his letter to Lambert of 2 September 1770.
2  In its strictest sense, see WL-1804-II, *Die Wissenschaftslehre, zweiter Vortrag im Jahre 1804,* Hamburg, 1986. This text is divided in two parts : a phenomenology and a theory of truth.
3  In his *Cartesian Meditations* § 10. Husserl said that Descartes doesn't cross the threshold that leads to phenomena and hence misses phenomenology.

with Husserl, philosophy's two fundamental motives – the "epistemic" and the "phenomenological" – are complementary and not mutually exclusive. Yet one may easily demonstrate that in Descartes, one has the "epistemic" without the "phenomenological", and in Heidegger we have the "phenomenological" as opposed to the "epistemic". Fichte's and Husserl's common desire that philosophy should be a rigorous science articulating a theory of truth and a description of phenomena seems to call for a systematic comparison of these two philosophers[4].

One may wonder, then, why I haven't chosen to confront Fichte with phenomenology ? Why have I chosen to confront Fichte with a philosopher who apparently is utterly aloof from the Fichtean theme of philosophy as rigorous science? To put it differently, why have I selected a phenomenologist who has criticized the "intellectualist" and "theoreticist" Husserl, and who has denounced his desire to constitute philosophy as a rigorous science as one of the remains of the old metaphysical mode of thinking? In what manner may Levinas be compared with Fichte – when, as early as his *Théorie de l'intuition*, he favored the "existential" over the "epistemic", the description of appearing over the determination of principles, the concreteness of man over the transcendental ego.

Certainly, he could be compared with Fichte. Some of his central themes are also to be found in Fichte's position. These include the critique of representation and the description of the Other as well as the themes of the finite and the infinite. But he *must* also be compared because these themes are central to both philosophies, however radically different they remain as regards the question of philosophy's status. This is the theme I wish to "foreground" here, in order to better raise the question of the "transcendental" in phenomenology. Indeed, as we shall see, what is essentially at stake in this comparison between Fichte and Levinas is the question of the meaning and status of the transcendental in phenomenology. Finally, Fichte is closer to Husserl than Levinas because he is a transcendantal philosopher. Before I turn to this point, I must examine the relation between Fichte and Levinas:

---

4   Jean Hyppolite's article – "La doctrine de la science chez Fichte et Husserl," Paris 1954, opened the way leading to this comparison.

## II. On the relation of Fichte and Levinas?

One must first try to describe the relation between Fichte and Levinas. This is not easy to do, since they are seldom compared. However, three central and constitutive elements in Levinas's thought are to be found in almost identical form in Fichte's philosophy. These three elements are the critique of representation, the description of the Other, and the extension to non-æsthetic realms of the problematics of the sublime with respect to the finite and the infinite. Let us consider these points separately.

### II.1. The Critique of Representation

While it is well known that Levinas sees his philosophy as a critique of metaphysical objectivism[5], Fichte's involvement with such themes is not really self-evident. And yet, the entirety of Fichte's philosophy may be read as a critique of representation[6]. Indeed, Fichte questions Kant's equation, according to which to know is to represent, and to represent is to make the object "figurable". For Kant, "figuration" – definded as circumscription or as the ascription of a limit – is the condition of the possibility of knowledge. In this context, knowledge refers to the figure, to delineation, and to the limit. For Kant, to know is to represent, and to represent is to make the object visible thanks to the schema that imposes a form, a contour – in other words, that creates a figure. Figuration becomes the sign of true knowledge, and the "non-figurable" remains in the realm of falsehood and deception.

Fichte questions the linking of figure and knowledge and of the limit and representation, and formulates the existence of modes of knowledge that go beyond a mere representation as "figuration". Concerning the determination of principles – what he defines as the "doctrine of truth" in the 1804 *Wissenschaftslehre* – Fichte unveils a cognitive process, which he calls the "illimitation of the limit". In this way, he describes the movement of reason that makes infinite that which is given as finite. One may illustrate this process with the geometrical figure of a triangle. I form a mental representation of a triangle. The triangle, defined by its

---

5 See for example : Levinas, Emmanuel: *Ruine de la représentation* 1959, in : *En découvrant l'existence avec Husserl et Heidegger*, Paris 1974.
6 This critique which, as with Levinas, opens onto the specific thinking of the Other. See Thomas-Fogiel, Isabelle: *Critique de la représentation, Etudes sur Fichte*, Paris 2000.

limits, is finite by essence. But this "line", or "limit", must be included into some vaster "space" in order to appear as a line or a limit. Indeed, were I unable to think beyond the mere limits of the triangle, it would not appear to me as a triangle – that is to say, as a finite figure. In other words, I must constitute a horizon within which the triangle may appear as a limit. By establishing this "perimeter" (*Umfang*) within which the limit may appear, Fichte says that the I "illimits the limit." It becomes clear that, in order to be properly thought, an object has to be thus infinitized. To know is not solely to limit and to set boundaries to an object. To know also consists in "infinitizing" and "illimiting".

## II.2. The Phenomenological Description of the Other

This cognitive process, which Fichte describes at the level of the "doctrine of truth", will find an equivalent on another level, which – in the 1804 *Wissenschaftslehre* – he calls phenomenology or the doctrine of phenomena. In other words, Fichte formulates a phenomenological description that illustrates a process previously unveiled as inherent to reason in his epistemic elucidation of principles. I am referring to his description of the appearing of the Other, as found in his *Foundations of Natural Right*. This text is the exact phenomenological equivalent of the illimitation of the limit described in the first *Wissenschaftslehre* (*1794*). First, Fichte reminds us what is traditionally understood by "understanding" a phenomenon. He writes that "to understand is to fix, to delimit and to determine."[7] The limit, or the act of drawing a limit, is a condition of understanding. But the whole demonstration that follows will try to establish that one may not understand the appearing of the Other, that is, one may not bound it within limits, or give it a definitive outline. The last stage in the description will make clear that a limit cannot be imposed or found. The face of the Other is precisely that which cannot be delimited and seems to lie beyond all ascribable limits. By attempting to determine the Other, one draws a limit that one will need to surpass immediately afterwards. Every progress in the analysis consists in transgressing a limit. Every moment in the demonstration rolls back the limit a little further. As successive attempts to reductively delimit fail, the Other becomes less clearly visible and the limits recede. As the demonstration progresses, what was initially to be delimited and understood

---

7  Fichte, Johann G.: *Foundations of Natural Right*, trans. by Frederick Neuhauser and Michael Baur, §6, Second Main dividsion, Cambridge 2000.

becomes ever less visible. The face of the Other resists all limitation or delineation. And this necessary failure to reduce the face of the Other to a mere figure is precisely the source from which, for Fichte, true knowledge may emerge. Indeed, it is because the body of the Other (*Leib*, chair) does not let itself be fixed or determined that it may be thought as the locus where the infinite of freedom expresses itself. Because he is a bearer of the infinite, the Other cannot be reduced to limits. This the reason why the demonstration must always roll back the limit and effect its illimitation – and this illimitation of the limit is what gives access to the knwowledge of the Other as a free being. In this context, the illimitation of the limit becomes one of the modalities of knowing. It then becomes rather easy to compare Fichte's precise description with Levinas's developments against objectivating thought, against "representation", which he means to surpass in order to account for the "irruption" of the Other[8]. Alterity, conceived as a trace of the infinite, is what allows one to outflank traditional philosophical thought as it were in order to finally feel the *eros* of genuine thought[9]. What we have in both Fichte and Levinas is this idea that objectifying representation may and must be outgrown by a thinking of the infinite of which the face of the Other is a manifestation. This "irruption" of the infinite in the field of philosophical thought must now be the focus of our attention.

## II.3. The Infinite in Philosophy

Let us first recall what, to my mind, is one of the most significant propositions of the *Wissenschaftslehre*, namely, that the movement of knowledge is the process of the sublime. The sublime is not to be relegated to the sole domain of the æsthetic: the sublime is the dynamic of the mind. Promoting the concept of the sublime to the level of a gnoseological process is done by each *Wissenschaftslehre*, and this "promotion" always guides us from the critique of objectifying knowledge to the definition of a knowledge beyond representation.

In Kant's third *Critique*, the sublime is defined as an attempt to "present the infinite". In this context, the sublime is beauty 's counter-con-

---

8 The irruption of the Other, such as one may find it exemplified in the face of the Other whose, "only meaning is irrecusable". Levinas, Emmanuel : *Autrement qu'être*, Paris 1978, p. 240. [Author's trans.]
9 "The face, against contemporary ontology, brings up a notion of truth that is not the unveiling of some impersonal neutrality". Levinas, Emmanuel: *Totalité et infini*, Paris 1974, p. 43. [Author's trans.]

cept[10]. The beautiful harks back to ideas of contour, delineation and limits, while the sublime proceeds inversely and attempts to present the infinite. The sublime presents itself as an anti-figure. But while the process of the sublime is an attempt to present the infinite, it is obviously not a positive presentation. It is quite telling, in this respect, that the statement Kant presents as an example of the sublime should be the Second Commandment[11]. Because the infinite cannot be contained in a finite figure, the sublime is a sign of the failure of figuration, of objectifying representation, and of the circumscription within defined limits. The sublime is this moment when figuration is rejected; since the sublime's task is to interweave the finite and the infinite into one self-same act, representation is not "available". On the contrary, it is to be questioned. In other words, for Kant the sublime questions the representable, while Fichte sees it as the very sign of the ongoing process of knowledge. If, among many possible other examples, one focuses on the structure of the *Wissenschaftslehre Nova Methodo*, the dynamic is that of the sublime. In the very first paragraphs, Fichte explains that the I cannot immediately apply the predicate "infinite" to itself – in other words, the infinite of freedom cannot be represented without being determined and limited[12]. Thus the contradiction between freedom and representation is born. It is the moment of failure for the Kantian analysis of the sublime so to speak. But this is a fruitful failure that breeds new concepts, such as the concept of the end and the categorical imperative. The interrelation of the finite and of the infinite as the dynamic of freedom and of the knowledge of freedom is not some unreachable ideal but the very process by which truth is being engendered. Intermediate concepts[13] are merely the truths given to us by this movement of rationality. Thus the infinite is not a being that stands without thought anymore, a being that thought would need to objectify, to determine, to limit, and, hence, inevitably, to negate. The infinite is the very process of thought. The infinite is what reason generates through its very *praxis*. And now, of course, this decisive importance of the infinite

---

10  In a word, beauty always proceeds from the object's form or figure, and the figure is a delimitation.
11  "You shall not make for yourself a graven image, or any likeness of anything that is in heaven above, or that is in the earth beneath, or that is in the water under the earth."
12  But this limitation seems to require that an object or a figure be constituted which, being inserted within precise limits, may become apprehensible.
13  For example the concept of the end, the categorical imperative, space and the Other in the WLnm.

obviously is one of the main characteristics of Levinas's thought. Being an ethical notion par excellence, the infinite, for Levinas, is the ultimate condition of possibility, which is itself a radical transcendence, extreme difference, absolute alterity. Contrary to the classical philosophies of identity and totality, Levinas aims to "foreground" a philosophy of difference, of the Other and of the infinite (see *Totalité et infini*). Thus emerges a true similarity between the two philosophies that hinges on this capital point that is the thinking of the infinite, or, to be more precise, that thinking is the infinite.

We may now claim the following similiarities about the positions of Fichte and Levinas. They share the same critique of representation, the same phenomenological description of the Other, the same value given to the infinite and the same promotion of the sublime. All these points are so central in their philosophies that one is now tempted to ask, not what makes their thoughts comparable but what makes them different. Naturally, the difference is radical and it explains why the two philosophers have never truly been either assimilated or compared. But this very difference, again, finds its source in a new and fundamental proximity that makes the comparison fruitful. It is this proximity I now wish to describe. I will return below to what I consider to be a radical opposition between their respective views.

### III. Similarity in the Two Theories of Meaning

#### III.1. Fichte's Theory of Meaning

Indeed, Levinas and Fichte share another decisive similarity: they both reject a strictly semantic theory of truth in order to make the Saying emerge within the Said – within what is being said. To demonstrate this, one must first sketch Fichte's theory of meaning. The *Wissenschaftslehre* bases a theory of meaning on the Saying (*Sagen*) and the Doing (*Tun*)[14]. The Saying (*Sagen*) is here to be understood as the content of philosophical discourse – say in Kant or Spinoza. So, if in the *Wissenschaftslehre* 1804 we find the expression adequation between "Tun und Sagen". We have equivalents in the *Wissenschaftslehre* 1794 in the expres-

---

14 It is the expression of WL-1804, for example p. 191. See also the *Introductions of 1798. About this relation between "Tun und Sagen" in 1804*, see Thomas-Fogiel, Isabelle: *Fichte, réflexion et argumentation*, Paris 2004.

sion " the conformity between the explication" and "what is explicated,"[15] or of course "what is done" and the "doing" ; or the famous opposition between "The posited ( *for example Setzen or " Ich gesetze* ",) and the positing (*Setzend*)[16] etc. This Fichtean Saying may thus be compared to what, beginning with Austin, is called the "propositional content". As for the Doing, it must be strictly understood as the act or the status of the enunciation: it is not what Kant says but, as proposed in the 1804 *Wissenschaftslehre*, "what he presupposes in order to be able to say what he says."[17] Thus in the proposition "I am not speaking," the Saying is what this proposition says, while the Doing is what makes it possible; in other words, the very act of speaking. In this case, one immediately notes that this very act falsifies the propositional content. In other words, the fundamental principle of Fichte's theory is what, in reference to Austin and Recanati, we now call the performative non-contradiction or pragmatic identity. Fichte thus develops a true and precise theory of meaning, based on the notions of Saying and Doing, which Levinas will redevelop as the theory of the Saying and the Said. The way they both account for the Saying within the Said is a capital point. Levinas will also reject all semantic theories of meaning and will introduce the dimension of the Saying within the Said. However, his theory of meaning will end up being the diametrical opposite of Fichte's. This is why we'll need to examine Levinas's theory.

### III.2. Levinas's Theory of Meaning

In *Autrement qu'être* Levinas uses the categories of the Said and the Saying in order to develop what he calls "the very significance of meaning." (la "veritable signifiance de la signification")[18] Always eager to get rid of Husserl's "objectivism", he attempts to refute Husserl's semantic intentionality. Indeed, for Husserl, the Said, conceived of as a theme, as what is being said, that is, as object, tends to supersede all other aspects.

---

15 GWL, p. 131.
16 See GWL, p 131, and also the beginning of the *Wissenschafltslehre Nova methodo* or *Fondations of Natural Right*, etc. (ed. Frederick Neuhouser, trans. Michael Baur, Cambridge Texts in the History of Philosophy) .
17 WL-1804, p. 18 of the German text. French editors : Aubier-Montaigne, Paris 1967, translated by Didier Julia " l'on étudie Kant ici non comme l'ont fait tous les kantiens sans exception en collant à la lettre [...] mais en s'élevant de ce qu'il dit réellement à ce qu'il ne doit pas *mais devrait présupposer pour pouvoir dire ce qu'il dit* ", p.34.
18 Levinas, Emmanuel : *Autrement qu'être*, p. 17

Husserl's aim could be described as an attempt to obfuscate the Saying in order to promote the Said. In this respect, he would be as positivistic as the members of the Vienna Circle. For Husserl, Levinas tells us, the correlation of the Said and the Saying is nothing but "the subordination of the Saying to the Said": "the Said dominates the Saying that enounces it."[19] But for Levinas "the Saying does not vanish in apophansis": one must revise the whole Western theory of meaning which is but the offshoot of the theory of objectivity, a corollary of "representationalism" and of the imperialism of "objecthood".

But one may ask what is the Saying if the Said is the theme, the object, the content? It is not the act performed by the subject. For Levinas, Saying is Speech addressed to the other, turned towards the other. It is before all Said, and hence before all object-oriented intentionality. The Saying will end up being defined as "supreme passivity of the exposition to the Other."[20] This exposition by which I offer myself up to the Other makes me infinitely vulnerable. This vulnerability is born of the "sincerity" with which I give myself up to the Other. "Saying to the Other" comes before "anything Said" and conditions it. Levinas writes: "It is necessary that one reach this Saying before the Said, or that one reduce the Said to it."[21]

This saying that always-already constitutes me and by which I connect with the Other by sincerely exposing myself, this "here I am" is the trace of the infinite that traverses me. This "Thou" of which I am the answer, this "Thou" that makes me become a "here I am", actually is, originarily, God's call. The analysis of the Saying thus leads us to what Levinas calls "the glory of the infinite." Ultimately, the Saying is how the infinite is being said within each one of us.

The successive substitutions in *Autrement qu'être* are clear. They lead us from the Saying to the Response to the Other, from the Response to Sincerity and from Sincerity to "the infinite saying itself". The significance is that of the Infinite, my saying bears its trace, just like Abraham's "here I am " bore God's call within itself.

It is thus confirmed that Levinas's theory of meaning is the Husserlian theory turned upside-down. The Saying comes before the Said. Semantics is thus relativized not by a theory of the act or a pragmatics, but by a rethinking of the sublime, which amounts to an "irruption" of the infinite

---

19  Levinas, Emmanuel: *Autrement*, p.19.
20  Levinas, Emmanuel: *Autrement*, p. 241.
21  Levinas, Emmanuel: *Autrement*, p. 241.

that disorganizes the orderly relations between what is said and the very fact of saying it.

We may now summarize these two thinkers' theories of meaning. What they have in common is that they both take into account the Saying in the Said. They both deal with a non-semantic dimension of meaning. But this convergence is the basis for a radical difference, for Levinas will end up producing a theory that is exactly the opposite of Fichte's. Their theories are diametrically opposed so that the one may be seen as the reverse of the other or inverted figure. The identity I described in my first part and the proximity I suggested in my second part lead to a radical opposition I now wish to describe.

## IV. The Inverted Figure. Identity or Performative Contradiction as Condition for the Advent of the Infinite

### IV.1. Fichte's Pragmatic Identity as Giving Access to the Infinite

Fichte's theory of meaning took into account the *Tun* in the *Sagen* and "foregrounded" a new principle of identity that was to become a model for all philosophical statements to come. Identity, strictly considered as the adequation of the utterance and the enunciation, or as the congruence of the Saying and the Doing, must be the philosopher's goal, if the philosopher wishes to reach truth and to avoid the contradictions that have wrecked all other philosophies – whether it be Spinoza's, Kant's or Jacobi's. The contradiction is not a contradiction in terms of formal logic, whether it be the traditional logic of predicates (A is A) or propositional logic (P implies Q). Neither is it a contradiction between two opposed elements, such as the Newtonian contradiction of physical forces that Kant called opposition, nor a contradiction between my proposition and the object it is supposed to convey. Actually, it is a contradiction between the act of saying X and what is being said of X – strictly speaking, a performative contradiction. This non-contradiction is the supreme law of reason that will generate the process of "infinitization" and illimitation described above. The identity of the supposing (posits) and the supposed is an act we perform. It is an originary act, with neither cause nor necessity, which is by the very fact that it is effected, performed and accomplished. The freedom of the first principle is the starting point and should also be the point of arrival. In our every concepts and productions, we must realize this identity, that is to say that, in one single act, we must think contradictory determinations (such as the posits of freedom and the knowledge of freedom). Realizing this amounts to an effectuation of the sublime process. It does not lead to failure but to the creation of new, intermediate concepts each of which expresses reflexive identity.[22]. For example, in the 1804 *Wissenschaftslehre*, the "*Urbegriff*" will serve to think the opposition between light and concept and will here again function as a hinge between the finite and the infinite. It is the realization of reflexive identity that leads to the sublime. There is thus a link, in Fichte's thought between the identity principle, the thinking of the infinite through the infinitization process, and the production of rationally verifiable concepts. Things are exactly the opposite in Levinas.

IV.2. Performative Contradiction as the Access to the Infinite in Levinas

For Levinas, it is the performative contradiction that allows the Infinite to irrupt into speech. The philosopher must accept the performative contradiction in order to allow the infinite to manifest itself. This is what Levinas, in *Autrement qu'être*, calls "the philosopher's retraction" ("dédit du philosophe"[23]). The philosopher must accept this gaping void, and should not attempt to fill it in by arguing for some impossible coherence[24].

The philosopher must accept this "retraction" in order to better signify "the nearness where the infinite occurs." Philosophy, by exhibiting its failure, by accepting this retraction, by renouncing this coherence, leaves room for another mode of expression: revelation and prophecy. The performative contradiction thus becomes the trace of God, the expression of the sublime. The performative contradiction helps us think the infinite within the finite, the unsayable at the very heart of what is said. The performative contradiction, actually, is the "presentation of the infinite" – a presentation which, in Kant's words, is given in the impossibility of presentation. This "retraction of the philosopher" leads Levinas back to prophetic utterance and leads him to call for philosophy to be superseded in religion. The successive substitutions in *Autrement qu'être* and *Etudes tal-*

---

22 In the *WL nova methodo*, for instance, the categorical imperative is the only non-contradictory way to associate freedom and knowledge, thus making it function as a hinge between the finite and the infinite.
23 Levinas, Emmanuel: *Autrement qu'être*, pp. 19–20.
24 Levinas writes : "Thinking the otherwise than being calls perhaps for more daring than the skeptic who does not fear to assert the impossibility of the utterance while he realizes this impossibility by the very utterance of it." In: *Autrement qu'être*, p. 84. [Author's trans.]

*mudiques* are clear: Levinas states the performative contradiction, accepts and overturns it, and makes of our impossibility to supersede it the very trace of God in us. We should give up philosophy in favor of religion, give up Husserl in favor of Isaiah – who is symptomatically mentioned in these pages of *Autrement qu'être* that claim the performative contradiction.

The difference between the two philosophers then appears clear. Fichte poses pragmatic identity as the condition of the advent of the infinite and the condition of philosophy. Levinas poses pragmatic contradiction as the condition of the irruption of the infinite and the "supercedence" of philosophy (the philosopher's retraction). We clearly have here theories that are diametrically opposed. And this strict inversion of the symmetrical pattern, to my mind, says something about the meaning of the transcendental in today's phenomenology. It is with this suggestion that I wish to conclude.

## V. Conclusion

It has become rather common, today, to oppose the transcendental Husserl, the "first" analytical and realist Husserl of the *Logical Investigations* and finally the "third", "genetic" or late Husserl, who prefigures today's existential themes. The introduction of Fichte in this debate will allow us to overcome these "ruptures" and to formulate differently the question of Husserl's coherence. Indeed, it seems to me that the three periods in Husserl's thought are the effect of his disciples' readings and not of his own position. Thus, Levinas – who introduced Husserl in France and influenced Sartre's and Derrida's interpretations of his work – has greatly biased Husserlian thought by stressing the rejection of the theme of philosophy as science, the rejection of reason, and the rejection of the transcendental. By promoting contradiction, Levinas chooses un-reason that leads us to religion. On the contrary, Fichte chooses reason, whose law is performative identity, and which enables us to maintain the goals of a philosophy considered as science. Comparing Fichte and Levinas thus allows or even compels us in retrospect to evaluate the true meaning of Husserl's work. Should we give precedence to the latest Husserl, as Levinas does – as well as Merleau-Ponty, Michel Henry and Jean-Luc Marion after him, and many other phenomenologists today – , or should we attempt, along with Fichte, to ponder anew the notion of philosophy as science? Such, in my mind, is the question raised by the topic we have been invited to reflect upon.

# The Other and the Necessary Conditions of the Self in Fichte's *Wissenschaftslehre* and Paul Ricoeur's Phenomenology of the Will

ARNOLD L. FARR

St. Joseph's University, Philadelphia

## I. Introduction

In the first volume of his phenomenological examination of the will Paul Ricoeur writes:

> Similarly we should encounter no problem in understanding that the basic active refusal is indiscernible from the self-positing of consciousness: it is by this decree – which we could call the third wish of absolute freedom – that freedom responds to that fundamental passivity which is the factual existence or the contingence of the Cogito. Consciousness refutes its own anxiety of possible nonbeing by a gesture of power. We need to reread Fichte in light of this idea: it is intolerable to find oneself existing and not necessary; we need to *posit* ourselves as existing. This initial demand which considers itself a cry of victory governs all *ideal derivations* which claim to attest the fecundity of consciousness. If I posit myself, I posit also my limits and my contingence at the same time as the basic determinations of life.[1]

Unfortunately, Ricoeur says nothing else about Fichte in this text and paradoxically seems to try to distance himself from Fichte in a couple of other texts. In his Preface to Don Ihde's book *Hermeneutic Phenomenology: The Philosophy of Paul Ricoeur* Ricoeur writes:

> The reflective philosophy to which I appeal is at the outset opposed to any philosophy of the Cartesian type based on the transparency of the ego to itself, and to all philosophy of the Fichtean type based on the self-positing of that ego. Today this mistrust is reinforced by the conviction that the understanding of the self is always indirect and proceeds from the interpretation of

---

1 Ricoeur, Paul: *Freedom and Nature*, trans. Erazim V. Kohák, Evanston 1966, pp. 465–466.

signs given outside me in culture and history and from the appropriation of the meaning of the signs.[2]

There are a few other cryptic references to Fichte in other texts by Ricoeur. However, none of them are accompanied by a clear explanation of the relevance of Fichte for Ricoeur's project. It is apparent that Ricoeur has an uneasy relationship to Fichte.

Ricoeur's references to Fichte occur in the context of his attempt to develop a phenomenology of the will. The purpose of this paper is to explore Ricoeur's phenomenology of the will in an attempt to answer the question, "why reread Fichte in light of Ricoeur's work"? I admit from the beginning that given the shear breadth and complexity of Ricoeur's phenomenology of the will, his seemingly infinite list of interlocutors, and the hermeneutic turn to which it leads, my exploration will be partial and to some extent dissatisfying. However, it is possible in the scope of this paper to shed some light on Ricoeur's cryptic references to Fichte and lay the foundation for further work on the Fichte/Ricoeur relationship.

## II. Problem of the Cogito

At the center of Ricoeur's phenomenology of the will and Fichte's *Wissenschaftslehre* is the problem of the cogito. Neither Fichte nor Ricoeur rejects the Cartesian cogito altogether but both philosophers found it too narrow to actually describe the duality or original duplicity of the I. Descartes makes the cogito the foundation of all human knowledge. However, this view is one-sided insofar as the I is not merely a knower but also a doer. The discovery of the I as thinking is also to discover the I as acting. The Fichtean claim that the I posits itself already depicts the I as engaged in an activity that is fundamental to any acquisition of knowledge. In Fichte's philosophy the cogito remains but is joined by the "I act". The I is a *Thathandlung*.

In the *Wissenschaftslehre* thinking and willing are coterminous. The absolute unity of thinking and willing is the original duplicity of the I. In fact, willing is so fundamental to the very being of the I that Fichte provides us with what appears to be a transcendental reduction to

---

2   Ihde, Don: *Hermeneutic Phenomenology: The Philosophy of Paul Ricoeur*, Evanston 1971, p. xv.

show that willing is primary. Fichte says in the first theorem of *The System of Ethics* that "I find myself as myself only as willing."³ Later he says:

> In order to find my true essence I must therefore think away all that is foreign in willing. What then remains is my pure being. This assertion is the immediate consequence of the propositions that preceded it. All that is left to examine is what may remain after one has made the requisite abstraction from what is foreign in willing. Willing as such is something primary, grounded absolutely in itself and in nothing outside of itself.

He continues:

> insofar as willing is something absolute and primary, therefore, it simply cannot be explained on the basis of any influence of something outside the I, but only on the basis of the I itself; and *this absoluteness* of the I is what remain following abstraction from everything foreign.⁴

In the above passages we have at once an agreement and disagreement between Fichte and Ricoeur. They both make willing primary and in doing so advocate the primacy of practical reason. Following Fichte, and the so-called French Fichte, Jean Nabert, Ricoeur moves away from the idea of the cogito as an epistemological subject. The I or self is an acting/willing subject who is from the beginning engaged in a practical project. However, it appears that Ricoeur is not as sure as Fichte that the absolute willing of the I cannot be explained by something outside of the I. Notice, I said that this appears to be the case.

In *Freedom and Nature* only one page over from where Ricoeur states that one ought to reread Fichte in light of his philosophy of the will he offers a criticism of idealism that seems to be aimed at Fichte. He writes:

> The hallmark of idealism is precisely this effort, taken up a thousand times over, to engender space, time, and contingence. This effort would not arise over again if it did not correspond to freedom's most basic wish, which is to respond to his own condition by positing itself as sovereign.⁵

Later:

> Any *ideal* derivation of consciousness is a refusal of its *concrete* condition.⁶

If the above passages are aimed at Fichte (which I think they are given comments about Fichte in other texts) then Ricoeur is guilty of a misread-

---
3   SE, p. 24.
4   Ibid., p. 30.
5   Ricoeur, Paul: *Freedom and Nature* p. 465.
6   Ibid.

ing of Fichte. That is, he rightly understands that the I wishes or desires to posit itself as absolutely free. But he fails to recognize that even Fichte did not believe that the I could posit itself as absolutely free. Any freedom that the I experiences is always a conditioned freedom. There is for Fichte and in Ricoeur's own words a non-coincidence in the I. There is a failure to achieve in Ricoeur's terms the desired totality or in Fichte's terms the desired unity. Therefore, Fichte's philosophy is a philosophy of striving wherein the I (because of its concrete condition) must strive to achieve that which it absolutely cannot achieve. More will be said about this later.

### III. Intentionality and the Human Condition: Between Sartre and Fichte

In the phenomenological tradition Brentano and Husserl made the decisive step beyond the Cartesian cogito with the concept of intentionality. Here, the emptiness of the I think is given content. There is no I think or consciousness without the I think something, something determinate. The concept of intentionality suggest that the I is active insofar as it is always directed by itself toward some object of consciousness. Here again we are at a place where there is agreement between Fichte and Ricoeur. Intentionality itself is a type of positing wherein the I not only perceives objects or representations in a mere passive way, but it actively directs its attention toward objects in the world. This self-directing activity is guided by a project that the I gives itself.

Like the Fichtean notion of self-positing, the phenomenological concept of intentionality implies that the self-directed subject is free and is the source of the contents of consciousness. However, Ricoeur fears that the Husserlian concept of intentionality leads to solipsism. Even the later Husserl in his turn to the "life world" cannot fully escape the possible fall into solipsism insofar as even the necessary Other is constituted by the transcendental ego.

With respect to intentionality there are two problems that must be addressed. First, the problem of intentionality and the human condition. Secondly, the problem of intentionality and the nature of the I from a Fichtean and Sartrean perspective.

Ricoeur's view of intentionality is far more Fichtean than he realized. Embedded in his view of intentionality is a philosophy of striving. Whereas Fichte portrays reason as striving for absolute freedom, Ricoeur depicts reason as striving for a totality, for fulfilled intentionality. This is the theme of the second volume of his phenomenology of the will (*Fal-*

*lible Man*) which he calls an empirics of the will. Ricoeur argues that human beings are the only creatures that we know of who presents an unstable ontological constitution of being greater and lesser than themselves.[7]

This unstable constitution discussed in *Fallible Man* is the duality of finite perspective and experience on one hand and transcendence on the other. It is also the duality of fulfilled and empty intentionality. Or even better and in more Fichtean language, it is the duality or the original duplicity of the real and the ideal. On Ricoeur's account intentionality is always partial and perspectival. Here we are reminded of Husserl's notion of intending an aspect or side of an object while consciousness fills in the part of the object not present for perception. For Fichte and Ricoeur, human beings are frustrated by their finitude. The human project is to overcome finitude or any limits to our freedom. However, this task is unachievable as both Fichte and Ricoeur frequently remind us.

The human condition as an unstable ontological constitution is the source of Ricoeur's suggestion that we reread Fichte, and it is also the point of tension between Fichte and Ricoeur. It also discloses to us the specter of a thinker who haunts Ricoeur's early project. That thinker is Jean Paul Sartre. I will address Fichte in more detail later. Here I want to say a few things about the influence of Sartre on Ricoeur's project. Ricoeur's phenomenology of the will is in some ways a reaction to Sartre's *Being and Nothingness*. In *Freedom and Nature, Fallible Man*, and especially in an 1956 essay entitled "Negativity and Primary Affirmation"[8] Ricoeur attacks Sartre's view that man is situated between being and nothingness.

Ricoeur rejects Sartre's view that at the heart of being lies nothingness and that this nothingness is the source of the power of negation which we call freedom. In "Negativity and Primary Affirmation" Ricoeur sets up the problem in this way:

> But what does it mean to start with reflection, with the act of reflection? It means precisely to start with the acts and operations in which we become *aware of our finitude by going beyond it.* Hence, it means to start with the connection between an *experience* of finitude and a *movement* which transgresses this finitude. This is where we shall find principal and fundamental negation, the one which relates to the very constitution of reflection. The experience of finitude will be shown to be implied in an act of transcending

---

7  Ricoeur, Paul: *Fallible Man*, trans. Charles A. Kelbley, New York 1986, p. 1.
8  This essay has been published in: *History and Truth*, trans. Charles A. Kelbley, Evanston 1965.

> which, in its turn, will show itself as denegation.
> Once this negative movement is brought into view, the properly ontological question will be elaborated: does denegation attest to a Nothingness or a Being whose privileged mode of manifestation and attestation is negation?[9]

Ricoeur's position is that freedom, the power of negation does not indicate that nothingness lies at the core of being like a worm at the core of an apple. Instead, freedom as the power of negation is denegation. That is, finitude itself is already a form of negation which is then negated by transcendence. Transcendence has as its source thought and willing. Therefore, it is not nothingness that lies at the core of the being that is human being, but rather, infinitude lies at the core of the finite like a worm in the core of an apple. In this sense Ricoeur is on Kantian grounds with respect to infinity, totality, completeness etc. as regulative ideas. Ultimately, it is not nothingness that lies at the core of the human being but affirmation. Denegation is affirmation.

It is here where Ricoeur develops a theory of finitude that sounds quite Fichtean. The first negation is the recognition of finitude. However, what is required for this recognition is difference and the Other. I will address this notion of the Other in Fichte and Ricoeur later. Here I want to continue my exploration of Ricoeur's phenomenology of the will as it is developed in *Freedom and Nature*. My goal here is to make more transparent the original duplicity or equiprimordiality thesis that is prominently featured in the very text wherein Ricoeur suggest that we reread Fichte. It is also in this text that he provides us with another way of dealing with the Sartrean problem of nothingness.

## IV. The Duality of the I – The Voluntary and the Involuntary

As we have seen above, for Ricoeur, the core of the self is constituted by something rather than nothingness. This something at the core of the self is itself a duality. The duality of the voluntary and the involuntary, or freedom and nature as discovered and explained by an empirics of the will which abstracts from empirical willing. Ricoeur begins with the voluntary and works toward the involuntary via a diagnostics which refers to

---

9   Ricoeur, Paul: "Negativity and Primary Affirmation," in: *History and Truth*, trans. Charles A. Kelbley, Evanston 1965, p. 306.

the process of uncovering intentional structures embodied in empirical descriptions.[10]

Just as Fichte attempts to explain precisely where the limits to human freedom lie in the *Grundlage* of 1794/95 by beginning with the concept of absolute freedom and then demonstrating that such freedom is unthinkable, indeed, he shows that freedom is always a limited freedom, Ricoeur begins with the voluntary and moves toward the involuntary. In the spirit of Fichte, Ricoeur argues that it is the understanding of the voluntary that comes first in man.[11] The involuntary (where the limits are encountered) makes the voluntary intelligible. Similarly, for Fichte the theoretical makes the practical thinkable.

The problem of the cogito haunts Ricoeur's discussion of the relationship between the voluntary and the involuntary. That is, the descriptive science of phenomenology discloses to us the structures of consciousness as willing, as voluntary. However, willing by necessity includes the involuntary. Ricoeur attempts to avoid what he sees as the path toward solipsism in Husserl by first reconstructing phenomenology within a Kantian framework so as to limit phenomenology. Secondly, he takes seriously the discoveries of the objective sciences. Ricoeur's method is a dialectical one wherein he allows one theory or type of theory to reveal the limits of the other and vice versa. He finds Husserlian phenomenology helpful for exploring the voluntary side of willing but not the involuntary side.

In both Fichte's and Ricoeur's account of willing the body is given a central role (something omitted by many other philosophies of the will). Ricoeur writes:

> The nexus of the voluntary and the involuntary does not lie at the boundary of two universes of discourse, one of which would be reflection concerning thought and the other concerning the physical aspects of the body: Cogito's intuition is the intuition of a body conjoined to a willing which submits to it and governs it. It is the meaning of the body as a source of motives, as a cluster of capacities, and even as necessary nature our task will in effect be one of discovering even necessity in the first person, as the nature which I am. Motivation, motion, and necessity are intersubjective relations. It is a phenom-

---

10 Ricoeur, Paul: *Freedom and Nature*, p. xv
11 Ibid., p. 5. Ricoeur writes: "Far from the voluntary being derivable from the involuntary, it is, on the contrary, the understanding of the voluntary which comes first in man. I understand myself in the first place as he says " I will." The involuntary refers to the will as that which gives it its motives and capacities, its foundations, and even its limits.

enological eidetics of the body as the body belonging to a self, and of its relations to the willing " I."[12]

In Ricoeur's phenomenology of the will the central problem is that of motivation. According to Ricoeur, all willing is motivated. This is also true for Fichte. The question is "what motivates the will of a free being?" It is here where we find ourselves on problematic grounds. For the rest of this section I will focus on the developments of the third part of *Freedom and Nature*.

After grappling with the relationship between the voluntary and the involuntary in the act of decision (the first cycle of the will where the body is the source of motives) and action (the second cycle of the will and where the body is the organ of movement) Ricoeur turns to the problem of consent (the third cycle of the will where the body is an invincible limit). It is in this third cycle of the will where we find the only reference to Fichte in the entire text of *Freedom and Nature*.

Ricoeur claims that "consenting is the act of the will which acquiesces necessity – remembering that it is the same will which is considered successively from different points of view: the point of view of legitimacy, of efficacy, and of patience."[13] In the final part of *Freedom and Nature* Ricoeur examines three ways in which necessity is experienced and the ways in which freedom responds to this experience of necessity.

Necessity is first experienced as character. The problem of character is also examined in *Fallible Man*. Character, as how I think and not what I think is closest to my will. Character is the *"limited openness of our field of motivation taken as a whole."*[14] It represents a dialectic of openness and closure of the I.

The openness of the I is the I's freedom to the extent that it represents the I's infinite possibilities and its general humanity. The closure of the I is indicative of the I's limitations and its particularity. The I is never all of humanity but always this specific I right here right now with its own finite perspective. Yet, it is more than this I right here right now. Although character is a limitation, in a Fichtean sense, this limitation is a necessary condition for freedom. The I must have closure to be an I but it is characteristic of the I to never completely accept this closure.

The fact that character is one of the necessary conditions for freedom is forgotten by the so-called objective sciences. Ricoeur argues that it is

---

12 Ibid., pp. 9–10.
13 Ibid., p. 341.
14 Ricoeur, Paul: *Fallible Man* p. 60.

the tendency of the objective sciences to treat character as if it is completely determined, indeed, human beings are often reduced to character types. However, the very act of defining oneself as a character type and accepting oneself as such is a type of self-positing that requires freedom. To say that "I am the type that" is to be self-conscious and to posit myself as a certain type of character. Ricoeur argues that to consistently think myself as object is already to deliver myself from it as subject.

Ricoeur's phenomenology of the will leads him to a long-term engagement with Freudian psychoanalysis since psychoanalysis also reveals to us one way in which we experience necessity. In this case, the experience of necessity is not conscious in the traditional sense, but rather, subconscious or unconscious. In short, the will is often driven by motivating forces that it is not aware of. To the extent that the I is motivated by hidden, unconscious, and involuntary forces the I is not free, or so it seems. However, the I is not completely determined by unconscious forces but merely limited.

I will avoid the details of the function of the unconscious in Freudian psychoanalysis in the interest of time. However, a few insights by Ricoeur must be mentioned. First, according to Ricoeur it is not permissible to view the unconscious as a thing alongside consciousness. Instead, the unconscious is a certain type of mental function, indeed, it is a part of consciousness that remains hidden from consciousness. Hence, his claim against Descartes, the I or cogito is never completely transparent to itself. Therefore, the I's consciousness of itself is merely partial.

The good news here is that the function of the psychoanalytic cure is to expand the field of consciousness thereby expanding the field of freedom. In psychoanalysis the analyst and the analysand are engaged in an intersubjective striving to expand the domain of freedom for the analysand. Even the decision to seek help from the analyst is an attempt to free oneself from a form of existence that one has already recognized as problematic and binding.

The third and final type of necessity that we experience is life itself. The structure of life wherein the will must assert itself is not of the will's own making. We may think here of the body and its structure and even the accident of one's own birth. Here Ricoeur argues that although life belongs to the involuntary, it does not belong only to the absolute involuntary. Instead, it belongs also to the relative voluntary.[15] He writes:

---
15 Ricoeur, Paul: *Freedom and Nature* p. 419.

> Thus I constantly experience within myself the mixture of two involuntaries: the absolute involuntary of life which gives me existence as consciousness – and thus is the *preface* to my humanity – *and* the involuntary relative to a life which seeks my decision and effort – and thus waits upon my humanity. There is the resolved *and* the unresolved. My life at the same time constitutes a part of those things which do not depend on me.[16]

The two types of involuntary bear witness to the ambiguity of life. Life is experienced on the one hand as a task and on the other as a resolved problem (or as given).[17] However, Ricoeur claims that the structure of life is an index of the absolute involuntary, the condition *sine qua non*. He also argues that I must give up harmonizing the subjective experience of willing and the objective knowledge of structure in coherent knowledge.[18] Here, Ricoeur, like Fichte recognizes the impossibility of the dream of reason, the dream of achieving an absolute harmony or totality. However, it is the nature of the I to posit itself, that is, to continue to assert itself as the absolute condition for its own activity. Fichte uses the language of self-positing which Ricoeur will use from time to time, but Ricoeur most often describes the self-positing of the I as refusal. In fact, it is in the section of *Freedom and Nature* entitled "Freedom's Response: Refusal" that Fichte makes his one appearance in Ricoeur's text.

In this context Ricoeur seems to believe that refusal is the affirmation of consciousness as absolute and he examines three movements of refusal that contain a misreading of Fichte. He writes:

> The initial moment of refusal is the wish for totality in which I repudiate the constrictions of character.[19]
> The second wish of absolute freedom is that of total transparence.[20]

Finally, there is the self-positing of consciousness wherein, "Consciousness refutes its own anxiety of possible non-being by a gesture of power."[21] Ricoeur then moves from refusal to consent. Consent is not passivity, but rather, the acceptance of the involuntary limits of life for the sake of the voluntary. Indeed, Ricoeur ends *Freedom and Nature* with a Fichtean type discussion of the type of freedom that is the only freedom possible for the human being, a limited freedom. In the very

---

16 Ibid., p. 419–420.
17 Ibid., p. 420.
18 Ibid., p. 420.
19 Ibid., p. 463.
20 Ibid., p. 464.
21 Ibid.

last section of *Freedom and Nature* he invokes the notion of Kantian limits and regulative ideas as necessary features of human freedom. Here I will briefly examine Ricoeur's misreading of Fichte.

## V. The Mystery of Being, Belief and Consent

Ricoeur's misreading of Fichte is one that we are all too familiar with. He takes Fichte's discussion of the self-positing I to mean that Fichte refuses to recognize the role of the involuntary in human life. Indeed, Ricoeur implies that self-positing is a rejection of the involuntary. It is my view that the gap between Fichte and Ricoeur is not that great. Ricoeur seems to be unaware of Fichte's equiprimordiality thesis, the unity of theoretical and practical reason, or the unity of the involuntary and the voluntary. It seems that Ricoeur never came to terms with the complexity of Fichte's system. Even the Fichte of the 1794–95 *Grundlage* posits the absolute I only to show that such is unthinkable. There is no I without the not-I. In other words, there is no voluntary without the involuntary.

It is rather ironic that Ricoeur attempts to develop phenomenology within Kantian limits. I have argued elsewhere that it is Fichte who is even more clear than Kant about where these limits lay. In spite of his misreading of Fichte, both Ricoeur and Fichte have much in common with regards to the limits of human knowledge and freedom. Both take seriously the Kantian view of limits or human finitude. We must also keep in mind the influence of Gabriel Marcel on Ricoeur. From the beginning Ricoeur was preoccupied with the mystery of Being. It is possible that at some level Fichte was also concerned about the mystery of Being. By "mystery of being" I am simply referring to the involuntary ground for the voluntary that always escapes our comprehension. Ricoeur captures this mystery in a dialectical manner when he states that "The involuntary is *for* the will and the will is *by reason* of the involuntary."[22] This is the quintessential paradox. The involuntary is for the will, it is to be mastered by the will. In Fichtean language, the world is the sphere of my duty made sensible.[23] On the other hand, the involuntary is the ground or condition for the will, it is that from which the will emerges.

---

22 Ibid., p. 86.
23 See Fichte, Johann G.: "On the Basis of Our Belief in a Divine Governance of the World", in: *Introductions to the Wissenschaftslehre and Other Writings*, trans. and ed. by Daniel Breazeale, Indianapolis/Cambridge 1994, p. 150.

To use Heideggarian language, *Dasein* or the I is thrown into being. The throwness of the I is absolutely involuntary. However, the I is thrown for the sake of throwing itself. I am the thrown and the thrower at once.

Ricoeur's use of consent and Fichte's use of *Glaube* in the *Vocation of Man* simply refers to the acceptance of the involuntary conditions for the voluntary. I accept my status as that which is thrown into existence so that I might become the thrower. For Fichte, *Glaube* is the acceptance of that which cannot be known but must be believed if the I is to continue its self-formative process. To act only when one has absolute knowledge of all of the conditions for one's acting produces a paralysis that makes any knowledge whatsoever impossible since I acquire knowledge only insofar as I act.

## VI. The Other that I am and the Necessary Conditions of the Self

In Ricoeur's phenomenology of the will the involuntary and the voluntary (the will) are intertwined to the point of impossible separation. Willing seems to require an originary involuntary ground but yet willing seems to stand beyond this ground as its own source. Ricoeur writes: "I recognize my body as body-for-my-willing, and my willing as project-based-(in part)-on my body. The involuntary is *for* the will and the will is *by reason* of the involuntary"[24] Here we find that the gap between Fichte and Ricoeur is not so great with regards to willing. Ricoeur's position is in agreement with Fichte's equiprimordiality thesis. The duality or original duplicity of the involuntary and the voluntary is very similar to Fichte's duality of passivity and activity in the I. The very constitution of the I requires that which is other than the I, the not-I.

Ricoeur's concept of the involuntary signifies the passivity at the heart of willing. Willing requires something determinate. For Fichte and Ricoeur, willing occurs only to the extent that human freedom encounters resistance. Ricouer grapples with this resistance at two levels. First, there is the level of physical resistance. That is, all willing is embodied willing. In his Translator's Introduction to *Freedom and Nature* Erazim Kohák writes:

---

24 Ricoeur, Paul, *Freedom and Nature* p. 85–86.

Since freedom is incarnate in nature, empirical description of nature is prima facie relevant evidence for philosophy. But since philosophy, as Ricoeur understands it, is intentional analysis of the *subject's* being-in-the-world, it has to approach empirical science "diagnostically," as a description of "symptoms," that is, description of the ways in which the Cogito becomes actual in the world, and apply to it its own question, the question of the underlying intentional structure manifest through the objective form. The term *diagnostics* refers to this process of uncovering intentional structures embodied in empirical descriptions.[25]

Here we find the decisive connection between the projects of Fichte and Ricoeur. Through out *Freedom and Nature* Ricoeur grapples with the objective sciences. While there is much to learn from the objective sciences about the human condition, they fall short of achieving an understanding of the human condition goes beyond mere determinism. The human person is treated as one object among many. That is, the objective sciences cannot account for the human experience of freedom. For Ricoeur, it is phenomenology with its examination of intentionality that makes it possible for us to give some kind of account of human freedom. Whether it be intentionality in Husserl, comportment in Heidegger, of self-positing in Fichte, we recognize in ourselves an active resistance to the limits placed on us by nature and even our social environment. However, as I stated earlier, Ricoeur believed that we must still take the objective sciences seriously to avoid solipsism. The recognition of freedom must entail awareness of the limits of that freedom.

The second level of resistance or limitation for Ricoeur is social as well as biological. Here my existence and self-hood is dependant on another human being. At the biological level I am dependant on another for my birth which includes heredity. Therefore, I do not choose the body that I am. In terms of the social I also inherit a web of social meanings and a language. It is this inheritance of social meanings that leads Ricoeur to eventually turn away from his phenomenology of the will and focus on myth and narrative. This turn does not concern us here. My point is that Ricoeur failed to realize the extent to which he and Fichte shared the same concerns.

Fichte was also concerned about a one-sided interpretation of the human condition that left the human person completely determined on one side with no account of human freedom, and free to the point of having no limitations on the other side. Fichte informs us that freedom

---

25 Ricoeur, Paul: *Freedom and Nature* p. xv.

without limitations is unthinkable. The famous criticisms of dogmatism and idealism and the tension between the feeling of necessity (Ricoeur's involuntary) and the feeling of freedom (Ricoeur's voluntary) in the *Introductions to the Wissenschaftslehre* are more than adequate examples of the concerns that Fichte and Ricoeur share. Ricoeur read Fichte as a resurrected Descartes, defender of the philosophy of the cogito. In fact, in his "Intellectual Biography" Ricoeur defines his project as an attempt to overcome the "Cartesian, Fichtean, and to a certain extent, Husserlian as well, ideal of the transparence of the subject to itself."[26] He failed to see that Fichte was as concerned as he to avoid the pitfalls of Cartesianism. For Fichte, the I as act is primary. However, activity requires a certain degree of passivity.

Like Ricoeur, Fichte shows how the I is limited at two distinct levels. First, the I is limited in terms of embodiment. Here there is a fundamental agreement between Fichte and Ricoeur. Both agree that although the body is a limitation, it is also a necessary tool for freedom. It is through the body that willing is manifest. No body to will equals no willing at all. The will, as embodied, encounters resistance from the external world. Fichte knew that resistance was a necessary condition for freedom. He writes: "The sensible world proceeds peacefully along its own path, in accordance with its own eternal laws, in order to constitute a sphere of freedom."[27] However, as a moral agent I must soar above the sensible world. This drive to soar above the sensible world does not mean that I can become disconnected from the sensible world as Ricoeur seems to understand Fichte. Rather, it means that I have a duty to soar above. This duty to soar above the sensible world does not remove me from the sensible world, rather, it puts me in conflict with it. I find myself striving to overcome that which cannot be overcome. Nevertheless, it is my duty to overcome the sensible world. In more existentialist terms and even in Ricoeur's language, my project is that of transforming the sensible world.

In this context, one would have to remind followers of Ricoeur who might be inclined to take up Ricoeur's attitude toward Fichte that Fichte's philosophy is a *strebungsphilosophie*. This is explained in the following passage:

---

26 Hahn, Lewis Edwin (ed.): *The Philosophy of Paul Ricoeur*, Chicago and La Salle, Illinois 1995, p. 37.
27 Fichte, Johann G.: "On the Basis of our Belief in a Divine Governance of the World," in: *Introductions to the Wissenschaftslehre*, p. 149.

Man's final end is to subordinate to himself all that is irrational, to master it freely and according to his own laws. This is a final end which is completely inachievable and must always remain so – so long, that is, as man is to remain man and is not supposed to become God. It is part of the concept of man that his ultimate goal be unobtainable and that his path thereto be infinitely long. Thus it is not man's vocation to reach this goal. But he can and should draw nearer to it, and his true vocation qua *man*, that is, insofar as he is a rational but finite, a sensuous but free being, lies in *endless approximation toward this goal*. Now if, as we surely can, we call this total harmony with oneself "perfection," in the highest sense of the word, then *perfection* is man's highest unobtainable goal. His vocation, however, is to *perfect himself without end*. He exists in order to become constantly better in an ethical sense, in order to make all that surrounds him better *sensuously* and – insofar as we consider him in relation to society – *ethically* as well, and thereby to make himself ever happier.[28]

Here we find a fundamental agreement between Fichte and Ricoeur and also the place where they part company. They agree with respect to humankind's struggle for harmony (Fichte) and totality (Ricoeur). They also agree that the harmony or totality that we strive for is unobtainable. However, for Fichte, this striving is not to be loathed, but instead, celebrated. One need only consult the sermonic conclusion of *The Vocation of Man*. For Ricoeur, this striving leads to a sense of guilt, a pathos. This is the topic of *Fallible Man* and *The Symbolism of Evil*.

The second level of resistance or limitation in Fichte is social as it is for Ricoeur. I-hood or self-hood is constituted intersubjectively. There is no I without the Other. The concept of a rational being that posits itself has no meaning apart from a realm of rational beings. In fact, Fichte's lectures and writings of 1796 and 1797 adds to the *anstoß* of the 1794/95 *Wissenschaftslehre* the notion of *aufforderung* (summons). The summons is a call to me by the Other to limit my freedom in a particular way. Simply put, if all human persons are to be free, all must limit their freedom for others. It is not my purpose to develop Fichte's argument here. I simply want to show that the gap between Fichte and Ricoeur is not so great with regards to the necessary conditions for self-hood.

It is not clear why Ricoeur failed to recognize the similarities between his conclusion regarding necessary conditions for the self and Fichte's. It seems to me that the problem might lie in method and the sources for their philosophizing. Fichte begins as a Kantian who set out to prove

---

28 Fichte, Johann G.: "Some Lectures Concerning the Scholar's Vocation," in: *Fichte: Early Philosophical Writings*, trans. and ed. Daniel Breazeale, Ithaca and London 1988, p. 152.

the truth of the Kantian philosophy by setting it on a more adequate foundation. Fichte's method was to begin with the absolute positing of the I only to watch the absolute I deconstruct itself thereby revealing its limitations. This beginning with the absolute positing of the I reveals the way in which the I is limited and free at the same time. What is revealed is a limited freedom. Once we have acquired an adequate understanding of the I and its capacity for only limited knowledge we also gain an understanding of what kind of scientific knowledge is possible for the I.

Ricoeur begins with Husserlian phenomenology and its focus on intentionality. As a dialectical thinker, Ricoeur puts phenomenology in dialogue with the objective sciences. He begins with two opposed views of the I or self. In this dialogue between phenomenology and the objective sciences a certain kind of self emerges. Ricoeur does not start with an investigation of the I itself, but rather, with competing theories about the I. It is in this theoretical conflict that the nature of the I is discovered as a dialectical unity of the voluntary and the involuntary. Hence, one should re-read Fichte as one studies Ricoeur's phenomenology of the will. However, Fichte should not be read a problem that is to be transcended but as Ricoeur's forerunner in the discovery of the necessary conditions for the self.

# Does the Methodology of Phenomenology Involve Dual Intentionality?
## Some Remarks on Conceptions of Phenomenology in Husserl, Fichte, Hegel, Sartre and Freud

Violetta L. Waibel

Universität Wien

### I. Preliminary Considerations

Despite obvious and considerable differences in the positions they held, Fichte, Hegel, Husserl, Sartre and Merleau-Ponty, Deleuze and Levinas, Heidegger, and, with some circumspection, even Freud and James may be said to have advanced phenomenological inquiry. If this is so, the question arises whether, to speak in the manner of Husserl, this claim is merely a misleading equivocacy or whether there are meaningful methodological similarities between the phenomenologies of the idealists and the phenomenological movement of the 20$^{th}$ century, that is the phenomenological movement as such that begins with Husserl but includes other more peripheral figures. I will consider this question briefly in the final remarks of this paper (VII).

After these preliminary considerations (I), this paper opens with a discussion of the founder of modern phenomenology, that is with Husserl (II). It then proceeds to examine Fichte's (III) and Hegel's (IV) idealistic conceptions of phenomenology and will thus be returning to an earlier period in the history of philosophy. Sartre (V), who avowedly developed his phenomenological ontology from Hegel and Husserl, but certainly also from Heidegger, is considered next. Because Freud's notions (VI) are the implicit subtext of Sartre's phenomenological ontology, he will also be included in the methodological examination of this paper. This is of particular interest because it was Husserl's constant wish to distance himself from the psychology of consciousness, even if he was thereby referring to the empirical psychology of his teacher Franz Brentano and not to Freud's teachings.

It is well known that the term phenomenology derives from the Greek, *"phainein,"* "to make visible" or *"phainestai,"* "to become visible" or "to appear" and from *"logos,"* "concept," or "doctrine." Phenomenology is thus a doctrine of appearance.

In Fichte's early *Wissenschaftslehre* there is already a focus on a doctrine of appearance, although his is a doctrine of appearance of the Absolute. The term "appearance" is here obviously not used in the sense Fichte was familiar with from Kant's critique of knowledge. Even though the notion of appearance is of central importance to Kant's critique of knowledge, it would not be appropriate to speak of a Kantian phenomenology.[1] For Kant inquires into the condition for the objective validity of judgment despite its subjective principles of knowledge. He is concerned with the grounds of the validity of the demands of knowledge and not with the question as to how objects in conscious experience appear to the sensing, perceiving and thinking subject.

Therefore, both Fichte's *Wissenschaftslehre* and Husserl's *Phänomenologie* may with regard to various questions that had previously been left unanswered be considered emendations of the Kantian *Kritik*. In this paper, I would like not only to explore the methodological potential of phenomenology but also to pursue the question of how Fichte's and Hegel's endeavors are to be judged in this respect. Fichte referred to the second part of the *Wissenschaftslehre 1804* as a phenomenology, and Hegel called his first main work, which was published in 1807, *Phänomenologie des Geistes*. It is generally known that Hegel may well have found this term in Johann Heinrich Lambert's book *Neues Organon*[2] whose fourth and last section treats the "phenomenology or doctrine of illusion" (*"Phänomenologie oder Lehre von dem Schein"*). Hegel's understanding of the term "phenomenology" differs significantly from what Lambert examines in that part of his *Neues Organon*. It is, however, remarkable that Lambert primarily examines optical illusion, thereby revealing the nature of both illusion and knowledge. It is well known that Hegel's *Phänomenologie* is

---

1   The article "Phänomenologie, phänomenologisch" in: Vetter, Helmuth (ed.): *Wörterbuch der phänomenologischen Begriffe*, Hamburg 2004, pp. 410–425, p. 410, makes reference to Kant's wish to work on a phenomenology that was to determine the limits of both sensibility and reason. He expressed this wish in a letter to Johann Heinrich Lambert.
2   Lambert, Johann H.: *Neues Organon oder Gedanken über die Erforschung und Bezeichnung des Wahren und dessen Unterscheidung von Irrthum und Schein*, Leipzig 1964 (Reprint: Philosophische Schriften, 10 volumes, Hildesheim 1965 ff., volumes 1 and 2).

considered a science of the experience of consciousness. It reveals the shapes of the appearances of consciousness, their incompleteness and inner moments of self-cancellation. As such there is an inner continuity in the way the term and method were employed by these early phenomenologies. In respect to that which reveals itself as an appearance, reflective consciousness defines the boundaries of what has appeared. Through reflection that which initially appears discloses concealed constitutive conditions of the object as it appears. These conditions revealed through reflection are the negation of that which was previously concealed. I mention Lambert here only briefly and will not deal with him in any further detail.

Fichte's conception can be compared with Husserl's because both focus on intentionality. Husserl is considered the founder of a theory of intentionality, yet it is also true that Fichte had dealt with this matter long before. However, instead of dealing with intentionality per se Fichte writes about the striving, the drives, the many and varied determinations of aims of subjectivity and finally about life itself.

For Husserl intentionality is one of the main elements which differentiate the phenomenology he founded from empiric psychology. Intentionality describes both the purposeful relation the subject entertains to the objects of its conscious experience, and its spontaneous interest in the objects of the world. Out of the manifoldness that perpetually presents itself to the subject something is always chosen, whether deliberately or wholly unintentionally, or through what Husserl refers to as the "original impression." Moreover, interest is always taken in something, attention directed to something, whether because it is especially loud, shrill, urgent, dominant, impressive, beautiful or repulsive, or whether a chosen aim or purpose has focussed both interest in and attention to something. Intentionality aimed at the world of objects is, however, not the main thrust of my inquiry; the main thrust is rather, if you will, the intentionality of intentionality, the intentionality of the phenomenological method and its systematic attractiveness.

II. Husserl's *Phänomenologie des inneren Zeitbewußtseins*

Phenomenology as it was founded by Husserl is a descriptive and highly detailed examination of conscious experiences. For Husserl every event of consciousness is intentional. Yet if it is considered true that each lifeworld relation to an object is intentional, and that therefore even the tiniest original impression is consciously or unconsciously oriented towards a purpose, then this orientation must also hold true for both the choice and development of a philosophical method.

The decision of the phenomenologists simply to engage in description is an epoché, a rejection of conventional philosophical strategy and its methodic intentional approach. Mere description excludes intentionality aimed at epistemological validity. Yet a specific kind of intentionality must be ascribed to mere description, if it can be assumed that an intentionality is inherent in each act of consciousness and thus also in each epistemological approach to the world. Mere description can therefore be seen as a derivative form of the originally intentional approach to the world. It is, moreover, the negation of the original intentionality and gives the object that is examined the opportunity to disclose itself in its character as both object and appearance.

Husserl's *Phänomenologie des inneren Zeitbewußtseins* is of particular interest because it is an exemplary inquiry into object-consciousness in general with respect not only to the object of time but also to the constitution and inner structure of consciousness.[3] This phenomenological inquiry is therefore particularly enlightening about Husserl's philosophical method which will thus not be considered in its entirety but rather with particular attention paid to one specific and important aspect.

It is remarkable that within the scope of his lectures *Zur Phänomenologie des inneren Zeitbewußtseins* (1905 and 1893–1917) Husserl speaks of a dual intentionality a number of times, and he reveals this intentionality in the course of his inquiry into temporal consciousness. This I find to be of particular interest. Such thinking is first introduced in paragraph 9 of the total of 45 paragraphs of the lecture as edited by Edith Stein. Husserl writes,

> We distinguish the permanent, immanent object from the object in its manner of appearing ("*Objekt im Wie*"), the object we are conscious of as actually

---

3 On Husserl's time analyses see Kortooms, Toine 2002: *Edmund Husserl's Analysis of Time Consciousness*, Boston. – Orth, Wolfgang (ed.): *Zeit und Zeitlichkeit bei Husserl und Heidegger*, essays by Rudolf Bernet, Kurt Rainer Meist, Elisabeth Ströker, Ulrich Claesges, Otto Pöggeler, Theodore Kisiel. Freiburg im Breisgau, 1983. – Piper, Hans-Joachim: *Zeitbewußtsein und Zeitlichkeit. Vergleichende Analysen zu Edmund Husserls Vorlesungen zur Phänomenologie des inneren Zeitbewußtseins (1905) und Maurice Merleau-Pontys Phänomenologie der Wahrnehmung (1945)*, Frankfurt am Main and Vienna, 1993. – Schnell, Alexander: *Temps et phénomène. La phénomènologie husserlienne du temps (1893–1918)*, Hildesheim 2004.

present or as past. Each temporal being 'appears' in some mode of running-off that changes continually, and in this change the 'object in the mode of running-off' is time and again a different one. We nevertheless say that the object, each point of its time and time itself are one and the same. We will not be able to term this appearance, namely the 'object in the mode of running-off', consciousness (just as we will not give the name 'consciousness' to the phenomenon of space, that is to say the body in its manner of appearing from this or the other side, from near or far). 'Consciousness', 'experience' relates to its object by way of an appearance, in which the 'object in its manner of appearing' is before us. We apparently must understand our discourse on 'intentionality' as ambiguous, depending on whether we speak of the relation of the appearance to that which appears or the relation of consciousness, on the one hand, to 'that which appears in its manner of appearing', and, on the other, to the appearance as such.[4]

This passage seems to me paradigmatic not only for Husserl's time analyses but also for the way in which phenomenologists conceive their method. The phenomenon is the intended state of affairs. The exact description of the state of affairs within the scope of the phenomenological inquiry shows that it is on the one hand the permanent, immanent object in itself, or the entity, and, on the other, the object which constitutive perception determines. Yet, even as determined, it is nevertheless relatively undetermined insofar as it is a transcendent idea in Husserl's sense and is thus also a concept. It is, moreover, relatively undetermined when compared with the always very specific, concrete manner in which it is given in the momentary experience of consciousness. This Husserl refers to as the "object in the mode of running-off." The phenomenological object of inquiry can thus sometimes be considered one way and sometimes another way, and it can thereby be determined more precisely.

It is important to note that Husserl not only discovers but reveals a dual intentionality in both the consciousness of remembered objects (§25) and in retentional consciousness (§35). Dual intentionality of remembered objects is grounded in both the original experience of an entity and in memory. Phenomenological inquiry elucidates that each process of remembrance involves a dual intentionality. Memory would not be memory, if, coinciding and yet distinguishable, both the now-consciousness of

---

4   Husserl, Edmund: *Zur Phänomenologie des inneren Zeitbewußtseins (1893–1917)*, ed. by Rudolf Boehm, HUA X, Haag 1966, pp. 26–27 (translation of Husserl quotations here and in the following by Diana Rosdolsky). – On Edith Stein's editorial work on Husserl's lectures see ibid the Introduction, pp. XX-XXIII.

the remembering subject and the original experience in actuality of that which is remembered weren't inherent in it.

Husserl's examination of dual intentionality seems to be of particular systematic interest. It is well known that for Husserl retention is a present phase in the perception of an object that is potentially modifiable in time, in which ideas are linked in actual consciousness to form, for example, a continuous melody or a thought expressed in words. Husserl clearly distinguishes retentional consciousness of the now-phase stretching over moments in time from that consciousness which he ascribes to the memory of a nearer or farther past. Within the context of his inquiry into the constitution of retentional consciousness, Husserl expressly differentiates between longitudinal and transverse intentionality. In terms of transverse intentionality, retention can be seen as a now-phase, in which a number of actual now-points succeed one another. This succession, however, is seen in terms of longitudinal intentionality. In the microscopic observation of object-constitution in the flow of consciousness, the object reveals itself in terms of transverse intentionality, namely through the distinguishable "identifying coincidences," as Husserl terms the constitution of the identity of a (modifying) object with itself over a period of moments in time. In contrast, longitudinal intentionality is a continuation in the flow of time, which, in relation to transverse intentionality, enables consciousness to experience and thus grasp identity or change from one moment to the next. He writes,

> Our seeing can, in one instance, be guided *through* the phases that 'coincide' in the continual progression of the flow and that are intentionalities of the tone. Yet our seeing can also be aimed at the flow, at a passage within the flow, at the transition of the flowing consciousness from the beginning of the tone to its end. Each profile of consciousness of the kind 'retention' possesses a dual intentionality: one of these serves for the constitution of the immanent object, of the tone. This is the intentionality that we term 'primary memory' of the (just sensed) tone, or, more precisely, the retention of the tone; for retention is a way of being still-conscious (*Noch-Bewußtsein*), a holding back, or, more precisely, retention, retention of elapsed tone-retention: it is continual retention in the process of a continual self-profiling, it is continual retention of continually preceeding phases.[5]

Thus one intentionality serves for the synthesis of that which is identical in the change, the other intentionality serves for the retention of differ-

---

5 Husserl, Edmund: *Zur Phänomenologie des inneren Zeitbewußtseins*, HUA X, pp. 80–81.

ences and modifications in the constituting process of the relevant context. Husserl summarizes,

> Therefore *two* inseparably united intentionalitities – mutually necessitating intentionalities – are interwoven in the one, unique flow of consciousness. By virtue of one of the intentionalities immanent time is constituted, it is an objective time, a real time in which there is duration and change of that which endures; in the other intentionality the *quasi*-temporal phases of the flow are subsumed. The flow always and necessarily contains within itself the flowing 'now'-point – the phase of actuality – and the series of pre-actual and post-actual (of the not yet actual) phases. This pre-phenomenal, pre-immanent temporality is constituted intentionally as the form of the consciousness that constitutes time and constitutes itself as such.[6]

In the *Ideen zu einer Phänomenologie und phänomenologischen Philosophie* (1930) the notion of dual intentionality leads to Husserl's distinction between noetic (constituting, real) and noematic (posited as constituted, ideal) intentionalities.

It can therefore be said that there are forms of object-relation, such as memory, which, invariably, even if only implicitly, involve a dual intentionality. This intentionality is made explicit through phenomenological inquiry. Moreover, Husserl's phenomenological inquiry into inner time consciousness reveals that every object-relation is necessarily, although implicitly, determined by a dual intentionality, namely by the concurrence of longitudinal and transverse intentionalities. Consciousness, which always relates to an object, is not generally aware of this relation. Phenomenology thus engages in the observation of the original experience of consciousness in an artifical manner, and it does this by parenthesizing the familiar steps in reflection and thus letting the object speak for itself. Each object-relation clearly and implicitly involves a dual intentionality which the phenomenological method discloses. That this in a certain sense holds true for the early phenomenologists will be demonstrated through an examination of Fichte's *Thatsachen des Bewußtseyns* (1810/11).

---

6   Husserl, Edmund: *Zur Phänomenologie des inneren Zeitbewußtseins*, HUA X, p. 83.

## III. Fichte's *Thatsachen des Bewußtseyns of 1810/1811*

In the *Grundlage der gesamten Wissenschaftslehre* of 1794/1795 Fichte had already revealed the intentionality of an apprehension of the world so constituted that everything aims at knowledge, and he had made this intentionality explicit, although with a wholly different terminology. When he speakes of the drives and the striving of the cognitive subject, Fichte emphasizes that striving is for him not merely the striving of the moral subject aiming to fulfil the demand, or "ought," of the moral law, but rather a striving aimed at both internal and external objects. In the *Grundlage des Naturrechts* of 1796/97 and in the *Wissenschaftslehre novo methodo* the concept of striving is replaced by that of aim or purpose. It is remarkable that in the further development of the *Wissenschaftslehre* Fichte speaks of a dual intentionality similar to what Husserl conceived, yet Fichte describes this intentionality with a different terminology. Fichte writes:

> The essence of all science lies in employing thought to ascend from any one thing perceived by the senses to its extrasensory ground [...]. In these lectures we are concerned with the first topic of this science, namely the phenomenon. We will describe the phenomenon systematically, and it is my duty to pay close attention to the observations you make.[7]

In both his observations of the facts of consciousness and of the phenomena, Fichte is particularly concerned with an interrelationship that reveals itself in knowledge realized in action, an interrelationship between the scope of knowledge as bound, or limited by the perceived object and that same scope disclosing itself to the subject perceiving the object.

Fichte maintains that the object is neither experienced as actual, nor intuited as ideal, but instead emerges from a synthesis of these two elements, a synthesis made possible by the thinking subject. Neither of these elements can exist separately. Fichte calls this synthesis, or merging, of these two elements of spiritual activity the "life of the spirit" (*Leben des Geistes*). Accordingly, he writes, "This consciousness, which merges into itself and forms a closed spiritual life moment is not simplex, but consists of the parts already mentioned, thought and self-intuition."[8]

---

[7] Fichte, Johann G.: *Thatsachen des Bewußtseyns 1810/11*, GA II/12, p. 21; SW II, p. 541 (translation of Fichte quotations here and in the following by Diana Rosdolsky).

[8] Fichte, Johann G.: *Thatsachen des Bewußtseyns 1810/11*, GA II/12, p. 26; SW II, p. 549.

Fichte's phenomenology seeks to demonstrate that knowledge of external objects consists only to a small extent of that which is actually given and is thus essentially the expression of self-determining freedom. He writes: "Knowledge as such in its inner form and essence is the *being of freedom.*"[9] The goal of his phenomenological inquiry is not only to observe but to identify those aspects of an idea of a concrete object that rest on perception and intuition and to isolate from these the aspects attributable to the autonomy of the spirit. One intentionality therefore describes the yielding of the perceiving subject to the object, and the other describes the active, constitutive performance of the not only perceiving but judging subject.

A color presenting itself to a subject is given. We can imagine the same color changed to a different one. Yet to perceive the color red as empirically given is not at all the same as conceiving blue instead of red by means of the power of imagination. Fichte's phenomenological inquiry examines the constitution of the object in consciousness, and he distinguishes those aspects of the object that are empirically given from those aspects that come into being through the autonomous activity of consciousness. For Fichte it is thus evident that the spatial extension of a colored surface is, essentially, a property that is merely conceived by the subject. For the given extension of an object is never perceived in itself but only by means either of the color or other surface property. Furthermore, Fichte argues that extension in thought is divisible to infinity. His argument is apparently based on the Kantian thesis of the ideality of space (and time). Extension is thus not an actual spatial property of an object but is ideally given as the form of spatial intuition which becomes perceptible to the senses by means of the color or other property of an object.[10]

Husserl's oberservation and scrutiny of empirical objects pays much greater attention to detail. Nevertheless for Fichte, too, the observation of the phenomenon reveals that there are indeed two aspects of the image of the object, or the phenomenon, namely the one that is actual

---

9 Fichte, Johann G.: *Thatsachen des Bewußtseyns 1810/11*, GA II/12, p. 27; SW II, p. 549.
10 On Kant's and Fichte's conceptions of time and space see Waibel, Violetta L.: *La reconstruction de la théorie kantienne de l'espace et du temps dans le 'Précis de ce qui est propre à la Doctrine de la Science' de Fichte*, in : *Années 1781–1801. Kant. Critique de la Raison Pure. Vingt Ans de Réception.* Actes du 5. Congrès international de la Société d'études kantiennes de langue francaise. Montréal, 27–30 septembre 2001, éd. Claude Piché, Paris (Vrin), 2002, pp. 213–223.

and thus bound or limited and the one that is ideal and thus free. This seems to reflect Husserl's dual intentionality which considers, on the one hand, the actual, empiric relation to the object, and, on the other, the process of consciousness.

With increasing complexity of cognitive performance reflection on the activities of consciousness permits an increasing amount of constitutive performance of the subject to be revealed in the consciousness. For Fichte this means that a greater scope of freedom of the spirit is disclosed. Through reflective interpenetration of consciousness mechanisms and object-related activity of thought the subject increasingly discloses itself as a being that is not confined to a causal chain – whether it be the affective mechanisms of perecption itself, or whether it be in the causal interplay of things – but rather as a being capable of activating a causal chain by itself. Reproductive imagination collects a wealth of images based on impressions and observations in order to create something by means of the freedom of "creative imagination" (*Bildungskraft*) – as Fichte now names the productive imagination – that emerges as a new possibility. Fichte's phenomenological inquiry into the subjective constituitive performance in consciousness thus apparently aims at exploring the full scope of freedom in thought and the freedom of self-determined intentionality.

The subject that is freed from the ideas of relatedness to an object explores the fields of thought freely available and is moreover able to investigate consciousness in its totality by means of reflection. Thus the subject acquires not only an inner intuition of its states of consciousness but also of its capacities. As in earlier versions of the *Wissenschaftslehre*, the concept of intuition is not limited to sensory objects of experience but pertains also to the self-representation of the subject. Where states of consciousness related to external objects are intuited, we speak of object-related knowledge of knowledge. Where, however, the capacities of consciousness are intuited which produce such states, we speak of knowledge of the principle of knowledge, which, as principle is absolute freedom.

The principle of knowledge can, however, only be intuited insofar as it is seen as that which inheres the states of consciousness. In this respect it is only the form of the states of consciousnesss ascribed to it. In itself it cannot be intuited but can only be thought. Insofar as the subject intuits itself as the instance of its states of consciousness, it is streaming like the phenomenality of its states. If, however, the subject is aware of itself as a being at rest and consisting in itself, as a being, which is the instance of all streaming states of consciousness, then it does not simply intuit itself, but it thinks itself beyond all states of coming and going, and sometimes not even present, as a perpetual being and thus as an ideational substance. Beyond the character of its substantiality, the subject is also the causal principle of its freedom. In this sense Fichte maintains that to think the principle not only must the substantiality of the I, but also its "accidents be left aside, and thus in no way held fast; therefrom emerges the thought of one principle, or ground."[11]

The totality of consciousness is for Fichte an organic whole that demands to be described in terms of such instruments as "analogy" and "image." Thus reflection on the *Thatsachen des Bewußtseyns* serves as an analogical model in the inquiry into the principle of knowledge and its self-description in the science of principle, namely the actual *Wissenschaftslehre*. Even the programmatic notion of an increasing transparency of consciousness through the *Wissenschaftslehre* is an image that underlines the intention to reveal that which is concealed in "normal" consciousness. What is not revealed in that which is given in "normal" consciousness, that is in intuition and thought, is the hidden presence of freedom and spontaneity. These are only freed in reflection on the facts of consciousness and thus permit free and creative intercourse with the binding and free elements of knowledge.

The term "transparency" points to an act of seeing that Fichte focusses on in his doctrine of principle. While Kant concentrates on the conception of all the organological connections inherent in an idea as a *focus imaginarius*, which represents the totality around which all the parts are organized, and from which the parts define themselves, Fichte operates with the epistemological primacy of the image and with an extended notion of intuition. The principle becomes transparent through a concomitant apprehension of its aspects in both their vertical (temporal) and horizontal (spatial) forms.

## IV. Hegel's *Phänomenologie des Geistes*

It is well known that Hegel's *Phänomenologie des Geistes* is considered a science of the experience of consciousness. In the following reflections I aim to show that it is possible to speak of a dual intentionality in Hegel's writings as well, an intentionality that is revealed through the *Phänomenologie*. I shall focus mainly on the introduction to the *Phänomenologie des*

---

11 Fichte, Johann G.: *Thatsachen des Bewußtseyns 1810/11*, GA II/12, p. 38; SW II, p. 564.

*Geistes*. Let us consider the words "science" and "experience." These words can be taken to represent two opposing parameters impelling the dialectical thought movement in Hegel's *Phänomenologie* forward. That which is dialectically juxtaposed as arguments pro and con is, on the one hand, knowledge as the criterion of knowledge, and, on the other, knowledge appearing in the various shapes of consciousness, a knowledge, which is, in turn, examined with respect to this criterion. It is generally known that for Hegel the shapes of the appearances of consciousness are provisional, partial, and even deficient when measured against the full truth of absolute knowledge. Yet it is remarkable that for Hegel absolute, otherworldly and unattainable knowledge does not draw to itself in endless approximation a finite, this-worldly knowledge of mere appearances. Rather, the criterion of the absolute can be said not only to be present to deficient knowledge but to inhere it. Therefore, absolute knowledge is not merely to be distinguished from deficient knowledge. More correctly, absolute knowledge and deficient knowledge form an original unity – however this process may be described – which can be separated into two elements of this unity.

Consciousness *is* originally the object of its experience. It is, as it were, originally a being of knowledge, of the conscious and of the known. Consciousness thus coincides with the object. It is object-knowledge, or, to use Hegel's famous formula: "'Now is Night.'"[12] Therefore we cannot speak, on the one hand, of object-knowledge, and, on the other hand, of that same object-knowledge as ascribing a subject to itself. It is only through the reflection of consciousness upon itself *as* consciousness that it is separated into the being-for-itself of the instantiated subject, and the being-in-itself of the known object. Consciousness' object-experience is knowledge that determines itself more closely when it examines both its own activity and itself in that activity. In this relation to itself, in this re-flection, consciousness comes to understand that its knowing grasp of things is an illusion of knowledge, and it comes to understand that knowledge as appearance is belief, supposing, error and doubt. Thus, in truth, truth reveals itself as untruth. In the reflection of the being-in-itself of truth, truth as being-for-itself reveals itself as untruth, untruth both as being-for-itself and as being-in-itself.

---

12 Hegel, Georg Wilhelm Friedrich, *Phenomenology of the Spirit (Phänomenologie des Geistes*, Bamberg and Würzburg 1807), translated by A.V. Miller, Oxford University Press 1977, p. 60.

> Consciousness provides its own criterion from within itself, so that the investigation becomes a comparison of consciousness with itself [...]. In consciousness one thing exists *for* another, i.e. consciousness regularly contains the determinateness of the moment of knowledge; at the same time, this other is to consciousness not merely *for it*, but is also outside of this relationship, or exists *in itself*: the moment of truth. Thus in what consciousness affirms from within itself as *being-in-itself* or the *True* we have the standard which consciousness itself sets up by which to measure what it knows.[13]

Where Husserl in his observation of the phenomenon sees two perspectives as two intentional aspects of an entity whose intrinsic structure represents the duality of one entity, whole and entire, Hegel, by constrast, is concerned with the comparison of the entity with itself. The comparison of an entity with itself creates a specific form of intrinsic duality which in the seeming oneness identifies two intentional, clearly distinguishable aspects, namely an actual relation to knowledge and knowledge as truth. Knowledge is in itself and out of itself its own truth. Hegel's central argument is that knowledge and truth are a unity and yet this unity allows a twoness to emerge which makes measurable comparison possible. That truth or untruth is measured by an external criterion is readily comprehensible. Yet how it is possible that consciousness is in itself this criterion, as Hegel states, is the systematically decisive question.

To Hegel's way of thinking, consciousness aimed at the object of its mental activity originally loses itself in its object, the object for the duration of its interest. This interest can be broken off, that is to say negated, and, generally, be taken up again. The possibility of breaking off interest in an object, which is at the same time a negation of the object-relation, and the possibility of taking interest up again emphasize that interest and its negation is a being-for-itself, a subjective activity of consciousness, distinguishable from the being-in-itself of the object. Primary intentionality aimed at wanting-to-know thus divides itself, upon examination, into two intentionalities, the being-for-itself of knowledge and the being-in-itself of the object.

> If we designate *knowledge* as the Notion, but the essence or the *True* as what exists, or the *object*, then the examination consists in seeing whether the Notion corresponds to the object. But if we call the *essence* or in-itself of the *object* the *Notion*, and on the other hand understand by the *object* the Notion itself as *object*, viz. as it exists *for an other*, then the examination consists in seeing whether the object corresponds to the Notion. It is evident, of course, that the two procedures are the same [...] that these two moments, 'Notion'

---

13  Hegel, Georg Wilhelm Friedrich: *Phenomenology of the Spirit*, p. 53.

and 'object', 'being-for-another' and being-in-itself', both fall *within* that knowledge which we are investigating. Consequently, we do not need to import criteria.[14]

The question must therefore be raised how it can be that truth and knowledge coincide when Hegel's *Phänomenologie* claims that at the same time the shapes of consciousness are one-sided and provisional and are therefore just exactly not the fulfilment of truth. Hegel is to be understood in the sense that each shape of consciousness is always a mode of knowledge, even if it is knowledge as appearance and therefore unmasked as mere opinion, deception or plain error. Each original relation consciousness entertains to the world involves intentional knowledge, even if only in the form of wanting-to-know. Originally, consciousness understands itself as known being, that is to say as knowledge. Original knowledge, which discloses itself against itself as mere appearance remains knowledge and at the same time becomes, for Hegel, the other of itself. In the other of itself, that is in every negation, something is necessarily present against which negation directs itself. In accordance with Husserl it can thus be said that in transverse intentionality knowledge as criterion, as form, is always present, and it is against this knowledge that certain forms of modes of knowing are differentiated. In longitudinal intentionality and in the close scrutiny of what the known object is, and how it may be described, it becomes clear which mode of knowing is involved in the actual appearance of knowledge. It is only in knowledge of truth that the actual status of the mode of knowing is revealed, a mode of knowing that is measured against knowledge in the full sense of the word. This knowledge in the full sense of the word, which is criterion, emerges in the other of itself, that is to say in the appearance of knowledge.

Hegel makes clear that in every "now" "the Now" is inherently present. In every wanting-to-know, knowledge – however deficient it may be – of what knowledge is, is present. It would otherwise not be possible for consciousness to know itself as deficient knowledge. Thus every experience of consciousness understands itself as knowledge. The appearances of consciousness represent determinacies, which, when seen from a higher standpoint, reveal their own negation, that is to say the negation as the other of itself. The determinacy of "now" is the determinacy of the singularity of this "Now" and, time and again, this "Now." In line with Husserl, the determinacy of these "Nows" reveals that they do not merely de-

---

14 Hegel, Georg Wilhelm Friedrich: *Phenomenology of the Spirit*, p. 53–54.

scribe the singularity, but that they also carry with them their own generality. In the use of "now" a singular "Now" is intended, but it is intended by means of a linguistic form of deixis, which describes the singular just as much as the generality. The "Nows" are "now", and they are the other of the "now." Close scrutiny of that which is known defines what the entity is, and what it is not. This scrutiny furthermore determines not only the exact relationship between the criterion of actual knowledge and what is held to be knowledge but permits provisional knowledge to be measured against absolute knowledge.

## V. Sartre's Phenomenological Ontology in *L'être et le néant*

Sartre is among the thinkers of the early 20th century who returned to ontology, although his was a phenomenological ontology. It is generally known that for Sartre there are three fundamental forms of being, namely the *en-soi*, the *pour-soi* and the *pour-autrui*, that is, the being-in-itself, the being-for-itself and the interpersonal being-for-others. Sartre emphatically welcomes the fact that phenomenology – whereby he is referring above all to Husserl's efforts in the field – has been able to overcome a large number of aggravating dualisms. The deep gulf between subject and object since Kant, which, according to Sartre, had been bridged only insufficiently by Schelling and Hegel, was now no longer relevant to philosophy. That gulf had been bridged by the new term, "phenomenon." The discussion of what Nietzsche had discredited as the backworlds (*Hinterwelten*) of the Platonists and Neo-Platonists had for Sartre been brought to an end. But so had both the old dualisms between empiricism and idea and between a visible, outer surface and an inner or actual being. All talk of inner and outer aspects of appearances and their objects and between potential and deed had also abated. These dualisms had, however, only been overcome to make room for new ones. Among these new dualisms were the ones Husserl had conceived between finite things that are grasped in an infinite number of object profiles, between transcendence and immanence, between objective time and the immanence of experienced time, and between the objectivity of things and immanent objects.[15] For Sartre the old dualisms are apparently the greater nuisance because

---

15 See Sartre, Jean-Paul: *Being and Nothingness. A Phenomenological Essay on Ontology* (*L'Être et le Néant. Essai d'ontologie phénoménologique*, Paris 1943), New York 1984, pp. 4–5.

to an experiencing mind they seem artificial, the mere result of a need for an explanation of knowledge such as transcendental philosophy can offer.

Sartre emphasizes both the genetic primacy of being over consciousness and the resultant dependence of that consciousness on the givenness of objects. Consciousness is always "consciousness of…". It is important for Sartre that this "consciousness of…" not be understood in terms of a relation. It is not a relation between consciousness and its content. To indicate this non-relationality in the phrases "conscience (de)…", "consciousness (of)…", Sartre parenthesizes the word "de", or "of". Consciousness is not distinguished from the object that is perceived or thought.[16] Self-consciousness too is "conscience (de) soi". It seems that Sartre thus essentially gets rid of disagreeable dualisms that had previously explained consciousness and turns instead to his notion of a pure, naturally given structure. Consciousness is therefore reconstructed on the basis of a state of experienced consciousness.

"Conscience (de)…", "consciousness (of)…", and even "conscience (de) soi", the consciousness of the self, is – according to Sartre's analyses – experience of an inseparable identity in the same sense as Husserl's original knowledge.

We thus find a double intentionality in Sartre's phenomenological reflections on things as well, and this permits us on the one hand to reflect upon objects of consciousness, on the other upon consciousness itself in its activity, making it possible for us to intend first the former, then the latter, of the two. Sartre considers phenomenology to demand new dualisms, and he comes up with his own formulae to describe them. Thus the *pour-soi* emerges as its own negation. Negation, and consequently both absence and nothing, occur only because of the being of consciousness. "Consciousness is a being, the nature of which is to be conscious of the nothingness of being."[17] Consciousness is what it isn't, and it isn't what it is. This is because consciousness first and foremost is that which it perceives, thinks, and so forth. It is its content and nothing more. Yet just when consciousness reflects upon itself as such, and thus grasps itself as such, it is no longer consciousness of a specific content but is its content, which reflects upon itself and which attempts to grasp itself. As soon as consciousness understands itself as grasping itself as such, it must, however, acknowledge that the previous content, the *en-soi*, has been substituted by the positing of another content, namely the

---

16  BN, pp. 14–15.
17  BN, p. 86.

*pour-soi:* it is therefore what it isn't, and it isn't what it is. The *pour-soi* reflects upon itself, understands that it reflects upon itself, and it is precisely because of this understanding that it is no longer *pour-soi* but *en-soi*. At any one moment it is its own past being.

Sartre is a phenomenological thinker who emphasizes simple, undivided and primordial experience of consciousness in its relation to an object. To the dualisms he uses to describe the being of consciousness – it is what it isn't, and it isn't what it is – countless other dualisms are in turn added. They clearly express the separating of states of consciousness in reflection, which, in all initial experiencing, is one. While Husserl not only describes but emphasizes a double intentionality in his philosophical discourse, Sartre's characteristically distinctive formulae describe this double intentionality in the reflection and mirroring activity brought about by time relations like the recall of something at any present moment, the imagining of something in the future at any present moment, and the envisioning of something past and many others. The relational forms of speech are instantaneously grasped, and their inner dimensions described by Sartre in his philosophical reflection.

## VI. Freud's Theory of the Dynamic Unconscious

In his own very specific manner Freud also undertook to reveal that which is concealed. In his essay *The Unconscious* (*Das Unbewußte*, 1915) and again in *The Ego and the Id* (*Das Ich und das Es,* 1923), Freud decidedly opposes the conventional equation of the psychical with the conscious. Such an equation, he maintains, necessarily disrupts psychical continuity.[18] For Freud the conscious represents only a part of the psychic apparatus, which, in fact, comprises far more than mere conscious experience. Freud thus posits the unconscious as a powerful part of the psyche, which functions according to its own laws, and exists alongside the conscious. There is, however, a constant reciprocal interplay between the conscious and the unconscious. Therefore, there is for Freud a systematically decisive difference between those contents of the conscious that are latent and can in fact be accessed, and those that are kept unconscious owing to repression. He distinguishes between the latent uncon-

---

18 See Freud, Sigmund: "The Unconscious," in: *The Standard Edition of the Complete Psychological Works of Sigmund Freud,* volume XIV, trans. James Strachey, London 1958, pp. 161–215, pp. 167–168.

scious – which he terms, "the descriptive unconscious" – and the dynamic unconscious. Only the latter is systemically relevant to his inquiry. Freud's main thrust is thus to show that ideas (*Vorstellungen*) do not remain in the dynamic unconscious by mere chance, but are kept there for a specific purpose by unconscious drives. These drives make repression of specifically selected ideas not only possible but actually help sustain that very repression. Freud stresses moreover that only ideas – not affects and emotions – can be considered contents of the repressed unconscious. This is because affects and drives not only seek discharge but are also liable to change.

Thus Freud maintains: "Thus an unconscious conception is one of which we are not aware, but the existence of which we are nevertheless ready to admit on account of other proofs or signs."[19] Two things are to be noted here. There is a vast area within the dynamic unconscious that is concealed, and there are obvious and explicit signs of that concealment, which jut out like the peeks of an iceberg from the sea of the dynamic unconscious. However, this is the perspective of someone capable of identifying these signs as signs of a concealed area of consciousness. It is therefore necessary to ask just how conscious phenomena can actually be recognized as signs, or forms of expression, of a consciousness that is concealed. What Freud is thinking of when he writes about such signs are dreams and neurotic symptoms that suggest an unconscious. To the subject, however, such signs are recognizable as signs of a concealed consciousness only because they seem an alien intruder to the familiar cogency of consciousness. As long as a person succumbs to the flow of conscious experience as a mere succession of ideas and actual experiences, consciousness contains nothing that seems in any way alien. Dreams are dreams, and fears are fears, we sometimes have more of them, sometimes less, we sometimes know of their existence, or explain the matter in a different way. It is only when a person becomes aware of, or experiences, certain disruptions in the normal course of things, or when his or her intellect, which continuously sorts, systemizes and classifies, is confronted with certain things that defy the order of the laws of the conscious, that what is considered alien actually reveals itself as such. Thus disruptions either of conscious experience or of the coherent structure of the conscious point to something that lies beyond the conscious. This, in

---

19 Freud, Sigmund: "A Note on the Unconscious in Psycho-Analysis," in: *The Standard Edition of the Complete Psychological Works of Sigmund Freud*, volume XII, transl. James Strachey, London 1958, pp. 260–266, p. 260.

any case, is plainly Freud's reasoning. A double intentionality is to be noted here. Occurrences within the psyche are perceived as merely revealing themselves. And it is moreover necessary to learn to interpret them as signs of something else. Signs point to that part of the psyche that is concealed – the dynamic unconscious – and if disruptions are to be understood, the concealed must be revealed.

Hence Freud points out that it is only by using inferences that we can have knowledge of and about the unconscious. Just as another person's psyche can only be inferred from our own, and its existence proven only by means of such an inference, so the existence of the unconscious can also only be inferred from certain psychic occurrences. Nevertheless, an explanation of psychic phenomena such as dreams and neurotic symptoms is made possible only by positing an unconscious. Freud therefore emphasizes that the goal of such a positing is a general explanation of psychic occurrences.

Since for the conscious the unconscious is concealed, Freud maintains:

> The nucleus of the *Ucs.* consists of instinctual representatives which seek to discharge their cathexis. [...] There are in this system no negation, no doubt, no degrees of certainty: all this is only introduced by the work of the censorship between the *Ucs.* and the *Pcs.* Negation is a substitute, at a higher level, for repression.[20]

Moreover, for Freud the unconscious is timeless and represents a preliminary stage in human development. Yet even if the contents of the unconscious are identifiable only in dreams and neurotic symptoms, this content is not an area of the psyche that lies dormant or has in some way been switched off, but rather one that is constantly active.

If we consider it a fact that the soul creates an area for itself not accessible to the conscious, then the question must be raised not only why this is so, but also how this is actually possible. And if we then accept the somewhat generalized response that numerous fears, not successfully overcome, explain why there is an unconscious, then we can maintain that the agency of censorship was introduced by Freud as a quasi-condition of the possibility of the systematically relevant dynamic unconscious. As Freud first showed in Chapter 7 of the *Interpretation of Dreams* (*Traumdeutung*, 1900), censorship regulates – or rather blocks – the permeable boundary between the conscious and the unconscious.

---

20 Freud, Sigmund: "The Unconscious", p. 186.

In his essay *The Unconscious,* Freud also reflects on those mechanisms he encountered in psychoanalytic practice that permit communication to occur between the conscious ego and the unconscious id, thus making it possible to break through the barrier of censorship and gain access to the unconscious. For Freud only that can become content of the unconscious which was previously conscious, and which, by way of signs that point to the existence of an unconscious can gradually be made conscious again.

## VII. Final Remarks

Phenomenological observation is, in a very essential way, reference to a state of affairs that is whole and entire. This state of affairs is a manifestation of consciousness. Yet scrutiny of the phenomenon of consciousness reveals that it is not whole and entire but rather taken apart into its constituent pieces before the reflective consciousness. The reason for this process is explained by Husserl's phenomenology of inner time consciousness in a very specific manner. It is not without good reason that Husserl began very early to try to understand both the temporality of consciousness and the phenomenology of temporality. To consciousness, which is temporal and thus in constant flux, that which is intially whole and entire does not remain whole. Just as temporality is taken apart into flux and rest with respect to an object, so the object is taken apart with respect to temporality into a being at rest and a being in flux. The specifically determined phenomenon, however, is taken apart into what it is and what it isn't.

It is thus a question of the scope of the problem that Fichte reconstructs the phenomenon with regard to intuition and thought, limitation and activity, but, above all, with regard to necessity and freedom, that Hegel examines the thing as it is in itself and as it is in the other of its determinacies or their negation, that Sartre made it his major concern to inquire into the interaction between being and nothingness, between being-for-itself and being-in-itself, and, finally, that Freud explored the interaction between the dynamic unconscious and the conscious.

As far as I can see there can be not talk of equivocacy between the phenomenologies treated in this paper. Phenomenologies are committed to a close scrutiny of the appearances in consciousness, to treat these appearances as primary events in consciousness, to render accessible concealed moments, visible at a primary level, in the being of the phenomenon, each according to their philosophical inclinations. In this respect it is apparently a necessary consequence that the phenomenological method carries with it dual intentionality. To reveal the highly informative, concealed elements of the visible phenomenon is, in the case of Freud's analyses, of particular interest. People may not understand the nature of threats emerging from repressed fears and anxieties that are kept in the dynamic unconscious and require professional treatment. Yet they have the need to understand and clarify seemingly impenetrable subjective states of consciousness. To be more familiar with the complex and seemingly impenetrable possibilities of conscious experience, whether they are amenable or not amenable to closer scrutiny, is a highly attractive objective of any phenomenology.

*Translation by Diana Rosdolsky*

# Fichte's Logical Legacy: Thetic Judgment from the *Wissenschaftslehre* to Brentano

WAYNE M. MARTIN

University of Essex

It is not usual to think of Fichte as a logician, nor indeed to think of him as leaving a legacy that shaped the subsequent history of symbolic logic. But I argue here that there is such a legacy, and that Fichte formulated an agenda in formal logic that his students (and their students in turn) used to spark a logical revolution. That revolution arguably reached its culmination in the logical writings of Franz Brentano, better known as a founding figure of the phenomenological movement. In logical writings that were published only posthumously, but that were fully elaborated in the decade prior to the publication of Frege's *Begriffschrift*, Brentano (together with his collaborator Anton Marty) developed a radically innovative logical calculus that was explicitly designed to overthrow the orthodox logical analysis of judgment and inference. At the center of this revolution was the notion of thetic judgment [*thetische Urteil*], a form of judgment upon which Fichte had insisted in the first published version of the *Wissenschaftslehre*, and which his students subsequently set out to accommodate within the framework provided by Kant's general logic. But thetic judgment proved resistant to such assimilation, and it was left to Brentano to use the analysis of thetic judgment in his attempt to topple a long-standing logical tradition.

In what follows I reconstruct the main episodes in this century-long drama in the logical theory of judgment. My discussion is divided into four sections. I begin with a review of Fichte's most explicit call for logical revolution, together with his introduction of the notion of thetic judgment, set against the backdrop of an anomaly within Kant's logical commitments. In the second section I trace the logical treatment of this anomaly among Fichte's philosophical progeny, in particular Johann Friedrich Herbart and Moritz Drobisch. The third section explores Brentano's position, and his more radical solution to the anomaly bequeathed by Kant. In the final section I return to Fichte, to consider to what degree these subsequent developments remained faithful to the logical agenda Fichte had projected.

## I. Fichte's Call to Logical Revolution

Logical concerns play a role in many of Fichte's writings. From his first prospectus for the yet-to-be-written *Wissenschaftslehre*, through to some of his final lecture courses, Fichte again and again returns to logical questions. One of the continuing themes of these logical remarks concerns the proper relation between logic on the one hand and transcendental philosophy (or simply *Wissenschaftslehre*) on the other. In the *Critique of Pure Reason*, Kant had famously proposed to use logical theory – and in particular the logical treatment of judgment – as a guide to his investigation of the structures and limits of knowledge. But from the beginning, Fichte proposed a different schema. Logical theory, he boldly pronounced in his essay "On the Concept of the *Wissenchaftslehre*" must *follow* from the *Wissenschaftslehre*, being built upon or even derived from the transcendental investigation of knowledge and objective representation.

> The special relationship between logic and the *Wissenschaftslehre* follows from the above. The former does not *provide the foundation* for the latter; it is, instead, the latter which provides the foundation for the former.[1]

This is a paradoxical agenda to be sure, as Fichte himself recognized. For it suggests that one must *derive* logical theory from some other body of doctrine.[2] Yet surely any such derivation would itself have to presuppose some principles of proof – i.e., a logic.

In a number of subsequent writings we find Fichte struggling with this paradox, to which I shall return in due course. But one thing is clear. To follow such a path is to undertake a rather direct reversal of the path of investigation followed in *The Critique of Pure Reason*. No longer can logical theory be taken for granted as a fixed and completed body of doctrine upon which we might rely in the transcendental investigation of the conditions of knowledge and the forms of subjectivity. For Fichte, the results of logic must remain provisional in advance of transcendental

---

1 SW I, p. 68.
2 "[E]very logical proposition and logic in its entirety must be deduced [*bewiesen werden*] from the *Wissenschaftslehre*" (SW I, p. 68).

inquiry, awaiting vindication by the results of the "science of science" – i.e., *Wissenschaftslehre*. Fichte explicitly endorses this result in the earliest writings, but it was some time before its full revolutionary potential came into view. Is it possible that the logic receiving its warrant from the *Wissenschaftslehre* might diverge from logical orthodoxy? Fichte himself certainly recognized this revolutionary possibility; indeed he insisted upon it – most explicitly in a lecture course he delivered twice in the last stages of his life. In the course advertised under the title *Transcendental Logic*, he criticized Kant for his uncritical reliance on logical theory, and called for a logical revolution to be carried out in Kant's name.

> He [Kant] was not so disinclined as he ought to have been toward common logic, and did not destroy it from the ground up as his philosophy truly required, and as we here undertake to do in his name.[3]

To carry through the spirit of Kant's project, and to make good on his own early promise not to take logic for granted, Fichte here insists that logical theory must be thoroughly reconstructed in the light of the new accounts of knowledge and subjectivity inaugurated by Kant's critical investigations.

What might such a reconstruction look like? What kind of logic would proceed from and reflect the approach to knowledge developed by Kant and Fichte? This is by no means a simple question, and I shall not here propose anything like a complete answer. In the late lecture course to which I have already referred, Fichte himself sketched out an agenda for this logical revolution, but it is not that agenda that I seek analyze here.[4] I propose instead to focus on a logical revolution that unfolded only after Fichte's death, but which drew on a logical proposal Fichte had already advanced in the first part of the first published version of the *Wissenschaftslehre*.

As is well-known, the opening of the 1794–95 *Grundlage* (GWL) takes as its point of departure certain fundamental principles of logic. Fichte there attempts to guide his readers and students to the first prin-

---

3  SW IX, pp. 111–112.
4  For a preliminary discussion of the logical proposals of 1812, see Martin, Wayne: "Nothing More or Less Than Logic: General Logic, Transcendental Philosophy, and Kant's Denunciation of Fichte's *Wissenschaftslehre*," in: *Topoi* 22:1, 2003, pp. 29–39. A recent issue of *Fichte-Studien* (Number 15, 1999) was devoted to themes in Fichte's transcendental logic, but on the whole Fichte's specifically logical doctrines have only recently begun to receive sustained attention from scholars and are still not well-understood.

ciples of the *Wissenschaftslehre* by challenging them to reflect on the logical principles of identity and non-contradiction. But Fichte also insists that these opening moves are not themselves intended as *proofs* of the first principles of the *Wissenschaftslehre*, since the first principles of *all* knowledge clearly cannot themselves be derived from anything more basic. So much is well-known, and has been much discussed. But what is rather less often noted is that Fichte himself returns to logical concerns at the *end* of his opening moves in GWL. At this point the direction of reasoning has indeed been reversed, in accordance with the radical position Fichte had proposed in his prospectus. Fichte no longer seeks to draw transcendental principles from logical ones, but proposes instead a revision of logic based on the fundamental transcendental principles he has identified.

> So much for the application of the foregoing to our system in general; but it has yet another and more important application to the form of judgments, which there are many reasons for not overlooking at this point. For, just as there were antithetic and synthetic judgments, so there ought, by analogy, to be *thetic judgments also*, which should in some respect be directly opposed to them.[5]

Fichte's proposal here is that the discovery of the first principles of the *Wissenschaftslehre* should itself lead us to recognize a new logical form of judgment: the thetic judgment.

Cataloging the various forms of judgment has long been a central part of logical theory. Just as the syllogistic figures specify the allowable forms of inference (the forms in accordance with which judgments must be combined in order to yield a valid proof) so the catalog of judgments specifies the allowable forms of judgment: the forms by which concepts can be combined to forge well-formed judgments of different logical types. In Kant's logic, the analysis of the forms of judgment is carried out with reference to the table of judgment forms. The table, which famously appears in the so-called "Metaphysical Deduction of the Categories" (A70/B95), provides a tool which can be used both to construct judgments and to exhibit their differential contributions to inference. Using the table, one analyzes a judgment by indicating one form from each of Kant's four trios. Hence "All men are mortal" (for example) is universal in quantity, affirmative in quality, categorical in relation, and assertoric in modality.

---

5 SW I, pp. 115–116; emphasis added.

In order to appreciate the significance of Fichte's proposed revision, it is important to recognize that all the judgments catalogued within the framework of Kant's table require a minimum of two concepts. With the concepts "man" and "mortal" I can in principle form twenty-seven distinct affirmative judgments using the table; but with "mortality" alone I can form none. As we shall see, this constraint seems to have a deep source in Kant's approach to the logic of judgment. At least within the limits of general logic, Kant treats judgment in general as involving a combination of representations; hence the very possibility of judgment depends on the availability of at least two representations that can be combined. Since the general logic of judgment deals only with general representations (i.e., not with intuitions), any judgment that is recognized in logic requires the synthesis [*Synthesis*] or combination [*Verbindung*] of at least two concepts. I shall refer to this as *Kant's synthetic construal of judgment.* The traces of the synthetic construal can be seen in some of Kant's very general characterizations of judgment,[6] in the specific forms of judgment he recognizes,[7] and in the formulation of his famous distinction between analytic and synthetic judgments.[8] It is also a construal of judgment that shapes his approach to the operations of the understanding more generally.[9]

In introducing the notion of thetic judgment, Fichte is effectively proposing a revision to the Kantian typography of judgment forms. But in doing so he is also recognizably developing one of Kant's own

---

6 "A judgment is the representation of the way that concepts belong to one consciousness universally, objectively. If one thinks two representations as they are combined together and together constitute one cognition, this is a judgment." (Ak. XXIV, p. 928).

7 The three forms of relation allowed under Kant's table of judgment forms are categorical, hypothetical, and disjunctive. In the first case one thinks "the relation of a predicate to a subject"; in the second one thinks the relation between two judgments; in the third one thinks "several judgments in their relation to each other." (KrV A73/B98). It would seem to follow that each of the recognized forms of judgmental relation requires a minimum of two concepts.

8 The proper specification of the analytic-synthetic distinction has been a matter of considerable controversy, but in the passage of the *Critique* which addresses this question explicitly, the distinction is defined only for judgments which involve pairs of concepts. See KrV A6/B10.

9 "Synthesis of a manifold is what first gives rise to knowledge. ... [S]ynthesis is that which gathers together the elements of knowledge, and unites them to form a certain content. It is to synthesis, therefore, that we must first direct our attention, if we would determine the first origin of our knowledge." (KrV A77/B103)

most famous leads. The point of departure in this case, however, is not general logic, but Kant's treatment of a particular argument in metaphysics: the ontological proof for the existence of God. As is well known, Kant insisted in the *Critique* that the ontological argument is spurious, since it illicitly treats "existence" as a real predicate. On its face, this sounds like a claim about the logical form of existential judgments. But it is not an insight that easily finds a place within the parameters of Kant's general logical theory. If 'exists' (the '*ist*' in '*Gott ist*') is not a real predicate, then how should we analyze the logical form of a singular existential judgment?

Kant's writings contain a number of suggestions about how to answer this question, though none are properly integrated into his general logical theory of judgment.[10] One such suggestion will be particularly important in what follows. In his discussion of the ontological proof, Kant seeks to accommodate existential judgment by distinguishing between two forms of positing.

> The proposition, 'God is omnipotent' contains two concepts, each of which has its object – God and omnipotence. The small word 'is' adds no new predicate, but only serves to posit the predicate *in its relation* to the subject. If, now, we take the subject (God) with all its predicates (among which is omnipotence), and say 'God is' or 'There is a God', we attach no new predicate to the concept of God, but only posit the subject in itself with all its predicates, and indeed posit it as being an *object* that stands in relation to my concept.[11]

At this point a terminological observation is perhaps in order. The German verb which is here translated as "posit" is of course "*setzen*" – to put or place. This in turn is the etymological equivalent of the Greek, "*thesis*," which is itself the root in "syn-thesis": to put or place together. Kant here proposes a distinction between two forms of judgment. Each is to be understood as a kind of positing or *thesis*, but the positing comes in two fundamentally different varieties. In relative positing I posit one representation *in relation to* another. In Kant's example, I posit the concept "God" in a certain relation to the concept "omnipotence." But in a judgment of existence I engage in a different sort of positing altogether. In effect I posit *God* (not the concept, but the divine being itself) as something which an-

---

10  I discuss several of Kant's claims about singular existential judgment in Martin, Wayne: *Theories of Judgment: Psychology, Logic, Phenomenology*, Cambridge 2006, pp. 42–55.
11  KrV A598–9/B626–7

swers to my concept. In an early essay Kant had even called this second form of positing "absolute positing" – a phrase with obvious Fichtean resonances.[12]

We must resist the temptation to enter further here into the rich details of Kant's position. The crucial point for our purposes lies in the affinity between Kant's second, non-relative form of positing, and the thetic judgment-form Fichte identifies in the opening passages of the *Wissenschaftslehre*. Fichte provides various formulations of the principles that are meant to provide "the foundation of the entire *Wissenschaftslehre*".[13] Some are symbolic ('I = I', 'I ≠ -I'); others discursive ('the I is posited absolutely', 'I am I'). The first two principles – the principles of self-positing and counter-positing respectively – are meant to express constitutive acts (or 'fact-acts' – *Thathandlungen*) of subjectivity. But they have as their correlates a pair of proto-existential judgments: '*I am*' and '*It is.*' That is, the first act involves positing my own existence as a self-determining, self-enacting subject; in the second act I posit the existence of something else, some not-I, which limits and determines the I. For Fichte the twin acts of positing and counter-positing comprise the basic transcendental-dialectical framework for finite rational subjectivity. And in these two proto-existential judgments we find the underlying conditions for all particular acts of judgment.[14] But in neither of these proto-judgments do we find a case of what Kant would call 'relative positing.' They do not involve the combination or synthesis of concepts, hence they find no natural place on Kant's table of forms. So if the apparatus of general logic is to accommodate them, then the catalog of basic judgment forms must be revised.

> A thetic judgment, [...], would be one in which something is asserted, not to be like anything else or opposed to anything else, but simply to be identical with itself [...]. The first and foremost judgment of this type is 'I am'.[15]

I shall return below (§4) to consider Fichte's own elaboration of the status of such thetic judgments. But I turn first to consider the problems they created for the generations of logicians who undertook the requisite revision of general logic.

---

12  Ak II, pp. 73–74.
13  SW I, p. 91 ff.
14  I discuss the function and status of these first principles in Martin, Wayne: *Idealism and Objectivity: Understanding Fichte's Jena Project*, Stanford, CA 1997, ch.iv.
15  SW I, p. 116.

## II. Moritz Drobisch and the Logical Accommodation of Thetic Judgment[16]

The first decades of 19th century German logic are now mainly remembered as a period of Hegelian dominance and radical logical proposals: dialectical logic, material logic, the purported rejection of the principle of non-contradiction. But alongside the Hegelian movement there persisted a logic that can best be described as *normal* by comparison. I use 'normal' here in a sense borrowed from Thomas Kuhn.[17] In mid-19th century Germany there was, in Kuhn's sense, a 'normal science' of logic, explicitly relying on a paradigm provided by Kant. Kant's logic provided a canonical accomplishment, a standard textbook for training practitioners, and a working apparatus for the logical analysis of judgments and inferences. At the same time it generated problems of normal science requiring solutions, with standards of success and failure established by the logical practice itself. In the phenomenon of singular existential judgment it encountered an anomaly to be resolved. So here is our question: how did the normal working logicians of the 19th century manage the apparent anomaly of singular existential judgment? How did a logic designed to handle judgments of the form 'S is P' handle judgments whose grammatical form is 'I am' or 'it is'? There are many voices in the history of this logical unrest; in what follows I focus my attention on two logicians in particular: Moritz Wm. Drobisch and Franz Brentano – a heroic logical normal and a logical subversive.

Moritz Drobisch (1802–1896) was, in effect, Fichte's logical grandson, by way of Johann Friedrich Herbart (1776–1841) – the founder and namesake of the 'Herbartian School' of logic. Herbart had studied with Fichte at Jena, and although he very prominently broke with Fichtean idealism, he nonetheless took up Fichte's call to logical revolution together with his notion of thetic judgment. At the heart of Herbartian logic was the claim that categorical judgments lack existential import. To say that Cyclops are one-eyed, for instance, or that square circles are impossible, is certainly not to assert the existence of Cyclops or square cir-

---

16 This section and the one that follows largely recapitulate material from Martin, Wayne: *Theories of Judgment*, pp. 55–73, which also incorporates a discussion of phenomenological issues pertaining to thetic judgment.
17 Kuhn, Thomas: *The Structure of Scientific Revolution*, Chicago 1962.

cles.¹⁸ An existence claim, Herbart proposes, must accordingly be recognized as an independent, non-categorical judgmental form. In these judgments, Herbart claims, there is only a predicate, introduced 'without limit or condition.'

> Everything changes in the representation of these judgments, where there is no subject for the predicate. There arises in this way an *existential proposition*, which one misinterprets if one treats the concept of being as the original predicate.¹⁹

Among traditional logicians, Herbart complains, these judgments have been neglected, even though they are well-represented in ordinary language and play a fundamental logical role. He goes on to introduce a set of examples which would receive considerable attention over the subsequent decades of German logic: *es friert, es regnet, es blitzt, es donnert* (it is freezing, it is raining, there is lightening, it is thundering). And he introduces new terminology to cover these judgments. They are, he claims, 'existential propositions' [*Existentialsätze*] or 'thetic judgments' [*thetische Urtheile*]. Their root form is not 'S is P' but rather 'it is P' or 'there is P' [*Es ist P*], where 'it' (*es*) functions not as a subject-concept but only to mark the empty place of the subject position.

Among the logicians of the Herbartian school, it became standard to credit Herbart with having "discovered existential propositions."²⁰ In retrospect we can see that he was introducing logical terminology to acknowledge a form of judgment upon which Kant had relied and Fichte had insisted. But it is one thing to name a new judgment form; it is quite another to integrate it into logical theory and a working inferential system. In Herbart's logic, existential judgments were quite literally tacked on as a final section in the logic of judgment, following a faithful replication of Kant's synthetic treatment in accordance with the table of forms. The task of integrating this addition was taken up in detail by Herbart's student and disciple, Moritz Drobisch. The chief work here is Drobisch's *Neue Darstellung der Logik nach ihren einfachsten Verhältnis-*

---

18 Herbart, Johann F.: *Lehrbuch zur Einleitung in die Philosophie*, Königsberg 1813, pp. 35–37.
19 Herbart, Johann F.: *Lehrbuch zur Einleitung in die Philosophie*, p. 111, emphasis added.
20 See for instance Drobisch, Moritz W.: *Neue Darstellung der Logik nach ihren einfachsten Verhältnissen, mit Rücksicht auf Mathematik und Naturwissenschaft*, 1836, p. 49; see also Brentano, Franz: *Psychologie vom empirischen Standpunkt*, Leipzig 1874, p. 211; citations refer to the pagination of the English translation by L. McAlister et. al., London 1973.

*sen*, which first appeared in 1836 and then in many subsequent editions over the course of half a century. The work falls squarely within the Kantian-Herbartian tradition, in its definitions and organization, in its many explicit references to Kant's logical apparatus and in its frequent claims to be following Herbart's innovations.[21] It is historically significant in part for its attempt to apply logic in mathematics (a Mathematical Appendix constructs mathematical proofs using Drobisch's logical apparatus), but for us its significance lies in its attempt to provide a Kantian logic that can systematically incorporate the thetic judgments that Fichte had proposed. In the changes made to the successive editions of Drobisch's text one finds a record of a crisis underway in Kantian logic.

Drobisch's central logical innovation lies in his distinction between two broad classes of judgment, which he dubs '*Beschaffenheitsurteile*' and '*Beziehungsurteile*.' These are difficult terms to translate, but for reasons that will become clear I render them as '*attributive judgments*' and '*referential judgments*' respectively. The distinction is incipient in the first edition of Drobisch's *Logic* (1836) but emerges fully in the second edition (1851), which Drobisch himself describes as 'a completely rewritten work, almost a new book.' My discussion follows Drobisch's third edition (1863), by which time the distinction had quite thoroughly reshaped his logical treatment of judgment.

Drobisch's point of departure is the Herbartian analysis of categorical propositions, which he treats as non-existential and intrinsically hypothetical in form.

> The judgments, 'God is just,' or 'the soul in not transitory,' no more include the claims that a God exists, or that there are souls than 'the Cyclops are one-eyed,' 'the Furies have snakes for hair,' or 'Ghosts appear at night' unconditionally posit the subjects: Cyclops, Furies, Ghosts. Rather, all these judgments say only that *if* one posits the subject then the predicate applies as a determination of its features [*Beschaffenheiten*]. [...] This important point was first recognized by Herbart.[22]

For Drobisch, an attributive judgment [*Beschaffenheitsurteil*] expresses a relation among concepts, specifying either its genus or some among its species, or attributing some property to its instances. But an attributive

---

21 For Drobisch's retrospective reflections on Herbart's accomplishments see Drobisch, Moritz W.: *Über die Fortbildung der Philosophie durch Herbart: akademische Vorlesung zur Mitfeier seines hundertjährigen Geburtstags gehalten zu Leipzig am 4. Mai 1876*, Leipzig 1876.
22 Drobisch, Moritz, W.: *Neue Darstellung der Logik*, 1863, pp. 59–60.

judgment does not take a stand on whether or not those concepts are instantiated. Because attributive judgments express a relation, they require a minimum of two concepts to serve as the relata. Symbolically, they are represented as 'S is P' or 'SxP', where S and P are concepts and x is a form of relation. Such judgments cannot be used to express an existential claim, insofar as the existence of an S is always implicit as an undischarged antecedent in a conditional. 'Cyclops are one-eyed' becomes 'If there is a Cyclops then it is one-eyed.' 'The soul is not transitory' becomes 'If there is a soul then it undergoes no change.' Generally: 'If S is, then S is P.' Existence cannot be treated as a predicate in an attributive judgment, for to do so would yield a tautology: 'If there is a Cyclops then it exists.'

How then is a judgment of existence to be formulated? Drobisch provides his answer in his treatment of referential judgments (*Beziehungsurteile*):

> The simple answer is: through condition-less judgments, that is, those in which the conditioning subject term is [...] absent altogether or in which there is only an empty place for one. [...] [T]here results the form of judgment:
> There is P [*es ist P*],
> where the small word '*es*' ('it' or 'there') indicates the empty subject position. We can call such judgments 'thetic' or 'absolute'.[23]

For Drobisch, 'S is P' and 'There is p' become the root forms for two broad families of judgment. We use attributive judgments to express relations among our concepts; we use referential judgments when existence is expressed. In each case the root form can be inflected and modified to express a whole range of more complex judgments. Drobisch's treatment concludes with a memorable catalog of thetic forms:

> Examples: There is lightening; it is raining, there is fire; there are forebodings; there is a God; there is no devil, there are no witches, and so on; there are religious, irreligious and agnostic men; there are neither fairies nor elves nor goblins; there is either providence or fate; it is true, that everything good is beautiful; it is not true that if virtue is not rewarded then all morality is an empty illusion.

'These thetic judgments' Drobisch insists, 'have an independent meaning, and should not be treated as categorical judgments.'

Drobisch's distinction between attributive and referential judgments allows what Kant's own logic did not: the formal recognition of judg-

---

23 Ibid., p. 60.

ments involving only a single concept. Drobisch integrates such judgments into logic essentially following Kant's own approach. Thetic judgments vary in all the usual ways: in quantity, quality, modality and relation. And they are subject to a range of principles of combination, both for producing complex thetic judgments from simple ones, and for combining thetic judgments in mediate and immediate inferences. In effect, Drobisch normalizes the anomalous phenomenon. He shows how the apparently anomalous case of singular existential judgment can be integrated into a Kantian formal representation of judgment and apparatus of inference. The generations of students who were taught logic from Drobisch's textbook learned a logical practice which recognized singular existential judgment as a distinct logical form of judgment governed by its own set of inference rules.

There is however an important sense in which Drobisch's accommodation of thetic judgment remained incomplete. For although his logical practice recognized and made use of existential judgments as judgments of a single concept, his definitions and general characterizations of judgment tended systematically to leave such judgments out of account, or even to exclude them. This is because, despite his expansion of logical forms, Drobisch perpetuates the traditional characterization of judgment in general as essentially involving the combination and division of conceptual representations. In his general introduction to the work he defines judgments as the combination and separation of concepts [*Die Verknüpfung und Trennung der Begriffe*][24] and at the opening of the division devoted to judgment, he requires of every judgment at minimum a subject, a predicate, and a copula.

> Every judgment consists therefore of three elements: 1) the subject, the concept concerning which the assertion is issued; 2) the predicate, which includes that which is asserted about the subject; 3) the copula, the form of the assertion, which is either affirming or denying, and either ascribes the predicate to the subject or refuses it [*das Prädikat dem Subjekt entweder beilegt oder abspricht*].[25]

The result is a curious imbalance in Drobisch's work. His logical practice recognizes and deploys a form of judgment which is excluded by own definition of judgment and by his general requirements on a well-formed formula. The tension we found in the Kantian position has here been sharpened into a formal inconsistency in symbolic logic.

---

24 Ibid., p. 11.
25 Ibid., §40.

Drobisch himself recognized the problem, and the traces of his struggle with it can be found in the many additions [*Zusätze*] and changes made to the later editions. Some of the changes amount to a merely cosmetic qualification of the principles which generate the problems. For instance, all the editions include the requirement that a well-formed judgment include both a subject and a predicate, but between the second and third editions Drobisch drops the word '*immer*' (always) from the sentence: '*das Urteil wird nämlich immer aus drei Stücken bestehen*'.[26] In a *Zusatz* introduced in the second edition, he suggests that judgments of one term (for instance: 'Cannonfire!' or 'Fire Alarm!') can be treated as enthymatic (*enthymematisch*, 1851, §46z), but he offers no suggestion about how the enthymeme is to be filled out in accordance with the form specified by his definition and formal requirements. In a note included from the third edition on he finally acknowledges the difficulty of providing a unified definition of judgment applying to the full range of forms he relies on: "It is not easy to provide a simpler explanation of judgment than the one given here. It always comes out dualistically, if it aims to be clear" [*Es fällt immer dualistisch aus*].[27] In short: in Drobisch's logical system, judgment seems at root to be two different things. In some judgments I sort and combine my representations; in others I say that something beyond my representations exists. Drobisch himself ultimately despairs of uniting these two forms in a single non-disjunctive definition.

In sum, Drobisch sought to resolve an anomaly in Kantian logic, by showing how the paradigmatic logical characterization of judgment could accommodate the thetic judgments upon which Fichte and Herbart had insisted. But the strategy Drobisch used was insufficiently radical. The logical accommodation ultimately failed, because it attempted to graft a form of judgment onto a core theory that tends systematically to exclude it. If judgment is essentially the combination of representational content then it cannot ultimately accommodate judgments that do not at root involve the combination of representations. It would fall to a more radical generation of logicians to make a more fundamental break.

---

26 Comparing Drobisch, Moritz W: *Neue Darstellung der Logik*, 1851, §39 to *Neue Darstellung der Logik*, 1863, §40

27 Drobisch, Moritz, W.: *Neue Darstellung der Logik*, 1863, §40z.

## III. Brentano's Thetic Logic

Franz Brentano is now best remembered as a founding figure of modern phenomenology, the one who vigorously introduced the problems of intentionality into the study of conscious experience, and appealed to 'intentional inexistence' to analyze its structure. Solving the problems bequeathed by Brentano's work became one of the organizing strategies not only among his many influential students (Husserl, Meinong, Twardowski, Marty) but also among philosophers of mind a century later (Chisholm, Dennett, Quine, Dretske, Fodor, Searle, McGinn …). But our interest here is rather in Brentano's work as a logician. Brentano's logical doctrines have not been widely discussed, and the neglect is in retrospect explicable.[28] His most detailed logical writings were published only posthumously in 1956, and his influence and accomplishment in this area, though significant, were doubly eclipsed: first by his role in the emergence of a distinctively phenomenological school, and then by the broader logical revolution to which Brentano had contributed but which ultimately over-swept him. (Brentano's main logical doctrines were first set out in 1874, and his calculus was elaborated in detail by 1877; Frege's *Begriffsschrift* was published in 1879.) Nonetheless, Brentano's logical accomplishments merit our attention. Why? Because in Brentano's logic the dispute over the logical representation of thetic judgments

---

28 For some excpetions to the general neglect of Brentano's logic, see Chisholm, Roderick: "Brentano's Theory of Judgment," in: *Brentano and Meinong Studies*, Atlantic Highlands, NJ 1982, pp. 17–36, and important discussions by Simons, Peter: "Brentano's Reform of Logic," in *Topoi 6*, 1987, pp. 25–38, and the Italian logician Poli, Roberto: "Ontologica e logica in Franz Brentano: giudizi categorici e giudizi tetici," in: *Epistemologia 16*, 1993, pp. 39–76, and "La teoria del giudizio di Franz Brentano e Anton Marty: giudizi tetici e giudizi doppi," in: *Epistemologia 21*, 1998, pp. 41–50. Two essays by Terrell, Burnham: "Franz Brentano's Logical Innovations," in: *Midwest Studies in Philosophy*, vol. 1, 1976, pp. 81–90 and "Quantification and Brentano's Logic," in: Chisholm and Haller (eds.): *Beiträge zur Brentano-Konferenz Graz, 4–8 September 1977*, Amsterdam 1978, pp. 45–65, deal with Brentano's treatment of quantification; for replies see Fischer, Kurt and Miller, Leon: "Notes on Terrell's 'Brentano's Logical Innovations'," in: *Midwest Studies in Philosophy*, vol. 1, pp. 95–97, and Chisholm, Roderick: "Brentano's Non-Propositional Theory of Judgment," in: *Midwest Studies in Philosophy*, vol. 1, pp. 91–95. Perhaps the most intriguing appropriation of Brentano's logical proposals is Kuroda, S.Y.: "The Categorical and Thetic Judgment," in: *Foundations of Language 9*, pp. 153–185, which uses Brentanian logic in the analysis of Japanese syntax and is still regularly cited in linguistic research.

turns subversive, directly challenging the longstanding characterization of judgment as synthesis. Brentano and his collaborators formulated the first modern system of inference that systematically eschewed any appeal to judgment as a synthesis of representational content.

Brentano's most celebrated work is his *Psychology from an Empirical Standpoint*, first published in 1874. The seventh chapter touches directly on logical topics, and Brentano already there stated the main elements of his logical treatment of judgment: he rejects the synthetic construal of judgment; he insists that all judgments are essentially thetic in form; and he provides (in overview) the formal argument required to establish these conclusions in detail. In order to see these logical positions fully elaborated, however, we must work from Brentano's posthumously published logic lectures from the 1870s (Brentano 1870–77), and from the work of Brentano's collaborators, particularly Franz Hillebrand and Anton Marty,[29] who worked closely with Brentano in the construction and elaboration of the new logical framework he had established.

In the logic lectures, the first glimpse of Brentano's revolution is symbolic. Where the tradition had identified 'S is P' or 'SxP' as the fundamental schema for judgment, Brentano proposes instead (A+) or (A-).

> The most universal schema for assertion accordingly reads: 'A is' (A+) and 'A is not' (A-). [...] This form of expression contains everything that belongs to a simple judgment: a name, which names the object of judgment [*das Beurteilte*], and a sign which indicates whether the object of judgment is to be acknowledged or denied [*anzuerkennen oder zu verwerfen sei*].[30]

For Brentano, the fundamental elements of a judgment are not a subject and predicate in synthesis but rather a name (A), together with an indication of affirmation (+) or negation (-). It is hard to overestimate the significance of this rupture in a tradition which had long followed Kant and Aristotle in defining judgment in terms of synthesis.

---

29 Hillebrand, Franz: *Die neuen Theorien der kategorischen Schlüsse*, Vienna 1891 and Marty, Anton: *Untersuchungen zur Grundlegung der allgemeinen Grammatik und Sprachphilosophie*, vol. 1, Halle 1908. Franziska Mayer-Hillebrand also deserves mention here; it was she who assembled the source documents into a single treatise.

30 Brentano, Franz: *Die Lehre vom richtigen Urteil;* published posthumously in an edition edited by Franziska Mayer-Hillebrand, Bern 1956, p. 98.

Brentano acknowledges straightaway that his approach marks a break from that tradition, and that he owes us some principled grounds for rejecting the longstanding logical precedent.

> This means a break with the traditional doctrine that every proposition consists of subject and predicate, and that the fundamental form (*Urform*) of judgment is 'A is (or is not) B'. One cannot repudiate so old a tradition unless one provides the grounds for one's divergence from it.[31]

This opens a forthright and explicit attack (prior to Frege's or Russell's) on the subject-predicate analysis of judgment – a logical position that he rather dramatically describes as '*die Hauptfehler*' of traditional logic: 'They [traditional logicians] remained of the false opinion that judgment is essentially a combination of representations.'[32]

Brentano states his case against the synthetic construal of judgment in section 75 of his logic lectures, and his argument draws on several lines of argument we have excavated. He credits John Stuart Mill with the recognition that synthesis is not sufficient for judgment, although the point can be traced at least to Hume.[33] In simply entertaining a compound concept ('a golden mountain') or in posing a question ('Was Mohammed a prophet of God?') we find the combination of concepts without judgment; hence synthesis cannot by itself suffice for judgment.

> We have seen that a combination of representations can take place without a judgment being given. J. St. Mill [...] already remarked that if I say 'golden mountain', this is a combination of representations [*Verbindung von Vorstellungen*], but nonetheless not a judgment. [...] Mill also showed that, whether I now believe or deny that Mohammed was a prophet of God, I must combine the two concepts 'prophet of God' and 'Mohammed' with one another.[34]

Recognizing this, one might then set out to discover what *in addition to synthesis* is required for judgment – whether by seeking out a particular form of synthesis (as in Kant) or by seeking some additional element present in judgmental synthesis (as in the appeal to the representation of 'objective validity' – a position Brentano associates with Mill). Brentano cites Mill's memorable remark: "To determine what it is that happens in the case of assent or dissent *besides putting two ideas together*, is one of

---

31 Ibid.
32 Ibid., p. 125.
33 I have discussed Hume's contribution to these issues in Martin, Wayne: *Theories of Judgment*, pp. 21–36.
34 Brentano, Franz: *Die Lehre vom richtigen Urteil*, pp. 98–99.

the most intricate of metaphysical problems."[35] But Brentano argues that such an approach is 'wholly misguided' [*vollkommen mislungen*]. This is because synthesis is not only insufficient for judgment; it is not necessary either. His argument on this point invokes the by-now celebrated examples:

> Not only does the combination of representations not suffice to bring about a judgment, it is often not even necessary. This can be seen from the so-called existential propositions: *es regnet, es donnert, es gibt ein Gott* (it is raining, it is thundering, there is a God).[36]

At least in the case of elementary judgments, Brentano argues, 'the multiplicity of elements [*Mehrgliedrigkeit*] is in no way a necessary property of judgment' (Brentano 1870–77, 101). Brentano accordingly draws his revolutionary conclusion: since the combination of representations is neither necessary nor sufficient for judgment, we ought to abandon the tradition which defines judgment in terms of synthesis: "We have shown that the combination of subject and predicate and other similar connections are in no way part of the essence of judgment".[37]

In articulating and defending this argument, Brentano both draws on but also forthrightly criticizes the Kantian-Herbartian tradition we have been tracking. As with most German logicians of this period, his treatment of the forms of judgment is peppered with commentary on Kant's table, and he credits Kant with recognition of the crucial point that existence is not a predicate, and with the treatment of existential judgment as positing. But Brentano ultimately describes the Kantian position as 'an unclear and contradictory halfway measure,' complaining that Kant 'allowed himself to be misled into classifying existential judgments as synthetic [as opposed to analytic] propositions.'[38] The problem is that Kant recognizes a form of judgment that requires no conceptual multiplicity, and yet at the same time applies the analytic-synthetic distinction, thereby presupposing a pair of concepts in judgmental synthesis.[39] Brentano's assessment of the Herbartian position is similarly

---

35 For Mill's argument see Mill, John Stuart: *A System of Logic, Ratiocinative and Inductive: Being a Connected View of the Principles of Evidence and the Methods of Scientific Investigation*, Book I Chapter 5, esp. section 1, London 1843.
36 Brentano, Franz: *Die Lehre vom richtigen Urteil*, p. 99.
37 Brentano, Franz: *Psychologie vom empirischen Standpunkt*, p. 222e.
38 Ibid., p. 211.
39 For Kant's insistent claim that existential judgments are synthetic, see KrV A598/B626.

mixed. He credits Herbart with the introduction of thetic judgment, thereby putting an end to longstanding requirement of conceptual multiplicity in judgment, but he criticizes him for treating thetic judgment as a rudimentary form 'alongside' [*nebenher*] the traditionally recognized categorical judgments.[40] For Brentano, such a position represents an insufficiently radical reform of the traditional approach: existential judgment is not to be treated simply as one form alongside others; it is much rather the basic form of all judgment.

This brings us to Brentano's second major innovation in the logical representation of judgment. For Brentano, the case of existential judgment is not simply a counterexample to the characterization of judgment as synthesis – an outlier against a general pattern of synthetic judgment. Its place is much more central than that. Ultimately, he argues, existential judgment is the root form of all judgment: "The fundamental form of judgment [*die Urform des Urteils*] is the thetic or absolute".[41] The argument for this thesis extensive and intricate. Where Herbart had argued that categorical judgment must be supplemented by thetic or existential judgment, Brentano argues that once thetic judgment is introduced, the categorical forms of judgment are strictly dispensable – reducible to complexes of thetic judgments. Establishing this result in detail takes up much of the text of the logic lectures. The first stage of the argument is to show that all the judgment forms recognized in Kantian logic can be 'translated' [*übersetzt*] or 'reduced' [*zurückgeführt*] to affirmative or negative thetic judgments or conjunctions thereof.[42] He then sets out to construct axioms of proof and inferential figures sufficient to capture all the traditionally recognized valid inferences, now making use of only thetic premises and conclusions. In short, he undertakes to transpose Kantian logic into a strictly thetic idiom.

The full details of this logical undertaking cannot be recounted here, but a few examples will provide a sense of the project. As we have seen, a basic judgment in Brentanian logic takes one of two forms: (A+) or (A-), either the affirmation or the denial of the existence of A. 'Pierre exists' accordingly becomes (P+); 'there are no goblins' becomes (G-). The traditional categorical forms are then treated as what Brentano calls 'double

---

40 See Brentano, Franz: *Psychologie vom empirischen Standpunkt*, p. 211 and *Die Lehre vom richtigen Urteil*, p. 124.
41 Brentano, Franz: *Die Lehre vom richtigen Urteil*, p. xviii.
42 See Brentano, Franz: *Psychologie vom empirischen Standpukt*, p. 213.

judgments' (*Doppelurteile*).[43] Some care must be taken with this term. The 'doubling' involved in a Brentanian double judgment is neither conjunction nor predication. It is not formed by combining two simple existential judgments (A+ & B+), nor by combining two concepts in a predicative unity, but rather by compounding the name or concept in a simple existential judgment. Hence for instance 'Some S is P' becomes (SP+); 'No S is P' becomes (SP-).

> The categorical proposition, 'Some man is sick,' means the same as the existential proposition, 'A sick man exists,' or 'There is a sick man.' The categorical proposition, 'No stone is living' means the same as the existential proposition, 'A living stone does not exist,' or 'There is no living stone.'

Some of the principles of the Brentanian translations are at first surprising. Using lower case letters to designate the negation of a concept, he proposes that the universal affirmative form of categorical judgment be rendered as follows: (Sp-). In this way the canonical affirmative judgment comes out as a negative: 'All S are P' becomes in effect: 'There are no non-P Ss,' or 'A non-P S does not exist.'

The results are sometimes cumbersome, and not always intuitive. Compare a classical inference with its Brentanian transposition:

| *Classical* | *Brentanian* |
|---|---|
| Some S are P | SP+ |
| All P are Q | Pq- |
| Some S are Q | SQ+ |

The validity of the transposed inference is certainly not as readily recognizable as that of the traditional schema, and this is not simply because of the familiarity of the traditional form. And matters get considerably worse when hypothetical and disjunctive syllogisms are involved, since every disjunctive or hypothetical premise must ultimately be recast as a sequence of negated existential conjunctions – an anticipation of Wittgenstein's truth tables. Brentano grants that his formulations may at times be awkward [*schleppend und unbequem*; Brentano, *Die Lehre vom richtigen Urteil*, p. 123], and allows that we may choose to acknowledge the traditional forms for simplicity of expression. But he insists that his

---

43 See Brentano, Franz: *Die Lehre vom richtigen Urteil*, p. 113.

translations show those forms to be dispensable; thetic judgment suffices for all the recognized inferences of classical logic.

Brentano's logic was destined to be surpassed and overshadowed before it was even published in any detail, but it nonetheless marks a watershed in the history of logic. In appearance it is utterly unlike any logic that preceded it; it operated with judgmental and inferential forms that differed fundamentally from those of its predecessors; and it provided the first modern calculus of proof that entirely renounced the construal of judgment as synthesis. Though now largely forgotten, it was the culmination of a century of logical foment.

But was it successful? There are of course different measures for the success of an inferential system. Certainly the Brentanian proposals were not without their difficulties. One of the most heated debates concerned Brentano's treatment of universal affirmative categoricals as existential negatives – the transposition of 'All men are mortal' into 'There are no immortal men.' This transposition raises particular difficulty in connection with the fictional contexts to which the Herbartian analysis had appealed. One of the basic inference rules in Brentanian logic is that a *simple* existential negative entails any corresponding *compound* existential negative: (C-) entails both (CA-) and (Ca-). (If there are no honest men then there are neither tall ones nor short ones.)[44] But now consider Brentano's treatment of a universal affirmative concerning a fictional object. In the Brentanian framework, a judgment about a Centaur or a Cyclops must be rendered as either an existential affirmative or an existential negative. This seems straightforward in the case of a simple denial that Cyclops exist, but what are we to say of the judgment that, e.g., Cyclops are monocular? Under the principles of Brentanian transposition, this comes out as 'There are no non-monocular Cyclops' (Cm-). That may seem fine until we recognize that 'Cyclops are binocular' must accordingly be rendered: 'There are no non-binocular Cyclops' (Cb-). By the inference rule governing existential negatives, (C-) entails both (Cm-) and (Cb-). Accordingly 'Cyclops are n-eyed' is true for any number n.

A more fundamental problem concerns the principled limits on Brentano's revolutionary ambitions. Brentano's stated aim was to bring about a thoroughgoing revolution in logic – 'a complete overthrow, and at the

---

44 "Jedes richtige negative Urteil bleibt richtig wenn man seine Materie um beliebig viele Determinationen bereichert." (Brentano, Franz: *Die Lehre vom richtigen Urteil*, p. 209).

same time, a reconstruction of elementary logic'.[45] While there is a sense in which he accomplished this, his revolutionary impulse was in the end fundamentally limited by the basic strategy of proof and legitimation that he adopted. As we have seen, Brentano effectively produced his logic by systematically translating or transposing the classically recognized forms. Moreover, his standard of adequacy for his completed system was in large part driven by his aim of capturing all traditionally warranted valid inferences.[46] These strategies amount to a significant drag on his revolutionary impulse – as if the would-be revolutionary council seeks to legitimate itself by appeal to the very government it denounces and overthrows.

Certainly if success is to be measured by influence then Brentano's logic can at best be deemed a limited success. There did briefly emerge in Vienna what we might well describe as new 'normal science' of logic, explicitly taking Brentano's logical proposals as its point of reference and repudiating essential elements of the Kantian paradigm. Brentano's own logic remain unpublished until long after his death, but Marty, Hillebrand, Kraus, Meinong and others elaborated his logical proposals and tackled some of the central problems that arose from them. Through the mediation of his student Twardowski, Brentano indirectly influenced important developments in 20$^{th}$ century Polish logic. For the most part, however, Brentano's influence in logic was limited to his immediate circle, and indeed the details of his logic were known only to those who attended his lectures in Vienna. The textbooks and problems of the new century would much rather take their orientation from the mathematical logics of Peano, Frege, and Russell.

## IV. Conclusion: Thetic Judgment and the *Wissenschaftslehre*

In the history we have reviewed here we find traces of Fichte's legacy in symbolic logic. With Brentano's logical calculus we find a systematic representation of inference that can aptly be described as a destruction of common logic "from the ground up," starting from the logical represen-

---

45 Brentano, Franz: *Psychologie vom empirischen Standpunkt*, p. 230
46 There were limitations to this aim, however. In particular, Brentano rejected those classical inferences whose validity turned on an assumption of existential import in the universal affirmative form. Hence, for instance, he rejects the classical inference rule of subalternation. See Brentano, Franz: *Die Lehre vom richtigen Urteil*, p. 205 ff; and for a discussion Simons, Peter: "Brentano's Reform of Logic," in: *Topoi 6*, 1987, pp. 25–38.

tation of judgment. In both the destructive and the constructive dimensions of his logical project, Brentano relies on the possibility of thetic judgment forms. Although Brentano himself makes scant reference to Fichte, his logical writings are peppered with references to Fichte's student (Herbart) and 'grand-student' (Drobisch). And as we have seen here, his core logical proposal can be traced back to a logical innovation Fichte himself had proposed in the *Wissenschaftslehre*. But even if we allow that Brentano's logic owes much to a logical tradition traceable to Fichte, it still makes sense to ask whether and to what extent these later logical developments remained true to the vision for logical reform that Fichte himself had projected. This is not a straightforward question to answer, in no small part because Fichte's own logical doctrines remain under-explored and poorly understood. By way of conclusion, however, I would like to indicate at least one crucial respect in which the logicians who took up Fichte's logical legacy came to depart from the notion of thetic judgment that Fichte himself had proposed.

Before tackling this issue directly, however, it will be useful to return to a paradox that we noted at the outset: the paradox in Fichte's demand that logic be deduced or derived from the *Wissenschaftslehre*. We have already considered the ways in which this program involved a reversal of Kant's own account of the relation between logic and transcendental philosophy, sowing the seed for a possible revolution in logic. But we have also had occasion to consider the apparent incoherence – or at least deep circularity – involved in such a demand. For how can one *derive* one theory from another without relying (either implicitly or explicitly) on some kind of logical standard or rules of inference? I shall not here propose a general resolution of this paradox, but it is worth taking note of at least one respect in which the history of thetic judgment might help us make sense of Fichte's paradoxical demand.

To see the crucial point here, it is important to distinguish among the characteristic tasks of logical theory. Traditionally, the central task of logical theory is to provide some kind of standard for validity in inference. The standard itself can take various forms – whether as a set of inference-rules or an accounting of canonically valid syllogistic figures, for instance. Secondly, a logical theory typically advances a catalog of fundamental logical truths; classically these comprised the core principles of identity, non-contradiction, and excluded middle. (Depending on the ways in which a particular logical system is devised, these two aspects of logical theory may be reducible to one.) But alongside these familiar tasks of logical theory there is an additional component which operates largely in the background, but which is in certain respects more basic. A logical theory must provide an accounting of the *elements* of inferences, and in particular an account of their underlying logical form. In modern logical systems, this task of logical theory is characteristically carried out by specifying a set of constraints or construction-rules for a well-formed formula; in classical logic it involved cataloging forms of judgment.

Now it is commonly said of logical theory that it is in the end no more that an elaborate set of tautologies. Kant himself held that general logic was analytic, and that its fundamental principle was nothing more than the principle of non-contradiction. This may be true for that portion of logical theory which enumerates logical truths or catalogs the valid rules of inference. But it is deeply misleading as an account of the logician's task of specifying the possible logical forms of judgment or the requirements on a well-formed formula. If, in the context of the modern predicate calculus, we say that the simplest atomic proposition consists of a name and a predicate, we are effectively laying down a stipulation, a requirement of well-formedness for any string of symbols that will be recognized as a truth-evaluable unit in our calculus. Such stipulations are not themselves grounded in or warranted by the principle of non-contradiction. Firstly, there is no contradiction in stipulating some alternate standard of well-formedness. But more importantly, these stipulations function as a constraint on anything that can be considered party to a contradiction, and in that sense operate prior to any explicit application of the standard of non-contradiction.

So what are these basic logical demands grounded in, if not the principle of non-contradiction? I don't believe that there is a simple answer to this question. Indeed I would propose that it is one of the tasks of the historian of logic to document and illuminate the complex ways in which those stipulations have changed over the course of two and a half millennia of logical theory. But *part of the answer* is surely that the logician's constraints on well-formed judgments or propositions are motivated and guided by the domains of theory which the logician seeks to model and assess. Probably the most familiar example of this sort of motivation is to be found in Russell's famous insistence on logical forms suited to express relations. This important change in the standard of well-formedness was motivated not by concerns internal to logic, much less by the need to avoid contradiction. Russell proposed a new set of construction rules for well-formed formulae because of his interest in a particular *application* of logic: its application in formulating and proving the truths of arithmetic. It was because arithmetic theory trafficked so heavily in relations that Russell sought a logical syntax suited to their representation.[47] In short: the kind of logic a man chooses depends on the kind of theory he sets out to reflect and articulate.

How does this apply to the case of Fichte's logical proposals? In 1794, Fichte took himself to be in possession of a radically novel and far-reaching *philosophical* theory: the *Wissenschaftslehre*. And just as Russell reconfigured the demands on a well-formed formula in response to his specific concern with arithmetic, so Fichte's logical concerns were driven by the need to accommodate the specific judgmental forms that figured in the *Wissenschaftslehre*. Here we find one non-paradoxical sense in which logic might indeed be derivative upon another body of doctrine. Before one settles on a standard for well-formed formulae or on a catalog of judgmental forms, one needs to know something of the judgments that actually figure in the bodies of theory with which one is concerned. In this sense, then, one must indeed let the formulation of the target theory run out ahead of the development of logical theory, which will in turn answer to its particular needs. And this is just what we find in Fichte's logical proposal concerning thetic judgment. The synthetic construal of judgment may have been adequate to the tasks of traditional metaphysics, but the science of *Wissenschaftslehre* gave prominence to judgments that were distorted if pressed into the traditional logical forms. Accordingly, Fichte proposed to let logical theory follow in the wake of transcendental philosophy, specifically by letting the shape of his philosophical theory revise the traditional standards for logical form.

But if this allows us to accommodate at least one element of Fichte's paradoxical demand for a "derivation of logic," it also brings into view some of the distance that separates Fichte's original logical proposal from the logical tradition to which it gave rise. As we have seen, Fichte's first and fundamental example of a thetic judgment is 'I am.' Now for a logician who has come to accommodate thetic judgment forms, such a judgment can be treated a simple substitution instance of the basic existential judgment-form, '_____ is' (A+ in the Brentanian calculus). The blank here might just as well be filled by 'the I' or 'God' or 'Pierre'; the logical form remains the same. This is of course just what we should expect from the characteristic methods of general logic: as Kant repeatedly insists, general logic abstracts from the matter or content of a judgment in order to attend only to its form. But if Fichte introduced the notion of

---

47  For an overview of the issues involved, see Martin, Wayne: *Theories of Judgment*, ch. iii.

thetic judgment in order to capture the distinctive logical form of 'I am' *as it figures in the Wissenschaftslehre*, then this sort of abstraction will inevitably miss its target. A thorough investigation of this matter must be reserved for another occasion, but two observations should suffice to indicate the nature of the difficulty.

The first point to note is Fichte's insistence that the distinction between the form and content of knowledge cannot be applied in the usual way to the first principle of the *Wissenschaftslehre*. In this special case, he holds, form and content are inextricably intertwined. This is a point that figures prominently in BWL:

> No proposition is possible without both content and form. There must be something about which one has knowledge, and there must also be something which one knows about this thing. It follows that the initial proposition of the entire *Wissenschaftslehre* must have both content and form. Since this proposition is supposed to be certain immediately and through itself, this can only mean that its content determines its form and its form determines its content. *This particular form can fit only this particular content, and this content can fit only this form.*[48]

It is not my purpose here to propose an interpretation of this tantalizing but deeply puzzling argument of BWL. But if we take Fichte's conclusion seriously here, then it should be clear that to treat 'I am' simply as a substitution instance of A+ is *not* to represent the logical form of the first principle of the *Wissenschaftlehre*.

A second observation serves to reinforce the first. To this point we have only considered one of Fichte's examples of a thetic judgment. But in the opening sections of GWL he in fact proposes three. 'I am' is the first of the three. Even in this case we now have reason to wonder whether this is properly interpreted as an existential judgment. But consider now the second and third examples: 'Man is free' and 'A is beautiful'.[49] Neither of *these* judgments would appear to be existential in form; yet Fichte treats both as thetic judgments. With this in mind it is worth recalling Drobish's catalog of thetic judgments (above, §2), which included not only examples like 'There is a God', 'There is no devil', and 'There is either providence or fate', but also 'It is true, that everything good is beautiful.' In the first three cases we seem to have existential judgments (affirmative, negative and disjunctive respectively), but the last example points to something quite different.

---

48 SW I, p. 49 (emphasis added).
49 SW I, p. 116–117.

Limitations of space preclude a full discussion of this matter here, but in the oddity of these non-existential thetic judgments I believe we find an important clue regarding the logical approach Fichte sought to draw from the results of the *Wissenschaftslehre*. In order to bring the issues into view, we can take our orientation from a contrast between two very general ways of thinking about the logical form of judgments. If we start from the traditional conception of a judgment as a combination or synthesis of representational content, then it will be natural to specify the logical form of a judgment by specifying the construction-rules one must follow in order to forge a unified judgment out of its constituent concepts. On this approach, it is compositional similarity that marks out discrete logical kinds. As we have seen, such an approach encounters an obstacle in judgments which arguably involve only a single concept, although in an important sense the approach persists in any specification of logical form by appeal to the rules for the construction of basic and compound formulae. An alternate strategy for thinking about logical form is to think rather about the inferential role of a judgment, or more narrowly, about the kind of argument or evidence that would be required in order to warrant it. We tend to think of this latter approach to logical form as a part of Frege's distinctive contribution to the development of modern logic, but there is reason to suspect that it has a considerably longer history. Now it should be clear that in many cases these two approaches to logical form will converge. In the compositional form of a conjunction, for instance, we find a clear reflection of its inferential significance. But the two conceptions of form are nonetheless discrete, and in particular cases may point toward very different strategies for logical analysis.

At this point it is worth attending to Fichte's account of the logical form of two non-thetic judgments: 'A bird is an animal' and 'A plant is not an animal'.[50] In each of these cases we have a pair of concepts, but the logical form differs. Why? Fichte's answer is instructive: their difference, he claims, consists in the difference in their respective 'grounds of correctness' [*Grund der Richtigkeit*]. There is a fundamental difference, as he puts it, in "what must be exhibited if the judgment is to be warranted sound" [*welche* [...] *aufgezeigt werden müssen, wenn das Urtheil bewiesen werden soll*]. The particular account Fichte gives of this difference is rather sketchy. Roughly, warrant for judgments of the first form requires that we indicate some "ground of relation" [*Beziehungsgrund*] between the

---

50 SW I, p. 116.

subject and predicate concept; warrant in the latter case requires some "ground of difference" [*Unterscheidungsgrund*] between the two. But what matters for our purposes here are not the particulars of these accounts but rather the understanding of logical form which they betray. For Fichte, it seems, the logical form of a judgment may be reflected in its compositional structure, but its measure lies in the form of warrant it projects and demands.

Now already it should be clear that on this approach, a judgment of one concept must have a different logical form from the two examples just considered. The result is overdetermined. If an existential judgment involves only one concept then obviously it cannot be warranted by specifying either a *Beziehungsgrund* or an *Unterscheidungsgrund* between its constituent concepts. In this sense the distinctive compositional structure of existential judgments may indeed alert us to the need to recognize novel logical forms of judgment. Ultimately, however, it is not the number of concepts that matters to Fichte, but rather the mode of proof that a judgment projects for itself. And it is here that we can indeed glimpse a principle of unity among Fichte's otherwise heterogeneous examples of thetic judgment. In terms of their compositional form, 'I am,' 'Man is free,' and 'A is beautiful' are quite disparate judgments. What unites them as thetic judgments, I suggest, is their distinctive inferential significance in the context of the *Wissenschaftslehre*. In particular, all three are such that *no possible inference* could suffice to warrant them, though they nonetheless make an unconditional demand upon our assent.

Obviously this is a suggestion that points well beyond the scope of the present paper. But I hope it suffices to indicate that the logical revolution Fichte required would have to go well beyond any mere tinkering with the table of judgment forms or the rules for a well-formed formula. The 19th century logicians who sought to accommodate thetic judgments retained a deep allegiance to a conception of logic which required abstraction from all content, and to a conception of logical form tightly linked to compositional structure. Accordingly their strategy for accommodating thetic judgments was to propose a set of construction-rules and inferential principles for modeling them. In doing so, they did indeed take a rather dramatic step away from the canonical treatment of judgment in general logic. But in the course of this normalization of thetic judgment, what was most radical about Fichte's proposal progressively slipped from view.

# Notes on Contributors

DANIEL BREAZEALE was born in 1945 and received his PhD in philosophy from Yale University in 1971. He is currently Professor of Philosophy and Distinguished Professor of Arts and Sciences at the University of Kentucky. He is one of the founders (or co-positors) of the North American Fichte Society and author of many scholarly articles on Fichte, Kant, Reinhold Maimon, Schelling, Nietzsche, and Sartre. He is also the editor and English translator of four volumes of *Fichte: Early Philosophical Writings*, as well as co-editor of numerous collections of papers on Fichte's philosophy. His research on German idealism has been supported by multiple grants and fellowships from the National Endowment for the Humanities and the Alexander von Humboldt Foundation.

MÁRIO JORGE DE CARVALHO studied in Lisbon, Vienna, Louvain-la-Neuve and Freiburg. He received his Master's Degree and his Ph.D. in Philosophy from Universidade Nova de Lisboa, the former with a dissertation on Heidegger and the latter with a dissertation on "Human Finitude". He is currently an Associate Professor at the Philosophy Department, Universidade Nova de Lisboa. He has authored numerous articles and papers on Plato, Aristotle, the Stoics, Swift, Kant, Fichte, Hegel, Husserl and Heidegger. In 2007, together with a colleague, he published a book on Kierkegaard (*Adquirir a sua alma na paciência*). In 2009, he published a book on Plato (*Die Aristophanesrede in Platons Symposium. Die Verfassung des Selbst*). He is currently preparing a book on the Stoic doctrine of oikeiosis (*Polythryletos oikeiosis*) and a collection of studies on Plato's *Philebus*.

SHARIN N ELKHOLY received her undergraduate degree from Antioch College and her PhD in Philosophy from the New School for Social Research in NY. She is currently an Assistant Professor of Philosophy at the University of Houston-Downtown and Coordinator of the Ethnic Studies minor. She is author of the book *Heidegger and a Metaphysics of Feeling: Angst and the Finitude of Being* (2008). Elkholy has numerous articles on the intersections of gender, race, phenomenology and ontology: "What's *Gender* Got To Do With It? A Phenomenology of Romantic Love", in: *Athenäum: Jahrbuch für Romantik* (1999 Yearbook) discusses aesthetic subjectivity and love in Fichte, Schlegel and Isadora Duncan; and "Friendship Across Differences: Heidegger and Richard Wright's Native Son", in: *Janus Head* (Summer/Fall 2007). She is currently working on an edited volume, *The Beats and Philosophy*, (forthcoming 2011).

ARNOLD FARR is Associate Professor of philosophy at the University of Kentucky. His research interests are 19th and 20th century continental philosophy with an emphasis on social/political philosophy, German idealism, Western Marxism, critical theory, and philosophy of race. His most recent book is *Critical Theory and Democratic Vision: Herbert Recent Liberation Philosophies*. He is also co-author and co-editor of *Marginal Groups and Mainstream American Society*. One of the most important moments of his career was the fall of 2005 when he founded the International Herbert Marcuse Society. This society is flourishing today. Another important moment was being asked to return to the University of Kentucky as a faculty member.

FEDERICO FERRAGUTO (born in Rome 1979) graduated summa cum laude from the University of Rome "La Sapienza" where he currently has a post-doc research position. He obtained a Ph.D. degree in Philosophy at the University of Rome "Tor Vergata". He has been post graduate visiting student at the University of Munich (Germany) and post-doc researcher at the University of Parma (Italy). His main research interests are: German Idealism, Philosophy of Religion, History of Philosophy. He has published *Filosofare prima della filosofia. Il problema dell'introduzione alla Wissenscaftslehre di J.G. Fichte* (2010); "Dimensioni trascendentali e speculative del problema dell'introduzione alla dottrina della scienza di J.G. Fichte", in: *Archivio di Filosofia* (2005); "L'elevazione al punto di vista trascendentale nella Wissenschaftslehre di J.G. Fichte. Aspetti metodologici e sistematici", in: Bertinetto, Alessandro (ed.): *Leggere Fichte* (2009).

GARTH W. GREEN is Assistant Professor of Philosophy of Religion at Boston University (USA). He holds a Ph.D. in Philosophy of Religion from Boston University. He has held fellowship and research positions at the Institut für die Wissenschaften vom Menschen (Austria), the University of Leuven (Belgium), the Institut Catholique de Paris (France), and the Istituto Italiano per gli Studi Filosofici (Italy). His first book, *The Aporia of Inner Sense: The Self-Knowledge of Reason and the Critique of Metaphysics in Kant*, was published with Brill in 2010. He has lectured widely in both Europe and the United States, and is the author of several articles, in each of his areas of concentration; in medieval neo-Platonism, in 19th-century philosophy of knowledge and philosophy of religion, and in 20th-century phenomenology. His current research concerns Kant's critiques of metaphysics and theology and Fichte's late philosophy of religion, or *Religionslehre*.

VIRGINIA LÓPEZ-DOMÍNGUEZ was born in Buenos Aires (1954), studied in the UBA and the Complutensian University of Madrid, where she received her Ph. D. with a dissertation on Fichte. She taught in this University during 30 years and was Vicedecan of the Philosophy Faculty 7 years. She translated works of German idealists like *Philosophy of the Art* and *System of the transcendental idealism* by Schelling, or *Review of Enesidem* by Fichte. Some of her philosophical essays are *La concepción fichteana del amor* (1982, awarded in Argentina) and *Fichte: acción y libertad* (1995). She left the University in 2008 to write fiction. Her novel *El Tacuaral* was awarded 2009 and published in 2010. www.virginiamoratiel.com.

WAYNE MARTIN is Professor and Head of the Department of Philosophy at the University of Essex in the UK. He is author of *Idealism and Objectivity* (1997) and *Theories of Judgment* (2006). He serves as General Editor of *Inquiry* and Series Editor of *Modern European Philosophy* (the monograph series at Cambridge University Press). He is the Principal Investigator of *The Essex Autonomy Project*, a large-scale, interdisciplinary research project investigating the ideal of self-determination in history, theory, and professional practice.

ELIZABETH MILLÁN is Professor of philosophy at DePaul University, Chicago. She works on early German Romanticism and Latin American philosophy. Her most recent publications include: *Friedrich Schlegel and the Emergence of Romantic Philosophy* (2007); with Bärbel Frischmann, *Das neue Licht der Frühromantik/The New Light of German Romanticism* (2008); "Borderline Philosophy? Incompleteness, Incomprehension, and the Romantic Transformation of Philosophy" in: *Yearbook on German Idealism 6* (2008). She is currently finishing a manuscript on *Alexander von Humboldt: Romantic Critic of Nature*. Her work has been generously supported by the Alexander von Humboldt Stiftung.

ANGELICA NUZZO is Professor of Philosophy at the Graduate Center and Brooklyn College (City University of New York). She has been recipient of a Mellon Fellowship in the Humanities (2007–08), an Alexander von Humboldt Fellowship (2005–06), and has been Fellow at the Radcliffe Institute for Advanced Studies at Harvard (2000–01). Among her publications are: *Ideal Embodiment. Kant's Theory of Sensibility* (2008); *Kant and the Unity of Reason* (2005), two books on Hegel *(Logica e sistema*, 1996; *Rappresentazione e concetto nella Filosofia del diritto*, 1990), and *System* (2003). She has edited *Hegel and the Analytic Tradition* (2010). Her numerous essays on German Idealism and Modern Philosophy appear in journals such as the *Journal of the History of Philosophy, Metaphilosophy, Journal of Philosophy and Social Criticism, Hegel Studien*, and *Fichte-Studien*.

ANTHONY N. PEROVICH is Professor of Philosophy at Hope College in Holland, Michigan (USA). He received his Ph.D. from the University of Chicago. He has edited a collection of Alan Donagan's papers, *Reflections on Philosophy and Religion* (1999), and has published numerous articles dealing with German Idealism and with the philosophy of mysticism.

CLAUDE PICHÉ is Professor of Philosophy at the Université de Montréal. He has written widely on Kant, German idealism and Neo-Kantianism. He is the author of *Das Ideal. Ein Problem der Kantischen Ideenlehre* (1984) and of *Kant et ses épigones* (1995). He has also (co-)edited *Kant actuel. Hommage à Pierre Laberge* (2000) and *Années 1781–1801. Kant : Critique de la raison pure. Vingt ans de réception* (2002).

GAETANO RAMETTA is Aggregate Professor of History of Contemporary Philosophy at the Department of Philosophy of the University of Padua. He has published several works about Idealism and Transcendental Philosophy. He is currently Director of the Seminar on Idealism and Transcendental Philosophy at the Doctorate School in Philosophy at the University of Padua. He is currently working on French contemporary philosophy, with particular attention on Deleuze and Foucault. He has published *Le strutture speculative della Dottrina della scienza. Il pensiero di J.G. Fichte negli anni 1801–1807* (1995); *La metafisica di Bradley e la sua ricezione nel pensiero del primo Novecento* [Bradley's Metaphysics and Its Influence on 20th Century Philosophy] (2006). In edition, he is Editor of *Les métamorphoses du transcendantal. Parcours multiples de Kant à Deleuze* (2009).

TOM ROCKMORE is McAnulty Distinguished Professor and Professor of Philosophy in Duquesne University and currently Distinguished visiting professor at the University of Peking. His writings mainly concern various aspects of European philosophy. His three most recent books are *Kant and Idealism* (2007), *In Kant's Wake: Philosophy in the Twentieth Century* (2006) and *Hegel, Idealism and Analytic Philosophy* (2005).

F. SCOTT SCRIBNER is Associate Professor of Philosophy at The University of Hartford (USA). He is most concerned with utilizing the resources of nineteenth century German Idealism for thinking about current issues in media technology. He has published numerous articles in this field, as well as a recent book: *Matters of Spirit: J.G. Fichte and the Technological Imagination* (2010).

JÜRGEN STOLZENBERG, Doctorate 1984, Habilitation 1993, 1998 Full Professor at the Department of Philosophy of the Martin-Luther University, Halle-Wittenberg. Corresponding Member of the Academy of Sciences at Göttingen; Fellow of the Carl Friedrich von Siemens Foundation, Munich; Member of the Board of the Kant-Society; Founding Member of the International Centre for Classical Research in the Klassik Foundation Weimar. Publications: *Fichtes Begriff der intellektuellen Anschauung* (1986), *Ursprung und System* (1995), *International Yearbook of German Idealism* (ed. with Karl Ameriks 2003 ff.), *System der Vernunft. Kant und der deutsche Idealismus* (ed. with H.-D. Klein u. W.G. Jacobs 2007). Many Articles on Kant and German Idealism, Neokantianism, Phenomenology (Heidegger), Aesthetics.

ISABELLE THOMAS-FOGIEL is Professor at Université Paris 1, Panthéon-Sorbonne (France) and University of Ottawa (Canada). Her most recent publications are: *Le concept et le lieu, figures de la relation entre art et philosophie* (2008); *Référence et autoréférence, étude sur le thème de la mort de la philosophie dans la pensée contemporaine* (2006) (American Translation by R.A. Lynch, *Reference and Self-Reference: On the "Death of Philosophy" in Contemporary Thought*, Columbia, University-press, 2010); *Fichte, réflexion et argumentation* (2004); *Critique de la représentation* (2000).

VIOLETTA L. WAIBEL is Professor of European and Continental Philosophy at the University of Vienna. She was previously Assistant for Transcendental Philosophy and German Idealism starting in 2004. Before she was Assistant for scientific research of the philosophy of German early romanticism at the University of Tubingen and of the origins of German Idealism at the University of Munich. Her most recent books are: *Hölderlin und Fichte. 1794–1800* (2000) and *System der Systemlosigkeit. Erster Teil: Die ›Fichte-Studien‹ Friedrich von Hardenbergs im philosophischen Kontext von Kant und Fichte. Zweiter Teil: Ein Philosophisch-systematischer Kommentar der ›Fichte-Studien‹ Friedrich von Hardenbergs* (forthcoming 2011). She is co-editor of the volume *Anatomie der Subjektivität. Bewusstsein, Selbstbewusstsein, Selbstgefühl* (2005) with Thomas Grundmann and others.

ROBERT R. WILLIAMS, Professor Emeritus of German, Philosophy and Religious Studies at the University of Illinois at Chicago, Past President of the Hegel Society of North America, Fulbright Research Professor at the University of Tübingen, Germany; author of *Hegel's Ethics of Recognition* (1998) and *Recognition: Fichte and Hegel on the Other* (1992), translator of *Hegels Vorlesungen über die Philosophie des Geistes 1827/8* (2007), and of many articles on German Idealism including Kant, Fichte, Schleiermacher. Current Project: Tragedy, Recognition and the Death of God: Studies in Hegel and Nietzsche.

www.ingramcontent.com/pod-product-compliance
Lightning Source LLC
Chambersburg PA
CBHW050848160426
43194CB00011B/2078